Society for the Propagation of Faith

Annals Of The Propagation Of The Faith

Volume 59

Society for the Propagation of Faith

Annals Of The Propagation Of The Faith
Volume 59

ISBN/EAN: 9783337201838

Printed in Europe, USA, Canada, Australia, Japan

Cover: Foto ©Lupo / pixelio.de

More available books at **www.hansebooks.com**

1. Right Reverend bishop TIMOLEON RAIMONDI, vicar apostolic of Hong-Kong

ANNALS

OF THE

PROPAGATION OF THE FAITH.

A PERIODICAL COLLECTION

OF

LETTERS FROM THE BISHOPS AND MISSIONERS EMPLOYED IN THE
MISSIONS OF THE OLD AND NEW WORLD, AND OF ALL THE
DOCUMENTS RELATING TO THOSE MISSIONS, AND TO
THE INSTITUTION OF THE PROPAGATION
OF THE FAITH.

This Collection serves as a continuation of the "LETTRES EDEFIANTES."

Vol. LVIII.—JANUARY 1895.—No. CCCXLIII.

DUBLIN:

PUBLISHED FOR THE CENTRAL COMMITTEE
OF THE ASSOCIATION FOR IRELAND,
22 PARLIAMENT STREET.

W. POWELL, PRINTER, 22 PARLIAMENT STREET.

1895.

GENERAL REVIEW

OF THE LABOURS OF THE

APOSTOLATE FOR THE YEAR 1894.

DURING the early months of the year 1894, the Catholic Church continued its onward course, and in comparative peace. True, some of our Missions had their trials, which, however slight, are always to be deplored; but we may say that for a long time the Apostolate had not had less to endure. These latter months, alas! have not fulfilled the happy promise of the beginning of the year, and from China, the Corea, and Madagascar come grave accounts and still graver forebodings.

Once more we are enabled to testify that religious rancours and prejudices are lessening amongst our separated brethren. In England, for example, it is no longer rare to hear clergymen acknowledge that, outside the legitimate authority of the Pope, the successor of Saint Peter, religious unity is impossible. There are some who do not hesitate in expressing the hope "that one day all men of good-will will unite, and that, of one common accord, all will enter into the pale of the Roman Catholic Church, to walk, like the first born of the Church, under the guidance of the Pastor of souls."

The Pope, whom Providence has given to the Church, has in a great measure contributed to this movement towards unity. No one could receive a greater tribute of admiration than has been offered him, even by his adversaries. There is not a single question of the hour that the brilliant intellect of Leo XIII. has not exhaustively treated in his imperishable Encyclicals. It is unnecessary to say that he has done much to forward the interests of the Apostolate. There have been, in fact, few Pontificates that have endowed the Church with so many new Vicariates-Apostolic, or which have laboured with such ardour for the union of the West with the East. Leo XIII. has opened his arms to these illustrious communities whose energies had been paralyzed by schism, and, leaving them their discipline, their rites, and their ceremonies, has asked of them but one thing: submission to the See of Peter. This is what has been so clearly explained by the Holy Father's Legate, his Eminence Cardinal Langenieux; this ardour for Christian unity it is that consecrated the meeting of the two Churches in the never-to-be-forgotten festival of the Eucharistic Congress; this ardour it is that will explain the recent re-union of the Eastern Patriarchs at Rome; and it is further proved by these projected, or already realized foundations of Seminaries and Universities which, even in far off India are destined to prepare a learned and enlightened priesthood, capable of imparting to their people both a solid piety and a perfect knowledge of religious matters.

In the midst of these efforts towards unity, trials have befallen the Eastern churches. An earthquake has caused consternation and ruin amongst them. It is true our communities have suffered greatly, and the Venerable Armenian Patriarch, Mgr. Azarian, has eloquently voiced their distress, but the buildings dedicated to schism and heresy have suffered far more seriously. The West has once more responded to the appeal of the East and, acting on the initiation of the Sultan, a committee was formed and the ruin has been repaired. We must not omit to mention the proofs of sympathy given by the East to Catholic France. At the time of the assassination of M. Carnot, Masses and funeral services were celebrated for the repose of the soul of the President of the French Republic. The East desired to draw yet closer the indissoluble bonds which unite it to the eldest daughter of the Church, to that nation which lead the van in the crusades and which, through its charity, merits to be always the guardian of the sacred Precincts.

In the Far East, the Society of Foreign Missions, Paris, always first in honour and in peril, has registered more than 30,000 adult conversions and 200,000 infant baptisms. Eighteen hundred pupils attend the large seminaries of its twenty-seven Vicariates. What we say of the Foreign Missions, Paris, we can also say of the Jesuits, who, in Madras and Kiang-Nan, are establishing flourishing Christian settlements, thanks to a zeal as enlightened as it is active; and of the Lazarists and Sisters of Charity who, even at Pekin have won the esteem and affection of the ministers and of the emperor himself; of the Belgian Missioners, who in Mongolia rise superior to trials and persecutions; of the sons of St. Francis of Assisi and of St. Dominic, and of the Milanese Fathers who, in India and in the poorest and most distant countries of China, have succeeded in making themselves loved and venerated : of all these we can speak in the same high terms. In September, 1894, the last named Society suffered a severe loss in the death of Mgr. Raimondi, who for twenty years was at the head of the Mission at Hong-Kong.

The devotion of all our Missioners is equal to the greatest difficulties that can arise. Let a pestilence come, as at Canton; let inundations come, as at Tonquin; let war come, as at Siam or in the Corea; wherever there is misery to be relieved, a cry of suffering to be heard, there our apostles will be found, and the Fathers Ambrose in Madura, and the Fathers Jozeau in the Corea will shed their blood, even while they pray for their executioners.

Africa is still the battlefield whereon our Missioners and explorers meet, and I may say our Missioners feel pleasure whenever they can place their experience at the service of these fearless travellers. In this way, Mgr. Augouard was one of Monsieur de Brazza's most valued auxiliaries; the Rev. Father Hacquard, a disciple of Cardinal Lavigerie's, guided the Attanoux Mission in the Sahara; Monseigneur Le Roy, whose name is so dear to our readers, undertook, this very year, an exploring expedition amongst the yet unknown tribes of Gaboon, whom he found ripe for the apostolate, and Father Planque's Missioners, of the African Missions, Lyons, aided by the Sisters of the same Congregation, upheld the reputation of the Church in Dahomey.

While the advanced guard of the apostolic army thus assures fresh conquests to the Church, other soldiers watch over those regions that are already evangelized: amongst the Catholic Copts, the Jesuits and native clergy are uniting their efforts, in order to give this venerable branch of the Church well-instructed young pastors. Sixteen Priests, amongst whom are nine doctors of philosopy and theology, already form a select little corps, destined to combat error and to forward the reign of truth. Amongst the Kabyles, a hospital, opened under the patronage of France and in the charge of Cardinal Lavigerie's White Sisters, bears witness to the marvellous power exercised in aid of civilization by the union of the Cross and the sword. These same Sisters have this year led their first caravans into the regions of the Great Lakes. As for the White Fathers, in the midst of the consolation they receive from their neophytes of the Victoria Nyanza, they have had to bow to the inevitable. England, sovereign of the greater part of the Mtesa kingdom, naturally desired that the Catholic Missions should belong to her own nationality. Rome, ever wise, and seeking in all human events but the spiritual good of peoples, has acceded to this request, and before long the Missioners from Mill-Hill will tread in the furrow opened for them by the sons of the great French Cardinal. As we write these lines, a terrible storm threatens the Madagascar Mission. It has at least given us cause once more to appreciate the valour of our Missioners. While all the European residents fled from Tananarive and took refuge in the stations along the coast, the Jesuit Fathers remained in the capital in order to give their faithful neophytes courage in the moment of danger. May God keep from all evil both pastors and sheep of this great Mission !

During the great exhibition at Chicago, the United States gave our Old World a new lesson in the highest etiquette. A general Catholic Congress was held there under the presidency of Cardinal Gibbons. Each diocese sent a deputy for every five thousand faithful, and the Seminaries, the Universities, and the various Associations had also their delegates. This Congress was followed by another religious assembly, to which representatives of every religion were invited. It was inaugurated by the Archbishop of Baltimore, who, in a clear and distinct voice, repeated the Lord's Prayer before thousands of auditors of all creeds.

Let us not leave America without a passing thought to the laborious Missions of the Oblate Fathers in Canada. God is bestowing on them the sweetest consolations. These poor savages, at first so rebellious against the preaching of the Word, begin to appreciate the patient devotion of their Missioners; they now leave their rude life of hunting and fishing, at intervals to come and hear the Good Tidings. Still, one trial has smitten this Congregation : it has lost one of the oldest members of the episcopate, the Archbishop of Saint Boniface, Mgr. Tache. It is thus God loves to try His friends, in order to show them that all glory and all strength are from Him. At the same time that, after an episcopate of forty-three years, He removed this venerable Prelate from amongst his affectionate people, He called to Himself, almost on the morrow of his consecration, Monseigneur Chausse, of the African Missions, Lyons. For both, the palm was ready. To the one, God gave the reward after a long struggle; to the other, He gave the recompense of the will, of good works ardently desired, and of labours that will be carried out by the elect of His choice.

In Oceania, the Marist Fathers continue to gather in the inheritance of the Blessed Chanel. Wherever his Brothers carry the Word of the Gospel, the prayer of the martyr precedes them, and whether in the Fidji Islands, or in Central Oceania, softens the hearts of these once cannibal nations. The same hopes lighten the labours of the Fathers of the Sacred Heart (Issoudun). Their Missions, twice abandoned, and twice re-commenced by different Congregations, are at last emerging from their period of trial. God smiles upon all who valiantly bear poverty, sickness, and, what is still worse, apparent sterility. To-day, these tribes call for more numerous labourers, and the young Society of Issoudun, aided by its auxiliaries, the Sisters of the Sacred Heart, find, in spite of their poverty, a success which the preachers of heresy, with all their riches, have not had. While the Sandwich Isles witnessed the erection of a statue to the heroic Father Damien, the apostle of the Lepers, a statue, erected by a Committee presided over by the Prince of Wales, Father Damien's emulator in devotedness, the Rev. Father Montiton, likewise a Member of the Society of the Sacred Hearts, died in Spain. For four years he aided Father Damien in his trying ministry. He would willingly have become a leper in order to end his life amongst his beloved sufferers. God, however, willed otherwise, and he had to resume his long journeys in Tahiti up to the day when, worn out more by fatigues than by age, he expired in retirement.

We cannot end this rapid summary without mentioning a few facts interesting to our Association. These are: the Colonial Exhibition at Lyons, where the Propagation of the Faith and its Museum held a distinguished place; the enthronement in the See of Lyons, the cradle of our Association, of a beloved and illustrious

Archbishop, Mgr. Couille, who, like his eminent predecessor, honours us with his kindest consideration; the death of the good Father Tissot, Superior of the Society of Missioners, Annecy, a religious family who evangelized India. A holy and amiable Religious, it was for our cause he preached his last sermon, one of the most eloquent which he ever delivered. Finally, the ever fruitful Mexican Mission of our Delegates, Mgr. Terrien and Father Devoucoux.

In conclusion, we ask our Benefactors for still more generous contributions. Besides the blessing of Heaven, we promise them the gratitude of the apostolate. The following, selected from amongst many others, is a letter recently written to the Councils of the Association, by the Bishops of the Province of Pondicherry:

"Before separating, there remains a duty dear to our hearts to be fulfilled, that of offering you our sincere respect and our profound gratitude for your boundless devotion to that Association which embraces with the same affection all the Missions, and aids them powerfully in extending more and more the reign of Jesus Christ. In this expression of our sincere and lively gratitude, God preserve us from forgetting all those pious Associates whose generosity keeps up the admirable Work of the Propagation of the Faith. This Association not only furnishes us with our daily bread, but enables us to support the manifold undertakings of our Missions. Yes, it makes us happy to acknowledge and maintain, before the entire Catholic world, that if good is done in the Missions; if catechumens and neophytes are increasing; if we have succeeded in founding charitable establishments which are the admiration of the pagans themselves; if we have been able to build churches which do the highest honour to religion, it is to the Association of the Propagation of the Faith that we owe all..."

MISSIONS OF ASIA.

VICARIATE-APOSTOLIC OF THE COREA.

Particulars of the Death of Father Jozeau and of the Situation of Christians in the Corea.

Mgr. Mutel, the venerable Vicar-Apostolic of the Corea, sends us, through the Seminary of Foreign Missions, Paris, the following letter. It contains the touching story of the assassination of Father Jozeau. Alas! unhappy days seem again the lot of this heroic and unfortunate Mission, and in face of this sombre future, we have need to remember that trials bring triumph to the Church, and to count upon the charity of our Associates to aid the chief and the Father of these noble Christian foundations in healing the wounds and comforting the sorrows of his children.

LETTER FROM MONSEIGNEUR MUTEL,
OF THE FOREIGN MISSIONS, PARIS, VICAR-APOSTOLIC OF THE COREA.

...Father Jozeau was, of all the Brethren, most in danger: several times the rebels entered his house and three times even confronted him; each time the Father had advanced, baring his breast and telling them to fire if they dared. His courageous bearing alone had made them retreat. But this strained condition of things could not last, and it is evident that Father Jozeau did not deceive himself in the least, for on the 16th July, he wrote at the head of his will:

"Living, as I do, in the midst of disturbances, I am in daily expectation of falling by the blow of some savage. It may be that my blood is necessary to prevent the massacre of my Christians; if this be so, I give it with all my heart, for the greater glory of God."

On the 14th July I received at Seoul the following despatch:
The Fathers and all the Christians are to die.

I then renewed, by telegram, the order already sent by letter in case of the situation becoming desperate:
Let the Fathers fly or come here.

As soon as he was made aware of this last order, Father Jozeau set out for the city of Tjyen-Tjyou, from which he was distant about fifty *lys*, and thence he started for Seoul. The two Fathers, Baudounet and Villemot, who were less harassed, resolved upon waiting a while. On the 27th, Father Jozeau set out on horseback, accompanied by a servant. Four other Christians followed on foot, but they were soon left behind by the Father, who had resolved to reach Seoul in four days. He passed the Kong-Tjyou river on the 28th at mid-day, and went to pass the night at an inn called Koan-tjyeng, forty *lys* further on.

The following morning, the 29th, he again resumed his journey, but scarcely had he gone a few *lys* when he encountered the Chinese army flying towards Kong-tjyou. The first battalions allowed him to pass; a little farther on, he encountered a group of Corean rebels, and it is very probable that it was at their suggestion that the Chinese general, who happened to be on the spot, had the Father arrested by his soldiers.

I must here remark that, since the 23rd of July, a great change had come over the spirit of the rebels, and perhaps also of the Chinese. By taking possession of the royal palace, and in laying hands on the king, the Japanese have wounded the national feelings of the Coreans to the quick; the rebels, who before that had taken the field in revolt against the authority of the king, acted from that moment as the defenders of his administration; they allied themselves with the Chinese, that they might revenge themselves upon the Japanese, and even upon the Europeans, whom the people believed to be more or less accomplices in the unjustifiable aggression. The Chinese, already partly beaten, and on the eve of being driven from their strongholds by the Japanese, willingly accepted the alliance of the rebel Tong-haks whom they had come to vanquish. They doubtless wished to make use of them as guides and purveyors for their fugitive troops.

The Chinese general, having caused Father Jozeau to be arrested, interrogated him through a Corean interpreter:

" —From what country are you ? "

" —I am a Frenchman."

" —Whence do you come ? "

" I come from Tjyen-la-to, in the neighbourhood of Tjyen-tjyou."

" —What was your business in Tjyen-la-to ? "

" —I have never meddled in anything, save to teach the Christian Doctrine."

" —Why have you left Tjyen-la-to ? "

" —I had to leave on account of the Tong-hak, who threatened me and the other Christians with death."

" —Have you seen any Japanese ? "

" —No."

" —Where are you going ? "

" —To Seoul."

" —As you are going to Seoul, we will return together to Kong-tjyou; there we will take the same route to Seoul."

Father Jozeau doubtless saw very plainly that a trap was laid for him; but, resistance being impossible, he let them lead him where they would. An escort of soldiers placed him in their ranks and forced him to go on foot, guarding him closely; from time to time uttering savage cries. Having journeyed on thus for some time, Father Jozeau, fatigued with the march and the heat, signed to his servant, who led the horse by the bridle, to approach the ranks; but they would not allow the Father to mount, and he was forced, whether he liked it or not, to continue his way of the Cross.

Before the traveller reaches the river Kong-tjyou, there is beside the road, at an inn called Kam-na-mou-kol, a small open pavilion kept up by the authorities of the town, and used as a sort of waiting-room for guests of distinction. There, mandarins going out of office are in the habit of exchanging the customary courtesies with those coming to replace them. The governor of Kong-tjyou, hearing of the arrival of the Chinese troops, sent a mandarin and the criminal judge to meet the general. The meeting took place in the pavilion.

After the first exchange of courtesies, the Chinese general entered the waiting-room and sat down, the military mandarin and the judge seating themselves on his right and left.

Father Jozeau, worn out with fatigue, stopped, like everybody else, in front of the inn, where a number of Coreans gathered round him through curiosity. No one dared to address a word to him on account of the soldiers. At last, the Father called out:

"—I am a French Missioner; I was arrested this morning by the Chinese, and I have eaten nothing all day; give me, I beg of you, a glass of wine."

The innkeeper at once offered a glass. The Father put it to his lips, but the soldiers did not give him time to drink it; they threw themselves upon him brutally, and the wine was partly spilled upon the ground.

At this moment the general desired that the Missioner should be brought before him. Father Jozeau thought the occasion favourable for explaining his case clearly to the two Corean magistrates and he attempted to enter the pavilion, but the soldiers pushed him back violently, and forced him to kneel on the bare ground, like a criminal in presence of his three judges. He was then questioned for a few moments. All I know is that the Father renewed before his judges his declaration:

"—I am a French Missioner."

Then the party resumed their march.

On arriving at the right bank of the river which it was necessary to cross in order to reach Kong-tjyou, the military mandarin and the criminal judge entered one boat, and the Chinese general another. Father Jozeau got into the boat with the general, who, outwardly at least, showed no signs of annoyance; but immediately the Chinese soldiers threw themselves upon the Father and dragged him by force into another boat, already filled with soldiers, and which crossed first.

Having landed, the Missioner was at once surrounded and secured by the soldiers who had crossed with him. All around, but at a little distance, was a crowd of Coreans who had come from the city, just to watch the troops pass by. There were some Christians amongst them, one of whom, at the first glance, recognized the prisoner as a Missioner, another knew him to be Father Jozeau, whom he had lately seen.

The ends of Father Jozeau's garments were all wet and covered with mud; he stood erect, in the midst of a circle of Chinese soldiers, in a tranquil, or rather in a resigned attitude. Sometimes he looked at them with the air of a fearless and innocent man; sometimes he raised his eyes towards Heaven, as if in prayer.

Presently, a soldier approached from behind, took the head of the Missioner between his two hands and made a violent effort as if to jerk it upwards; the onlookers think that the soldiers wished to stretch the victim's neck, in order to render it more supple for the stroke of the sword.

Almost at the moment the Father was seen to bound into the air; some think that he was suddenly stabbed in the loins by the soldiers, and that the sharp agony made him bound thus, others think that he tried to tear himself from the hands of his executioners in order to throw himself into the river and endeavour to save his life by swimming. But he was held by four of the soldiers who, seizing his arms, drew them behind his back; the Father fell forward. Instantly, other soldiers struck him with their swords; the first blow fell upon the neck, the second upon the head itself, and the brains gushed forth. The victim only expired at the fifth sword-thrust, though the head was almost separated from the body. He was also wounded about the arms and legs. This was about five o'clock in the evening of Sunday, the 29th July. The place of the murder was the strand on the left bank of the river, a spot which serves as the place of execution for noted criminals at Kong-tjyou.

Father Jozeau (John Moses), was born at Boissiere-Thouarsaize Canton of Parthenay (Deux-Sevres), on the 8th February, 1866. Arriving in the Corea on the 16th February, 1889, he worked there zealously for five years and a half, and fell victim to his devotedness, at the age of twenty-eight years and a half.

The Father's servant was present at his execution; he was there, a few paces from the scene, all the time holding the horse by the bridle. The Chinese seemed to be paying no attention to him, when a Tong-hak, who was with them, cried out:

"—And this rascally servant, where is he?"

Hearing these words, the poor man attempted to fly; but he had only gone a few steps when he was caught be the Chinese soldiers who gave him two sword cuts in the neck. He fell, but as he still breathed, they despatched him with two gun-shots which lodged in the back. He was a recently converted Christian whom Father Jozeau had engaged in the town, simply for this journey. He leaves a widow and one child six years of age.

The boats containing the Chinese general and the Corean magistrates did not touch the left bank of the river until after this double murder; they distinctly saw the bodies of the two victims, without seeming to pay any attention to what had just taken place. A Chinese soldier, who came up after the execution, searched Father Jozeau's clothes and took away his crucifix, his scapulars, and his rosary. Seeing this, the two Corean Christians fancied that this soldier was also a Christian, but they were soon undeceived by observing the wretch kick the Father's corpse to the edge of the river and leave it there, half immersed in the water.

For two days and two nights the Christians sought in vain a chance of laying the abandoned remains of the Missioner in the earth, but the continual passage of troops and the concourse of sightseers prevented them. At last, on the night of the 31st July, or the 1st of August, having succeeded in eluding observation, they dug a grave, in the best manner they could, in the sand, not far from the river, where they laid the venerated remains of the Father, whose body they simply wrapped in a mat.

Father Baudounet, who remained at Tjyen-tjyou, having learned the murder of his fellow-Missioner, on the 4th of August, sent the governor of Kong-tjyou the following telegram:

"*Father Jozeau has been killed on the banks of the river: for what reason? What has become of his body?*
"*Baudounet, French Missioner.*"

The latter sent his people to arrange for the interment of the Missioner, but, finding the Father already buried, they interred the remains of the servant.

On the 5th, the governor replied by the following strange despatch:

"*There is a rumour that when the Chinese soldiers crossed the river, they executed a Japanese and that a local mandarin has had is body interred.*
"*Governor of Kong-tjyou.*"

This is one of the administrative lies customary amongst the Chinese and Coreans.

Équator (Southern America). — Indians of Napo.

Without taking into consideration the immense loss that a Missioner such as Father Jozeau is to us, I may say that his death has been to the Mission the greatest of all its trials. The Tong-haks, who hitherto had not dared to raise their hands against the Missioners, began at once to hunt them like wild beasts, while as to the Christians, their position has become intolerable. In the two provinces of Tjyen-la and of Tchyoung-tchyeng, there is not perhaps a single Christian village that has not been pillaged and ruined. The inhabitants have all fled, and we sorrowfully ask ourselves, will there be a single survivor of these eleven thousand Christians?

VICARIATE-APOSTOLIC OF SIAM.

Evangelization of a Tribe of the Laos on the left shore of the Me-Kong.

This Mission, more extensive than all France, has been, for two centuries, evangelized by the Priests of the Foreign Missions, Paris. It consists of 20,000 Catholics, 62 Christian settlements, all provided with churches and schools, 86 European Missioners, and 11 native Priests. The Siamese Laos, mentioned in this correspondence, represent the inhabitants of the central mountainous district of the kingdom.

NARRATIVE OF M. XAVIER GUEGO,

OF THE SOCIETY OF FOREIGN MISSIONS, PARIS, MISSIONER TO SIAM.

The Sos.—Diplomacy and Diplomatist.—Simplicity and Poverty.—A good Mayor.—A troubled night.

IF the Laotien tribe of whom I am about to speak bear, in our mischief-loving French language, a name which strongly incites to laughter, I pray the reader not to make any puns. This tribe, then, is called the tribe of the *Sos* (1). If the name sound badly in our ears, it is pleasing to the heart of the good God, for many of these poor people are already His, since they are Christians.

Five years ago, when I first ventured to take up my residence amongst them, all, or nearly all fled to the forest, like the veritable savages they were. Indeed, at the time of which I speak, the neighbouring Laotiens only spoke of the Sôs by the slighting name of *Kha*, or wild men of the woods. At this first visit, notwithstand-

---

(1) A play upon the sound of the word *sot*, foolish, silly, which in French has the same pronunciation as Sos, the name of the tribe of Laos above alluded to.

ing all my advances, I could not induce them to come and see me in the modest dwelling I had had built in the very midst of their village; so I was obliged to leave, utterly unsuccessful. I therefore employed other means. Having returned to my headquarters, which at the time was the Island of St. Francis Xavier, called Done (the White Island), I sought amongst my Christians a diplomatist who should go amongst these poor Sos, and tame them somewhat. I happened to have precisely the proper person, a Christian whose father and mother were Sos. My resolution was quickly taken. I proposed that he should spend a month amongst his countrymen; he hesitated at first, but the promise of a crown piece quickly made him change his mind. Little by little he made friends with the Sos, and at the end of the month he returned triumphant to announce to me that his compatriots were anxious to be taught.

Not daring to confide too implicitly in the fine promises of my envoy, I sent on my catechist, who also spent a month in the Sos village and came back enchanted with the simplicity of the people, whereupon I myself set out once more to visit them, and, as I went along, I earnestly recommended them to their angel guardians. I walked all day and, about five o'clock in the evening, I arrived, worn out with fatigue, at my little hut, which also served as a place of meeting for the common prayer.

The interior was in perfect keeping with the exterior; there was neither chair nor table, it was absolutely bare.

On arrival, the chief of the village dons his best raiment in my honour, and when he reaches my hut prostrates himself in salutation. Immediately after come two, three, four other visitors, and before long I count as many as twenty, but not a single woman or child. With a few kindly words, I try to put them at their ease, but only partially succeed: there they crouch, scarcely daring to look me in the face. I ask them if they know any prayers, and they immediately begin to recite, as well as they know how, "*In* the name of the Father," the "Our Father," and the "Hail Mary." After this, the mayor of the village sends his son with my supper; he brings me a ragout of, *I don't know what*, in such a dirty porringer that I could not bring myself to touch it, although I may remark in passing, I am not very delicate in the matter of food; I therefore contented myself with two raw eggs, but even these were half hatched! This was my first supper.

When it was time for prayer, I gave the signal by striking on a piece of bamboo which served by way of bell. About twenty assembled, four or five of whom were little girls, but how piteously miserable was their attire!!! In all the time I had been in Laos, I had never seen anything so poor.

I intoned the few prayers which they knew, their responses seeming a mere gabble. In the midst of the service, a venemous serpent brushed against my feet, seen by all except myself, who only noticed it when prayers were over. Having despatched it, I thanked my good angel for having thus preserved me, recalling the words of the prophet: *Super aspidem ambulabis*...Yes, he whom God watches over, is well guarded.

As my beloved auditors for the most part knew nothing of the Laotien tongue, the catechism lesson was very short, but sufficient to show me that I should have enough to do in teaching them. When they had gone away, I stretched myself upon the little mat which served me as a bed, my shoes, wrapped in a piece of stuff, doing duty as a pillow. To be sure, one had been brought to me, but it was so greasy that I dared not lay my head upon it!

As I had forgotten my mosquito-net, there was not the slightest use in trying to sleep; it was still in vain, the mosquitos would not allow it, and I had nothing for it but to walk about. Towards one o'clock in the morning I again tried to sleep; still impossible. I then invented a last resource. I muffled myself in three pairs of pantaloons and three coats, I put stockings on my feet and hands, and I enveloped my head in an enormous turban, leaving only my mouth and the tip of my nose exposed. Thus swathed, I was at last enabled to sleep. In the morning, the tip of my nose was crimson with blood, but my lips had been respected.

At daybreak, my new catechumens, coming of their own accord for prayers, found me enveloped in my singular accoutrements. In France, they would have laughed; my Sos did not as much as make a remark. I taught them a little catechism, and immediately after they brought me my breakfast, which was not one whit more palatable than the supper of the night before; but there is virtue in the maxim:

"Whether you feast, or whether you fast,
Keep a light heart to the last."

All the same, I tried to do honour to my repast, but certainly I did not commit the sin of gluttony.

An Official Visit.—The Demon Guardian.—Hesitation and Triumph.—Honour to the Virgin Mary!

After breakfast, I went to pay a domiciliary visit to the village mayor. Heavens! what a hovel!...And yet, it was what they call a fine residence. My attention was attracted by the *thene phi* (altar of the guardian demon). This was a little shelf, placed against the partition and covered with all kinds of fetiches representing a toad, an elephant, a dog, etc....Pretending not to understand, I ask the mayor what is that.

"Father and benefactor, these are the tutelary gods of my house and of the whole village."

I begin to laugh, and advise him to get rid of all these little demons, promising him to put something better in their place.

"Father and benefactor," answers my good friend, "I am afraid lest the *phi raksa* (guardian demons) of my ancestors should avenge themselves if I abandon them; and then, what would people say? for it is to me they have given the charge of feeding and caring the guardian demon. My house is the altar for the whole village."

Not wishing, at my very first visit, to hurt the old mayor's feelings, I insisted no further, promising myself to return to the charge. On quitting this little hell upon earth, I went to take a walk through the village, but on seeing me, the children, and even some of the elders fled. I understood by this that the moment had not yet come for exhibiting my illustrious person. I therefore returned, quite saddened, to my house, and stretched myself upon my mat, to try and make up for my sleepless night...This time all went well; like a miller without care or without work, I had a good sleep of over three hours.

In the evening my auditors returned, accompanied by many other villagers; there were even some women, but they could not understand anything, as they did not know three words of the Laotien tongue. However, their presence was a good omen for the future. On that evening, I spoke to them of the good and bad angels, ridiculing the worship of those fetiches I had seen in the mayor's house.

"—Take my advice, my friends, and throw those powerless pieces of wood into the fire, and adore none but the great God I have come to announce to you."

"—Father and benefactor," the old mayor then replied, "do you consider what you are saying?...If ever one of us should dare to do as you advise, he would be punished on the spot. There does not pass a month, or even a week that the protecting genius does not require a sacrifice; sometimes it is a fowl, sometimes a pig, and often he even demands a buffalo; now, in spite of all these costly sacrifices, the protecting genius still troubles us in various ways; what would it be, then, should one of us dare to overthrow his altar?"

"—But," I answered, "if One more powerful should take you under His protection, what have you to fear from all the demons together?...Well, then, I assure you that if you will believe me, not only will the devil be powerless to cause your death on the spot, but he will no longer even annoy you."

"—Father and benefactor," again answers Mr. Mayor, "*jane* (I am afraid); I dare not take down the *thene* (altar)."

"—Then let me do it; I am not afraid. Here, to prove that all these little demons are powerless, to-morrow morning I will have all these ugly images brought here, before the *vote* (church), and that by these two children beside me (my two servers at Mass)."

The whole night was spent in deliberation. I could hear them from my house, but I understood nothing, as they spoke in their own language, which has no resemblance whatever to the Laotien tongue. There must have been a debate, their talk was so animated.

Being unable to sleep, both on account of the noise they made and because of the mosquitos, I began to recite my rosary, praying my angel guardian to plan, along with the good angels of my catechumens, the overthrow of the fetiches. The result was a marvellous success.

The next morning, all my brave Sos came to me, saying:

"It shall be as the Father and benefactor wishes."

The morning prayer ended, I send my two little mad-caps to hunt up the lair of the devil, with all its fetiches, decorations of flowers, garlands, etc. No need to tell them twice. No sooner said than done; in an instant the fetiches are taken from their altar and brought in an old basket very much the worse for wear, but still too good for its contents. While one lights the fire that is to consume these wooden idols, the other amuses himself poking them with a stick, and crying:

"Ugly old horned devils, make off as fast as you can, if you do not wish to be roasted!"

I laughed heartily, but my poor Sos stood there, quite terror-stricken.

After the execution, I went myself to install a statue of the Blessed Virgin in the spot where the demon had so long reigned; I blessed the house of the head of the village and I remained eight days longer amongst my beloved catechumens, to strengthen them against their fear lest the devil should come back to trouble them.

"Above all," I said to them, "repeat these words often : ' Mary, be thou our guide.' "

. I returned to my headquarters, the Island of Saint Francis Xavier, where I had left my catechist, alone, preparing the neophytes for confirmation.

The Life of a Missioner.—A First Communion.—The apostle Mayor.—A Danger avoided.—A singular vision.

Once more at home, I sent my catechist to take my place amongst the Sos and continued myself the instructions for confirmation. There had been no confirmation on the island the previous year, so that it was very trying work, the candidates being numerous.

In order the better to instruct them, I divided them into two bands, and taught them the catechism as often as four or five times a day, and it frequently happened that at the end of the day I suffered from extinction of voice; but the night and a good refreshing sleep would cure the throat, and the next day I began again as courageously as ever. About twelve days before that fixed on for the ceremony by the Rev. Father Prodhomme, the Pro-Vicar, I commenced the examinations. There were the *very good*, the *good*, and the *passable*, as in all examinations. I had already questioned about eighty, when the Pro-Vicar arrived, the full number to be confirmed being ninety-one. I need scarcely say it was a day of rejoicing for the whole island. From the communion rails to the very door of my little church, the aspirants for confirmation were ranged in two lines and there were, moreover, six first communions. Ah! how such festivals compensate the poor Missioner a hundredfold for his labours!

A few days after this happy event I once more set out in order to visit other outposts, but, as the object of this letter is to make you particularly acquainted with my beloved Sos, we will return to them at once.

During the few months that I had left them in the hands of my catechist, all had gone on admirably. My worthy mayor had preached the propaganda amongst his countrymen, and the inhabitants of two other villages, forming, with his own, a triangle, had inscribed their names as catechumens. The three villages united make a population of about five hundred souls, so you may imagine my joy on hearing this news. As the village of our good old mayor was, so to speak, the precursor of the two others, I placed it under the patronage of St. John the Baptist, the Precursor of Our Lord, the second village under that of the apostles Saint Peter and Paul, the third under that of the Immaculate Conception. The entire village of St. John the Baptist, with the exception of four or five families, were studying enthusiastically, the most fervent of all being the mayor, who begged to be at once baptized, along with his whole family: they were especially anxious, on account of an incident which had very nearly destroyed my hopes of all three villages. This is what happened:

Quite close to the village of Saint John the Baptist, is a pond, well stocked with fish, but said to be haunted by the devil. Formerly, whenever my new catechumens went there to fish, they never failed to offer sacrifice. Now, since I had burned their fetiches, they simply went to set their nets, without showing the slightest reverence for the spirit of the pond.

All the pagans were astounded that no accident happened in consequence of such daring. But behold, one fine day the mayor's son falls suddenly ill; he begins to rave and struggle like one possessed. Upon this, everyone cries out that the tutelary genii are avenging themselves. The unhappy boy, between fits and ravings, was two days without either eating or drinking; at last, on the third day, he fell into a sort of lethargic sleep. The whole village was for offering a sacrifice to the devil, otherwise the poor patient must die. If my catechist had not been there, they would certainly have offered sacrifice to the spirit of the pond and there would have been many defections. But, God be thanked, the invalid recovered, and this is what he has often related to me since:

"While I slept, two *phi* (devils) came to me and summoned me to go with them, saying that their chief had sent them for me, and that they must bring me, whether I would or no. As I refused to go, the stronger of the devils thought to seize me in his arms, both of them cursing me and reproaching me for having burned my fetiches."

"—But," I answered them, "it was not I who burned them: it was the good Father."

"—Why didst thou not prevent it? Build us here, on the very border of the pond, a new altar, or we will drag you away to our chief."

"I asked to be allowed to go and first consult the good Father, and, if he would permit it, I would build the altar. The demons advanced to seize me, when a great black man appeared; he stopped them and said, with a sneer:

"—Leave him there, let the impious one alone, and, above all, let him not bring the Father here, for then we should suffer still more."

This is the story my brave Sos has often related to me. Whatever truth may be in what he says, certain it is that since this incident all are studying more indefatigably than ever. We may well say that all things tend to the greater glory of God.

During my absence, my catechist had constructed an altar and had enlarged the shed which served as my church, and henceforth I had the consolation of celebrating the Holy Sacrifice of the Mass. I had brought with me my poor little chapel, poor indeed, as it only contained two sets of altar furniture, one black and one white. I had left my other requisites at the Island of St. Francis Xavier, in order that my fellow Missioners, who are stationed at half an hour's distance, on the right bank of the Mekong, might go there from time to time to say Mass during my absence.

In the Village of Saint John the Baptist.—Baptism of the Tribe.—Plunderers and Plundered.

I sent my catechist to Saints Peter and Paul, and I myself continued to prepare first thirty catechumens in my village of Saint John the Baptist; since the incident above related, these villagers were most anxious to be baptized. This was no easy matter. The men, as yet, did not perfectly understand me, but the women and children, having rarely heard the Laotien tongue spoken, could not understand at all.

In this work I was assisted by a young Sos whom I had brought with me to the Island of St. Francis Xavier, on the occasion of my first visit. This, my "catechist extraordinary," set himself to instruct the women and children, and it was a pleasure to listen to them, now speaking in Sos, now in Laotien. For my part, I had the men, that is to say, the flower of our students. In the evening, after prayers, I would gather all around me and teach catechism in common, during which time my new auxiliary was busy apart, teaching two old men who were half deaf. God knows the trouble and fatigue it cost me to prepare these first fruits of the Sos tribe for baptism. I gave as many as five catechism classes each day, and that for more than six weeks.

At last the long-wished for day arrived. I had chosen the feast of St. John the Baptist, patron of the village. Having prepared the souls of my dear children as best I could, there still remained a last work, that of clothing them properly, for none of them possessed anything but rags. I purchased fifteen francs worth of stuff, which was enough for the adults; as for the children, I was obliged to put off their baptism a little longer, that is to say, until I should be able to provide enough of stuff for even slight clothing.

On the very day of our patron's feast, or pardon, as they say in Brittany, a new obstacle presents itself. Word is brought to me that fifty or sixty pounds of rice had been stolen during the night from one of my catechumens. I at once sent off in pursuit of the thieves, who had been discovered; there were four of them. I had them brought into the town, where they were locked up and condemned to pay a fine of forty crowns to the owner of the stolen rice. The owner, however, according to an absurd custom existing from time immemorial in the tribe, would not take the benefit of the fine; he would only consent to receive the minimum price of his rice, and, moreover, he was obliged to disburse three or four crowns to pay those who had brought the thieves to the town; therefore, nothing remained for him. My gentlemen judges made no scruple of pocketing the greater part of forty crowns. Besides, as a general rule, the Laotiens, knowing this custom of the tribe, profit by it to commit all kind of thefts and depredations amongst the Sos... But to return to the festival, from which this incident diverted us a moment.

I administered, then, baptism to eighteen adults, at whose head were our old mayor, his son, and all his family. After the dejeuner, my newly baptized children, with their godfathers and godmothers, whom I had brought hither from the Island of Saint Francis Xavier, came to pay their respects to me and offer me a number of presents: bananas, sugarcanes, fowl, frogs, etc., etc., and I distributed rosaries and medals to them... How happy we all were, Father and children! At two o'clock we recited the Rosary, after which, I went to bless the houses, even the mayoralty house (do not, if you please, forget for a moment that it is but a hovel). I gave a little statue to each family, to be put in the place of the fetiches, and, finally, I blessed the cemetery, where already repose two good old men whom my catechist had baptized on their deathbeds. Thus the living and the dead had a part in the festival. Once more, what a happy day! In truth, are not Missioners the spoiled children of Providence!

In the Village of the Holy Apostles.—Art in its Infancy. Terror and Confidence.—Stratagems of Charity.

The following day I set out on horseback to visit the other village of Sos catechumens whom I had placed under the protection of the Holy Apostles. My catechist had already been there for two months and had built for me a sort of chapel-house. In this village are twenty-five families, twenty-two of whom are under instruction, but, my God, how untamed these poor pagans were! As soon as they saw me (this was the first time I entered that village), the women, the children, and even a great many of the men, fled to the forest, and God only knows in what attire! In fact, these poor Sos are absolutely ignorant both of weaving and sewing. The few rags in which they are wrapped are usually only the cast-offs of the Laotiens, and for these they exchange small grass mats, the only work of art known to their women. They spend five or six days plaiting a single one, which will be sold for two or three pence. With seven or eight of these little mats they can buy themselves a sort of petticoat which is fastened round the waist and reaches below the knees; this is the whole dress of the women; as for the men, their's is still more primitive ... And yet, to do them justice, they are fairly good blacksmiths, especially when we consider the very imperfect implements they employ.

When night came, I saw as if shadows stealing into the village on all sides; they were the fugitives returning to their huts. A few men, however, came to pay me a visit, in company with the mayor, who made rather a good impression on me. I tried to win them, to handle them with gloves on, as we say, in order not to startle their timid natures.

Next morning, I offered up the Holy Sacrifice, about twenty men and three or four women assisting. While making my thanksgiving I left them with my catechist, then I came to converse with them, but they scarcely dared to speak to me, still less, look me in the face. Were they frightened at my beard? or at what? I do not know. Having exchanged a few words, I desired them to come, after breakfast, in great numbers to the catechism.

"—Good Father," answered the mayor, "it is impossible. In a few minutes all, save the old and the infirm, will disperse to one place or another, to sow the fields, to gather faggots in the forest, etc."

"—Well, at least," said I, "try and come in the evening. I want, my friends, to teach you how to be happy, even in the midst of your poverty."

"—Father," replied my old friend, the women and children do not understand the Laotien language."

"—But that will come little by little."

"—The women, particularly, not having proper clothing, dare not present themselves."

Seeing here a favourable occasion for winning their good graces:

"—Very well," said I, "to-morrow morning I will give the poorest amongst them material to make clothes."

And I at once sent off to purchase 12 francs worth of stuff. Next day, two or three women only came to ask for them; and why did not the others come? Would you believe it? They were afraid that I might afterwards say that they were in my debt and at the end of the account I should seize on them as slaves ... In fact, here amongst the Laos it is not rare to find poor slaves, the principle of whose debt did not exceed two or three francs; I have even met some who were enslaved for stealing a hen. My brave Sos therefore feared a trap, and left me there, with my presents of stuff.

For several days my congregation was the same as in the beginning. I tried a new method. I sent my two choir boys to take walks in the village, advising them to bring back the children to play with them. All in vain. The little savages, not knowing a word of the Laotien tongue, fled into the forests as fast as their legs would carry them. What am I to do, I said to myself, to catch these uncatchables? I tried yet another method which had some little success. I fill my pockets with tobacco and go through the village; still they run away. I go farther, I enter the cabins. Here, I find an old man, there, an old woman; before saying anything, I laughingly hold out a handful of tobacco; they understand this at once and stretch out their horny hands to receive my little gift.

All my tobacco goes thus. In the evening, the labourers coming back from the fields soon heard of my generosity, and several at once came to ask me for a pipeful of tobacco, which I was delighted to give them. Next day, I went through the same process, I even added to my ambulatory bazaar.

I also brought needles, thread, stuff, etc., which I distributed to the grandmothers. To be brief, I ended by taming these poor savages a little. After having remained two weeks in their village, I returned to my Island of Saint Francis Xavier, but, in order to continue their religious instruction, I left behind me a young man whom I had brought with me and my two choir boys. A month later, the young catechist arrived at the Island, quite discouraged and saying nothing could be done with these savages; that since my departure they no longer attended the catechism classes.

"—Come, come," said I, "you do not know how to set about it; in a few days you shall return there with me, and you will see that we shall do wonders."

But the young man was so downcast that he would have no more to do with me.

I therefore looked out for another assistant and once more set out, passing through the village of Saint John the Baptist, where my temporary catechist prepared the neophyte for confession. He told me that all came to catechism with the greatest regularity. He had only one complaint to make, which was, that his food was insufficient, so I gave him some fishing-tackle and he was perfectly content.

Having heard the confessions of my new Christians, I at once left for the village of the Holy Apostles, of which I had had a sad account. My old acquaintances, the mayor amongst them, hastened forth to welcome me with:

"—Father, we know three prayers already."

"—That's good," said I, "we shall see this evening. Be sure you all come."

And, in fact, my auditors were more numerous than ever, there being even a good many women, who this time were properly clothed; in the end, they had taken the stuff which I had desired my catechist to distribute amongst them. After the devotions, I questioned several of them and found they could repeat the "Our Father," and the "Hail Mary," which they had learned from my two acolytes. I congratulated them on their knowledge, and particularly on their good will.

My good angel then suggested an idea which was worth its weight in gold. As there were a great many children in the village, I asked the mayor to send them to me that they might learn by themselves during the day. The old man started objections at once; they hadn't proper clothes; some must go to the pastures and tend the herds; others must remain at home to mind the little brother or the little sister; they could not understand me, and then ...

"—Stop there, old grandpapa;" said I, "as for the clothes, I'll

ÉQUATOR (Southern America). — Missionary-house at Archidona.

undertake to find them; as for the herds, they can go graze a little later, and they won't be one bit the less well fed; finally, let the scholars bring the little brothers and the little sisters with them; if they cry too much, the school shall be closed; if it is possible to quiet them, we will do it with some dainties. As for the rest, grandpapa, don't imagine I shall keep the children too long: you shall see that in a few days the little madcaps will be enchanted to come to school. They don't know the Laotien tongue; that is an additional reason why they should come, for I will teach it to them."

Next day my mayor arrives, himself bringing the little scholars. Thirty children, boys and girls, several of whom carried either a little brother or a little sister on their backs. I gave each one a little piece of stuff... you should see the delight of all these little people!... To gain my pupils' hearts, I did nothing for several days beyond making them chant some prayers. It was enchanting to see them making the sign of the Cross! They made it in thirty-six different ways!... It was nearly right when I guided the hand, all laughing at each other, like the happy little innocents they were. When they were somewhat at home with me, I began to teach them the A, B, C, dividing them into three sections, two of which I handed over to my choir boys, reserving the third for myself. The programme was carried out: sometimes a little A, B, C, sometimes a few prayers, and sometimes catechism.

All was going on splendidly, when home sickness seized on my two little teachers. It was all in vain to preach to them, to promise them a rosary, a little brass cross; all in vain, I was obliged to send them back to the Island.

Behold me, then, alone, in the midst of my pupils, the boys to the right, the girls to the left, and you have the picture. It was often necessary to call them to order, for the noise was unendurable, the smallest of all, astride on the backs of their elders, adding their share to the racket. In fact, my poor throat suffered, and my sense of smell also went through a martyrdom. But I consoled myself by thinking that before long the souls of these little ones, purified in the waters of baptism, would exhale a delicious perfume.

In the evening, after the public prayers, I taught catechism to the men and women, who came in ever increasing numbers, while the afternoons were spent in an attempt to teach the old men and women and the sick. How often, on such occasions, have I been obliged to repeat the same thing twenty times over! Ah! how frequently I petitioned the good Saint Francis de Sales to obtain for me one ounce of patience and of gentleness!

I remained a little over a month in the midst of this select audience. I do not know if the good God was content with me, but for my part I thanked Him with all my heart for having enabled me to induce these poor people, so lately mere savages, to come and listen to me, especially as they were then in very poor circumstances: in fact, they were in extreme want at the very time. After having recommended my dear catechumens to their good guardian angels, I confided them to my new catechist who had come from the Island of Saint Francis Xavier.

Escaped with a Fright.—In the Village of the Immaculate Conception.—Discouragement.

Thence I directed my steps towards another village, the largest and most populous of my three Sos districts. This village contained sixty or seventy families, and my principal catechist or seminarist had been there for a month, with two children to whom he was teaching their prayers.

Thither the devil wished to accompany me and tried to play me an ugly trick. The road was excessively difficult and, in descending a ravine, I had a fall which must have had serious consequences if my horse had not stopped on the instant. As it was, I remained hanging by the legs in the midst of a clump of thorns. My groom, who followed, should have hurried to my assistance, but he remained there looking on at my struggles to free myself from the brushwood, and only got off his horse when I ordered him to dismount. When he came to my assistance, I was already on my feet, but with torn garments and limbs lacerated by the thorns. I drew the rags of my clothing together, as best I could, and continued my journey; as for my wounded legs, time cured them.

As I have already said, I had placed this village under the protection of the Immaculate Conception. On my arrival, the inhabitants received me well, and I found that the greater number had already inscribed their names as catechumens. My catechist had built a fairly good chapel-house for me, and everything inspired me with hopes of full success. During the fortnight I remained in this village most of the inhabitants attended the catechism classes pretty regularly; but the great number of Laotien villages which are likewise desirous of being under our care would not allow of my making a longer stay, and after my departure this Sos village fell off from its first good dispositions. The enemy of all truth sowed the tares, and the authorities of the district succeeded, by all kinds of lies and calumnies, in making them return to their old superstitions. Still, seven or eight families persevered, and last year I had the happiness of baptizing them. With the grace of God and with patience, I hope to see the return of all the deserters, especially as the two principal men of the village are amongst those who have been baptized.

Holy Death of the old Mayor of St. John the Baptist.—Last Words: the Harvest is ripe, but Labourers and means are wanting.

Before ending my story, let us return for a moment to the village of St. John the Baptist. The last time that I went there I found the good old mayor confined to bed attacked by a dysentery which refused to yield to any remedies. The moment he saw me, he threw himself at my feet, saying that he had a presentiment that his end was near.

"—Yes, good Father, I feel that I am dying, but I am happy, because I have been baptized. I have already divided my herds amongst my children. As for money, I have none, save a few crowns that have been borrowed by my *thai bane* (compatriots, neighbours). As there is no written evidence of the debt, I ask that you, good Father, will call my debtors together and let them acknowledge or deny their debts in your presence. I am afraid that were I dead, my children might cause my memory to be cursed by exacting more than is due to me, or that, on the other hand, my debtors might injure my children by denying their debts."

I summoned all the debtors before me, and not a single one denied his obligation. Thus, all the old man's temporal affairs were happily arranged.

"—Father," said he, "I now wish to make my last confession: I ask to be allowed to make it this evening . . . I desire to have no more worldly distractions, but to prepare for death...I have heard the catechist teach that there is a sacrament still greater than that of baptism, the *sin maha sanit* (the Sacrament of the Eucharist): oh! might I not receive it!"

And he then began to tell me all he had learned about the Holy Communion. In order to satisfy his pious longing, and not to sadden Our Saviour's Heart by depriving His zealous servant of this Pledge of eternal life, I spent three days explaining this Divine Sacrament, of which he had understood but the letter; then I gave him Holy Communion. The good old man! with what sentiments of love and fervour did he, for the first and last time, receive his Divine Master! The following day I administered Extreme Unction, for his malady grew worse. He lingered eight days longer, then rendered up his pure soul to his Creator, one Sunday while I was celebrating Mass.

Thus expired this good old mayor, who had always assisted me, to the utmost of his power, to win over his fellow-countrymen to the cause of Jesus Christ. I have no doubt that Our Saviour granted him His Mercy.

You see here how my ministry amongst the Laos tribe has begun. Now, friend reader, what do you say of my beloved Sos? As for me, I am enchanted with them. I have amongst them two hundred and seventy-five Christians living. Ah! why are there not more of us to work amongst our Laos, and why have we not more abundant means! The harvest looks ripe on every side, but the harvesters, and the means of gathering it in, are wanting. On the left bank of the vast Mekong river, I am alone, with one young student from Bangkok, while I have twelve stations.

From one end of the year to the other, I may say I do nothing but travel, sometimes on foot, sometimes in a boat, oftenest on horseback. At each post, my only presbytery is a little spot adjoining the poor shed which serves as my church: miserable enough. But can I complain, when Our Lord is no better lodged! Last year I had 201 baptisms, the year before that I had 361; this year I have had but 101, and yet God knows if I have not worked hard. But, as you have seen, I am often obliged to help, in their great poverty, these poor outcasts of fortune.

May I then be permitted to recommend our work to the prayers and charity of pious souls.

MISSIONS OF AMERICA.

VICARIATE-APOSTOLIC OF NAPO.

The following letter from the Rev. Father Detroux is a tribute to the memory of Garcia Moreno, the illustrious President of Equator. It shows what influence those in high places can exercise for the moral good of their subjects. Happily, the valiant Society of Jesuits still continues its onward course, with the enlightened devotion which characterizes all its Missions.

LETTER FROM THE REV. FATHER M. DETROUX
OF THE SOCIETY OF JESUS.

Missions amongst the Savages.—Difficulties of Travelling.

IN 1869, the Mission of Napo was, after a century of interruption, once more confided to the care of the Jesuit Fathers. It is situated in the eastern part of the Republic of Equator, and has for limits on the north and north-east the diocese of Pasto, in Colombia, on the south-east the diocese of Chachapoyas in Peru, and to the south and south-west the Prefecture-Apostolic of Canelos and Macas, from which it is separated by the Tiger river.

The principal residence is Archidona, the capital of the province, situated in southern latitude 53° 46, and 45° 39 eastern longitude, in the meridian of Quito, on the left bank of the Misbagualli. The distance from Quito is about thirty leagues, which cannot be got over in less than eight days, on account of the difficulties of the road. The first day's journey can be made on horseback, as far as Papallacta, a civilized Indian village which forms the limit of the diocese of Quito. Here the Missioner must put his soutane in his portmanteau, don a light coat, short pantaloons, sandals on his feet, and, straw hat on his head and staff in hand, set out across hills and through ravines. He is often up to the knees in mud, especially in the rainy season.

A few Indians carry the baggage necessary for the six or seven days' march which separate Papallacta from Achidona, for along the whole route there is not a single habitation to be met with, save a little cluster of houses at Baeza, an ancient town, situated about midway on the journey. On this account, it is also necessary each evening to improvise a hut made with four stakes, two large and two smaller, fixed in the ground and joined together at the top with branches of trees, upon which are spread palm leaves, to serve as a roof. It is hardly necessary to say that this roof does not always suffice to keep out the torrents of rain which frequently fall during the night. There are also a number of rivers to be crossed, either by swimming, aided by a stout Indian accustomed to the passage, or by crossing a bridge consisting simply of a couple of trees thrown across. Sometimes it happens that the river is so swollen after some storm, that the traveller is obliged to stop and wait upon the banks for three or four days before venturing the passage; and woe to whoever is thus surprised without the necessary provisions!

Beginning Evangelization.—First Fruits.—Hopes.

From its very inception, the Jesuit Fathers received from his Holiness, with the consent of the government of Garcia Moreno, charge of the entire Oriental Mission, which is now divided into four Prefectures-Apostolic. Our schools were flourishing, and our Missioners were ardently and successfully working for the evangelization of the poor Indians.

The following was received by us from the Minister of the Interior on the 21st September, 1870. The letter shows what confidence was placed in us by the government:

"The excellent results obtained by your zealous apostleship amongst the barbarians of these regions, renders it the duty of the government to express to you their great satisfaction and deep gratitude. They are a proof that God protects and guides you. The actual state of the Indians makes it impossible to establish any definite rule, but as social life is impossible without a certain authority being established, his Excellency the President of the Republic has arranged as follows:

1st. The Reverends, the Missioner Fathers, will appoint authorities, under the title of alcades (governors), in each village, confiding to them the maintainance of order and the administration of justice in their respective districts;

2nd. The Reverend Fathers, the Missioners, may accept the resignation of the authorities, or may revoke their appointments in the case of non-fulfilment of duty, and may appoint others in their places;

3rd. Schools shall be established in each Reduction, at the cost of the Government, for the instruction of children, not only in catechism, Spanish, reading, writing, and arithmetic, but also in the most useful trades, in singing and instrumental music. At least one hour daily shall be devoted to the teaching of trades. Schools will also be established for girls, as soon as there are ladies in the country capable of teaching. Fathers of families shall be obliged to send their children to school, and the class-hours shall be so divided that the children will not be fatigued or wearied of them. Their application to be stimulated by prizes and honours.

4th. Sunday schools will be established for adults, who shall receive primary instruction for two hours on all holy days.

5th. The Reverend Fathers, the Missioners, will always receive from the Government the support and protection necessary for the carrying out of the holy work with which they are charged, and, should circumstances require it, they will have the aid of the public forces for their defence and protection."

All went on so marvellously well in the Missions that, in his message to the Chambers, in 1873, Garcia Moreno felt justified in writing:

" Upon the banks of the Napo, where the Missioners have established themselves, with the approbation of the Government, true civilization, the civilization of the Cross, is steadily making its way, and the schools founded by the apostolic zeal of the indefatigable sons of the Society of Jesus, are preparing an era of light and prosperity for these rich, but wild regions. The Mission is in a flourishing condition and promises well for the future."

And certainly these hopes would not have been vain, had Garcia Moreno, the especial protection of the Missions, lived.

The following was written by the Rev. Father, the Vicar-Apostolic, in 1875:

" Up to the present, we have built nine churches, proportionate in size to the several populations.

" Not to mention each Reduction in particular, I will confine myself to that of Archidona. Its two thousand inhabitants are, unfortunately, scattered in little groups of families over a district of several miles, intersected by greater and lesser rivers, and full of impenetrable forests and ravines. Each family cultivates its field and follows the occupations of hunting, fishing, and the manufacture of a sort of coarse thread. When offered wages, the natives also help in the harvesting.

" These people assemble each Saturday around the church and the Missioners' house, remaining there in groups all Saturday afternoon and Sunday morning. The re-union brings about a little market, and each head of a group gives the Missioner an account of the principal events of the week. Baptisms generally take place during these re-unions and all disputes are settled. On Sunday we say Mass, the Christian Doctrine is chanted and the Missioner gives an explanation of the catechism. At mid-day the adults go home to their distant huts, not to return until the following Saturday, unless some festival occur during the week. The children attend catechism every day, the greater number of the boys living constantly near the Fathers, and sleeping in a place assigned for this purpose near the church. It is upon these latter the hopes of the Mission are founded. Their good conduct and their studiousness, joined to a most docile character, make it possible to rule them with almost as great regularity as if it were a college in a civilized city. There are at present 217 at Archidona.

"We observe a marked difference between the Indians who have grown old in their nomad habits and the rising generations. The old folks are outwardly submissive, and sometimes even servile to an exaggerated degree, but in their hearts they preserve, and occasionally betray, their old ideas and their evil intents, opposing a dogged resistance to all the Missioners' plans, in order that they may continue in their untrammelled and lazy life. The children, on the contrary, are sincerely affectionate. These poor little ones read, write, learn elementary arithmetic, translate from Spanish into Quitchua, and are remarkable for their application and rapid progress. In my last journey to Quito, I brought with me two little Indians who exhibited their writing and read aloud from a book handed to them, and translated some paragraphs into their own language, although they were rendered somewhat nervous by the presence of the Archbishop and other distinguished personages of Quito."

The Missioner does not confine himself to directing the village schools and conducting the religious exercises of each week; he also visits the inhabited districts within a wide radius of the church, attending to the old, the infirm, and the dying. I do not think that a single child died unbaptized throughout our whole Mission, and we may even say that no one dies without receiving the sacraments, if we except those who are absent on the long journeys which are the delight of the Indians.

Such was the flourishing condition of the Napo Mission in 1875. " Nine thousand savages," exclaimed the illustrious President of Equator, on the last page of his missive, dyed with his blood, " nine thousand savages, led to a Christian and civilized life, speak in eloquent terms of what we owe to the Church and to the Religious Orders."

Trials.—Death of Garcia Moreno.—Revolt of the Indians.

Such happiness could not last. Garcia Moreno fell, and with him, for a time at least, the prosperity of the Mission was at an end. As we know, the death of the illustrious President took place on the 6th of August, 1875. Shortly before this, smallpox had broken out amongst the Indians, who at once fled in terror, to their huts amongst the mountains, where they lived as much isolated from each other as possible, such was their fear of contagion. Consequently, even before the death of their especial protector, the Missioners found themselves completely deserted by the Indians and d prived of all human aid. They had no food save a little yuca and what bananas they could gather in the abandoned fields, and had to go out to gather wood for their cooking fire. They were even obliged to refrain from celebrating the Mass, for want of the wine necessary for the Sacrifice. The news of the death of the President having become known, and the soldiers having returned to Quito, the Indians revolted against the Missioners, in order that they might henceforth live according to their inclinations.

Yet, little by little, by incessant labour and sacrifices, the Missioners succeeded in again uniting the Indians and in continuing their work of civilization. Yet all through they had much to suffer from the White traders who, far from aiding them, incited the poor Indians to revolt, while they themselves annoyed the Missioners in a hundred ways.

From the time the Jesuit Fathers arrived on the scene, the malice of these disturbers of the peace, the traders, has been ever on the increase. Towards the end of August, 1892, three White men, who had come from Archidona, repaired to Conception, where they had arranged to meet the Indians. They fell upon and disarmed the two soldiers who were there, took possession of their rifles, and both White men and Indians, some seventy in number, marched upon Loreto. Some of the rebels were armed with rifles, the rest with cutlasses. About five o'clock in the afternoon of the 30th of August, they took possession of the public square, and at once directed their steps towards the residence of the Chief, whom they seized and tied. Meantime, the Indians of Loreto joined with the rebels, thus forming a body of two hundred men, who then attacked the residence of the Missioners (at the time occupied in the schools), beat them severely and brought them in custody to the Chief's house, where they momentarily expected to be put to death.

At daybreak, remembering that the Blessed Sacrament remained in the chapel and was exposed to outrage, Father Guertas asked the rebels to allow him to celebrate Mass, in order that he might consume the Sacred Host, but his request was in vain. He, however, succeeded in obtaining permission to go, along with his companion, to the chapel, and, as all were fasting from noon of the previous day, Father Guertas opened the door of the Tabernacle, as best he could, his hands being tied, gave Holy Communion to his companions, and consumed the Blessed Eucharist.

Immediately after this religious rite, the rebels set about executing the second part of their project, which was, to bring their prisoners, tied as they were, throw them into a canoe, and let them float at the mercy of the current. It would be impossible to describe the agony of the victims during the four or five hours march towards the river.

Fortunately, a party of soldiers arrived in time to save them from death.

Reorganization of the Mission.—Its present Condition.

It would be impossible to realize the disastrous consequences of this rebellion, especially amongst the Indians of Loreto. Of the two hundred children who had previously frequented the school, it is doubtful if there are twenty attending to-day. As for the Indians of Archidona, they attend Mass regularly every Sunday and willingly give up their children to our care. All the Missioners' hopes are therefore founded on them.

Above two hundred and thirty boys attend the Fathers' school daily, and two hundred girls attend that of the Sisters. More than fifty children are fed and clothed at the expense of the Mission.

The Indians themselves recognize the superiority of the children reared with us: in fact, there is a complete change in them, as the Rev. Father Tovia has reported to the President of the Republic.

We hope to found similar establishments in the other Residences, for this is the only means of forming truly Christian generations.

MISSIONS OF OCEANIA.

ARCHDIOCESE OF WELLINGTON.

We owe the charming letter which we are about to read to a Marist Missioner whose praises we have no need to sound, for the readers of the *Annals* doubtless remember the touching incident the account of which we published from his pen four months since, and the subscribers to the *Missions Catholiques* have not forgotten the *Maori Tales*. This number, appearing at the season of the touching festival of Christmas, will give all the charm of reality to the following pages.

LETTER FROM THE REV. FATHER COGNET,

MARIST FATHER.

Christmas amongst the Maoris.

AMONGST all Christian peoples, "Christmas" holds the favourite place of all the festivals of the year; there is none which awakens so many sweet recollections, so many pious feelings, such pure joy. Only to name Christmas, is it not enough to recall that happy eve when, united around the traditional yule log which slowly burned upon the hearth, the family circle of other days waited, in joyous impatience, for the holy hour of midnight? Is it not enough to bring back the echo of the gay converse in which we little ones loved to have the larger share, while our mothers, to "quiet" us, half whispered the promise of a long coveted toy? Is it not enough to awaken, from the very depths of memory, I know not what faint peal of bells, I know not what mysterious flare of torches flitting along the roads, I know not what sweet strains of canticles re-echoing from the valley, what dim vision of stars twinkling above a world wrapped in a white mantle of snow? And the Crib of the God King, Jesus! Symbol and compendium of the hopes of the world! And the Christmas-tree, symbol and compendium of the simple hopes of childhood! This unity of mysteries, recalled by so many touching customs, does it not give a special, I had almost said unique cachet to this festival, a cachet that makes it popular the world over? "Noel! Noel! behold the Christ has come!" chanted the angels, inviting the Shepherds of Bethlehem to join in their act of faith and hail with them the advent of the Divine Emmanuel! And for eighteen hundred years, amongst all Christian people, the old have said to the young, and child repeats to child: "Noel! Noel! behold the Christ has come!"

Protestantism has never attempted to lessen the influence of this festival on the popular mind. It has left it as it found it; and to-day English, Germans, Americans, and Australians know no more beautiful festival than Christmas; rich and poor, public officials and private individuals, all celebrate it joyously, usually adding their good wishes for the coming year. Devotedly attached, as they are, to the customs of their forefathers, the English on that day make a great show of religious observances, which inspires us with some salutary reflections: many Protestants who never set foot within a church during the year, would think they had transgressed all rules of decorum if they absented themselves on that day. It is absolutely only the scum of English society that scoffs at the pious tradition of Christmas.

Side by side with these European splendours, perhaps my readers will look with pleasure on the modest but interesting first attempts of our Maoris of the Antipodes to join in the chorus of praise and adoration which rises yearly from all parts of the world towards the Crib of Bethlehem. Having several times had the happiness of assisting at these never-to-be-forgotten festivals, I will try to describe their organization and the manner in which they are conducted.

Civil Celebrations.—Receptions and Addresses.

I must first remark that custom has already given a somewhat civilized character to all our native usages, yet, in spite of this tendency to progress, a tendency which detracts greatly from the originality of the native festivals, there still remain details curious enough to be worthy of note.

The Maoris are an eminently practical people; they possess the organs of order and precision; they understand admirably how the division of labour quickens work, and, amongst them, the preparations for each festival are usually completed a long time beforehand. Christmas is celebrated by each village of a district, every village taking its turn, and a tribe would feel disgraced if it allowed its turn to pass. At the same time that this family festival draws hearts closer and furnishes a good occasion for talking over and arranging many things, it affords us, Missioners, the great advantage of meeting several tribes together, of living amongst them for some days, and of dispensing to them, while they take their leisure, the Gospel treasures we have brought them.

It was the 21st December, 1890. I was then at Kauaeroa, near Hiruharama, on the Wanganui river, where Christmas was to be celebrated that year. A long time before, an invitation had been sent to all the tribes of the district, summoning them to meet at the spot where, in 1852, the revered Father Lampila, their first apostle, had built his first church, and baptized his first neophytes.

The idea of a "jubilee" was therefore added to the usual motives for this assembly; and, as he who had organized this festival was a chief who lived in perfect harmony with all his neighbours, the invitation addressed to the tribes could not but be well responded to.

This chief, named Werahiko, was in their eyes the representative of an epoch of fervour, when Faith reigned supreme upon the shores

ÉQUATOR (Southern America). — PUCAURCU, village of Napo.

Lyon, imp. A. Rey.

of the Wanganui; having himself served the Mass of the former Missioners, and remaining to this day the best friend and right hand of their happy successors, his name sounded everywhere like an echo of the past, and like a call to Baptism and to a life of virtue. You can, then, easily understand how desirous we were to co-operate, to the utmost of our power, in making the festival a success. So, while the Rev. Father Soulas organized a band and was busy training his boys, I went visiting through the villages, beating up as many guests as possible for the occasion.

The Maoris of the town of Kauaeroa had charge of the *immediate preparations.* Some pitched and fixed the tents, which they then ornamented with flowers and green branches; others went eel-fishing amongst the rapids, fishing with long osier nets or traps, hollowed out in the shape of funnels; finally, others went through the fields, one killing an ox, another a sheep, another a certain animal which I shall not name, but which Saint Anthony has made celebrated. There were veritable hecatombs! In their carelessness of to-morrow and their enthusiasm of the moment, our natives sacrifice all, without a thought of the future.

The 24th December was the day fixed upon for the inaugural meeting. In the morning I had opened and blessed a pretty Maori house, the happy completion of which had served as the pretext for the feast, and a few hours later all the tribes of our Riviera arrived in their barks, singing as they rowed. It is a curious and interesting sight to watch a debarkation under such circumstances. To begin, when the first signal is given of the approach of a canoe, a salvo of musketry is fired in welcome. Then, from place to place, burst forth prolonged cheers, announcing the general joy, and, while the echoes are still repeating these noisy manifestations, the pirogues are discharging their crews. The provisions brought as an offering to the friendly tribe are piled upon the bank. Then, a procession is formed and the new arrivals present themselves before the assembly, who thereupon proceed to the ceremony of the "tangi." In the Maori country, friends never meet but that the first words exchanged are in remembrance of the dead whom they mourn, a touching custom, with which we are very careful not to interfere! When they have wept freely, they seat themselves around and the chiefs give themselves up to a perfect tournament of eloquence, or they chant the praises of the dead and announce the reason of their visit. This ended, they all draw closer to each other, and the "hongi" takes place. This ceremony consists in rubbing noses, while they press each others hands firmly, and the guttural organs emit an indescribable little cry which somewhat reminds one of a mouse caught in a trap and already half strangled. It is quite pathetic. Then the meeting is over: the new arrivals mix with the former and take possession of the tents or houses which have been assigned to them. If more boats arrive, then the whole company re-assembles to meet them.

Such are the usual proceedings of the first day: it is spent in receptions and speeches, though sometimes, in the midst of the civilities, a dispute arises out of nothing at all. For example, on this very occasion that I have undertaken to describe, two Hiruharama chiefs set to, *coram publico*, and entered on a regular joust of abuse, all about the merest trifle. Then, suddenly, at the very moment when the spectators anticipated something quite different, behold! the better man of the two (named Tohiora) addresses his adversary and says brusquely : "*Listen, I have said all I had to say. Now, shake hands, for to-morrow will be Christmas-Day !!!*" Loud applause hailed these noble words, and the other chief had to comply with a good grace, in order not to incur the ill-will of the tribe.

A few minutes after this incident, we all went in a body to welcome *Major Kemp* (Taitoko) and *Topia*, the two principal personages of the district. The former owes his title to the courage and ability he showed in commanding the natives regiments who rallied to the support of the Colonial Government during the late wars. He has two flags carried before him: one which he received as a reward for his services, and one carried at Moutoa, which is riddled with balls and is still stained with the blood of his brave men. Topia is the actual chief of Hiruharama, and is the standard bearer of Catholicism in New Zealand, for his father, the famous Pehi Turoa, was the first chief of note who protected our cause.

In order to give a grand reception to these typical representatives of our Antipodes, the whole tribe acted a mock battle, and our little band made the air resound with its most joyous music. In a word, the welcome was a perfect success.

After the ceremony of the "tangi" had taken place, our noble visitors pronounced two fine discourses, which I may sum up thus: "*All hail to Christmas! Glory to Christ, who has given peace to the world! Glory to the Church and to the Priests, who have spread the Faith amongst our people! Glory to Father Lampilla, the first Father of our tribes! We are here assembled to bear witness that his work and his memory still live,*" etc., etc.

While those eloquent speeches were being delivered, the young folk, ever restless and lively, amused themselves in the adjoining meadows. Some practised gymnastics, after their own fashion; others again improvised *camelots*, and played at keeping shop.

As for us Missioners, shut up in our tents, we spent our time in preparing those who were to be baptized, who were about to receive Holy Communion, and those about to be married, all of which sacred duties kept us busy until the night was far advanced. There was no other care to trouble us. In Europe, on such an occasion, it would be necessary to secure the assistance of the police, and, alas! provide for any deplorable casualties that might occur. But here, in the midst of these so-called savages, there is nothing of the kind to fear. So true is it to-day that the worst savages are not to be found in the woods, but at the corners of the most crowded streets, and even in the finest drawingrooms.

The Religious Celebrations.

In the morning, the religious services took place; but, alas! in Maori-land we cannot yet aspire to the holy grandeur of the midnight Mass. In place of spacious and beautiful churches, it is usually at the end of a *whare russanga* (house of assembly), that our modest altar, decked with flowers and leaves, is humbly raised. And yet, simple as it is, it must be very pleasing to the Divine Infant, for it is often surrounded by souls as upright and holy as those of the shepherds of Bethlehem, and, moreover, this altar represents the first homage offered by a conquered people to the Divine Conqueror of the world, Jesus: in this lies its chief beauty.

Besides, it must not be thought that our natives are quite devoid of artistic taste. We sometimes find them arrange really pretty decorations with interwoven flowers, ferns, and green boughs. And then, how is it possible not to be struck with a sentiment of deep admiration on hearing them sing the "*Adeste Fidelis!*" that canticle that so well expresses all the joys of Christmas! But yesterday, these same lips were stained with blood; they unclosed only to sing the praises of the demon . . . and to-day, behold them breathing canticles of holy love! A few minutes later, and you will see these long files of men and women approaching to present themselves at the holy altar. Draped in their mantles of ceremony, all these, the elect of the Holy Eucharist, will come to offer the tribute of their pure and simple faith to Jesus, the King.

Banquets.—Distributions of Provisions and of Presents.

After the refreshment of the soul comes that of the body. On these state occasions, the Maoris display a remarkable aptitude for organizing a banquet. If there is less of refinement and luxury in the preparation of the dishes, there is a truly Homeric abundance, and an incredible variety of viands amongst these " savages." For example: on these gala days, a favourite dish is an ox roasted entire in the earth, with its skin and horns. Flanking this " head dish " is a row of porkers, cooked in the same fashion, with potatoes, turnips, cabbages, etc., to say nothing of the game and fish which necessarily figure in a Maori bill of fare. Add to all this " *taros*," " *ignames*," confectionery, fruits, well-made and well-flavoured cakes, and, to wash down the whole, plenty of tea, or, should it be preferred, clear, fresh water. There is no table in the banqueting hall, but a white cloth, spread upon mats laid on the ground, takes its place. All seat themselves Japanese fashion, their backs against the wall, the centre of the room being reserved for the serving of the guests, which is done by the young men, who are well dressed and perform their duties with a courtesy that is perfect. The food is carried round in little baskets woven of the leaves of the *phormium tenax:* each guest receives his own basket.

But we must not be in too great a hurry to satisfy our appetite; a good Maori never neglects, in public especially, to say his *Benedicte* aloud. On important occasions, the honour of repeating this prayer is always reserved for the Priest; the Protestants themselves never find fault with this custom, to which they adhere as faithfully as we do ourselves. If the Catholic Priest be present, his *Benedicte* holds " valid " and is not repeated ; if, on the contrary, the Protestant minister takes it upon himself to fill this rôle, many of our Catholics, having listened in silence, are tempted to begin again. They say, in their homely style : " *to dine without the sign of the Cross, is as if one set out to fish without a net !* " It is, perhaps, in order to avoid this slight that our " Protestants " are careful to add a *grace* at the end of the *Benedicte*. It certainly is the surest means, for who could answer for its not being forgotten, were it put off to the end of the feast?

How much I could still tell you about these joyous festivals, which remind us of the "love-feasts" of the early Christians. The cordiality that reigns, the joy that overflows from all these souls, set one dreaming. Oh! what a happy people these would be if the Catholic Faith could win them to its beneficent yoke, calm the ardour of their passions, and purify all their inclinations!

But every Maori feast has its practical ending, which is a general distribution of viands and presents. I cannot omit speaking of this, for it is one of the most distinctive and salient characteristics of Oceanean manners.

I have already observed that, in coming to the assembly, each tribe was careful to bring its quota of provisions. The principal chiefs, above all, make it a point of honour to display their liberality. Contrary to our European socialists, whose maxims are but so many falsehoods, our "savages" of the Antipodes know well that, in order to have something to share, they must first have a common fund, and afterwards they must vie with each other to increase it. Then, when the moment has come for the distribution of the common wealth, they know perfectly well how to do it good temperedly and in proportion to individual rights. I do not say that there is never injustice or recrimination; but, if there be, the authority of the chiefs is there to put an end to disputes and re-establish peace.

At the close of the festivities, whatever provisions remain are to be distributed amongst all the tribes present. Wonderful to relate! Those who live in the interior of the Island and far from civilization, are the most favoured. If there be any rarities, or any delicacies unknown in their distant regions, our Christian tribes are careful to set these delicacies aside for them. This is a custom we delight in.

encouraging, for these graceful acts have often the effect of softening enmities and of awakening, in the most ignorant tribes, a desire for a more civilized life, with the advantages resulting from it.

What I especially admire is the extraordinary unconcern with which our Maoris ruin themselves for years to come, for no other reason than to sustain their ancient renown for hospitality. Thus, a hundred times have I seen collected, for distribution to their visitors, forty, fifty, and even seventy tons of flour, flocks of sheep and droves of pigs, piles of bed-covering and clothes, in a word, all sorts of food products and useful articles. The standard of the tribe floats above these valuables, which are left thus exhibited, for several hours, and in presence of all. Then the herald of the principal chief advances and, in a resounding voice, proclaims:

"*Ears! Be attentive and listen! In honour of Christmas, and in memory of our joyous reunion, these riches have been placed here, to be the lot of the most honoured amongst us!...*"

The Maori functionary then names the chief for whom all this wealth is destined, and returns to his place. The chief in question, who thoroughly understands the law of etiquette, passes on the honour to another, and so on, until all the principal persons of the assemblage have come forward and defiled before the "tahua" or presents. The Missioner himself is not forgotten, but he takes care to be represented by his catechist, who acts and speechifies in his place. Finally, the same herald who had opened the proceedings reappears upon the scene, and, amidst the applause of all, proposes that these treasures shall be divided amongst those assembled. Upon this, he calls several assistants to his aid, and the allotments are soon made, with the most scrupulous justice. When all this is well arranged, the herald, armed with a long wand, proclaims and points out the portion of each tribe: in order to vary his discourse somewhat, he embellishes it with humorous observations, in which there is a home-thrust for every recipient.

Scarcely has he concluded, than the meeting breaks up and all are on the road, carrying their booty and, as fast as possible, regain their native villages, where, for about a week they "swim in plenty," after which the ordinary thread of life is taken up. But the children do not forget Christmas, and perhaps a fortnight after, dreaming of the cakes and other delights of the festival, they ask their mothers: "*won't Christmas soon come again?*"

And the mothers answer, smiling: "*Alas! Christmas comes but once a year!*"

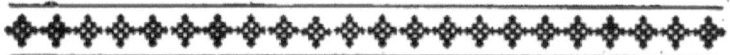

CHRONICLE OF THE WORK.

FEAST OF SAINT FRANCIS XAVIER, PATRON OF THE ASSOCIATION.

On Monday, 3rd December, the Rev. Father Didon, of the Order of Preachers, will deliver a discourse in the Primatial Church of Saint John, in favour of the Association of the Propagation of the Faith. His Grace the Archbishop of Lyons will preside.

BLESSING OF THE NEW OFFICES OF THE *MISSIONS CATHOLIQUES.*

On Thursday, the 9th of October, His Grace the Archbishop of Lyons was to have blessed the new offices of the *Missions Catholiques.* At the last moment, his Grace was obliged to absent himself from the ceremony, for which he himself had fixed the date, and begged Monseigneur Gouthe-Soulard, who was passing through Lyons, to take his place in the sacred functions.

Monsieur Hamel, President of the Central Council, Paris, had kindly consented to represent his colleagues at this family festival at which, together with all the Members of the Central Council, Lyons, there were present the President, the Count des Garets, Messrs. the Vicars-General of Lyons and Aix, and the President of the Administrative Council of the *Nouvelliste,* in whose house the *Illustrated Bulletin of the Association of the Propagation of the Faith* has been accommodated with spacious offices, free of expense.

Words the most precious to our hearts, and the most encouraging to us in our labours, came to crown the ceremony and to fulfil our dearest wishes. The Holy Father, and the Cardinal-Prefect of the Propaganda, whose official organ is the *Missions Catholiques,* wished to identify themselves with the Festival of the Association. The following are the telegrams sent from Rome on the morning of the 9th of October, to the Director of the journal:

"I hasten to announce to you that the Holy Father, from the depths of his heart, grants a blessing to the inauguration of the new offices of the journal *The Missions Catholiques*.

"The good accomplished by this journal for many years past, justifies the benevolent interest manifested by the Sovereign Pontiff, and His Holiness expresses his hope that it may develop more and more and continue its powerful assistance to the great work of the Propagation of the Faith throughout the world.

"CARDINAL RAMPOLLA,
"*Secretary of State.*"

"My sincere congratulations and good wishes that the work of the Bulletin may ever increase in prosperity and merit in its new offices.

"CARDINAL LEDOCHOWSKI,
"*Prefect of the Sacred College of the Propaganda.*"

We are, then, carrying out the wishes of the Holy Father and of the Sacred College of the Propaganda, in once more recommending the *Missions Catholiques*. On the 1st of January next, our Illustrated Bulletin begins it twenty-seventh year with remarkable articles on Madagascar, the Corea, Gaboon, etc. It this year offers, as a prize, to all its subscribers, a large map of the Sahara, a map which has been highly praised both by the Minister of the Colonies and by the Minister of Public Instruction.

Each year's numbers make a fine in-folio volume of 600 pages, with 200 illustrations.

We remind our readers that a specimen number will be sent free to all persons applying for it. The subscription is 10 francs (8s. 4d.) for France, and 12 francs (9s. 7d.) for the Postal Union. Address Monsieur le Directeur, *Missions Catholiques*, 14 Rue de la Charite, Lyons.

OUR ALMANACS FOR 1895.

It gives us pleasure to announce to our readers that the almanacs which we publish, have won the distinguished approbation of the Holy Father and of His Eminence the Cardinal Prefect of the Sacred Congregation of the Propaganda.

LETTER FROM HIS EMINENCE, CARDINAL RAMPOLLA, SECRETARY OF STATE TO HIS HOLINESS.

I have received your letter of the 23rd of October, and with it the almanacs of the *Missions* and of the *Propagation of the Faith.* In compliance with your desire, I hastened to present them, in your name, to His Holiness, who expressed his satisfaction and, moreover, is graciously pleased to send you his apostolic benediction.

In thanking you for the copies especially intended for myself, with pleasure I avail myself of the occasion to renew the expressions of my regard and esteem.

Rome, 27th October, 1894.

Signed: M. CARDINAL RAMPOLLA.

AUTOGRAPH LETTER FROM HIS EMINENCE CARDINAL LEDOCHOWSKI, PREFECT OF THE SACRED CONGREGATION OF THE PROPAGANDA.

I beg you to receive my best thanks for your letter of the 23rd inst., and for the two almanacs accompanying it. I consider them very successful, and I foretell for them a large circulation. They are a first-class production from your new offices.

M. CARDINAL LEDOCHOWSKI.

NOTES ON BOOKS.

"*LES MISSIONS CATHOLIQUES*" IN THE 19TH CENTURY,

By Monsieur LOUVET, Missioner in Western Cochinchina.

This magnificent work of 600 pages, illustrated with 200 engravings, is on sale at the offices of the Propagation of the Faith, and at the offices of the *Missions Catholiques*, 14 Rue de la Charite. It is a splendid book for a New Year's gift. Price, in paper cover, 15 francs; bound, 25 francs: carriage extra.

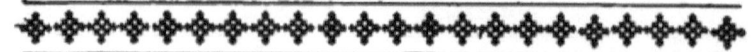

NEWS OF THE MISSIONS.

THE NEW SUPERIOR-GENERAL OF THE MISSIONERS OF ANNECY.

The General Chapter of the Congregation of Missioners of Saint Francis de Sales, assembled at the Mother-House at Annecy, has elected as Superior-General in the place of the lamented Father Tissot, of pious memory, the Very Rev. Father Eugene Gojon, Missioner of Saint Francis de Sales, who went to India eight years ago. The suffrages of his fellow-Missioners reached him at Gopalpore (diocese of Vizagapatam), where he fulfilled the various duties of Director of the Catholic station, of Chaplain to the Sisters of Saint Joseph, of Superior of the budding Seminary, of Master of Novices, and Professor of literature, philosophy, and theology. The newly-elected Superior is forty-five years of age.

GOOD NEWS FROM THIBET.

Monseigneur Biet has received the following telegram from Pekin through the Minister of Foreign Affairs:

" Re-establishment of the Missioners of Thibet in all their posts, at the expense of the Chinese government. Suitable indemnity for all losses suffered by the Mission for the last six years."

We heartily rejoice with Mgr. Biet in this almost unhoped-for result, and ask of God the conversion of this poor Thibetian people, hitherto so rebellious against the workings of grace.

THE PERSECUTION IN CHINA.

Monseigneur Potron, of the Minor Observantines, Titular Bishop of Jericho, and Procurator to the Franciscan Missions, writes to us from Paris:

"I send you a passage from the despatch received from Mgr. Benjamin Christiaens, Vicar-Apostolic of Southern Hou-pe:

"'Violent persecution in Ly-tchou-an. Many killed. Assist us. Particulars by letter.'

"As soon as I shall have received these particulars I will forward them to you."

✠

NECROLOGY.

MONSEIGNEUR RAIMONDI,
VICAR-APOSTOLIC OF HONG-KONG.

The *London and China Telegraph* announces as follows the death of this Prelate, who was at the head of the Mission of Hong-Kong for the last twenty years :

"We regret to announce the loss sustained by the colony of Hong-Kong in the death of an old and highly respected resident, Mgr. Raimondi, head of the Roman Catholic Mission in Hong-Kong. At the decease of Father Luiz, in 1867, he was appointed Prefect-Apostolic, and subsequently, on the 22nd of November, 1874, he was consecrated Bishop at Rome under the title of Bishop of Acanthe. For the last seven years his health was failing and his physicians had ordered him to sojourn a time in Australia. He returned to Hong-Kong apparently restored to health, but the improvement produced by change of air was only temporary; the Prelate again fell ill and did not rally. He died at the Mission-House, Glenealy, on the 27th September. A solemn *Requiem* Mass was celebrated at seven o'clock on the morning of the 28th September, and the funeral took place at four in the afternoon. Mgr. Pinaud officiated, and all the European colony made it a point of honour to be present. Captain Stirling represented Sir S. Robinson, governor of the colony."

MGR. NERAZ,
BISHOP OF SAN-ANTONIO (UNITED STATES).

As we go to press we learn the death of this Prelate who, for the last thirty years, administered the diocese of San-Antonio. Mgr. John Claude Neraz was born in the diocese of Lyons, 12th January, 1828.

We recommend to the prayers of our Missioners and of our readers the souls of several noteworthy Benefactors of the Association of the Propagation of the Faith, Mr J. J. Speersen, Director of the Orphanage of Terninck, near Antwerp, who died a holy death the 6th October, 1894 : Mlle Angela Dosal, of Mexico, Mr. D. Miguel Barquin, of Irapuato, Mr. D. Manuel Escudero y Perez Gallardo, Mexico.

DEPARTURE OF MISSIONERS.

The following are the names of the Missioners of the Society of Foreign Missions, Paris, who embarked at Marseilles, 2nd September, 1894: Messrs. Andrew Eloy, of Arras, for Southern Tonquin; Seraphin Godet, of Poitiers, for Northern Cochinchina; Émile Cherriere, of Tulle, for Southern Tonquin; Emile Devise, of Viviers, for the Corea; Julien Geoffroy, of Nancy, for Eastern Cochinchina; Marcel Lacroute, of Bayonne, for the Corea; Seraphin Iffly, of Metz, for Southern Burmah; Charles Ackermann, of Metz, for Cambodia; Theophilus Bohn, of Strasburg, for Southern Burmah; John-Mary Le Garrec, of Saint-Brieuc, for Yun-nan; Francis Harnois, of Saint-Brieuc, for Tokio; Henry Hay, of Cambrai, for Western Cochinchina; Clement Lemoine, of Coutances, for Tokio; Yves Moysan, of Saint-Brieuc, for Northern Burmah; Germain Barnabe, of Rhodes, for Yun-nan; Louis Valleet, of Viviers, for Eastern Cochinchina.

—Embarked at Marseilles, on the 30th of September, for the Mission of South-eastern Tche-ly (China), the Rev. Father Albert Wetterwald, S.J., and on the 29th of October five Fathers of the same Society embarked at Marseilles for the Mission of Kiang-nan (China). They were the Rev. Fathers Louis Froc, Rene Desnos, Xavier David, Celestine Frin, and Joseph Lebez.

—On the 3rd November, 1894, six of the Marist Fathers embarked at Marseilles: the Rev. Fathers Goutenoire and Cognet, of Lyons, returning to their Missions in New Zealand; Barrallon, of Lyons, and Hily, of Quimper, on their journey to the Vicariate-Apostolic of New-Caledonia and the New-Hebrides; and the Rev. Fathers Thierry, of Angers, and Calviac, of Rhodes, for their destination in the Vicariate-Apostolic of the Fidji Islands.

CONTENTS.

GENERAL REVIEW OF THE LABOURS OF THE APOSTOLATE DURING THE YEAR 1894. . . . 3

COREA.—*Letter from Mgr. Mutel.*—Particulars of the death of Father Jozeau, and account of the present situation of the Christians in the Corea. . . . 10

SIAM.—*Letter from M. Guego.* — Evangelization of a tribe of Laos on the left shore of the Me-Kong.—The Sos.—Christian vil'ages.—A singular vision.—The devices of charity. 18

NAPO.—*Letter from the Rev. Father Detroux.*—Missions to the savages of the Republic of Equator.—Difficulties of the journey.—Beginning and progress of evangelization.—Trials.—Present state of affairs. . . 38

WELLINGTON.—*Letter from the Rev. Father Cognet.*—Christmas amongst the Maoris. . . 46

CHRONICLE OF THE WORK. . . . 57

NEWS OF THE MISSIONS. . . . 60

NECROLOGY.—Mgrs. Ruimondi, Neraz; Monsieur Spiessen. 62

DEPARTURE OF MISSIONERS. . . . 63

2. Most Rev. Gregorios Youssef, greek patriarch of Antioch

1895.  1895.

ENCYCLICAL
CHRISTI NOMEN

IN FAVOUR OF THE

ASSOCIATION FOR THE PROPAGATION OF THE FAITH.

The Press, while tendering the tribute of its respect and attachment to the great Pontiff who governs the Church, has devoted special attention to the Convocation of Eastern Patriarchs at Rome and to the momentous decisions arrived at during their solemn deliberations. The Holy Father had already paved the way for the realization of his projects by sending His Eminence Cardinal Langeniux to Jerusalem in the capacity of Legate from the Holy See : in fact, it seemed to the Pontiff that the time had come for making a supreme effort for union with the Eastern Churches ; that the time had arrived to create an enlightened and eminent body of clergy, by founding, in the country of Chrysostom, seminaries for the education of Oriental Priests ; to honour these ancient and venerable Liturgies, contemporaneous with the Apostles and other apostolic men of the first centuries of the Christian era ; in a word, to insure to these ancient Churches their individual existence and autonomy, subject to the authority of the Roman Pontiff. It was with this end in view that, some weeks ago, he addressed to the entire Catholic world an Encyclical in which he laid down exact rules and limitations for the guidance of the Latin Priests associated with the Eastern Clergy.

To-day, in another Encyclical, Pope Leo XIII recommends the Work of the Propagation of the Faith to all the Patriarchs, Archbishops, and Bishops of the Universal Church. This important document we hasten to publish.

This call from the Holy Father is all the more urgent as he appeals to our Association to aid him strenuously in the accomplishment of his great projects, and, as he does not wish that the other Missions throughout the world should suffer from any diminution in the alms which we allocate to them, he conjures the faithful to supply the deficit which the newly created wants of the East will necessarily cause in our annual budget.

Discretion has hitherto kept us silent on the subject of this important fact, already announced in the journals. But, so early as the 15th November, 1894, his Eminence Cardinal Langenieux, in his capacity as Legate from the Holy See, laid before the Central Councils of Lyons and Paris the following letter, so flattering to our Association, a letter in which the Supreme Pontiff unfolds his projects and announces the publication of the Encyclical.

TO OUR BELOVED SONS, THE PRESIDENTS AND DIRECTORS
OF THE CENTRAL COUNCILS OF THE ASSOCIATION
OF THE PROPAGATION OF THE FAITH
AT LYONS AND AT PARIS.

DEARLY BELOVED SONS,

You have so frequently given proofs of your devotion to Holy Church and of your attachment to Our person that We gladly seize upon every occasion of expressing both Our sentiments of affection towards you and Our paternal gratitude. It is pleasing to Us to testify anew Our full confidence in you, and Our firm conviction that your zeal will not shrink before any labour, when there is question of seconding the Apostolic action of the Holy See for the extending of the reign of Jesus Christ upon earth, has inspired us with the design of associating you in a work which is peculiarly dear to Us—the regeneration of the Eastern Churches. Events, of which you are already cognizant, have awakened Our solicitude for the venerable Churches, so long weakened by troubles, and it happens at this moment that a Providential concurrence of circumstances enables Us to extricate them from their difficulties and place them in a position to exercise a useful and fruitful Apostolate in the midst of dissentient Eastern nations. As you well understand, such an undertaking necessitates numerous foundations of native seminaries for the education of the Clergy, of churches, schools, monasteries, and institutions of every kind. Therefore, like the Divine vine-dresser of the Gospel who, when the vintage season was come, went out to seek labourers for His vineyard, We seek helpers, and it is Our happiness to count you, beloved Sons, amongst Our most zealous auxiliaries.

His Eminence Cardinal Langenieux, Archbishop of Rheims, who last year was Our Legate at Jerusalem, will let you know in what manner and to what extent you may be called upon to lend Us your assistance. But it is Our desire that the new burden which We beg you will take upon you, shall in no way be injurious to the Catholic Missions whose providence you are. Therefore, it is Our intention to solemnly recommend the Association of the Propagation of the Faith to the faithful throughout the entire world, in order that it may be enabled to respond to Our wishes as regards the East, without being obliged to diminish its beneficent influence in other parts of the universe. Meanwhile, dearly beloved Sons, as a pledge of the Divine benediction, We grant affectionately, in the Lord, to you and your zealous Associates, Our Apostolic blessing.

Given at the Vatican,
15th November, 1894.

LEO PP. XIII.

ENCYCLICAL CHRISTI NOMEN.

VENERABILIBUS FRATRIBUS PATRI- ARCHIS, PRIMATIBUS, ARCHIEPI- SCOPIS, EPISCOPIS ALIISQUE LOCORUM ORDINARIIS PACEM ET COMMUNIONEM CUM APOSTOLICA SEDE HABENTIBUS

TO OUR VENERABLE BRETHREN, ALL PATRIARCHS, PRIMATES, ARCHBISHOPS, BISHOPS, AND OTHER DIGNITATORIES IN PEACE AND COMMUNION WITH THE APOSTOLIC SEE,

LEO PP. XIII.

LEO XIII., POPE.

Venerabiles Fratres Salutem apostolicam benedictionem.

Venerable Brethren, Health and Apostolic Benediction.

Christi nomen et regnum in gentibus quotidie latius proferre, atque devios discordesque invitare ad Ecclesiae sinum et revocare, hoc nimirum, quemadmodum sentit animus sanctum in primis esse officium muneris supremi quod gerimus, ita jamdiu est curis Nostris studiisque, apostolica urgente caritate, propositum. Hanc Nos ob causam sacras tueri ac multiplicare expeditiones, quarum potissimum ope christianiae sapientiae lumen ad errantes diffunditur, ad easque sustendandas auxilia in catholicis populis corrogata submittere, nulla unquam ratione cessavimus. Fecimus id praesertim, datis anno pontificatus tertio encyclicis litteris *Sancta Dei Civitas*, eo concilio ut praeclaro Instituto a *Propagatione Fidei* ampliorem catholicorum quum pietatem tum liberalitem,

To bear the Name of Christ to new peoples and daily to extend His Kingdom amongst nations, to draw within the Fold those who are straying outside, and to bring back to the bosom of the Church those who have become hostile to it, is undoubtedly one of the most sacred obligations of the sublime charge confided to Us; inspired by Apostolic charity, this duty has long been the subject of Our thoughts and of Our earnest solicitude. Therefore, We have never failed to favour and to multiply those Holy Missions which spread the light of the Christian Faith amongst those peoples who walk in darkness, and we have never ceased our efforts to stimulate the charity of the faithful by whose alms the Missions are sustained. This We did in an especial manner,

conciliaremus. Tunc persequi qortando libuit, quam ipsum modicis initiis ingressum ad quantam amplitudinem brevi tempore provenisset; quibus vel laudum testimoniis vel indulgentiae muneribus Decessores Nostri illustres, Pius VII., Leo XII., Pius VIII., Gregorius XVI., Pius IX., idem ornassent; quam multum ex eo adjumenti sacris per orbem terrarum Missionibus allatum jam esset et quam uberiora forent deinde expectanda. Neque exiguus, Dei beneficio, respondit hortationi fructus; quum sane, Episcoporum navitati et instantiae obsequente largitate fidelium, benemerentissimum opus hisce etiam proximis annis amplificatum videamus.—At nova jam subest graviorque necessitas, quae effusiores in hanc rem spiritus manusque catholicae caritatis desideret, vestramque acuat, Venerabiles Fratres, sollertiam.

Nam, quod probe nostis, per apostolicam epistolam *Praeclara*, junio superiore editam, visum est Nobis Dei providentis servire consiliis, vocando et incitando gentes quae ubique sunt ad fidei christianae unitatem; illud tamquam summum votorum optantibus, ut aliquanto per Nos maturetur promissum divinitus tempus, quo *fiet unum ovile et unus Pastor.*—Singularibus autem curis interea spectare Nos ad Orientem ejusque Ecclesias, multis nominibus insignes et venerandas; ex ipsis nuperrime

by Our Encyclical: *Sancta Dei Civitas*, the aim of which was to increase the love and generosity of Catholics for the noble Work of the Propagation of the Faith. On that occasion, We were pleased to exalt by Our recommendations an Association of which the humble beginnings were succeeded by a development so rapid and marvellous; an Association upon which our illustrious predecessors, Pius VII., Leo XII., Pius VIII., Gregory XVI., and Pius IX., lavished praise and spiritual favours; an Association which had given such efficacious aid to the Missions throughout the entire world, and which promised them still more abundant assistance for the future. Our words, thank God, have had the most happy results. The faithful have responded generously to the earnest appeal of the Bishops, and of late years this most meritorious Work has made remarkable progress. But at present, still more urgent needs call for increased zeal and generosity on the part of Catholics, and demand of you, Venerable Brethren, the most enlightened activity.

As you have learned from Our Apostolic Letter *Præclara* of June last, We believed We were acting in obedience to the inspirations of Divine Providence in urgently inviting all the nations of the earth to the unity of Christian Faith, and We should attain the full realization of our desires

intellexistis litteris apostolicis, quas perscripsimus de disciplina Orientalium conservanda et tuenda. Inde etiam satis compertae sunt vobis institutae rationes, quas, collatis diligenter consiliis cum Patriarchis earum gentium, exploravimus, aptius ad exitum profuturas. Neque tamen dffitemur, banc omnem causam difficultatibus implicari magnis : quibus eluctandis si quidem impar est virtus Nostra, totam nihilominus fiduciae constantiaque vim, in quo maxime oportet, sitam habemus magno in Deo. Qui enim rei mentem Nobis et initia providus dedit, vires ipse opemque ad perficiendum summa cum benignitate certe sufficiet: atque hoc est quod enixis precibus ab ipso implorare contendimus, idemque ut fideles omnes implorent vehementer hortamur. Divinus vero, quae fidenter expetimus, adjumentis quum humana prorsus accedere sit necesse, eis idcirco quaerendis et suppeditandis, quaecumque videantur ad id quo spectamus conducibilia, peculiares quasdam curas aequm est a Nobis impendi.

Namque ut Orientalibus, quotquot discessere, ad unicam Ecclesiam reditus muniatur, videtis, Venerabiles Fratres, opus esse in primis parari ex eis ipsis idoneam sacrorum ministrorum copiam, qui doctrina et pietate abundantes, ceteris optatae unitatis concilia suadeant; catholicae insuper sapientiae vitaeque

were it permitted Us to hasten the coming of that time promised by God when "There will be but one fold and one Shepherd." With what paternal love Our thoughts dwell upon the East and its illustrious and venerable Churches, you have been made aware by Our Apostolic Letters bearing upon the necessity for preserving and upholding the discipline of the Eastern Communities. This affectionate solicitude on Our part has also been manifested to you by the measures adopted by Us after conference with the Patriarchs of these nations. Nevertheless, We do not deceive Ourselves as to the great difficulties in the way of this undertaking, and Our own inability to surmount them; We, therefore, with unlimited confidence, place all Our hope for the success of Our efforts in God. It was His wisdom which inspired Us with the thought and which encourages Us to attempt its realization; His Sovereign goodness will assuredly give Us the strength and the means to accomplish Our desire. Our earnest prayers are unceasingly offered to obtain of Him this grace, and We urgently exhort the faithful to join their supplications to Ours for the same intention. But, to that aid from on High which We confidently implore, we must add human means, and We shall neglect nothing that lies in Our power to discover and to point

institutionem quam maxime evulgandam esse, atque ita impertiendam, ut proprio nationis ingenio accommodatius conveniat. Quare providendum, ut sacrae educandae juventuti, ubicumque expediat, pateant instructae congruenter domus ; ut plura numero praesto sint gymnasia alia alibi pro locorum frequentia ; ut sua cujusque ritus cum dignitate exercendi praebeatur facultas ; ut optimis edendis scriptis manare ad omnes germana religionis notitia possit. Ista et similia efficere quantae sit impensae futurum, vosmet facile intelligitis ; simul intelligitis tam multis rebus et magnis non posse Orientales Ecclesias omnino per se ipsas occurere, nec posse tamen a Nobis, his rerum angustiis, quam vellemus opem conferri.—Restat ut apta subsidia praecipue opportuneque ex eo petantur, quod modo laudavimus, Instituto ; cujus quidem propositum cum illo plane cohaeret quod Ipsi nunc animo destinamus. At simul vero, ne apostolicae Missiones, derivatis partim in alienum usum quibus aluntur praesidiis, quidquam accepturae sint detrimenti, magnopere instandum est, ut eo largius Catholicorum in ipsum influat liberalitas.—Similem autem cautionem rectum est adhiberi, quod attinet ad affine et perutile Institutum *a Scholis Orientis*, alias auctum commendatione Nostra ; praesertim quum, mo-

out the proper measures to be employed in order to attain the much desired result.

To bring back to the One True Fold all the Eastern peoples who have separated from it, nothing is more essential, as you, Venerable Brethren, well know, than, in the first place, to recruit a numerous clergy from amongst the Easterns themselves, a clergy commendable for doctrine and for piety and capable of inspiring others with a desire for union ; secondly, to multiply, as much as possible, institutions in which science and Catholic discipline shall be taught in accordance with the peculiar spirit of the nation. It is, therefore, the moment to establish, wherever practicable, special houses for the education of youths destined for the Church, and also colleges proportionate in number to the importance of the populations, in order that each Rite may be carried out with dignity, and that, by the diffusion of their best books, the faithful may acquire a knowledge of their national religion. The realization of these projects and others of a like nature will, you can easily understand, necessitate a great outlay and, as you are also aware, the Eastern Churches cannot, of themselves, meet so many and such heavy charges ; moreover, it is impossible for Us, in face of the difficult times through which We are passing, to contribute to

deratoribus ejus aperte pollicitis, paratum similiter sit, de stipe a se cogenda, Nobis, quantum copiosius licuerit, in idem subministrare.

Id est igitur, Venerabiles Fratres, in quo vestra singulariter officia exposcimus : neque dubitamus quin vos, qui Nobiscum religionis et Ecclesiæ causam sustinere et provehere modis omnibus assidue studetis, egregiam Nobis sitis operam navaturi. Efficite sedulo ut in fidelibus curae vestrae commissis ipsa *a Propagatione Fidei* Consociatio, quanta maxima possit, capiat incrementa. Pro certo enim habemus fore, ut multo plures dent ei libenter nomen et largam pro facultate conferant stipem, si per vos plane perspexerint quae sit eiusdem praestantia et quam dives spiritualium bonorum copia, quantaque inde rei christianae emolumenta sint in praesens optimo jure speranda. Id certe homines catholicos debet movere penitus, quum noverint nihil se posse Nobis facere tam gratum, neque sibi Ecclesiaeque tam salutare, quam sic votis obsecundare Nostris, uti tribuere studiose certent unde ea, quae Orientalium bono Ecclesiarum constituimus, re ipsa convenienter feliciterque praestemus At Deus, cujus unice agitur gloria in christiani nominis amplificatione et in sancta ejusdem fidei ac regiminis conjunctione, Nostris benignissimus adspiret desi-

these expenses as largely as We would wish. All that remains for Us, then, is to ask, within the bounds of moderation, the greater part of the necessary subsidies from the Association of which We have spoken above in such laudatory terms, and whose aim is in perfect accord with that which We have so much at heart. But, in order not to prejudice in any way the interests of the Apostolic Missions by depriving them of a portion of the resources upon which they depend for their very existence, We cannot too strongly urge the faithful to increase their bounty to this Association in proportion to our needs. It is likewise permissible to recommend the similar and useful work of the *Eastern Schools*, the directors of which have also promised to apply the greater part of the alms which they shall receive to the same object.

For all these reasons, We especially solicit your aid, Venerable Brethren, and We have no doubt that you will give us efficacious assistance, you who, with constancy and zeal, sustain with Us and labour by every means to promote the cause of religion and of the Church. Do, then, all that is in your power to extend the Association of the Propagation of the Faith amongst those confided to your care, We feel certain that a much larger number of the faithful would willingly inscribe their names

deriis, faveat coeptis: ejus autem lectissimorum munerum auspicem, vobis omnibus, Venerabiles Fratres, et Clero populoque vestro Apostolicam benedictionem amantissime impertimus.

and make offerings more generous in proportion to their means, if, instructed by you, they clearly understood how noble a work this is, how abundant are the spiritual riches attached to it, and what advantages the cause of Christianity may confidently hope from it at the present day.

And assuredly, Catholics wil be profoundly touched when they learn that nothing can be more pleasing to Us and more useful to the Church than that they should enter into a zealous rivalry in collecting the funds necessary in order to bring about the successful accomplishment of the projects we have formed for the welfare of the Eastern Churches. May that God, whose glory alone is concerned in the spread of Christianity and in the unity of Faith and spiritual government, deign in His goodness to bless Our desires and favour Our undertaking; and, as a pledge of the most precious Heavenly favours, We lovingly grant Our Apostolic Benediction to you, Venerable Brethren, to your clergy and to your people.

Datum Romae apud S. Petrum die 24 decembris anno 1894, Pontificatus Nostri decimo septimo.

Given at Saint Peter's, Rome, the 24th December, in the year 1894, the seventeenth of Our Pontificate.

LEO PP. XIII.

LEO XIII., POPE.

Never yet has our Association, so often favoured and recommended by Roman Pontiffs, received such a testimony of exalted and sovereign good-will, publicly expressed before the whole Catholic world. We feel assured that the entire Episcopate, from which we have received so many proofs of sympathy, will echo the words of the Head of the Church and that the charity of the faithful will make ample response to the voice of the Pastors. We shall then have the honour and the happiness, while seconding the vast projects of His Holiness Leo XIII. for the East, of offering even still more considerable resources to the other Missions.

MISSIONS OF ASIA.

VICARIATE-APOSTOLIC OF THE COREA.

Notwithstanding that we have already devoted a portion of the preceding numbers of the *Annals* to the Corea, the Sino-Japanese war, which continues to attract the attention of Europe to this country of the Far East, makes it our duty to give preference to communications coming from this distant Mission. The map which we publish will enable readers to trace his route, while reading Monsieur Villemot's dramatic and touching narrative.

We call attention to the fact that the *ly*, frequently mentioned in this letter, is a Chinese land measure equivalent to about four hundred and fifty yards.

LETTER FROM MONSIEUR P. VILLEMOT,

OF THE FOREIGN MISSIONS, PARIS,

To Monseigneur MUTEL, Vicar-Apostolic.

Premonitory Dangers.—Flight and Exile.

WE have already slightly sketched for your Lordships the gloomy days through which the two Missioners of the Tjyen-La-To have just passed, but as you wish for more ample details, we hasten to obey.

On the 28th July, I received a note from Father Baudounet, announcing to me that Monseigneur had telegraphed to him an order either to fly or to go to Seoul. "Father Jozeau," said he, "has just left, hoping to pass the enemy's lines before they shall be completely closed. For my part," added the Father, "I still wait at Tjyen-tjyou, in the hope that the Japanese will soon come, as is rumoured, and I may, perhaps, be able to protect our poor Christians."

As my district was not yet actually attacked, and as I also desired to have more reliable news as to the movements of the rebels, I determined to go at once to Tjyen-tjyou.

I left on the morning of the 29th. On the way, I met several bands, who let me pass without a word. Arrived at the inn at Pong-san, I awaited dinner in the public room, my servant being seated on the ground before the door. Suddenly, a man entered the courtyard, carrying on his back a bundle of arms, lances and rifles swathed in straw. Looking around and perceiving my horse with his European saddle, the man began to gesticulate, jumping and twirling about and uttering loud cries. There was something in his motions that reminded one of these wild dances that the "man-eaters" are said to execute around their victims.

"—He is a *Tong-hak*," cried my servant, "we are lost."

"—Don't be afraid," I replied, "he is only a madman; if he comes in here, we shall be able to defend ourselves."

The man had left the courtyard and had rejoined seven other individuals who were seated round a jar of wine. When they had drunk plenty, he said to his companions:

"—There is a European here in this inn; let us kill him at once;" and, addressing himself to a crowd of onlookers: "The Corea for the Coreans," cried he; "no strangers here!"

He was already advancing with his companions when several o the villagers, no doubt fearing that my death would get them into trouble, restrained them, swearing by all their gods that there was no European there, that the horse with the European saddle belonged to a merchant from the capital, who was well known to them, etc.

Being somewhat stupefied by drink, they allowed themselves to be persuaded; one of them, drawing a line in the dust before the door, traced some cabalistic characters. The men halted a moment, as if awaiting an inspiration, and . . . went off.

I did the same, but by another road. At the gates of the town of Tjyen-tjyou, the soldiers on guard, doubtless taking me for a Japanese, seized their rifles and aimed at me; some persons who observed my peril, cried out to hold fire, and when I had declared my name and nationality, I was allowed to pass. Arrived at the Father's dwelling, I learned the full gravity of the situation and the misfortunes that had already befallen.

On the morning of the 31st., two terrified Christians arrived from my village, announcing the massacre of Father Jozeau: he had been killed by the Chinese, at the instigation of the Tong-haks, both on account of being a Missioner and a Frenchman. The Christians were of opinion that it would be perilous for us to remain at Tjyen-tjyou; that as soon as the Father's death became known to the rebels, their audacity would increase. They therefore besought of us to retire during the night to some Christian village in the mountains, and it was with heavy hearts we were obliged to become exiles.

That evening, disguised as Coreans and wearing the large hats peculiar to the labourer, we quitted the town, walking with difficulty along the ill-made roads, rendered still more unpleasant by recent rains. In the morning, we arrived at a little Christian village, where the poor people were unable to restrain their tears at seeing us in such a piteous plight. Having rested a while and having warmed our limbs, benumbed by the cold and the dews of morning, we retired to a shed at some distance from any dwelling in order to be out of sight of the pagans in the neighbourhood. The next night it was necessary to move on farther to another Christian settlement, where we could with more security await better days. There, we were lodged in another shed, built against the mountain, that we might the more easily escape in case of danger. Besides, how could we possibly spend whole days shut up in a Corean hut during the hot season?

Departure for Seoul.—Obstacles.—In a Cavern.—Job's Comforters.—The Feast of the Assumption.

The day after our arrival, we learned that the news of the poor Father's death had spread through the town like wild-fire; the rebels openly proclaimed that they had killed him and that the two other Missioners should share the same fate. We were also told that the Japanese, being occupied elsewhere with the Chinese, would not come into our province.

Seeing this sad state of affairs, being unable in any way to protect our Christians, recognizing also that the present situation was likely to continue unchanged for some time, that, in spite of their kind-heartedness, we were a heavy charge upon our neophytes, and that they were exposed to greater danger on our account, we determined upon going to Seoul. But how, without being recognized, travel more than five hundred lys of a road filled with daily-increasing bands of rebels, who were stopping and rifling all passers-by? It was then that we wrote to acquaint your Lordship of the situation in which we were placed, seeing no chance of safety but in the arrival of some French man-of-war which might take us up on the coast, about a hundred lys from the place where we were. The messenger set out, having our note carefully hidden in his hair.

From that time forth nearly every one of the villages was searched; then the Christians, becoming still more fearful for us, and also wishing to insure their own safety, brought us to a cavern while they themselves withdrew in little bands to the mountain. At night, we had not only the cold of the woods to fear, but we had also the dread of tigers, which are very common in these districts. But our good Mother was watching over us. Two or three times a day we were supplied with food: our lives somewhat resembled those of the hermits of old, but that news from the outer world reached us. Alas! the bearers were Job's comforters. On the 12th., the news was that a band of Tong-haks had just entered the village we had left, but, finding nothing to make them comfortable, they retreated, giving notice that they would soon return. On the 13th., we learned that the governor of Tjyen-tjyou had sent away the soldiery, thus leaving the town to the mercy of the rebels; we got word also that these latter were looking after us, that they said we were hidden in the *tong-myen* (this was true), and that we could not escape them. Next day, the news was that my house had been entered and the doors broken, and that, moreover, they had put a Christian to the torture to make him confess where I was concealed.

On the eve of the Assumption we killed a viper close to our rock, and in the evening, by the light of a little lamp, we saw another within the cavern, gliding among the branches of trees that formed our couch, but we could not catch it. Feeling rather uneasy, we returned to the village. The damp of the cavern and the badly prepared food had weakened us, and we were anxious to regain a little strength ; we found that our Christians had also returned for the feast of the Assumption.

In spite of the gaiety we strove to assume in order to encourage our flock, they were very sad, thinking of former times. The previous year, I had come to this same settlement in order to celebrate this festival. Alas! what a change! How numerous the faithful then were; I had celebrated the holy Mass in the open air, under a canopy decked with flowers and green boughs; all had received the Blessed Eucharist, a few Baptism : and then the future seemed so promising, while to-day we could not even offer the holy Sacrifice, but prayed in hiding, as in times of persecution. And yet the Blessed Virgin would not allow the day to pass without a proof of her protection : this was the return of our messenger announcing the arrival of the man-of-war.

"—She is anchored," said he, "not far from the Port of Maryang, in the province of Tchyoung-Tchyeng, but how are the Fathers to get there? It is twenty leagues from this, and the few Christian villages along the route are deserted; everywhere the Tong-haks... and the river to be crossed! The coast itself is watched; scarcely had I left the boat which brought me to land (it was night) than I fell into the hands of the guards, who brought me before the mandarin of the port. They supposed me to be a traitor in the pay of the foreigners. In order to get out of the scrape, I invented a story, which was more or less believed, and after two day's imprisonment they released me, warning me not to return, under pain of losing my head."

We set out for the Man-of-war.—A Singular Cavalcade.

In spite of the difficulties and perils of the journey, we still determined to undertake it; the hunted life that we had led for the last fifteen days was undermining our strength and we could not go on with it. A plank was thrown out to save us, and we must seize it. One of our people called to mind that he knew some boatmen in a little port that was easy enough of access; perhaps, by an offer of money, he could induce them to take us. Twice already, it is true, we had sent Christians to try and find a boat in case we could only reach the ship by water; their search had always been fruitless. But this time we had better hopes and we were anxious to push on at once. Moreover, Syeng-Poul, the village in which we were, was becoming dangerous as a dwelling, the Christians repeating to each other in terror the *Tong-hak* words: "the Europeans are in these *Tong-Myen* mountains."

Once more we set out upon the road. We went to Si-rang, Kol, a little hamlet of only three houses, hidden in the depths of an almost inaccessible mountain gorge. Here live a few Christians, so poor that our arrival was a sad inconvenience: there was so little of either rice or barley that at the end of two days their store was exhausted, but, fortunately, Providence came to our assistance. On the 17th., a servant from Father Baudounet's house arrived, quite elated. He was the bearer of a letter addressed from Seoul.

COREA. — Mandarins and Satellites.

to the governor of Tjyen-tjyou, wherein, in very severe terms, he was ordered to provide us with an escort as far as Chemulpo. "We send," the letter said, "a ship to your province; the voyage will thus be made safe and easy."

This good news was joy for ourselves and for our Christians; it seemed to us as if there was about to be an end to our trials, and that, once arrived at Seoul, we should be able to assist our beloved neophytes. After another night's journey, we were back again at Tjyen-tjyou.

We at once apprised the governor of our presence. He sent one of his councillors to let us know that the ship would be at Syeng-tang-i (a little port upon the river, eleven leagues from Tjyen-tjyou), and that he would have us escorted by one of his pretorians. As we remarked that the rebels would pay very little heed to the government authorities, he replied that he had just been speaking about us to their chief (with whom he was on friendly terms), and that the latter had promised to send an inspector with an escort of armed men. On the 19th., we were ready to set out in the morning, wishing to do in one day the eleven leagues which separated us from the river: but we were delayed by the governor, who had not prepared his despatches for Seoul, and we did not leave until ten o'clock. The cavalcade was a pitiful sight enough. The pretorian marched sadly along on foot, having been unable to procure a mount, as all the horses were in the hands of the Tong-haks; we followed in a hand-chair, and behind us came the inspector, proudly mounted upon a little ass and escorted by two riflemen, their arms upon the left shoulder, an open umbrella upon the right! Two Christians followed at a distance, that they might be witnesses of whatever should happen.

It being broad day, we could see for ourselves the sad state of the province. At every instant, we encountered bands of insurgents: each village resembled a military station; the Coreans saluted each other by new titles: it was no longer my Lord, Sir, etc., but brigadier, sergeant, corporal; they spoke ostentatiously of their late exploits: tortures, plunderings, etc. Whenever our bearers stopped to rest, these fellows pressed threateningly around us, and were barely kept back by those who accompanied us. At the town of Ik-san, there were at least two hundred of them assembled, and here, more than at any other part of the journey, the danger seemed imminent, the people calling out that we must be beheaded, so, although it was already past sunset, we went farther on before we halted for the night. From the mat on which we stretched ourselves in the open air, we at four different times saw bands of rebels passing before the door of the inn.

Next morning, at daybreak, we set out, in the hope of finding the boat promised by the governor. What was our disappointment at discovering that it was not at the port indicated! We were the victims of the carelessness of this magistrate at Tjyen-tjyou; he had been written to from Seoul informing him that the vessel would approach as near as possible to Tjyen-tjyou, and, without making the slightest inquiry, he had assured us that she would be at Syeng-taug-i. But of what vessel had he then received intimation? Upon our representing that a French man-of-war had come to Ma-ryang, he replied: "That is not the ship in question, but a special boat, sent by the Corean government."

Seeking for our Ship.—A Corean barque.—Trials and Danger.—An unexpected Saviour.

Seeing that we had been tricked, we wished to go straight to Ma-ryang by land, but none of our people would consent, saying that our safe-conduct did not hold good for the province of Tchy-oung-Tchyeng, that we should certainly be killed, and they refused to accompany us. We were then obliged, though much against our will, to make the journey in Corean junks. The inspector and his riflemen, who had only received orders to go as far as Syeng-tang-i, parted from us, but, through kindness, they gave directions to another Tong-hak to accompany us as far as the port of Toun-tchyang.

The news of the arrival of two Europeans spread abroad and some Christians, inhabitants of these countries, came to bid us farewell. When the junk had sailed and we were already out of sight of our starting point, there, on the shore, at a bend of the river, stood a little band of Christians. Poor children, they wept to see us leave, and our hearts were filled with sombre thoughts.... How profoundly sad were our feelings!

Scarcely had we gone a few lys when a violent southerly wind arose, rendering navigation impossible: the bark drew water at every seam and the waves increasing at every moment, we were obliged to land; it was the shore of Tchyoung-tchyeng-to! Our people, terrified at finding themselves in this province, did not know where to hide, so they were delighted when a boat's crew consented to carry us to the opposite bank of the river, but we were so tossed about that all were sick. It was already late when we arrived at Kon-Kai; we had eaten nothing since morning, and were delighted to get a porringerful of cold rice, for we were so anxious to push on that we would not await the preparation of a meal.

We wished to travel by land as far as possible, so the pretorian made us take hand-chairs. But having gone a few lys, the bearers made some objection or other, and left us there: we had to make the best of a bad bargain, and it was already far on in the night when we reached Sye-hpo on foot.

Our brave companion of a rebel had received orders to accompany us all the way to Koun-tchyang, but no doubt he thought the charge too troublesome when he found we should have to go on foot. He had, therefore, courageously made off. Fortunately, we had with us an astute partisan; this was a cousin of the pretorian's who, learning how difficult a charge had been confided to his relative, had followed us incognito. As cunning as he was audacious, he had extorted from the Tjen-tjyou Tong-hak his commission as inspector. Thanks to this theft, we were enabled to extricate ourselves from many a difficulty, beginning with our arrival at Sye-hpe.

The natives of this village appeared anything but pleased at our coming; from one inn we were sent to another: no rice, no barley, no accommodation for the night: everywhere the same refrain. These people, who were all on the side of the rebels, could only be mastered through the authority of one of their chiefs; our improvised inspector saw this and, thanks to his flow of eloquence, rice, barley, and even a fowl appeared. Better still, early the next morning a little junk was ready: as we were no more than three or four leagues from Koun-tchyang by river, while the distance by land was two or three times greater, we were again obliged to proceed by boat. The wind, at first favourable, again turned, and we feared a repetition of the storm of the preceding day. Our attention was attracted by a pretty little sailing vessel of European build, anchored not far off, and our crew told us it was really a European boat, recently bought by a Corean, and it was coasting between Chemulpo and Syeng-tang-i.

"—The storm is rising," said our boatman, "we shall be in danger on this little barque: wind and tide are against us; the river at this point is nearly a quarter of a mile wide and there is not even a place to touch at. But this is a good chance; seeing that the government has given orders that you should be brought to Seoul, we can, according to the Corean laws, oblige this vessel to convey you as far as Ma-ryang, and, if necessary, even to Chemulpo."

Without placing too much hope in these fair promises, circumstances forced us to hail the vessel; the crew lowered the ladder and received us kindly enough. After an interchange of courtesies, the pretorian asks ·

" —Where is the master ?"

" —At Seoul," is the reply.

" —And the captain, the pilot ?"

" —In the province of Kyong-syang."

" —And the crew, where are they ?"

" —We are only three here, the rest are gone, we know not where."

On hearing such evident lies, our man gets angry, shouts, storms. Then, seized with fear, they acknowledge that the pilot and the sailors are in a village a few lys away.

" —Very well," answers the pretorian, " when the wind drops you must seek them ; meanwhile, cook us some rice."

It was about ten o'clock, and we had not broken our fast. What a meal that cook served ! Bad rice cooked in tainted water, and ... nothing else ! There was no other food on board. Though hungry as dogs, we could not swallow even a spoonful ... and all the time a perfect torrent of rain was pouring upon our heads : this, however, somewhat calmed the wind, and two sailors landed with the pretorian in order to lay in some provisions and bring back the crew. The rain soon recommenced. Crouched in the cabin, into which the water filtered on every side, thinking over the past, we were not without anxiety for the future: I did not feel too sure about this pretty barque ; all at once, I perceived a manuscript under a package: it was a *Summary of the Tong-hak Doctrine.*

" —Oh, ho ! " said I to Father Baudounet, " here is an affair ..., we are in a regular trap ; there is little doubt but that the crew are on the side of the rebels. If they want to kill us, they can easily do so, were it only by letting us die of hunger..., there are only a few handfuls of rice remaining, and you know how it tastes ! ... "

The weather having calmed, we walked sadly up and down the deck, from time to time swallowing a few mouthfuls of the fetid water, to try and appease our hunger.... Night came, and there was no sign of the boat. At last, through the haze a barque appeared..., it came alongside and the pretorian came on board, trembling with rage :

"—These beggars," said he, "are all Tong-haks; not only did they refuse to come with me, but several times they tried to kill me. An old man amongst them wished to have me put upon my trial ; I defended myself as best I could, swearing by all the devils that I also was a Tong-hak, and, as proof of what I said, I showed them the inspector's commission, which I fortunately had in my pocket. On seeing this, they calmed down, consenting to grant me my life, but would not hear of my returning to the vessel. I succeeded in escaping from the house where they had met and fled to a neighbouring village where, after much supplication, I was taken on board this barque, which is on its way to the opposite side of the river."

Having listened to the account of this adventure, we wanted to leave at once in the little junk in which we had come that morning, and which, fortunately, had not returned, but it was impossible to induce its crew to move ; they put forward endless pretexts for not obeying, their plan evidently being to escape alone, under cover of darkness. The return of the storm with redoubled force, proved our safeguard : neither could the boatmen leave nor the Tong-haks arrive. The tempest did not cease until about 9 o'clock the next day, and by that time hunger, which pricked all alike, decided even the most unwilling ones to make for the shore. Thanks to God, the waves were calmer and, the tide serving, we landed, without accident, near a little fishing village, not farther by land than forty lys. (a little more than three miles) from Koun-tchyang. Weary of junks, barges, and barques, we voluntarily made this journey on foot, and it was now, especially, the pretorian's cousin proved his value. In three or four villages through which we passed, he succeeded in getting a porter to carry our little baggage, but it was no longer to the *chief of the village* we addressed ourselves, but to the *brigadier*. Finally, we reached Koun-tchyang.

A crowd of men, boys, even women formed a cortege around us, and their numbers increased at every street corner. The doors of the inns were all shut in our faces, seeing which, we entered the first courtyard we came to. The master of the house was rather taken aback by our coolness, yet did not dare to say anything, besides, we assured him that we would move on shortly. In a moment, the crowd invaded our retreat, men, children, all wearing a collar or bracelet like those of the bonzes; we were to them like curious animals, and their remarks, sometimes comical, sometimes uncomplimentary, made us smile. At any other time, a few severe words would quickly have dispelled the rabble, but this was no time for severity, and our followers sought rather to hide themselves than to protect us. Learning that we were French, and that a man-of-war had come to meet us, they began to be afraid and gradually withdrew.

While this was going on, the pretorian had gone to seek the petty mandarin of the place who, poor man, frankly avowed his inability to aid us. Fortunately, our pseudo Tong-hak met with one of the chiefs of these people, and once more his eloquence was so persuasive that the chief promised a junk which should bring us that very evening to Ma-ryang. Wishing to take advantage of this good chance, we at once bought rice and fish for the evening meal and installed ourselves in the boat. This was six o'clock in the evening of Wednesday, 22nd August. It was, therefore, four days since we had left Tjyen-tjyou, and we had only advanced eleven leagues!

Saved! — Fresh Mishaps.

We forgot our past sufferings in thinking that we should soon arrive at our destination. Forty lys only now separated us from Ma-ryang; here, a French boat must be awaiting us, for, according to our courier, it had promised to remain from fifteen to twenty days; now, this was but the twelfth day. Our junk was new, the boatmen good fellows, it was therefore with a joyous heart that we weighed anchor. The sun had set; the sea, smooth as glass, bore our barque gently along, and thus a few miles were passed when, suddenly, a harsh noise like a rent came from the hold: we were upon rocks. The pilot and his companions then acknowledged, quite simply, that they did not know the coast; that if they had ever gone before to Ma-ryang, it was by another route. Luckily, the junk was stoutly built and there was scarcely any wind, otherwise, we should have had a genuine shipwreck this time.

This incident caused our people to feel anxious, for we had to cast anchor and await daylight before proceeding. Once more we were obliged to bear misfortune cheerfully, though we seemed to have a presentiment of fresh misfortunes. For mattress, we had the straw mat that covered the deck, a bowl reversed for pillow, a mat for counterpane, and thus we passed the first night on the open ocean. In the morning, the wind being somewhat favourable, the large straw sails were set and, with some little effort, we were once more under weigh.

We had passed the large island of Kai-tjyou, and already we could see Ma-ryang. All eyes sought the long desired vessel. We imagined we saw it everywhere! But, alas! we constantly discovered that what had been a ship, pitilessly turned into a rock or a junk, or sometimes even proved simply to be the effect of imagination.

At ten o'clock, we entered the port of Ma-ryang; as it was low tide, we hailed the villagers to come out to us with a little boat, but on seeing Father Baudounet's long beard and our black habit, they fled as fast as they could into the mountains..., men, women, children, all fled. There was no use calling out to them that we were neither Japanese nor Chinese, nor pirates nor thieves, they would listen to nothing, but escaped at their utmost speed. As the water was not deep, one of our men contrived to land and tackled a little boat, by means of which the pretorian, in full uniform, landed, together with two or three boatmen; seeing this, the bravest of the natives, who had only hidden, came to meet them.

They then learned that the French vessel had actually anchored near the coast; that she had remained nine days, but had left three days ago. What a disappointment! No money, no food; we could not believe such a thing possible. Thinking that during the day the commandant was exploring the neighbourhood but that at night he would return to his post, we resolved to wait. Having sought out the petty mandarin of the district, we explained our position to him.

"—It is impossible for you," said he, "to proceed to Seoul by land, on account of the rebels; as for going by sea, it is no longer practicable: besides the bad weather which threatens, there are no junks here to take you; perhaps your vessel will come back. For greater certainty, a messenger might go as far as Chemulpo..."

One of our men went, promising to return on the fourth day. That day we spent upon the mountain, on the look out, and several sentinels watched all night, but nothing was sighted. We therefore made up our minds to wait the four or five days.

At night we slept out of doors upon the floor of the verandah, on account of the vermin and the heat indoors, but the flooring was so narrow that, in order to economise space and to make the most of our one blanket, we were obliged to lie with the feet of one to the head of the other. The whole day long we spent upon the mountain top.

Mishaps.—From barque to barque.—From tempest to tempest.—A poor welcome.

On Friday, the Tong-haks invaded the village; warned of the danger, and hidden behind the long grass, we awaited the turn of events. They contented themselves with taking a few prisoners, without giving any reason for acting thus, and then withdrew. They were aware of our presence in the neighbourhood, and, next day, several hundreds of them assembled within a league of our retreat. The mandarin, uneasy on our account, sent out spies, who, mixing amongst them, soon learned their intentions.

"—There are two Europeans at Ma-ryang," said they; "it appears that they are waiting for a boat to take them back to their country: they have with them two Coreans who have certainly embraced their religion; a little later, they will return with soldiers, and, these Christians acting as their guides, our whole country will be upset: it would be, perhaps, dangerous to kill the Europeans, it might bring us into trouble, but we may at all events kill those who are with them; they are only Coreans, and no one will call us to account."

This being repeated to our people, they were seized with a regular panic: there was no use in trying to reason with them, they would listen to nothing. The pretorians, their chief at their head, took part with them, beseeching us to make off with our lives and those of our followers and thus spare the village a serious misfortune.

"—What have you to gain by remaining here?" they said, "await the French vessel? Do you not see that she has left for good, since, by day or by night, there is no sign of it; if your messenger has succeeded in reaching Chemulpo, he cannot be back in less than two or three days. Go on to the port of Ouen-san; one of our junks, returning from her voyage, can bring you there, and when your ship comes we will let your countrymen know where you are."

Very unwillingly, we were obliged to make up our minds to leave Ma-ryang. The junk was got ready, and the mandarin shared with us the little rice remaining to him, the stores having been plundered by the rebels. Not having any money to pay the innkeeper, we left our bed-clothes in pledge and were about embarking in the junk, when a little Japanese sailing vessel was sighted, on its way, it appeared, to Chemulpo.

"—It will be much quicker and more convenient to go by this junk," said the chief pretorian, "you will be at Ouen-san in a few hours."

Thinking the vessel belonged to Coreans, we asked to have it brought-to, if possible. It was hailed, and came to shore; what was our astonishment to see that the whole crew consisted of two out-and-out Japanese. A strong smell of fish, salt, dried, and smoked, exhaled from their boat. We told them that we wished to go at once to Ouen-san, and they willingly consented to bring us there. We pushed off from Ma-ryang, but, instead of making for Ouen-san, they sailed in quite an opposite direction.

"—Where are you going?" we asked.

"—To Kang-Kyeng-i (Kang-Kyeng-i is a village on the banks of the river, about thirty lys above Syeng-tang-i)."

"—To Kang-Kyeng-i! But we don't want to go there at all; you promised just now to take us to Ouen-san; we must go there at once."

"—No, when we shall have sold all our fish we will go there."

A Corean junk, passing at this moment, extricated us from this dilemma; the crew were fishermen from Ouen-san, returning to heir homes, and they consented to take us on board.

Our new boatmen were Tong-haks. To try and win their hearts, we killed a chicken (a gift from the sub-mandarin of Ma-ryang), which we shared amicably together. A good Tong-hak, it seems, should never eat chicken, but these were not too scrupulous, so, seated around the pot, bowl of rice in hand, each one pulled out for himself a piece of the chicken, having no other implements but our fingers.

Meanwhile, the junk made but slow progress. Ouen-san is between seven and eight leagues distant from Ma-ryang, but there was so little wind that after fifteen hours' journey we had not yet arrived. It was all in vain the boatmen beat their tambourine and hung out their grand flag, the god of the winds paid no attention to these honours, and the night surprised us in the midst of a maze of little islands, where we were obliged to anchor, through fear of hidden rocks. All these islands are inhabited, and, in the silence of the night, there arose a great clamour from each village; it was the evening prayer of the Tong-haks.

In the morning, we landed on the island of Ko-tai-to, which, according to our boatmen, was the most favourable spot whence to sight and signal our ship. The natives of this island received us with scant courtesy and, in order to pay for our dinner, we were obliged to give up all the rice we had, as they refused point blank to give us the smallest credit.

"—Go to the mandarin," said they, "he can feed you if he likes."

Now, this mandarin happened to be on another island, whither we were conveyed in a boat. It was low tide and, not wishing to make a detour in order to reach the port, the boatmen simply landed us at the foot of a rock. If we had been badly received elsewhere, at Ouen-san we met a worse reception, if that were possible. To be sure, we presented but a sorry figure; not having a change of clothing, the garments we wore were in a piteous state after such a campaign.

The sub-mandarin of the district gave us a better reception than his people had afforded us. He lent us a sum of money, and promised to have watch continually kept and to let us know as soon as a ship should be sighted. The look out was magnificently situated: to the south, was seen all Ma-ryang, and to the north, the course of vessels coming from Chemulpo is visible as far as the eye can reach. With money, we could have bought plenty of rice, but as we were too poor, we had to use it mixed with barley.

We passed peacefully, though somewhat anxiously, the whole of Monday and Tuesday, seated at the look-out ... and nothing appeared! Wednesday, the same disappointment. This was the seventh day since the departure of our messenger. Then, sick from disappointed hopes and weariness of mind and body, convinced that our courier had been arrested by the rebels or that the ship was unable to come to our rescue, we decided to continue our journey as best we could. A junk had just come in and the mandarin had engaged it to bring us as far as Chemulpo. Having laid in some provisions and the wind being favourable, we once again risked meeting misfortune: we had not long to wait. Once out of port, the sails swelled and we were making good way when we felt a violent shock: our helm had struck a sunken rock; the shock had dislocated the unfortunate rudder and the pilot was nearly flung into the water. We were obliged, then, to stop and repair the damage. Amongst Coreans, such an affair is, in the first place, the subject of long discussions, each one giving his advice; finally, tacking on a bit of wood here, a bit of wood there, they repaired the damage, after a fashion.

Next morning at daybreak, a Japanese man-of-war passed within a few lys of us We made signs of distress, even letting off one of the rockets which the commandant of the French man-of-war had given to our courier, but the vessel continued on its course ... We resumed ours, as best we could, but before long, the wind was against us and a torrent of rain poured down upon our heads. Crouched in a corner, a large sheet of oil-paper on our shoulders, by way of waterproof, we stoically awaited the end of all these misfortunes A Corean junk catches as much rain in the hold as on the deck. In vain our boatmen beat the tambourine, offered rice to all their devils, hung out their finest colours, still the rain went on.

The following night, the wind having changed, we once more set sail and all went well for a while, but in the morning the tempest rose again. Our little skiff danced like a cockle-shell upon the foaming waters; our terrified companions hid their faces, that they might not see themselves die, they said, and the boatmen and ourselves were not free from anxiety, for the day and night were terrible. In despair, and determined to tempt fortune, the boatmen hoisted the two sails and weighed anchor. In the twinkling of an eye, we were carried off by a whirlwind and ... as if by a miracle, we were out of danger. They were then able to steer and, after many a struggle, finally reached the port of An-heung.

Once more, our provisions were nearly exhausted, so we must look out for some safer and more expeditious means of reaching Seoul. Two Japanese men-of-war were lying not far from the port; if we could only send a letter to the commandant, we thought, he would surely welcome us on board and furnish us with means of going to Chemulpo. With this idea, we went to seek the mandarin of the district. He was a pursy, ricketty little old man, who received us seated in the midst of a heap of medicine bottles and soforth, for ministering to all the wants and ailments of his poor body. He welcomed us politely, promised everything, and ... did nothing. First, he promised us that he would himself send a letter, but night came and the sea ran so high that he decided on waiting until morning.

When the morrow came, no one would go near the Japanese vessels, swearing, that if they went near such engines of war, they should infallibly be killed ... We must then take some other step; we decided that, cost what it might, we would risk the journey by land. The mandarin approved of our resolve and sent one of his followers to accompany us; this was Sunday, 2nd. of September; fifteen days had therefore elapsed since we left Tjyen-tjyou, and we had still three hundred and eighty lys to travel!

It was nearly night when we arrived at Htai-an, and yet we were only too well remarked. A crowd surged around the courtyard of the house in which we lodged, vociferating threats of death; it may be that they took us to be Japanese. Learning that we were French, and their ideas of geography being somewhat confused, they fancied France to be a kingdom adjacent to China, and even a dependency on the Celestial Empire. No longer looking on us as enemies, they calmed down and gradually dispersed. We were then able to seek the mandarin, who made us the most flattering promises: not only would he lend us money for the journey, but he would do his very utmost to procure a mode of conveyance for us, and we went to rest, without, however, putting too much faith in these fine words. And in fact, by morning, all was changed. The money upon which he counted, could not be had, his treasurer, it seemed, had carried off the keys; the horses were all in the hands of the Tong-haks. Indignant at such a breach of faith, we sent him our passports, with the message:

"We do not know if you still respect treaties; in any case, keep this safe-conduct, given us by your king; whether we perish or not upon the way, it will yet be brought against you."

This language made him reflect; he at once sent us the money had promised, and provided us with an escort as far as the neighbouring town of Sye-san.

Thenceforth, our woes were at an end. In spite of fatigue, we finished the journey gaily; avoiding the most populous places, we slept at the small inns, and besides, the Tong-haks, not being numerous, let us pass quietly. At last, on the evening of the 6th September, we reached Seoul, forty days after I left my residence, to begin a journey which is usually accomplished in six days.

MISSIONS OF AFRICA.

VICARIATE-APOSTOLIC OF NORTHERN NYANZA.
(CENTRAL AND WESTERN OUGANDA).

The extraordinary number of conversions which, during these last few years, have taken place amongst the Negroes of the Nyanza region, has decided the Propaganda to increase the Vicariates-Apostolic in this country. Three new Vicariates have been founded: Northern Nyanza, Southern Nyanza, and the Upper Nile. The two first are in the charge of the White Fathers of Algiers, the third is in the hands of the English Missioners from Mill-Hill. The greater number of Missionary centres established by Cardinal Lavigerie's Missioners belong to the Vicariate of Northern Nyanza, and it is there, as we shall see by the following letter, that the Faith is making the most satisfactory progress.

LETTER FROM THE REV. FATHER ACHTE,

To Monseigneur Livinhac, Superior-General of the White Fathers.

Foundation of a Mission in Unyoro.

Notre-Dame de la Garde (Bukumi-Unyoro),
15th July, 1894.

YOU have already learned through Monsieur Hirth that we have at last succeeded in penetrating into the great kingdom of Unyoro and in establishing there our first Mission centre. He has also acquainted you with the fact that I was chosen for this new foundation.

1. Right Rev. Henry Hanlon, bishop and apostolic vicar of Upper Nile   B.

I rejoiced in the thought of going to plant the Cross in a country into which no Catholic Missioner had ever penetrated; still, I must confess that it was not without heartfelt sorrow that I parted from my Brethren and all our neophytes at the station of Our Lady of Victory. But is not the Missioner's motto

"Forward, for God and souls!"

This thought comforted me, and I set out for the new countries to be conquered for Jesus Christ.

Departure and journey.—Hunter and Huntress.—Catholics and Protestants.—God the Master of hearts.—The compact of Blood.

After Easter, I turned my steps towards Villa-Maria, where I was to find Father Houssin, who had been appointed to found the new Mission along with me. There, this good Father had already made his preparations for a journey of three months, not a very great labour, for we could only bring with us what was absolutely indispensable. In fact, we wanted for many things which else would be counted as necessaries. But poverty has its advantages, and the poorer we are in worldly wealth, the more we may count upon God.

After five days' rest at the flourishing station of Villa-Maria, we began our journey and, after halting twice, arrived at the Kotonga. We crossed it on the shoulders of our negroes, who were up to the neck in water, which means, that we had the pleasure of a little bath. We next entered an uninhabited country where we spent our nights in the open air. In the forest, we met one of our Christians, the blind Tobias Seboa, out hunting with his people. A rare thing, is it not, to see a blind man carrying a rifle and ... hunting antelopes and lions! Amongst his followers was a woman who, also, like her master, carried her gun, and I made her tell us of her latest exploits: she had just killed a lion and three antelopes, and she assured us that she never misses her aim. What is still better, she says her prayers and knows her catechism right well.

We next reached Bivekula, a small district of the province of Singo. This district was ceded to the Catholics after the inquiry into the persecution of 1892 had suggested to the English residents, MacDonald and Portal, the thought of indemnifying our poor Christians for their losses, at least, to a certain extent. There we learned that the English officers at Kampala had once more ordered a general levy of Baganda Catholics and Protestants, in order to invade Unyoro. Cunningly enough, they had this time distributed amongst the soldiers all the provinces bordering upon the frontier in the kingdom to be conquered, and, as usual, the Baganda Protestants had the lion's share. The Catholics murmured, but once more they were obliged, as usual, to be resigned. The terrible trials through which they have been passing these years back, have strengthened their faith, and, if they have lost confidence in man, their trust in God is all the stronger. The Catholics, therefore, only got the country of Kikukule, bordering on Bwekula.

But it is not enough to grant upon paper countries already occupied by a numerous and warlike people. Kikukule declared bravely: "If the Bagandas want my country, let them come and take it; they know we have good guns and impregnable caves."

The Catholics were left to their own resources, while the Protestants had with them two Englishmen, Captain Gibb and Sergeant Grant.

. The road to Unyoro, therefore, seemed closed against us for the moment, but this very moment was the decisive one for the cause of our holy religion. We determined to besiege Heaven with our poor prayers, and to try if we could not obtain a footing in the country before the arrival of the army. I therefore sent a courier to Kikukule, offering him our friendship and assuring him that, as Missioners of the True God, we were solely Ministers of peace and conciliation, and that we had nothing to do with the impending war.

God, the Master of hearts, inclined that of Kikukule in our favour. The courier was well received, several messengers, bearing words of ever-increasing good-will, passed between us, and, finally, an interview was granted, on condition that I should bring with me three men only. The interview took place at night, at the confines of the two countries and upon the summit of an immense rock. This rock was surrounded by Banyoros, who kept up immense fires which enabled the chieftain's officers to watch our slightest movement. At the sight of these preparations, I asked myself for a moment had I not pushed confidence even to temerity, and might they not fall upon me and massacre me. Secretly recommending myself to God and to my good angel, I took my seat facing the chief who was awaiting me. The interview began, at first cold and embarrassed enough; then, kindly words were exchanged; finally, from kind to cordial words we proceeded, from proverb to proverb; and we ended by proposing the compact of blood, a proposition which was accepted on both sides. A large knife was brought and each of the contracting parties pricked himself upon the breast; my blood dyed a coffee berry, which Kikukule swallowed; another grain was crimsoned with the blood of the aged savage, and this I swallowed, though not without repugnance.

The deed was done. We were brothers for life, and the most horrible maledictions were invoked upon the head of him who should violate the sacred compact of the brotherhood of blood.

The conditions agreed to previous to the carrying out of the ceremony of this compact were as follows: 1st. Kikukule should give us a favourable reception in his country and give liberty to all who should desire to pray; 2nd. We should do our utmost to prevent his country from being pillaged.—I then proposed to him to give in his submission to the English officers.

God had then looked with pity on Unyoro, and this country was about to receive the light of the Gospel.

Entry into Unyoro.—A peaceful conquest.—Notre-Dame de la Garde.—First catechumens.—Public Prayer.

I hastened to return to Bwekula in order to take up Father Houssin and make an effort to penetrate into Kikukule's district before the arrival of the Catholic army, and, on the 8th of May, we entered Unyoro, two days in advance of the Baganda army. When the latter crossed the frontier, the villages were at once deserted, and all the women and children hurriedly took refuge in the immense caverns with which this country of granite mountains is honey-combed. After much hesitation, Kikukule harkened to our advice, consented to all the propositions made by the leader of the army, accepted Cyprian Mwekula as his hierarchical chief and sent in his submission to the English fort. The Banyoros looked upon us as the authors of the peace, and it was to us they attributed the preservation of their plantations and villages, saved from certain destruction. What they dreaded above all was the carrying off of their women, who, in these countries, are always the most precious and the most coveted booty. I had previously obtained a formal promise from the principal chiefs, all neophytes, that they would neglect nothing in their power to prevent their men from seizing the women and children. They were loyal to their word.

Nevertheless, those pagans who had followed the army, like vultures on the look out for prey, carried off and hid four women. The Banyoros notified Father Houssin of this, and he informed the leader of the army. The women were at once sought out and given up, and this act did much to win for us the affection of the natives.

The Protestants, even with the assistance of the English officers and their Nubians, only succeeded in ravaging the provinces allotted to them, carrying off the women and children. Only one Muganda chief succeeded in establishing himself in the district apportioned to him. The success of the Catholic army aroused the jealousy of the Protestant chiefs, who could not help comparing their own conduct and acts with those of Cyprian and his followers, but they consoled themselves with their plunder and the shameful human booty they dragged in their train.

The submission of Kikukule being gained without striking a blow, our Catholics returned to their homes, and we, on our side set to work to construct our residence upon a hill situated half a league from the capital of the Munyoro chief, and whence we can plainly see the huts of his village. Kikukule has granted us a fairly large plot of ground, in which there are four good banana fields and three springs of limpid water.

It was during the month of May Unyoro was opened to us and, thanks to the visible protection of the Blessed Virgin, that which under ordinary circumstances would have proved an insurmountable obstacle to the foundation of a Mission in this country, had singularly facilitated it. And, moreover, it was during this same month that we received our first native catechumens. Through a feeling of gratitude which you will easily understand, we have placed our Mission under the protection of the Queen of Heaven: the station is called Notre-Dame de la Garde, in Kiganda language "Bukumi-la-Garde." May the Virgin Mary, who has given us this country, guard it for us; may she especially guard it against that heresy which has already made attempts to invade the land.

Not being able to build up, Protestantism seeks to destroy. In fact, barely a fortnight ago, a powerful Protestant chieftain came during the night to Kikukule in order to frighten him and induce him to go to worship amongst the Protestants, assuring him that we should not fail to destroy his country, being the enemies of the English officers.

It is by such calumnies they have already deprived us of the friendship of the king of Toru and closed his kingdom to us.

From the moment of our arrival, although very busy with the building of our huts, we began teaching the natives the catechism. At first, as generally happens, the Word of God was listened to with a certain curiosity, but no very deep impression was made. It was not until the feast of Pentecost, the 13th of May, that their hearts seemed really touched by grace, for on that day, in fact, fifteen youths earnestly asked permission "to pray," and one month later I had distributed a hundred medals to those who could repeat for me the *Pater*, the *Ave*, the *Gloria*, and the *Credo*. In August, fifteen of Kikukule's pages knew all their prayers.

I then thought it time to send one of the catechists to the chieftain's residence, there to inaugurate the custom of common prayer morning and evening, at the roll of the drum. In the evening, the catechist notified all his catechumens that they should be awakened in the morning by the beating of the drum whereupon they should at once assemble for prayer. Next morning, at daybreak, the drum is heard, about a hundred youths rush to the appointed spot; Kikukule, suddenly awakened by the drum, and the rush of hurrying feet, seizes his rifle and calls "to arms!"

"—What! am I betrayed by the Bagandas?" he shouted.

He remembered an unexpected attack of which he had been the victim. An English officer, surprising him when asleep, had one day burned his capital before he had time to assemble his warriors. But when he heard the prayer he understood and returned to his mat, anathemizing the involuntary authors of his fright. He, however, bears no ill-will and, as he promised, leaves all free to pray; but as for himself, he prefers his sorceries, and to all my urging simply answers that he is too old. He is no fanatic, nevertheless, and as he often comes early of a morning to Bukumi, he seats himself upon a stone and listens, like the rest, to the explanation of the catechism.

Amulets have lost their prestige in the neighbouring villages and have, with many, been replaced by the miraculous medal, already more or less worn everywhere. Unfortunately, our extreme poverty with regard to medals as well as all else, forces us to refuse the urgent requests of our beloved Banyoros. During the first month, I gave this little mark of distinction to every Munyoro who knew the *Pater*, the *Ave*, the *Gloria*, and the *Credo*. But since then, I can only give it to those who know all the morning and evening prayers. Oh! how I regret not having a few thousand of these medals.

Male and Female Sorcerers.—A courageous Catechumen.—Character of the Banyoros.—Missioners, Missioners!

By a somewhat brutal act, which, fortunately, led to no serious consequences, the men and women sorcerers have seen their fear-inspiring authority diminish and, in many cases, totally disappear in the country. All the Banyoros hold the superstitious belief that, were they to insult or strike a sorcerer, they should infallibly perish the following night. Now, quite lately, in Kikukule's capital, a sorceress conceived the unfortunate idea of trying, by her infernal incantations, to win back to the devil a group of youths who were at the time busily occupied learning their prayers. Dismissed politely, at first, she returned to the charge, uttering horrible imprecations against them. Upon this, a young man of about twenty-five years of age arose, and, in presence of a hundred pagans and some thirty catechumens, he pronounced these words :

"—The Father says that our divinities are demons who burn in fire, and that they have no power over those who, like me, believe in God and pray to Him. Well, then, look at me, all of you; I will be an example. If the Father speaks truly, I shall live; if he lies, I shall die this very night."

At these words, and to the great stupefaction of the bystanders, he gave a violent blow upon the cheek to the sorceress, who staggered back a pace or two, foaming with rage. Unnecessary to say, the young man was alive next morning, and is now one of our most fervent disciples.

To-day, July the 15th., after two months of Mission labour, I have already thirty-five catechumens who are half way through the catechism. In a month hence, they will know it all and we must then satisfy their ardour by giving them lessons in reading and writing, while we await the expiration of the period of probation, four years, which we are in the habit of imposing upon them before admitting them to baptism.

The Banyoros are, in general, of a gentle nature, but in the presence of strangers they evince a reserve which has the appearance of distrust. Of all the chiefs who have come to visit us, not one appeared sympathetic at first. It is not until the second or third visit that the ice melts and the tongues loosen, and then only do we find that they are as good laughers and as indefatigable talkers as our Bagandas. To see their care of the sick, one would say they are much more compassionate of heart than these latter. In our hospital there are already forty huts and nearly a hundred cases, for the most part persons maimed by wounds caused by the *funza*. These invalids are cared by Father Houssin with a patience and kindness truly maternal. This charity, so new to them, excites their admiration and inclines their hearts to listen to our teachings.

To this characteristic gentleness the Banyoros unite great bravery.

The Banyoros have not the cruel custom of mutilating their people, as was the former practice of the Bagandas, whether by the gouging out of both eyes, the cutting off of the ears, nose, lips, hands, or even of all the limbs together. But, instead, they are accustomed to extract the eye-teeth and the four molars of the lower jaw. Boys and girls arrived at the age of eleven or twelve years are obliged to conform to the fashion by submitting to this painful sacrifice, which is followed by a great feast and four days' rejoicing for the whole family. But this fashion has had its day in our neighbourhood, and the catechumens are only too glad to abandon it. How often have we heard young lads of ten or twelve cruelly joking their elders! And one day a young chieftain of four villages even came to me quite seriously, asking a remedy that should make his teeth grow again.

Our ministrations are not exclusively confined to the Banyoros. The Bagandas of the Bwekula province, who are at too great a distance to go to Villa-Maria, inhabit a vast district which is served by us. Here we have neophytes to the number of three hundred, and have already enrolled the names of about four hundred catechumens who know the whole catechism and who are awaiting baptism, but I have not yet been able to ascertain even the approximate number of the other catechumens.

You may judge from this slight sketch how ripe is the harvest in Unyoro. But how little can two poor Missioners do towards the evangelization of such a vast country! Our voice can only make itself heard in the districts around us, and we can do nothing to enlighten those souls who are at a distance; above all, are we powerless to prevent the pernicious spread of heresy, which, so strong in its temporal wealth and policy, everywhere takes advantage of its strength to force itself upon the people. Ah! Missioners! Send us Missioners!

OUR DELEGATES TO MEXICO.

Each year we make a point of giving our Benefactors an account of the works accomplished by our Delegates in Mexico; this is for us a debt of gratitude. It gives us pleasure once more to thank them for the zeal and devotedness they have evinced for our Work.

LETTER FROM MONSEIGNEUR TERRIEN,

To the Presidents and Directors of the Central Councils of the Association of the Propagation of the Faith.

THE fifth year of your Delegates to Mexico has been a laborious one, but, in return, how especially blessed has it not been by God! In 1894, the alms received by us reached a hitherto untouched figure; and what an ineffable consolation it is for us to be enabled to offer you this abundant sheaf, each ear of which is destined to nourish so many hungering souls who yearly have recourse to your charity, and who depend entirely upon the Association whose almoners you are for their daily bread and for the means necessary to carry on their holy Mission.

Bodily fatigue, mental pain, trials of every sort have not been wanting, but the Divine Master, whose goodness is infinite, has often lightened our burden and has deigned to crown our Mission with unlooked for success. Ah! this is because God wills that His Work shall be accomplished, and if He permits the struggle, it is that we may gain the more merit.

We have this year won for our beloved Association of the Propagation of the Faith seven new dioceses, which will figure in the *Annals* for the first time, occupying a distinguished place beside their elders in Europe. While preaching through these dioceses, we have not neglected the collection, and even increase, of the budget of the Association in those other dioceses where it was already known and appreciated. And we are happy to announce to you to-day that, after five years of hard labour and Apostolic visitations, almost the entire of the Mexican Republic, three times larger than France, has heard the voice of your Delegates and has responded to their call.

Of the twenty-seven dioceses of Mexico, five alone are not represented in the *Annals*, time, or other circumstances, having prevented our visiting them, but the remaining twenty-two will this year take their place in the glorious work of the Apostolate.

Linares, or Monterrey, Saltillo, Zacatecas, Durango, Oaxaca, Colima, and Cepic were for the first time visited by your Delegates: the first five I myself traversed, the other two were visited by the Rev. Father Devoucoux. In every town having an episcopal residence and in several other important localities, we left our Association organized, each locality having its respective Committee, acknowledged by the ecclesiastical authorities and composed of the most influential and zealous ladies, having at their head an enlightened and active Priest, appointed Diocesan Director of the Association.

We can only congratulate ourselves upon each choice we have made, and the alms received through the coteries of Ten appointed by us prove that the various committees are working with as much wisdom as enthusiasm.

We do not confine ourselves to working up simple Associations of Tens, which would yield a comparatively unimportant result, but, wherever we go, we endeavour, by means of domiciliary visits, to obtain extra annual offerings from the wealthy families; and I must point out to you that in this direction our success has exceeded our hopes, especially at Zacatecas and at Durango. In fact, sixteen persons in the first named diocese, and twelve in the second have been so good as to put down their names for the sum necessary to support a Missioner in perpetuity to the infidels. At Zacatecas, I proposed to a family of eight persons to thus adopt a Missioner in perpetuity, and I was witness of a most heroic action. My proposition was enthusiastically received, but the first general impulse was succeeded by a momentary silence; each one seemed to reflect, doubtless under the influence of Divine Grace, for immediately after there was an outburst of generosity, a generosity worthy of envy, for each one, following the impulse of his heart, cried out: "Father, I wish to take a Missioner in *perpetuity* for myself."

And thus, instead of one subscription I received eight, and that from one family alone.

The angels in Heaven must have looked down with admiration on this touching spectacle! As for me, I did not know how to express my gratitude; I simply stammered forth the words of the Great Apostle: "your names are already written in the Book of Life."

I must, however, remark that I did not at once receive all the offerings promised me: as a rule, all my benefactors are most willing to aid the Association of the Propagation of the Faith, but, not being able to pay a considerable sum at once, they give it to me by instalments. Thus it is that the dioceses visited during the preceding years still annually collect a fair sum; for in Mexico, more than elsewhere—such is human inconsistency—the Associations of Tens produce very little result and will cease completely once we leave the country.

Not only have persons devoted to pious works responded to our appeal, but merchants and business men have not remained insensible to our call. I was all the more touched by this, seeing that Monterrey Saltillo, Zacatecas, and Durango have just passed through a terrible crisis of five years of drought, causing awful suffering to the poorer classes! But God has at last sent them abundant rain, it may be in recompense for their charity.

After more than ten months of separation, my fellow Missioner and I met at Mexico, towards the end of October. During the few days that we spent together, Father Devoucoux gave me an account of his labours in the diocese of Colima and Tepic, bordering on the Pacific, where the Association has likewise been made known for the first time. Mgr. Atenogene Silva, Bishop of Colima, and Mgr. Ignatius Diaz, Bishop of Tepic, received him with the utmost cordiality, not only giving him permission to quest in their dioceses, but each furnishing him with a special letter of recommendation. Our Association has everywhere been established and organized, the Parish Priests receiving Father Devoucoux with fraternal hospitality, and co-operating, to the utmost of their power, in the inauguration of the Work.

Apart from these new foundations in the seven dioceses just mentioned, and which occupied six months of the year, the rest of the time was spent in consolidating and adding to the receipts of the Association in those districts where we had already introduced and organized it. For this purpose Father Devoucoux and I again visited, seperately, the principal cities of the dioceses of Puebla and Vera Cruz, everywhere meeting the same good-will and love towards the Missions.

Finally, three dioceses which we have not yet visited, will nevertheless be inscribed in the roll of the *Annals*: Merida, Tchuantepec and Sinaloa, though each sends but a trifling sum. It is to be regretted that time did not allow of our going as far as Yucatan; the Bishop, being favourably disposed towards the Association, which has been dear to him from childhood, would have received us warmly.

In concluding this account of our labours for the year 1894, I will say a word as to the results obtained in Mexico. This year, as heretofore, Mexico will occupy the foremost place. I have many munificent benefactors there, and since my arrival some fifty families have made a point of sending me large offerings, destined for the support of a Missioner. I do not give you any name in particular, as I should have to cite all the principal families.

In conclusion, I will tell you of a thought which has often occurred to me during the twelve years I have spent travelling through the Republics of Latin America. In Europe, even now, it is thought that money is found in such abundance in the New World that one has but to hold out the hand in order to obtain all that is desired, and thus many are simple enough to believe that the alms we receive cost us little trouble or labour... I do not wish to undervalue the generosity, the disinterestedness of these rich Spanish-American countries; on the contrary, I have always joyfully proclaimed their charity, for one never addresses himself in vain to the hearts of their inhabitants; but in the America of to-day, as in Europe, if we would succeed, we must work, we must stir ourselves, we must be men of action. If, on arriving in Mexico with my numerous letters of recommendation to all the principal personages of the Church, I had, in my character as

Official Delegate from the Central Councils, been contented myself with introducing the Association of the Propagation of the Faith, and merely making known the aim of my Mission by means of articles in the Catholic journals, by sermons, and by conferences, and if then I had remained tranquilly at home, awaiting the alms of the faithful, I should have done nothing and I should have had a completely fruitless Mission. But your Delegates understood the work confided to them and, in order to bring it to a successful issue, they undertook long, wearisome, and perilous journeys, preaching continually and undergoing many privations, that they might attain their end, never allowing themselves to be cast down by trials or disappointments. The Divine Master has blessed their good-will, their labours, their sacrifices: to Him alone be all praise, all glory, now, and for ever (1).

(1) The following are the names of Directors of Committees in those dioceses visited by us this year, but whose names I have omitted to mention in my report:

1. Archdiocese of Monterrey, or Linares: the Abbe Alfredo Davalos; the present Archbishop is D. Jacinto Lopez;

2. Diocese of Saltillo: the Abbe Hermenegildo Figueroa; the present Bishop is D. Santiago Garza Zambrano;

3. Diocese of Zacatecas: the Abbe Juan J. Richard; the present Bishop is Bonaventure Portillo;

4. Archdiocese of Durango: the Abbe José M. Landa; *sede vacante*;

5. Archdiocese of Oaxaca: the Abbe D. Mariano Palacios; the present Archbishop is D. Eulogio Gillow;

6. Diocese of Colima: the Abbe Mariano T. Ahumada; the present Bishop is D. Atenogenes Silva;

7. Diocese of Tepic: the Abbe D. Louis Quintero; the present Bishop is D. Ignacio Diaz.

CHRONICLE OF THE WORK.

Festivals of the Association.

As usual, the festival of the Patron of the Association has been celebrated with the utmost solemnity by the two Central Councils of Lyons and of Paris. At Paris, the ceremony took place, according to custom, in the Seminary of Foreign Missions, and the Pontifical Mass was sung by His Lordship Monseigneur Crouzet, Vicar-Apostolic of Abyssinia, the whole Council assisting.

At Lyons, His Grace the Archbishop himself said Mass in the morning, in presence of the Council. In the evening, Father Didon lent to our Association the aid of that eloquence so highly appreciated in Lyons since its first brilliant success, twenty years ago. On seeing this assemblage, amongst whom were magistrates, officers, the élite of society, one fancied himself transported to the days when Pere Lacordaire preached the Lent in the ancient Primatial city.

The power and spread of the Catholic Church, such is the subject of a discourse in which the orator seeks out the principle, the law, and defines the object of this marvellous extension.

We are the less willing to take the bloom off this beautiful discourse by a dry and incomplete analysis, inasmuch as the Rev. Father Didon has given us the incomplete text. This we have published, and we offer it to all who, having been present, would wish to refresh their memories, as well as to the less fortunate who were unable to hear those eloquent words.

In order to procure the discourse of the Rev. Father Didon, address: Offices of the Association, 12, Rue Sala, Lyons, and 20 Rue Cassette, Paris, or the Office of the *Missions Catholiques*, 14, Rue de la Charite, Lyons. Price at the Office, 5d., by post, 6d.

4.   Statue of the Father Damian at Louvain.   B.

To sum up, let us add that in our opinion the celebration of our festivals with great solemnity is the best means of promoting the interests of an institution whose field of action is vast as the world, itself. In fact, to bring together the faithful, and even all friends of progress and civilization; to tell them of the labours, the trials, the conquests of our heroic Missioners; to contrast the inferiority of our resources with the end to be attained, all this widens the circle of this Work of Providence, and multiplies the number (always but too small) of our friends and benefactors, and the appeal will be the better responded to because it comes from one possessing influence and authority in the Christian pulpit.

Monsieur Louvet's Book, Catholic Missions in the Nineteenth Century.

The readers of the *Missions Catholiques* will call to mind the very remarkable articles from the pen of M. Louvet, of the Society of Foreign Missions, Paris.

These articles, some of which appeared in the Illustrated Bulletin of the Association, have been collected in a magnificent volume by the Maison Desclee of Lille.

Catholic Missions in the XIXth Century, is the title of the work. Besides letters from His Grace the Archbishop of Lyons, from the Cardinals of Toulouse, Paris, and Rhodes, from their Lordships the Archbishop of Aix and the Bishop of Autun, this great work is honoured by a Brief addressed to the Director of the *Missions Catholiques*; the following is the translation:

TO OUR DEARLY BELOVED SON THE DIRECTOR OF THE *MISSIONS CATHOLIQUES.*

LEO XIII., POPE.

Beloved Son, health and Apostolic Benediction.

The news of the publication of a *History of Catholic Missions in the XIXth Century*, the conscientious and brilliant work of an eminent Missioner of the Seminary of Foreign Missions, Paris, has given Us heartfelt joy. This is, indeed, a work the diffusion of which will be eminently useful. Its aim is to develop the Apostolic Missions by recalling the great acts of their Apostles; their labours, and their intrepidity; and, truly, nothing can be better calculated to inspire a desire to imitate them. But, above all, does it exalt this Apostolic See, which, according to the command of Christ the Redeemer, has never ceased to teach all nations, inviting to enter, and gathering into the Fold of Christ those sheep who do not as yet belong to the Flock. Therefore, We cordially bestow unstinted and well-merited praise upon this work which in France lends such valuable aid to the Catholic Missions, the medium through which the book is published. To you, dearly beloved Sons to all you zealous fellow-labourers and particularly to the author of this work, We most affectionately grant Our Apostolic Benediction as a proof of Our fatherly love.

Given at Rome, near St. Peters, 3rd of December, of the year 1894, and the 17th of Our Pontificate.

LEO XIII., POPE.

We call attention to the fact that the Holy Father, as a mark of delicate attention towards the Association of the Propagation of the Faith, has deigned to sign the Brief with his own hand.

This magnificent infolio volume of more than six hundred pages, and containing above two hundred illustrations, is, for the friends of the Apostolate and the Associates of the Work of the Propagation of the Faith, as a monument raised to the glory of this nineteenth century which, with all its faults, has yet given rise to a magnificent expansion of the truth throughout the world.

It is therefore good and valuable reading, from every point of view, that the author, M. Louvet, presents to our friends, and we hope that they will cordially respond to our appeal. It is not necessary to say that the work will be sold for the profit of the Missions.

Price: in paper cover, 15 francs (12s.), carriage and packing, 2 francs (1s. 8d.) extra.—Bound, 25 francs (£1 0s. 0d.). If sent by mail, carriage according to distance.

An edition, limited to one hundred, has been printed upon extra fine paper: price, at the Office, 30 francs (£1 4s. 0d.).

Address of the Offices of the *Missions Catholiques*, 14, Rue de la Charite, Lyons.

We would remind our readers that, on demand, a *specimen* number of the Bulletin of the *Missions Catholiques* will be forwarded free.

NEWS OF THE MISSIONS.

EUROPE.

THE EASTERN PATRIARCHS AT ROME.

Our readers are aware that, since his advent of the Pontifical Chair, Pope Leo XIII. has always evinced a special predilection for the Eastern Churches, and has sought a means of bringing back to unity with Catholicism these millions of Christians belonging to those Rites, so venerable yet separated from the communion of Rome.

At the close of last year the Holy Father convoked at Rome the heads of each of the United Churches, and at a series of conferences held at the Propaganda, the Venerable Patriarchs were invited to give the aid of their enlightened experience and wisdom to the study of a project for union, the glorious realization of which is so much desired by His Holiness.

One of the noblest figures seen at the Patriarchal Synod was the Venerable Mgr. Gregory Youssef, who for thirty years has governed the Greek Melchite Church. Born in Alexandria (Egypt), on the 17th October 1823, he pursued his studies at the Greek Pontifical College, Rome; when barely thirty years of age he was appointed Bishop of Ptolemais, and on the 28th March 1865 he was promoted to be Patriarch of Antioch. We give a portrait of Mgr. Youssef.

CONSECRATION OF MONSEIGNEUR HANLON.

We announced the division of the Victoria Nyanza Mission into three vicariates-apostolic. We publish the portrait of the Bishop of one of these new vicariates.

Mgr. Henry Hanlon, titular Bishop of Tejo and Vicar-Apostolic of the Upper Nile, was consecrated by His Eminence Cardinal Vincent Vannutelli, at Rome, in the church of St. Sylvester *in capite*, which is served by the English Paulist Fathers. This Prelate belongs to the English seminary of Foreign Missions, Mill-Hill, near London.

HONOURS PAID TO A MISSIONER.

All our readers remember the Rev. Father Damien, who died a few years ago, a victim to his devotion to the lepers of the Island of Molokai.

The Belgian city of Louvain has just erected a statue in his honour.

The ceremony, which was honoured by the presence of the Archbishop of Mechlin, Cardinal Goossens, and of Monsieur Burlet, Prime Minister of Belgium, was magnificent. The Collegiate Church of St. Peter's was splendidly decorated for the occasion with banners and bannerets, the forty flags of the Catholic societies of Louvain being on either side of the high altar. Mass was celebrated by Father Pamphile, Member of the Congregation of the Sacred Hearts.

After Mass, an imposing procession, accompanied by bands and banners, went to the park St. Donat, where the monument to Father Damien has been erected. Senator Descamps-David, President of the Organizing Committee, was the first to speak in laudation of Father Damien's charity.

Next, the President of the Ministerial Council rose, amidst unanimous applause, to render honour, in the name of the government, and in most eloquent language, to the heroism of the modest Apostle of the lepers and to thank England for having associated herself with this festival, through her Belgian representative. "Let no one wonder," said the Prime Minister, "at the part we take in these celebrations: the government is proud of our national glories, and what glory is purer or nobler than that of the martyr of Molokai!"

Finally, Mgr. Goossens expressed his thanks to the government and to all present: "I tender these thanks," said His Eminence, "not in my name, but in the name of Jesus Christ, the Eternal Priest, Who, by His immolation on Calvary, has been, for eighteen hundred years, the inspiration and the Model of all sacrifices;—the fruitful Mother of Holy children, happy in and proud of their trials; in the name of that religious family that received into its bosom him who in the world was called Joseph de Veuster, and prepared him in silence and prayer for the sublimity of his apostolate; finally, I offer my thanks in the name of the clergy of the entire archdiocese, who love to take to themselves some little share in the glories of this day, for from their ranks came Father Damien."

MISSIONARY CATECHISTS.

The Association of Mary Immaculate was born of the compassion of Christian women for the miserable condition in which the great majority of women, so lamentably degraded in infidel countries, are abandoned, owing to the great difficulties Missioners find in extending to them the salutary influence of their apostolate.

Prejudices, mistrusts, jealousies, and inveterate customs usually keep the wife shut up and unable ever to speak to a man, save in the presence of her husband. "This powerlessness of the Missioner to assist all these poor souls, whom he would gladly save at any cost," writes the Rev. Father Dejean, from China, "is a martyrdom to which he had never looked forward, and is far more painful than that after which he sighs."

Moved by the sad condition of pagan women, generous Christian ladies conceived the idea of placing under the powerful patronage of Mary Immaculate a work of prayers and sacrifices, the aim of which was to obtain the salvation of these four millions of poor women. For this object, the first members of the Association met in Paris, on the 4th June 1880, the feast of the Sacred Heart of Jesus, when the Association of Mary Immaculate was founded.

United shortly afterwards to a similar work instituted for the East by the Sisterhood named "The Mother of God," the Council presented a petition to the Sovereign Pontiff, in order to obtain the Apostolic benediction for the budding work, and to open in its favour the treasury of Indulgences, which prayer was accordingly granted by a Rescript on the 17th June 1882.

The first result of so many prayers was to inspire a number of Christian women with a heroic resolution to fly to the aid of their pagan sisters, to go amongst them wherever the Missioner could not penetrate, to teach them the Christian Doctrine, under the Father's direction, and to bring them, little by little, to the True Faith, to the love of Jesus and Mary.

Priests and other pious persons, desirous of consecrating themselves to this apostolic work, or those, yet more numerous, who are unable to go on the Mission, yet who may desire to furnish the alms necessary for the support of a Missioner, will obtain all necessary information either at the head-quarters of the Association, 48, Rue de Bourgogne, Paris, or at the Novitiate, 7, Avenue de l'Archeveche, Lyons.

ASIA.

A MISSIONER TO CHINA ALMONER TO A FRENCH ADMIRAL'S SHIP.

A Franciscan Missioner at Eastern Chan-tong, writes from Tche-fou:

"I lately had the happiness of saying Mass for the crew on board the French admiral's vessel, the *Bayard*. At half-past eight o'clock, a little steam launch, displaying the French colours, came to fetch me. We were received by the admiral and his staff, and I was at once conducted to the Chaplain's room, in order to prepare to celebrate Mass.

"Need I say how I was moved! After four years and a half, I found myself, as it were, upon French soil. It was the national flag that floated above us; these were French officers who assisted at Mass; how it all made my heart throb! The most impressive moment was at the Elevation: the kneeling soldiers, the drum beating the never-to-be-forgotten procession air, the clarion ringing out the same notes; it was magnificent! I concluded the Mass in indescribable ecstasy. All around contributed to the effect, and never shall I forget the grand spectacle which presented itself to my gaze. The sacrifice of peace, in the midst of the trappings of war; the pardon of our sins by a God of Love, offering Himself up under the Eucharistic veil; the supports of the temporary altar, those formidable guns, ready to punish every offence against the nation; the contrast could not fail to strike me. But all things come to an end, and soon there remained nothing of the scene I have described, save the celestial merits and blessings drawn down upon us by the Holy Sacrifice.

"The admiral wished us to be present at the inspection of the sailors, which takes place every Sunday, and on that day it happened that promotions were to be announced; there were seventy-two for promotion. These latter were ranged in line and the whole crew filed past them; the admiral complimented them in simple words, saying: 'I congratulate you, boys; I myself rejoice in your happiness, and I hope you will continue to walk in the path you are treading, that you may be worthy defenders of the glorious flag of your country."

"The parade ended, the admiral himself explained to us the manipulation of the cannons and torpedos; finally, dinner was announced; all the officers of the quarter-deck who had assisted at Mass, were invited and the admiral was most attentive to his guests. They plied us with questions about China, and we gladly gave them all the information that our experience of the country enabled us to supply."

CONSECRATION OF MONSEIGNEUR SCHANG.

The Rev. Father Pacificus d'Aincreville, of the Observantines Minors, writes from Chefou, to Mgr. Stephen Mary Potron, titular Bishop of Jericho:

"The consecration of Mgr. Cesaire Schang has just taken place with unusual pomp. The new Prelate is a native of the diocese of Metz; he has received the dignity of titular Bishop of Vaga, and has been put in charge of the government of Eastern Chantong. This new vicariate, which is situated at the north-eastern extremity of China, is composed of three prefectures, dependent upon the *Tao-tai* (governor), resident at Chefou.

"The ceremony took place on the feast-day of the founder of our Order. A fortnight ago, admiral Dupuis, commanding the naval division in the Far East, arrived at the port of Chefou, and was delighted to place his crew, his military band and his colours at our disposal. Thanks to these, both our church and our residence wore an unusually festive appearance, the Pontifical and French flags floating in the place of honour. Monseigneur Schang is the first French Franciscan Bishop in China since the days of the French Revolution."

PROGRESS OF THE FAITH IN SU-TCHUEN.

Monsieur Jean Pontvianne, of the Foreign Missions, Paris, Procurator for Western Su-tchuen, writes from Tchen-tou:

"China and Japan are at war. What will be the result for this poor empire? I cannot hope for much, for, in China, it is easy enough to recruit troops of men (I do not say soldiers); but when it comes to disbanding them, then terrible revolutions break out.

"In spite of all, we still hold good our footing, even advancing, little by little. Each year sees our numbers increase.

"This year, we began a large building at Tchen-tou; our first residence was too small, and, besides, it was half eaten away by insects.

"When the new residence shall be finished, we shall make some repairs in the old one, with a view to making it suitable for our normal school, where we shall educate young Chinese for our service, either to act as schoolmasters or as apothecaries.

"But all this takes a good deal of money, and, now that I am bursar to the Mission, I am not free from anxiety as to how we shall meet so many expenses. Certainly, it is not for myself in person that I solicit aid, it is for my beloved Mission."

THE HOSPITAL OF GO-CONG.

Sister Benedict Joseph, Superioress of the hospital of Go-cong, writes to us:

"Our hospital at Go-cong, now three years established in the midst of an exclusively pagan district, owes its existence to the Rev. Father Abonnel. During six months, this Missioner travelled through the thirty-eight villages of the surrounding districts, in order to collect the money necessary for a plot of ground. In this he finally succeeded.

"Our first five Sisters took possession of this spot, where a large wooden house was being erected, and they were obliged to lodge themselves and their baggage in the straw hut of a leper. This poor creature was their first conquest: a fortnight later, they sent him to heaven. What work was necessary in order to make the place habitable! Fortunately, the administrator was a kindhearted man; he placed prisoners at the disposal of the Superioress for the construction of and thatching of straw huts, which were soon occupied by some forty patients of both sexes. Other cottages were built to serve as an orphanage for abandoned children or orphans, but the site soon proved too small. All this was organized in one year. It is clean and very well for a beginning, but there was no church, save a hut in ruins, the wood-work of which was all worm-eaten. There, the Missioners said Mass provisionally. All our resources were employed in order to build a large brick house which, later on, will serve for the sick, and which at present we use as chapel and parochial church; one part of the building is reserved for a school, attended by ninety children of pagan families.

"I am in want of ten thousand francs to rebuild, in the simplest manner, a room sixty-eight yards long by eleven wide. The present straw house is too low; our Sisters who are there are always ill of fever, and some of them are very bad.

"Through the hospital, many conversions have taken place, and others are preparing. On his arrival here, the Father found forty Christians, scattered amongst the thousand souls of the surrounding district. To-day, there are two hundred, and as many catechumens."

AFRICA.

CATHOLIC MISSIONS AT MADAGASCAR.

The preparations for an expedition against Madagascar have obliged the Jesuit Fathers to quit their flourishing stations in the interior of the Island. To remain after the announcement of the ultimatum to the Hovas through the French plenipotentiary, Monsieur Le Myre de Villers, would not only have been imprudent, but would have proved fatal to the Catholic Mission at Madagascar, composed, as it was, entirely of French subjects.

At this time, when the French expedition to Madagascar is setting out, our readers will peruse with more than ordinary interest the summary of the work of the Mission for the year 1894, sent to Tananarive by Mgr. Cazet, of the Society of Jesus, Vicar-Apostolic of Madagascar.

The number of baptisms of adults was 1,197; baptisms of children, 2,888; confessions, 128,561; communions, 92,097; confirmations, 2,158; extreme-unctions, 221; marriages, 354.

The total number of Catholics is 136,175; the number of posts or stations, 443; of churches, 88; of chapels, 277. The schools are frequented by 26,739 pupils. The Mission supports two leper houses. It employs the young convert Malgaches in various workshops where are carried on printing, binding, joinery, a forge, tinwork. Finally, the Fathers direct an astronomical, meteorological, and magnetic observatory at Tananarive.

The following are engaged in the Mission :

Missioners	51
School-masters (one of whom is a native)	4
Coadjutor Brothers	18
Christian Brothers	16
Sisters of St. Joseph of Cluny	27

THE MISSIONS OF DIEGO-SUAREZ.

Canon Murat writes to us from Diego-Suarez, on the 28th of November, 1894 :

"On the eve of All-Saints I returned to our poor Mission of Diego-Suarez, accompanied by Monsieur Florian Clain, a young Priest from the Seminary of the Holy Ghost. Where, one year ago, I was alone, we are now three Priests. Monsieur l'Abbé Foliquet, who, during my absence, had served the Mission, with great wisdom and with perfect devotedness went, on the 7th of November, to install himself at Anamakia, there to found a new station. The governor and I accompanied him there, as did also our three catechist Missioners of Mary Immaculate, who had arrived three days before. The presbytery at Anamakia was not yet quite finished, but now it is fairly well arranged, though there is neither chapel nor school. Quite close to the presbytery, and in the centre of the village, a site is reserved for the future church.

"Unfortunately, the colony is just now passing through a difficult time. The public treasury is empty and can do nothing for us; business is paralyzed by the rumours of war, and the colonists and labourers are in extreme misery. No indemnity has been granted to the victims of the cyclone, and I have been obliged, at my own expense, to repair the Sisters' house, the roof and verandahs having been carried off by the storm. These repairs have cost no less than 2,600 francs. In what a state did I find my poor presbytery! And this miserable shed which serves as the church of Antsirana, what a disgrace to us that it should be seen by natives and strangers who pass our way. It is small, it is hideous, it is uninhabitable from 7 o'clock in the morning, on account of the terrible heat, attracted by the iron-work. I have brought from France the plan of a large, handsome church, the building of which I should like to commence as soon as the rainy season is ended, and I have confidence that, to the few thousand francs I have already received for this work, the generosity of the French, and of Catholics in general, will make up the sum necessary to crown the edifice. We count upon a paternal Providence.

"The Jesuit Fathers of the Madagascar Mission have been forced to leave the Hova country, and two of these exiles have come to us, to aid us with their long experience and indefatigable zeal. One of these, Father Augustine Murat, is my brother, and the arrival of two others is announced. God be praised!"

AMERICA.

THE MISSIONS IN ARCTIC AMERICA.

The Rev. Father Corre, Oblate of Mary Immaculate, and at present in France, writes to us from Vannes:

"I recently received from our Missions, and especially from Mgr. Grouard, news which has given me great pleasure. All is going on well as regards evangelization, and the hopes we have of converting the Esquimaux, and our enterprises in the matter of steamboats for transport are most successful. Already, the *Saint Joseph* made its trial trips on Lake Athabaska in autumn last, and the builder, whom I found at Selkirk, in the neighbourhood of Winnipeg, has succeeded in beginning this winter the stocks for the second boat, which will make the journey from St. Isidore to the frozen sea by the Mackenzie River. What happiness if, by means of these boats, we should not alone be able to avoid the excessive cost of transport which the English Company imposes upon us, but also insure freer communication with our Missions and our tribes!

"I am longing to see both once more and to resume my Missionary life! France is beautiful and good; but our new family in that distant land is dear to us also, for the good reason that it has cost us many sacrifices!"

TWO NEW CHEVALIERS OF THE LEGION OF HONOUR.

At the suggestion of the Colonial Minister, Mgr. Soule, Archbishop of Leontopolis, administrator of the diocese of the Basse-Terre (Guadeloupe), and Madame Briere (Sister Elise), of the Congregation of St. Paul, Chartres, Superioress of the leper-house (Guadeloupe), have been created Chevaliers of the Legion of Honour.

OCEANIA.

A FIDJIAN CATHEDRAL.

Mgr. Vidal, Marist, Vicar-Apostolic of the Fidji Islands, writes to us from Suwa:

"Our cathedral is at last actually begun. It was Mgr. Redwood who, during the trip which he made to Fidji in company with Mgr. Primes, blessed and laid the first stone. Three Bishops at a time in Fidji! Here was an opportunity for an imposing ceremony. Our architect is a Missioner from New-Caledonia; he has already built several magnificent churches, and Mgr. Fraysse has kindly spared him to me for a while.

"But the funds with which to build this cathedral? Alas! they are precisely what are wanting. After the trials of the famine which visited us last year, we are not in a condition to undertake such a costly work; but this work has been suspended for two whole years on account of that famine: we must re-commence it if our projected church is not to be an object of public derision.

"We therefore count more than ever upon your charitable assistance, without which we must long continue to use our old wooden chapel, which is most unsuitable, as it does not accommodate more than a third of our Catholics, consequently, the remaining two-thirds cannot properly assist at the services."

APOSTOLIC LABOURS AMONGST CONVICTS.

Our readers are aware that a certain class of criminals are sent to New-Caledonia. Mgr. Fraysse, Bishop of Abila and Vicar-Apostolic of New-Caledonia, lately said that the power of the Blessed Virgin over these convicts is truly wonderful. When the Missioner meets amongst these prisoners poor souls some who, in their last moments, exhibit sentiments of the most sincere religious devotion, he invariably finds that, even in the midst of their errors, they yet preserved some devotion for the compassionate Advocate of sinners; one has never left off his scapulars; another has always kept his medal. The following story, told by the Venerable Prelate, is very touching.

"A poor exiled convict was dying of lung disease. Nothing in his manners indicated that he had any different sentiments from those of his companions in the penitentiary, yet, before long, it was observed that every Saturday, at three o'clock in the afternoon, he went regularly to place a bouquet in the chapel, before the altar of the Blessed Virgin. When his illness forced him to go into hospital, his companions wondered if the bouquet would still be offered. Now, every Saturday, at three o'clock, a fresh bouquet was found at Mary's feet. The invalid had charged the infirmarian to procure these flowers for him and to lay them in their place. The exile died one Saturday, at the very moment when the bouquet was being offered in his name, for the last time, and doubtless Mary herself received, at the gates of Paradise, this soul, just purified by the Sacraments."

✠

NECROLOGY.

As we go to press, we learn the death of His Eminence Cardinal Desprez, Archbishop of Toulouse. We cannot forget that this illustrious Prelate was formerly Bishop of *La Reunion;* he consequently belonged to our Work, and has a right to the prayers of our Associates. Neither do we forget that he was one of our most liberal benefactors, and that he was always happy to evince his good-will towards us. Amongst other proofs of this, we cite a letter which he lately wrote to us, showing how highly he approved the publication of Monsieur Louvet's work.

"With your letter, I received an advance copy of the work therein announced.

"I was anxious, before replying to you, to begin the reading of this great production, and I now hasten to send you, along with my thanks, my sincere congratulations. You are about to give us, in chronological and geographical order, an instructive and edifying epitome of the *Annals of the Propagation of the Faith* and of the *Missions Catholiques*.

"With all my heart, I bless your noble efforts, they will add one more proof of the ever fecund vitality of our holy Mother, the Church.

"✠ *Florian*, Card. DESPREZ,
"Archbishop of Toulouse."

MONSEIGNEUR COLOMBERT,

VICAR-APOSTOLIC OF WESTERN COCHINCHINA.

A telegram has just announced to us the death of this valiant Prelate, who died at Saigon, on the 31st. December, 1894.

Mgr. Colombert was born on the 19th. March, 1838, at Sainte-Marie-du-Bois, diocese of Laval. He first studied at the Laval Lyceum, which he soon left for the little Seminary of Precigny, and was shortly after advanced to the Great Seminary of Mans. Thence he left for the Seminary of Foreign Missions, Paris, where he spent two years.

On being ordained Priest in 1863, he set out for Western Cochinchina. At first placed in charge of the parish ministry, he quickly showed rare administrative abilities and was called by his Vicar-Apostolic, Mgr. Miche, to fill the posts of Secretary and Procurator to the Mission. In 1872, the venerable Prelate asked to have M. Colombert appointed as his coadjutor, consecrated him Bishop of Samosate, and, at his death, which occurred a year later, left the new dignitary in charge of the ecclesiastical government of Western Cochinchina. Since 1873 Mgr. Colombert was titular Vicar-Apostolic.

His long episcopacy has been a glorious one for the Mission. By the erection of a fine cathedral and of numerous churches, the founding of schools, hospitals, and various works organized with the aid the Sisters of Saint Paul (Chartres) and of the Christian Brothers, Mgr. Colombert has left nothing undone by which he could advance the glory of the Sacred Name of God; he leaves his Mission in a prosperous state, but his death will long leave a void in the hearts of his Missioners and of his flock, who reposed the utmost confidence in him.

We recommend to the prayers of our Missioners the soul of the Very Rev. Canon Pradel, Secretary to the bishopric and Honorary Canon of Carcassonne, and who was Treasurer of the Association of the Propagation of the Faith. Also the soul of Monseigneur Fernandez de Sotomayor, Parish Priest of the cathedral of Carthagena, and Treasurer of the Association for this diocese (South America) (Colombia).

DEPARTURE OF MISSIONERS.

A considerable number of Missioners of the Congregation of the Holy Ghost and the Sacred Heart of Mary embarked lately for the African and American Missions.

On the 3rd October, for Senegambia: the Rev. Fathers Cros, of Perigueux; Patry, of Seez. On the 25th October, the Rev. Fathers Renault, of Nantes; Ferreol, of Clermont; Parolas, of Chalons; Bodo, of Quimper; Wintz, of Strasburg; Peres, of Quimper; Royer, of Clermont; and on the 10th November: the Rev. Father Kunemann, of Strasburg.

—Embarked for Sierra-Leone, on the 25th September: the Rev. Fathers Lorber, of Strasburg; Mertel, of Paris.—25th October, for Lower Niger: Rev. Father Ganot, of Nancy.—On the 25th September, for Gaboon: the Rev. Fathers Heinis, of Strasburg; Hee, of Seez; Dreano, of Vannes. On the 25th November, the Rev. Father Reeb, of Strasburg.—On the 9th September, for French Congo: the Rev. Fathers Levadoux, of Clermont; Herpe, of Vannes. On the 25th October, the Rev. Father Koffel, of Strasburg.—On the 25th October, for Oubanghi: the Rev. Fathers Goblet, of Seez; Nio, of Vannes; Leclerq, of Beauvais.—On the 6th October, for the Lower Congo: the Rev. Fathers Ferchaud, of Rennes; Simeon, of Albi.—On the 20th September, for Cunene: the Rev. Fathers Muraton, of Clermont; Kauffmann, Kohler and Reymann, of Strasburg.—For Cimbebasia: the Rev. Fathers Keiling and Goep, of Strasburg.—On the 12th November, for Zanzibar: the Rev. Fathers Joseph Kornemann and Schneider, of Strasburg; Haberkorn, of Fribourg (Baden).—On the 12th November, for Nossi-Be: Father Holder, of the diocese of Strasburg.—On the 12th September, for Haiti: Fathers Jehl and Goetz, of Strasburg;

Rouxel, of Saint-Brieuc. On the 25th October: Fathers Limbour, of Quimper; Montel, of Clermont.—On the 10th October, for Trinidad: Father Wilhem, of Strasburg. On the 24th October: Fathers Nicholas Brennan, of Ossory; James Goodman, of Dublin (Ireland).—On the 11th October, for Para (Brazil): Fathers Disard, of Clermont; Fritsch, of Strasburg.—The 10th October, for Peru: Father Bertrand, of Strasburg.

Embarked at Havre on the 8th September, for the United States: Fathers Willms, of Cologne; Hehir, of Killaloe; Sand, of Luxembourg; Olfen, of Cologne. The 11th September: Fathers Nolan, of Killaloe; Kirby, of Cashel; Plunkett, of Dublin.

—During the course of the year 1894, thirteen Jesuit Missioners embarked at Marseilles for Madura, Madagascar, or the Mauritius. They were, for Madura, Rev. Fathers Boutelant, Dubreuil, Enderlin, Whitehead, Prince, Bosch, Perrain, Kortz and Carty. For Madagascar or the Mauritius, Fathers Neyroles, de la Chapelle and Kœnig.

—Embarked at Marseilles, the 6th December, on board the *Oungarang* for Soerabaya, Island of Java (Dutch Indies), Fathers Avellin and Theodore, of the Institute of Saint Louis, Oudenbosch (Holland).

—Embarked at Marseilles, 25th November, the following Missioners of the Society of Foreign Missions, Paris:

Messrs. Joseph Couillaud, of Angers, for Northern Burmah; Anthelme Excoffon, of Chambery, for Siam; Julius Duguet, of Besançon, for Cambodia; Leo Richard, of Rennes, for Siam; Louis Pavageau, of Lugon, for Southern Burmah; Louis Corbel, of Vannes, for Western Tonquin; John Baptist Blancheton, of Clermont, for Western Cochinchina; Louis Aubazac, of Puy, for Kouang-Tong; Charles Nain, of Autun, for Malacca.

—Embarked at Marseilles on the 9th December, the following Missioners, Members of the same Society:

Messrs. Paul Morin, of Autun, for Pondicherry; Louis Brenguier, of Rhodes, for Nagasaki; Abel Combes, of Langres, for Pondicherry; Julius Cochet, of Mans, for Mysore; John Marin, of Lyons, for Coimbatour; John Faveyrial, of Clermont, for Osaka; Louis Moriniaux, of Rennes, for Southern Thibet.

REPORT

Of the Receipts and Disbursements of the Irish Branch of the Association for the Propagation of the Faith, for the Year ending January the 1st., 1895.

RECEIPTS.		DISBURSEMENTS.	
Amount in Bank, on 1st. January, 1894, £2,085 3 1		Paid by order of Council of Paris to several Missions & Dioceses,*	£2,105 14 7
On Hands, 1st. January, 1894,	£138 18 8	Law Costs:— In re Halligan's Bequest, Probate Duty,	£400 0 0
Received from the 1st. of January, 1894, to the 1st. of January, 1895,	£16,951 9 9	Estate do.,	£128 0 0
		Legacy do.,	£1,213 13 2
		Expenses of Administration, Rent, Printing, Stationery, Carriage of Annals and pictures, Postage, Advertising, &c.,	£1,100 7 5
		In Bank, 1st. January, 1895,	£2,207 10 3
		Deposit Receipt,	£12,507 18 6
		On Hands,	22 7 7
	£19,775 11 6		£19,775 11 6

Names of the Dioceses, and the sum which each has respectively contributed during the year to the Funds of the Association.

DIOCESES.

	£ s. d.		£ s. d.
Armagh,	12,556 1 5	Amount brought over,	15,564 7 2
Achonry,	2 11 10	Galway,	4 13 4
Ardagh,	2 6 8	Kerry,	66 18 1
Cashel,	99 14 2	Kildare,	298 14 6
Clogher,	1 1 8	Killaloe,	1 0 0
Clonfert,	2 2 6	Kilmore,	4 0 10
Cloyne,	274 4 4	Limerick,	601 18 2
Cork,	42 5 9	Meath,	87 9 2
Derry,	3 11 8	Ossory,	17 15 6
Down and Connor,	552 14 8	Raphoe,	2 3 4
Dromore,	50 1 8	Ross,	138 13 4
Dublin,	1,929 5 8	Tuam,	1 1 8
Elphin,	5 8 4	Waterford,	162 14 8
Ferns,	42 16 10	Total	£16,951 9 9
	£15,564 7 2		

* The Central Councils of Paris and of Lyons reserve to themselves the exclusive right of allocating the grants to the several Missions throughout the world; but they have been always most generous in the distribution of the funds to those Foreign Missions in which Irishmen form a great portion of the Catholic population. The Society has, for many years past, allocated annually the large sum of Forty Thousand Pounds to those countries in which most of the Catholics are either Irish or the children of Irish Parents.

Central Committee-Rooms, 22 Parliament Street, Dublin.
January 1st, 1895.

CONTENTS:

The Encyclical *CHRISTI NOMEN* in favour of the Association of the Propagation of the Faith. . 65

Brief from the Holy Father to the Presidents and Directors of the Central Councils of the Association of the Propagation of the Faith. . . 66

The Encyclical *CHRISTI NOMEN*, text and translation. 68

The Corea.—*Letter from Monsieur Villemot.*—Dangers encountered by Messrs. Villemot and Baudounet during the Sino-Japanese war.—Incidents of their flight through the districts in possession of the rebels.—Tragic and moving details. 75

Northern Victoria Nyanza.—*Letter from the Rev. Father Achte.*—Foundation of a Mission in Unyoro. — Some account of the country and its inhabitants. . . 96

Our Delegates to Mexico.—*Letter from Monseigneur Terrien.*—Abundant fruits of the Mission of Mgr. Terrien and the Rev. Father Devoucoux. . . . 106

Chronicle of the Work. . . . 112

News of the Missions. 115

Necrology. 124

Departure of Missioners. . . . 125

Report. . . . 127

make their insufficiency more marked, since each year new stations are opened, new Vicariates established. As usual, the harvest is abundant, and we may now say that labourers are numerous; will not the charity of the faithful respond to all this devotedness with the same ardour and in like proportion?

True, the future seems full of promise when we study the subscription list and compare it with that of preceding years; we then see that our Association is throwing out yet more vigorous branches in Alsace-Lorrain, in Belgium, in Germany, in Italy, in Spain; or we remark that the Committee of ladies see their efforts blessed in Mexico, whose generous faith has crowned with such satisfactory success the labours of our beloved Delegates to that country, Mgr. Terrien and the Rev. Father Devoucoux. Then, in Asia and Africa, do we not see the newly-converted savages at once enrolling themselves in the Association of the Propagation of the Faith and making the most touching offerings? And yet must we acknowledge that it is with regret we see the United States, formerly so devoted to noble works, losing interest in the cause of the apostolate and, to quote the words of a New York journal, sending but very modest offerings to a Work which contributed so largely to the creation and development of their glorious churches!

We hasten to add that we are not complaining, for even in the United States the future seems brighter. In fact, we know with what filial love the great Republic responds to the appeals of the Supreme Pastor; we know the generous part she has always taken in the Work of Peter's Pence, and we therefore feel assured that in promulgating the Encyclical and recent appeal of Leo XIII. in our favour, her illustrious Bishops will give a fresh impetus to the Work of the Propagation of the Faith; they will organize it wherever it does not exist, and, guided by their experience, they will advance its interests by those means most congenial to the national spirit of their people.

In fact, it is in the Encyclical that we place our hopes. It is to us one proof the more of the confidence and affection of the Holy Father, but, may we be permitted to say, it poses a problem for which charity alone can find the solution : to consecrate a large sum to aiding the Pope in realizing his magnificent projects for the union of the Eastern Churches, and, at the same time, in no way diminish our allocations to those Missions already receiving aid, such is the programme we have to carry out.

The great Pontiff believes that he may count upon the Universe the Universe will respond freely to his appeal : the rich will increase their offerings, the poor will be faithful in handing in their weekly "halfpenny," and even should this alms be beyond their means, still smaller sums will be thankfully received by us. As his Lordship the Bishop of Saint-Flour says in his admirable pastoral, " these drops of dew will have a high and sacred value for the apostolate, for they will be the sap of its heart, and, so to speak, the life of its charity. Taken separately, they are of little value ; gathered together, they form a stream ; mingling, they gain the proportions of a river and the power of working wonders."

PARTICULARS OF CONTRIBUTIONS
FROM EACH DIOCESE TO THE INSTITUTION
During the Year 1894.

EUROPE.

FRANCE.

Diocese of AIX	...	21,684f.	32c.
,, Ajaccio	...	8,670	50
,, Digne	...	9,080	90
,, Fréjus	...	21,641	70
,, Gap	...	11,497	81
,, Marseilles	...	56,437	05
,, Nice	...	11,470	12
,, ALBI { Albi 24,375 91 / Castres 14,860 ,, }		39,235	01
,, Cahors	...	20,391	97
,, Mende	...	20,541	29
,, Perpignan	...	10,025	74
,, Rodez	...	74,341	,,
,, AUCH	...	38,507	50
,, Aire	...	33,667	80
,, Bayonne	...	51,862	26
,, Tarbes	...	18,672	60
,, AVIGNON	...	25,571	68
,, Montpellier	...	47,729	55
,, Nimes	...	23,623	83
,, Valence	...	25,470	20
,, Viviers	...	48,211	92
,, BESANCON	...	50,510	68
,, Belley	...	42,687	68
,, Nancy	...	33,561	80
,, Saint-Dié	...	39,380	97
,, Verdun	...	25,082	,,
,, BORDEAUX	...	68,737	54
,, Agen	...	14,275	,,

Diocese of	Angoulême	...	...	9,555f. ,,c.
,,	Luçon	...	...	41,155 75
,,	Périgueux	...	...	17,182 63
,,	Poitiers	...	...	34,834 50
,,	La Rochelle	...	...	14,511 70
,,	BOURGES	...	...	6,577 70
,,	Clermont-Ferrand		...	77,048 72
,,	Limoges	...	...	15,829 05
,,	Le Puy	...	...	83,472 75
,,	St. Flour	...	...	24,646 45
,,	Tulle	...	...	10,927 12
,,	CAMBRAY	...	...	186,776 50
,,	Arras	...	...	50,764 69
,,	CHAMBERY	...	...	10,256 65
,,	Annecy	...	...	32,557 50
,,	Maurienne	...	...	7,015 75
,,	Tarentaise	...	...	10,622 05
,,	LYONS	...	...	418,297 48
,,	Autun	...	...	55,826 83
,,	Dijon	...	...	27,211 89
,,	Grenoble	...	...	79,704 35
,,	Langres	...	...	21,497 72
,,	St. Claude	...	...	22,202 80
,,	PARIS	...	...	279,502 ,,
,,	Blois	...	...	50,174 20
,,	Chartres	...	...	22,142 20
,,	Meaux	...	...	6,425 30
,,	Orleans	...	...	16,680 60
,,	Versailles	...	...	32,956 95
,,	RHEIMS	...	...	46,123 ,,
,,	Amiens (1)	...	...	34,478 90
,,	Beauvais	...	...	8,738 84
,,	Châlons	...	...	12,376 50
,,	Soissons	...	...	31,652 45
,,	RENNES	...	...	124,982 10
,,	Quimper	...	...	132,304 90
,,	St. Brieuc	...	...	150,000 ,,
,,	Vannes	...	...	42,999 43
,,	ROUEN	...	...	62,592 35
,,	Bayeux	...	...	57,400 04
,,	Coutances	...	...	68,113 65
,,	Evreux	...	...	13,599 55

(1) Including a donation of 100 francs from Abbeville.

Diocese of Séez	...	...	46,689f.	42c.
,, SENS	...	...	19,875	70
,, Moulins	...	...	25,754	,,
,, Nevers	...	...	13,578	50
,, Troyes	...	...	8,869	,,
,, TOULOUSE	...	...	64,009	55
,, Carcassonne	...	...	22,826	02
,, Montauban	...	...	16,445	,,
,, Pamiers	...	...	10,616	05
,, TOURS	...	...	13,615	20
,, Angers	...	...	71,095	50
,, Laval	...	...	66,941	70
,, Le Mans	...	...	30,094	80
,, Nantes	...	...	141,185	05
			3,895,834f.	85c.

PRINCIPALITY OF MONACO.

Diocese of Monaco ... ... 2,800f. ,,c.

ALSACE AND LORRAINE.

Diocese of Metz	...	...	196,169f.	25c.
,, Strasburg	...	...	180,501	31
			376,670f.	56c.

GERMANY.

Diocese of COLOGNE	...	...	110,586f.	56c.
,, Münster	...	...	43,763	09
,, Paderborn	...	...	30,896	45
,, Trèves	...	...	56,196	84
,, POSEN and GNESEN		...	19,618	,,
,, Culm	...	...	4,145	50
,, Breslau	...	...	26,219	48
,, Hildesheim	...	...	79	08
,, Weimer	...	...	6,856	25
,, FRIBOURG	...	...	18,750	20
,, Fulda	...	...	8,265	52
,, Limbourg	...	...	5,469	35

Diocese of Mayence	... ...	2,502f.	90c.
,, Rottemburg	... ...	58,433	93
,, MUNICH	... ...	138	25
Vicariate-Apostolic of Saxe	{Bautzen 1,277 50 / Dresden 1,066 25}	2,343	75
		389,265f.	17c.

SWITZERLAND.

Diocese of Bâsle	{Bâsle 32,935 60 / Tessin 2,220 ,,}	35,155f.	60c.
,, Coira	... ...	20,364	86
,, St. Gall	... ...	12,312	15
,, Lausanne	{Lausanne 13,232 74 / Geneva 5,618 85}	18,851	59
Diocese of Sion	{Sion 7,209 62 / St. Maurice 9,223 05}	16,482	67
		103,116f.	87c.

AUSTRIA.

Diocese of GORITZ and GRADISCA ...	95f.	60c.
,, Laybach	481	45
,, Parenzo and Pola ...	117	40
,, Trieste	260	,,
,, LEOPOL	4,007	25
,, Prezmysl	1,327	,,
,, Tarnovia	1,682	05
,, OLMUTZ	1,227	55
,, PRAGUE	1,504	92
,, SALZBOURG	3,372	80
,, Brixen	6,823	90
,, Gurk	50	90
,, Seckau	1,275	35
,, Trent	8,633	25
,, VIENNA	6,539	90
,, Polten	333	60
,, Linz	3,670	10
,, AGRAM	26	,,
,, ZARA	81	60
,, Ragusa	333	10
,, Cracovia	9,785	15
	51,628f.	87c.

HUNGARY.

Diocese of GRAN	...	...	1,821f. 45c.
,, Funfkirchen	...	...	8 ,,
,, Grand Varadin	...	...	3,552 ,,
			5,381f. 45c.

BELGIUM.

Diocese of MALINES	...	...	79,112f. 94c.
,, Bruges	...	...	68,370 03
,, Gand	...	...	65,000 ,,
,, Liège	...	...	52,416 95
,, Namur	...	...	36,832 ,,
,, Tournay	...	...	69,517 35
			371,249f. 27c.

HOLLAND.

Diocese of UTRECHT	...	...	5,771f. ,,c.
,, Bois-le-Duc	...	...	58,422 20
,, Breda	...	...	5,800 ,,
,, Haarlem	...	...	11,177 37
,, Ruremonde	...	...	23,279 95

LUXEMBURG.

Diocese of Luxemburg (1)	...	...	25,140 ,,
			129,590f. 52c.

BRITISH ISLES.
IRELAND.

Diocese of ARMAGH	...	...	163,901f. 75c.
,, Ardagh	...	...	58 35
,, Clogher	...	...	27 10
,, Derry	...	...	89 60

(1) The receipts for 1893 comprise a donation of 1200f., "Anonymous from Eppeldorf."

Diocese of Down and Connor		13,818f. 85c.
" Dromore		1,252 10
" Kilmore		101 05
" Meath		2,186 45
" Raphoe		54 15
" CASHEL		2,492 70
" Cloyne		6,855 40
" Cork		1,057 20
" Kerry and Aghadoe		1,672 60
" Killaloe		25 "
" Limerick		15,047 70
" Ross		3,466 65
" Waterford and Lismore		4,068 35
" DUBLIN		48,238 40
" Ferns		1,071 05
" Kildare and Leighlin		7,468 15
" Ossory		444 35
" TUAM		27 10
" Achonry		64 80
" Clonfert		53 10
" Elphin		135 40
" Galway		116 65

ENGLAND.

Diocese of WESTMINSTER		10,396f. 40c.
" Birmingham		3,261 80
" Clifton		2,566 75
" Hexham and Newcastle		2,008 15
" Leeds		489 90
" Liverpool		6,526 50
" Middlesborough		538 05
" Newport and Menevia		2,278 50
" Northampton		98 90
" Nottingham		182 70
" Plymouth		1,259 25
" Portsmouth		2,652 10
" Salford		781 50
" Shrewsbury		2,068 "
" Southwark		2,653 75

SCOTLAND.

Diocese of ST. ANDREW and EDINBURGH		27f. 30c.
" Aberdeen		2,997 05
" Argyle and the Isles		561 05

Diocese of	Galloway	...	...	1,164f. 20c.
,,	GLASGOW	...	...	5,685 05
				321,990f. 40c.

SPAIN.

Diocese of	BURGOS	...	...	4,400f.	,,c.
,,	Calahorra	...	...	305	80
,,	Léone	...	...	855	15
,,	Palencia	...	...	2,700	,,
,,	Santander	...	...	2,469	15
,,	Vittoria	...	...	40,785	49
,,	COMPOSTELLO		...	1,333	,,
,,	Lugo	...	...	351	,,
,,	Mondonedo	...	...	789	,,
,,	Orense	...	...	2,784	,,
,,	Oviedo	...	...	4,575	,,
,,	Tuy	...	...	1,165	,,
,,	GRENADA	...	...	1,955	42
,,	Almeria	...	...	1,500	,,
,,	Carthagena	...	...	100	,,
,,	Jaen	...	...	26	,,
,,	Malaga	...	...	16	20
,,	SARAGOSSA	...	...	3,200	,,
,,	Huesca	...	...	734	90
,,	Pampeluna	...	...	3,173	45
,,	Tarazona	...	...	1,125	90
,,	SEVILLE	...	...	5,285	50
,,	Badajos	...	...	2,750	,,
,,	Cadiz	...	...	326	25
,,	Barcelona	...	...	10,699	50
,,	Lerida	...	...	973	,,
,,	Tortosa	...	...	62	75
,,	Vich	...	...	900	,,
,,	TOLEDO	...	...	1,066	15
,,	Coria	...	...	122	,,
,,	Cuenca	...	...	131	75
,,	Madrid	...	...	27,825	30
,,	Placencia	...	...	1,801	88
,,	Siguenza	...	...	50	,,
,,	VALENCE	...	...	49	,,
,,	Majorca	...	...	1,856	50
,,	Orihuela	...	...	931	60
,,	VALLADOLID		...	1,084	55

Diocese of	Avila	1,000f.	,,c.
,,	Ciudad Rodrigo	270	,,
,,	Salamanca	2,025	30
,,	Segovia	618	,,
,,	Zamora	314	87
,,	Ciudad Real	793	35
Vicariate-Apostolic of Gibraltar		350	,,
		135,631f.	31c.

PORTUGAL.

Diocese of	BRAGA	11,275f.	82c.
,,	Braganza	307	64
,,	Coimbra	1,929	79
,,	Lamego	103	36
,,	Oporto	4,081	74
,,	Viseu	851	17
,,	EVORA	175	77
,,	Beja	142	,,
,,	Faro	908	21
,,	LISBON	3,727	23
,,	Guarda	5,823	67
,,	Portalegre	108	09
,,	Angra	2,704	71
,,	Funchal	828	62
		32,962f.	82c.

ITALY.

Diocese of	ROME	17,266f.	25c.
,,	Albano	194	33
,,	CAMERINO	536	10
,,	FERRARA	1,116	88
,,	PERUGIA	1,153	98
,,	Acquapendente	375	27
,,	Alatri	97	80
,,	Amelia	92	48
,,	Anagni	53	61
,,	Ancona and Ulmana	218	19
,,	Assisi	89	35
,,	Bagnorea	160	83
,,	Citta di Castello	293	97
,,	Citta della Pieve	287	85

Diocese of	Civita Castellana	89f.	35c.
,,	Corneto and Civita-Vecchia	44	81
,,	Fabriano and Matelica	285	92
,,	Fano	268	05
,,	Ferentino	268	05
,,	Foligno	111	69
,,	Gubbio	294	56
,,	Iesi	252	69
,,	Montefiascone	127	02
,,	Norcia	178	70
,,	Orvieto	415	48
,,	Osimo and Cingoli	178	70
,,	Poggio Mirteto	26	81
,,	Recanati and Loretto	321	66
,,	Rieti	70	23
,,	Segni	22	84
,,	Terni	388	68
,,	Terracino	82	65
,,	Tivoli	190	10
,,	Todi	94	62
,,	Viterbo and Tascanella	214	53
,,	BOLOGNA	1,340	25
,,	Faenza	299	83
,,	FERMO	446	75
,,	Macerata and Tolentino	522	70
,,	Montalto	171	56
,,	San Severino	96	64
,,	RAVENNA	300	22
,,	Bertinoro	116	16
,,	Cervia	60	45
,,	Cesena	214	86
,,	Forli	344	,,
,,	Sarsina	160	83
,,	URBINO	191	21
,,	Cagli and Pergola	217	10
,,	Montefeltro	288	54
,,	Pesaro	714	80
,,	Senigaglia	268	05
,,	Urbania	89	85
,,	CAGLIARI	274	95
,,	GENOA	22,141	10
,,	Albenga	1,287	85
,,	Bobbio	898	45
,,	Tortona	3,903	34

Diocese of	Vintimiglia	...	621f.	20c.
,,	SASSARI	...	190	40
,,	TURIN	...	85,962	15
,,	Acqui	...	883	,,
,,	Alba	...	1,390	,,
,,	Aosta	...	3,648	75
,,	Asti	...	7,010	,,
,,	Coni	...	2,103	,,
,,	Fossano	...	2,000	,,
,,	Ivrea	...	10,960	,,
,,	Mondovi	...	5,444	,,
,,	Pignerol	...	2,750	,,
,,	Saluzzo	...	3,254	,,
,,	Susa	...	840	,,
,,	VERCELLI	...	8,603	,,
,,	Alexandria	...	660	,,
,,	Bielle	...	6,370	,,
,,	Casal	...	3,680	,,
,,	Novaro	...	10,146	40
,,	Vigevano	...	1,643	30
,,	UDINE	...	2,094	35
,,	MILAN	...	25,097	58
,,	Bergamo	...	5,500	,,
,,	Brescia	...	4,406	72
,,	Como	...	1,210	92
,,	Cremo	...	125	46
,,	Cremona	...	3,117	59
,,	Lodi	...	1,872	09
,,	Mantoue	...	125	83
,,	Pavia	...	1,437	79
Patriarch of	VENICE	...	1,570	80
Diocese of	Adria	...	402	75
,,	Bellune and Feltra	...	581	60
,,	Ceneda	...	179	,,
,,	Chioggia	...	31	50
,,	Concordia	...	127	20
,,	Trevisa	...	149	75
,,	Veroua	...	1,919	80
,,	Vicenza	...	1,118	45
,,	LUCCA	...	2,479	65
,,	Arezzo	...	163	94
,,	Cortona	...	165	12
,,	Montalcino	...	129	42
,,	Montepulciano	...	75	87
,,	Parma	...	372	,,

Diocese of	Plaisance	...	1,566f.	,,c.
,,	FLORENCE	...	2,187	24
,,	Collo	...	321	30
,,	Fiesole	...	332	82
,,	San Miniato	...	392	70
,,	Modigliana	...	182	97
,,	Pistoja and Prato	...	1,367	32
,,	PISA	...	937	10
,,	Livourna	...	1,532	95
,,	Pescia	...	274	89
,,	Pontremoli	...	409	78
,,	Volterra	...	371	28
,,	SIENNA	...	17	85
,,	Chiusi and Pienza	...	205	32
,,	Grossetto	...	89	25
,,	Massa-Marittima	...	166	60
,,	Sovano Pitigliano	...	174	24
,,	MODENA	...	49	,,
,,	Guastalla	...	186	,,
,,	Reggio	...	6,323	,,
,,	AQUILA	...	460	,,
,,	CATANIA	...	8,491	15
,,	Aci Reale	...	2,700	,,
,,	Aquina, Soro, and Pontecorvo		185	,,
,,	Aversa	...	605	20
,,	Cava and Sarno	...	1,083	,,
,,	Nocera	...	183	17
,,	Penne and Atri	...	67	20
,,	Trivento	...	597	50
,,	Valva and Sulmona	...	124	,,
,,	ACERENZA and MATERA		110	,,
,,	Venosa	...	48	60
,,	BARI	...	100	,,
,,	Bojano	...	142	,,
,,	Cerreto	...	34	50
,,	Larino	...	354	30
,,	CAPUA	...	354	34
,,	Cajazzo	...	75	50
,,	Calvi and Teano	...	267	35
,,	Caserta	...	298	65
,,	Isernia and Venafro	...	38	95
,,	Sessa	...	42	,,
,,	CHIETI	...	874	,,
,,	Vasto	...	216	,,

Diocese of	MESSINA	...	...	1,035f. ,,c.
,,	Nicosia	...	...	181 50
,,	MONREALE		...	546 10
,,	Caltanisetta	...	...	465 ,,
,,	Girgenti	...	...	433 ,,
,,	NAPLES	...	...	14,379 92
,,	Nola	...	...	25 20
,,	Pouzzoles	...	...	138 ,,
,,	OTRANTO	...	...	175 ,,
,,	Lecca	...	...	200 ,,
,,	PALERMO	...	...	1,246 25
,,	Mazzara	...	...	472 40
,,	Trapani	...	...	668 70
,,	REGGIO	...	...	200 ,,
,,	Catanzaro	...	...	73 ,,
,,	Nicastro	...	...	44 ,,
,,	Oppido	...	...	100 ,,
,,	SALERNA	...	...	535 ,,
,,	Diano	...	...	55 ,,
,,	Nocera and Pagani		...	152 15
,,	Nusco	...	...	30 ,,
,,	SORRENTO	...	...	6,004 13
,,	Castellamare	...	...	1,000 ,,
,,	SYRACUSA	...	...	230 65
,,	Caltagirone	...	...	21 20
,,	Noto	...	...	74 40
,,	Piazza	...	...	595 20
,,	TARANTO	...	...	114 77
,,	Castellaneta	...	...	270 ,,
,,	TRANI	...	...	214 ,,
,,	Andria	...	...	430 ,,
Abbe of	Mont-Cassin	...	...	50 60
,,	Monte-Vergine	...	...	80 ,,
				336,621f. 89c.

THE LEVANT.

Diocese of	Malta	...	...	14,130f. 75c.
,,	Gozzo	...	...	413 50

GREECE.

Diocese of	ATHENS	...	...	250f. ,,c.
,,	NAXIA	...	...	75 ,,
,,	Santorin	...	...	110 40
,,	Syra	...	...	180 30
,,	CORFU	...	...	200 ,,

TURKEY IN EUROPE.

Vicariate-Apostolic of CONSTANTINOPLE	4,267f.	15c.
Diocese of SCUTARI	211	50
,, Sappa	27	60
,, Candia	200	,,

ROUMANIA.

Diocese of BUCHAREST	250f.	,,c.

MONTENEGRO.

Diocese of ANTIVARI	112f.	,,c.
	20,428f.	20c.

RUSSIA AND POLAND.

Different Dioceses of Russia	1,706f.	75c.
Diocese of WARSAW	618	78
	2,325f.	53c.

Different countries of the North ... 328f. ,,c.

ASIA.

Diocese of SMYRNA	725f.	50c.
Delegation-Apostolic of Syria	976	20
Patriarchate of JERUSALEM { Jerusalem 2,447 50 / Seminary of St. Anne 166 40 / The Island of Cyprus 146 ,, }	2,759	90
Diocese of COLOMBO	242	20
,, Jaffna	344	,,
,, Hyderabad	77	,,
,, PONDICHERRY	682	70
,, Mysore	456	88
,, Coimbatour	70	,,
Vicariate-Apostolic of Southern Burmah	453	60
,, ,, Northern Ho-nan	50	,,
Prefect-Apostolic of Kouang-Tong	712	25
	7,550f.	28c.

AFRICA.

Diocese of ALGIERS	10,460f.	60c.
,, Constantine	4,840	90
,, Oran	5,803	08

UPPER-NIGER. — Wood of the mission at Assaba.

Vicariate-Apostolic of Sahara	100f.	„c.
Diocese of CARTHAGE	2,735	„
Prefecture-Apostolic of Tripoli	247	40
Delegation-Apostolic of Egypt	2,679	50
Prefecture-Apostolic of Tantah	106	50
„ „ Lower Niger	27	„
Vicariate-Apostolic of Western Cape	850	90
Prefecture-Apostolic of Cimbebasia	84	„
Vicariate-Apostolic of Congo	30	„
Prefecture-Apostolic of Congo	34	„
Mission of Cunène	33	„
Vicariate-Apostolic of The Two Guineas	32	„
„ „ Madagascar	57	75
„ „ Oubanghi	28	„
Diocese of Port-Louis (Maurice)	1,242	„
„ Saint Denis (Reunion)	125	„
Prefecture-Apostolic of Senegal	727	„
Vicariate-Apostolic of Senegambia	200	„
„ „ Sierra-Leone	160	„
„ „ Northern Zanzibar	60	„
	20,553f.	63c.

NORTH AMERICA.

CANADA.

Diocese of Antigonish	2,943f.	40c
„ Charlottetown	70	65
„ St. John (New Brunswick)	400	„
„ MONTREAL	745	95
Vicariate-Apostolic of Pontiac	641	25
Diocese of QUEBEC	597	20
„ SAINT-BONIFACE	450	25
„ Saint-Albert	624	„
„ TORONTO	2,501	„
Prefecture-Apostolic of St. Peter and Miquelon	500	„

UNITED STATES.

Diocese of BALTIMORE	3,519f.	17c.
„ St. Augustine	305	„
„ BOSTON	26,058	40
„ Burlington	407	21
„ Hartford	7,131	50
	10	

Diocese of Manchester	...	...	3,436f. 45c.
,, Portland	...	...	5,747 85
,, Providence	...	...	5,620 15
,, CHICAGO	...	...	8,220 ,,
,, Alton	...	...	2,110 ,,
,, Belleville	...	...	1,224 50
,, CINCINNATI		...	2,707 05
,, Cleveland	...	...	4,814 55
,, Fort-Wayne	...	...	151 90
,, Grand Rapids	...	...	2,076 70
,, Louisville	...	...	4,296 ,,
,, Vincennes	...	...	1,335 ,,
,, DUBUQUE	...	...	5,326 ,,
,, Davenport	...	...	8,257 50
,, MILWAUKEE		...	4,696 63
,, Marquetta	...		1,328 45
,, NEW ORLEANS		...	255 65
,, Galveston	...	...	103 85
,, Little Rock	...	...	655 ,,
,, Mobile	...	...	130 ,,
,, Natchez	...	...	598 ,,
,, Natchitoches	...	...	280 20
,, San Antonio	...	...	2,556 70
Vicariate-Apostolic of Brownsville		...	268 ,,
,, ,, Indian Territory		...	159 45
Diocese of NEW YORK	...	...	5,566 10
,, Newark	...	...	1,213 60
,, Ogdensburg	...	...	1,202 05
,, Syracuse	...	...	1,721 40
, Helena	...	...	185 ,,
,, Nesqualy	...	...	257 ,,
,, Erié	...	...	1,510 ,,
,, SANTA-FE		...	1,520 ,,
Vicariate-Apostolic of Arizona		...	680 ,,
Diocese of SAN FRANCISCO		...	4,623 75
,, Monterey	...	...	683 60
,, Sacramento	...	...	505 ,,
,, SAINT LOUIS		...	2,400 ,,
,, Kansas City and St. Joseph			915 ,,
,, Kansas City (Kansas)		...	2,546 ,,
,, Duluth	...	...	274 40
,, Saint Cloud	...	...	102 ,,
,, Sioux-Falls	...	...	646 62

MEXICO.

Diocese of DURANGO	32,526f.	20c.
,, Sinaloa	506	20
,, GUADALAJARA	71,030	60
,, Colima	5,074	40
,, Tepic	21,170	,,
,, Zacatecas	18,788	10
,, LINARES	7,676	30
,, San Louis of Potosi	5,135	80
,, Saltillo	2,152	20
,, MICHOACAN	7,434	90
,, Leon	11,289	,,
,, Queretaro	7,799	56
,, Zamora	26,968	50
,, MEXICO	136,217	05
,, Cuernavaca	1,822	30
,, Puebla	26,848	20
,, Tulancingo	6,756	80
,, Vera-Cruz	36,861	85
,, OAJACA	4,544	10
,, Merida and Yucatan	1,104	,,
,, Tehuantepec	316	40
	565,274f.	54c.

CENTRAL AMERICA.

Diocese of San José and Costa Rica	3f.	20c.
,, PORT OF PRINCE	794	,,
,, PORT OF SPAIN	3,189	,,
,, Roseau	461	80
,, Lowlands (Guadaloupe)	1,483	,,
,, St. Peter (Martinique)	7,448	35
	13,379f.	35c.

SOUTH AMERICA.

NEW GRANADA.

Diocese of Antioquia	26f.	,,c.
,, Panama	747	,,
,, Popayan	445	,,

VENEZUELA.

Diocese of CARACAS	1,693f.	25c.

10 *

GUIANA.

Prefecture-Apostolic of French Guiana	878f.	,,c.

ECUADOR.

Diocese of QUITO	120f.	,,c.
,, Guayaquil	704	95
,, Port Viejo	1,645	37

BRAZIL.

Diocese of Rio Janeiro	1,640f.	,,c.

ARGENTINE REPUBLIC.

Diocese of BUENOS-AYRES	980f.	,,c.
,, Cordova	2,364	,,
,, Parana	344	20

URUGUAY.

Diocese of Montevideo	5,909f.	80c.
	17,497f.	57c.

OCEANIA.

Diocese of ADELAIDE	1,180f.	50c.
,, HOBART	352	10
,, MELBOURNE	704	20
,, SYDNEY (1)	1,025	,,
,, WELLINGTON	1,597	15
,, Auckland	1,222	10
Vicariate-Apostolic of the Navigator Islands	220	60
,, ,, Sandwich Islands	3,129	75
,, ,, Tahiti	652	,,
	10,083f.	40c.

(1) Received from the Marist Fathers

GENERAL REPORT OF RECEIPTS IN 1894.

EUROPE.

Diocese of France	8,895,834f.	85c.
— Monaco	2,800	„
— Alsace and Lorraine	376,670	56
— Germany	389,265	17
— Switzerland	103,116	87
— Austria	51,628	87
— Hungary	5,381	45
— Belgium	371,249	27
— Holland	129,590	52
— British Isles	321,990	40
— Spain	135,631	31
— Portugal	32,962	82
— Italy	836,621	89
— The Levant	20,428	20
— Russia and Poland	2,825	53
From different Dioceses of the North	328	„

ASIA.

From different dioceses of Asia . . 7,550f. 23c.

AFRICA.

From different dioceses of Africa . 30,553f. 63c.

AMERICA.

Diocese of North America	565,274f.	54c.
— Central America	13,379	35
— South America	17,497	57

OCEANIA.

From different dioceses of Oceania 10,083f. 40c.

Total, 6,820,164f. 43c.

From various dioceses of Italy, whose receipts for 1894 having arrived after the accounts were closed, will be carried over to 1895:

From Rome	...	...	19,397f.	71c.
Diocese of Acquapendente	...	...	400	,,
,, Alatri	...	...	66	80
,, Amelia	...	...	91	,,
,, Ancona	...	...	225	50
,, Assisi	...	...	155	,,
,, Bagnorea	...	...	180	,,
,, Bertinoro	...	...	140	,,
,, Bitonto	...	...	89	70
,, Bologna	...	...	600	,,
,, Cagli and Pergola	...	...	150	,,
,, Camerino	...	...	500	,,
,, Cesena	...	...	188	75
,, Citta di Castello	...	...	1,080	60
,, Cerreto d'Esi	...	...	70	,,
,, Genes	...	...	600	,,
,, Cerneto and Civitavecchia	...	...	48	53
,, Domodossola	...	...	20,000	,,
,, Fano	...	...	265	81
,, Fermo	...	...	501	,,
,, Ferrara	...	...	1,100	,,
,, Forlimpopoli	...	...	80	,,
,, Fossombrone	...	...	86	,,
,, Fabriano	...	...	451	25
,, Faenza	...	...	290	,,
,, Gubbio	...	...	690	,,
,, Imola	...	...	1,200	,,
,, Iesi	...	...	240	,,
,, Ischia	...	...	274	90
,, Matelica	...	...	816	,,
,, Montalto	...	...	190	32
,, Montefiascone	...	...	72	10

Diocese of Nocera	... ...	198f.	,,c.
,, Orto	... ...	96	,,
,, Pesaro	... ...	770	,,
,, Poggio Mirteto	... ...	80	,,
,, Ravenna	... ...	430	,,
,, Recanati	... ...	248	40
,, Rimini	... ...	481	72
,, Ripatransone	... ...	150	,,
,, Rossano	... ...	100	,,
,, Rieti	... ...	80	,,
,, San Severino	... ...	86	60
,, Sarsina	... ...	94	54
,, Segni	... ...	26	,,
,, Senigaglia	... ...	350	,,
,, Terni	... ...	450	,,
,, Tivoli	... ...	156	20
,, Todi	... ...	116	48
,, Tolentino	... ...	275	,,
,, Urbino	... ...	210	,,
,, Viterbo	... ...	202	50
,, Norcia	... ...	100	,,

MISSIONS OF ASIA.

PREFECTURE-APOSTOLIC OF KOUANG-TONG.

The Prefecture-Apostolic of Kouang-Tong, which was the scene of the following dramatic episode, is one of the flourishing Missions of Southern China. It contains above 30,000 faithful, 50 European Missioners, 10 native Priests, and 140 churches or chapels. The Bishop, Mgr. Chausse, resides at Canton.

LETTER FROM MONSIEUR LE TALLANDIER,
APOSTOLIC MISSIONER,

To Monseigneur Chausse, Prefect-Apostolic of Kouang-Tong.

Martyrdom of a Christian and four Catechumens.

CAN-CHUÑG is the Christian settlement which met with the greatest obstacles at the time of its foundation, on account of the hatred of the most influential members of that family to which the catechumens in this village belong. However, the future seemed to promise peace, and when I left for Canton, in order to make my retreat there, I thought myself justified in telling the nearest Missioner, Monsieur Fleureau, that I felt no uneasiness in leaving my district. God had willed it otherwise.

In order to succeed in their designs, the heads of a family had communicated with a Christian, a connection of theirs, in the neighbourhood. On the 4th October, this Christian came from them, the bearer of conciliatory messages to the catechumens. But our neophytes had had too much reason to doubt their enemies and put no faith in these advances.

On the following day the autumnal sacrifices took place, and the village functionary (a sort of bailiff), went officially to invite our people to the customary feast. Seven of the catechumens yielded and accepted the invitation, namely, Foun-Ii, Shing-Tin, San-Tin, Sy-Cheung, A-Sam, Tang-Li, and A-Pat.

They were cordially welcomed in the temple of ancestors. A table was laid for them and they were invited to be seated.

"The reconciliation would not be complete," was hypocritically added, "if the whole family were not here."

And again they sent the messenger for Foun-Ii's father and mother, and even for his grandmother, who was eighty-three years old. After some hesitation, they also went to the Tsytong.

Scarcely had they crossed the threshold, when the door was shut upon them, then fifty young men, all armed, suddenly rose and surrounded the table where the Christians were seated. Tsok-Chiu, the foremost in rank, called upon them to give up their faith. Shing-Tin replied that they would rather die. Tsok-Chiu continued to urge them.

"You are only losing your time," said Sy-Cheung (the only one of them baptized), "we are Christians, and Christians we will remain."

At these words, the ruffians rushed forward, brandishing their arms, and Sy-Cheung was the first to fall, his head smashed in, his abdomen torn open by a blow of a *chang-tsiu* (a sort of spade).

Astounded by this unexpected attack, the others, in order to escape the blows, pushed through the crowd and fled in all directions, but they were soon overtaken and fell in their turn, their skulls smashed, their bodies bruised, their limbs broken.

Foun-Ii was in the arms of his mother and his grandmother, who protected him with their bodies, but he was torn from them and fell mortally wounded; then, at the sight of these mangled bodies, bathed in blood, the murderers stopped, terror-stricken; the pagans in the crowd protested timidly; the heads of the family, who had given orders for the massacre, began to reflect:

"What is to be done?" said they, "some of these wounded men are dying; we must inform the authorities of the affair."

For they well knew the hatred of the latter for everything pertaining to Christianity. Two of the ringleaders, still carrying their bloody *chang-tsiu* in their hands, repaired to the magistrate's house, where a catechist had been before them, but had been very badly received by the chief official.

"I have nothing to do with the affairs of the Christians," the latter had said to the catechist; "the Fou family can look after their own affairs and take such measures as they think proper with their relatives."

The murderers got the best possible reception.

"Get rid of all traces of the murder," he said to them: "finish off the wounded and burn the bodies."

Having deliberated and consumed a quantity of wine, in order to excite themselves for the carnage, the murderers resolved to act according to the advice of the chief official. There was plenty of wood and, to make the fire burn better and more quickly, they sent out for some petroleum, while a dozen young men undertook to dig a deep trench in the inner court.

There now remained but the work of despatching the wounded. Shik-Chao pointed out that in order to render the operation quick and complete, they must first bleed their victims and remove all soft parts: the intestines, heart, and lungs, and to this horrible work he set himself, with several others, for a sum of five thousand *sapeques*. Armed with enormous knives, they bend over their victims and execute to the letter the infamous project suggested to them.

Foun-Ii, Shing-Tin, Si-Cheung, and A-Sam were already cut in pieces, and they were about to seize Tang-Ii when an old man interposed:

"—Enough of blood;" said he, "do you want to destroy this whole family?"

His words made some impression; but Shik-Chao, drunk with wine and with blood, hastened forward:

"—Leave these people alive!" said he, "what are you thinking of! They would be only so many witnesses against us."

"—I will do my utmost," replied Tai-Hom, "to prevent them from bearing witness against us."

"—Very well," answered several voices; "but your own head will answer for them."

"—I will answer for them with my head," said the honest pagan.

"—Very well!" said Shik-Chao, "let him have Man-Fong (Foun-I's father), his wife, Tang-Ii, and A-Pat. But there are only four bodies here, and we must have five. Where is San-Tin?"

The wretch then went up to the garret, armed with a lance, caught sight of San-Tin stretched upon the ground, ran him through two or three times and kicked out the body, which, in its fall, struck against the top of a half open door and fell heavily on the ground.

One of the details of this atrocious scene was, that Sy-Cheung's son, A-Kwan, a child of fifteen years of age, had been obliged to look on at these executions.

The night had fallen and the furnace in which the bodies were to be consumed was ready, two or three layers of wood, saturated with petroleum, being placed in the bottom. The murderers, their hands and clothes covered with blood, caught up, by handfuls, the entrails and lungs, which they threw in first; then came the other parts, above which were heaped fresh faggots, and, the whole being sprinkled with petroleum, the pile was kindled.

Before long the flames arose in the midst of the darkness of the night, lighting up the whole neighbourhood, and even casting their sinister reflection upon the distant mountains, while throughout the village there reigned the silence of death. Shik-Chao and Hon-Tsay, like two demons, spent the whole night by the fire, stirring it up with long bamboos.

By daybreak the infernal work was done, and there remained nothing more than a smouldering heap of embers which contained but the ashes of the burned bodies. At least, so thought the executioners. They removed the first layer of charcoal, but, O wonder! the hearts and skulls were intact. These were quickly taken out of the furnace, the skulls smashed and packed, along with the hearts, in baskets which were removed through the opening in the roof. The ashes, the cinders, the upper layer of earth, which still bore traces of the fire, were in turn taken up and disappeared through the same opening, and, in less than an hour, the pit was filled up with fresh earth, brought from outside.

It was still necessary to remove the blood-stains from the place of the murder. They were dug up with a spade and covered over with sand. By this time it was broad day. The doors were at last opened and all were free to leave. Man-Fong, his wife, and the old grandmother returned sadly to their dwelling, but Tang-Ii and A-Pat, being unable to walk, were carried away in hand-chairs.

Where have the precious remains of the victims, their heads and their hearts, been hidden? As yet, no one knows. All that is known is that the ashes and cinders were thrown into the neighbouring river.

However, on the evening of the 5th., Foun-Ii's wife lodged a complaint before the mandarin, who received it very badly. Still, he promised to make inquiries, and by next evening the officials sent out for this purpose had already returned, affirming, on their honour as government employees, that nothing unusual had occurred at Tan-chuhg. To be sure, in order the better to convince them, the murderers had given them, by way of argument, from two to three hundred piastres, which they brought back carefully tied up in their baggage.

On the 7th., Foun-Ii's wife, accompanied by Shin-Tin's wife, again presented herself at the Prefecture. The mandarin was moved. 'He would go," he said, " to the place and see for himself."

On the morning of the 8th., he had not as yet left.

Foun-Ii's wife, Shin-Tin's, Sy-Cheung's son, an eye-witness, and, finally, A-Sam's mother came to ask for justice. Being unable to escape their importunities, the mandarin set out on the 9th., followed by the relatives of the victims.

At last the mandarin arrived, and found the chief magistrate of the place, the accomplice of the murderers, ready to receive him and surrounded by four hundred hired ruffians from Kouang-si, ostensibly, that they might add to his dignity, but, in reality, employed to seize upon the relatives of the victims. Being unable to lay hands upon them, the brigands were obliged to be content with loading them with abuse.

After breakfast on the morning of the 10th., the mandarin went to the temple and, as soon as he had entered, turning to the crowd :

"—Is it possible," he asked, " to find a witness who was present at what took place upon the 5th. ? "

" —Yes," answered one of the Christians, " there is Foun-Ii's grandmother."

"—Let a chair be got and have her brought here," said the mandarin.

The poor old woman, who had been witness of the massacre of her eldest grandson, at first refused to go to the pagoda.

" —They no doubt want to murder me also," said she.

When it was explained that the mandarin desired her presence, she allowed herself to be brought to the temple.

Interrogated by the magistrate, she answered all his questions with perfect accuracy.

"—I am," she said, "the mother of Man-Fong. I was here on the 5th.; they tore my grandson from my arms to put him to death."

"—How did you hold him?" asked the mandarin.

Listening only to her motherly heart, the good Christian pressed the mandarin to her bosom. The latter, with tears in his eyes, disengaged himself gently and asked:

"—Whereabouts did your grandson fall?"

"—Here," she answered, pointing with her finger to a spot close by.

"—Remove the sand," ordered the mandarin.

The work was begun and, in the interstices of the pavement, were seen dark spots, the remains of the blood which had been scraped off.

Leading the mandarin to another spot:

"—It was here Shing-Tin fell."

Farther on:

"—Here is where A-Sam fell."

In the three places indicated were found the same traces of blood.

"—But," said the mandarin, "they were five."

"—True," replied the Christian, "but San-Tin had gone to the upper storey, and it was there he was massacred. Let the great man see for himself. His body fell upon this door, the head hanging to one side, the feet to the other, and the door is stained with his blood."

The proofs were plainly to be seen, but, to make more sure, the mandarin directed the removal of the newly turned up earth which covered the pit where the bodies had been burned, and he there found the remains of charred bones, which he carefully gathered up. On the spot where the murderers had smashed the skulls, he found several teeth.

Tsan-Khan, Shui-Cheung, Sik-Chao, and Hon-Tsay, who had had the audacity to come for the purpose of justifying themselves, were obliged to follow the mandarin, and they are now in prison, but the remainder of the gang have not yet been arrested.

It may be that at head-quarters it is thought the Sun-i mandarin showed too much zeal!

Shall we obtain justice? These widows and grandmothers, women of from seventy to eighty years of age, will they in the end obtain from the Chinese judges compensation sufficient to prevent their dying of hunger? It is very doubtful. If, as there is every reason to fear, our petitions should be unsuccessful, these victims will have to be supported at the expense of the local Missioner. May some charitable souls be guided by the generous impulse of their hearts and come to the assistance of these poor Christians! Those who were their support upon earth preferred to die rather than renounce their God; I feel confident that in Heaven above they will pray for those who aid their desolate relatives.

MISSIONS OF AFRICA.

PREFECTURE-APOSTOLIC OF THE UPPER NIGER.

Our Associates will read with interest the satisfactory details contained in the following letter from the Rev. Father Zappa. They will see how zealously and successfully the Fathers of the African Missions (Lyons) enlarge their field of Apostolic labour upon the right bank of the great river of Guinea, and, at the same time, increase their Stations and the number of adorers of the True God.

LETTER FROM THE REV. FATHER ZAPPA,

SUPERIOR OF THE NIGER MISSION,

To the Very Rev. Father PLANQUE, Superior-General of the African Missions, Lyons.

IT is with a heart full of the most lively gratitude to God that I sit down to give you an account of the progress made by our Prefecture of the Niger during the course of the year. Twelve months ago, I could only give you the picture of a station just emerging from a period of trial; but now I shall have to give you the history of numerous recently founded posts, nearly all established at the same time; of several offshoots which we have been enabled to plant in a virgin soil, in the midst of exclusively pagan peoples.

I will speak little of Assaba, our principal post, for you saw it last year, already on the way to prosperity; you have before now rejoiced on learning that the old bamboo chapel had been replaced by a church, a modest one, to be sure, but still a marvel of beauty

CANADA. — House near the Mackenzie River.

in the eyes of our good savages. As for our neophytes, we have the great happiness of seeing them persevere in the right road and show a zeal and an activity which surpass our most ardent hopes: not a single one has left us; on the contrary, all, with perfect accord, have done their utmost to add to the number of the faithful.

A few facts will enable you to understand the progress made in Assaba.

A poor slave, the father of a numerous family, had for nearly two years attended our chapel, never failing to bring his children. We learned the road to his cabin and our Sisters often went to visit him, under pretext of bringing some medicaments, but, in reality, to have an opportunity of instructing him. He listened attentively to all that was said, yet never uttered a word which could give us the smallest hope of success.

Was it indifference? No. Insensibility? Not that either: God, who sounds the hearts of men, was witness of the struggle that went on in the depths of his soul. I sought one day to know what he thought of the truths of our holy religion and what he proposed to do:

"—Father," was his only reply, "I see the road, but my foot is not yet ready to enter upon it."

He had, in fact, a great obstacle to surmount: he had several wives. Now, if we consider the situation of a poor pagan who has all his life been witness of such customs, we can easily understand his slowness and his hesitations.

Still, his heart was upright, and, after long months of struggle, grace conquered. One Sunday, instruction being over, he came and, with a resolute air, knocked at my chamber door. On seeing his face, I easily divined the motive of his visit, besides, he had scarcely entered than, forestalling all questions:

"—Father," he said, "the road is straight and my foot is about to enter upon it. Twice, already, have I harvested my *ignames* (two years have passed) since my foot led me for the first time to the church, and since then I have been like the man who, seated in the long grass by the road-side, follows with his eye the people going to market, without ever having the courage to imitate them. But I am about to rise: this very day I will assemble my wives in order to tell them that I wish to prepare to receive the water of Life. Their feet shall never more pass the threshold of my cabin, and they shall be to me as strangers, with the exception of the one you will tell me to keep. And you, Father, pray for me, that this promise may remain always in my heart."

He kept his word, in spite of the railleries of the members of his family. God, on His part, has given him the grace of baptism and, moreover, of the most lively faith. It was not long before this was tried.

On Holy Thursday, only a few weeks after his baptism, I was watching beside the altar when I saw our neophyte enter. He knelt down near the Blessed Sacrament, which was exposed, and began to murmur his prayers. Little by little, his voice rose louder and louder, and soon I could hear his admirable discourse to Our Lord. On the following day he was to approach the Sacrament of Penance for the first time, and the thought greatly agitated him: he feared not being worthily prepared. Animated by this sentiment, he addressed himself to God as if he actually beheld Him with his corporal eyes.

"Our Father, my God, to-morrow my mouth will open to confess to the Priest the faults of my heart. The Father has told me what I must do, but Thou, Thou knowest that my head does not understand all that my ear hears; give me Thy hand, give It to me as Thou didst on the day the water of Life was poured upon my head. If Thou aidest me, then I shall be able to wash my heart clean. The Father has told me that when I can make a good confession, I may receive Thee within my breast. That is most wonderful, but to-day I do not wish to speak of that to Thee, I

—only ask Thee to stretch out Thy Hand to me, that I may do well that which I have to accomplish to-morrow."

He said a *Pater* and *Ave* devoutly, rose quietly, reached the chapel-door, took up his pick and his cutlass, which he had left in the entry and went on to his plantation.

God granted his prayer by giving him that sublime simplicity which is, in His eyes, the only wisdom. For my part, I was profoundly moved, and I left the chapel, my heart full of admiration for the faith animating his soul.

I could tell you of other interesting conversions, but I will only dwell upon this one truth, that it is works of charity alone which touch, prepare, and finally decide our pagans. I have always noticed that these great changes are summed up in the following formula, the logic of which the most ignorant pagan can appreciate: "Thy hand performs good works, therefore, thy mouth utters good words."

Now, from this point of view, it is almost entirely to our excellent Nuns that we must look for the secret of these happy conversions. They have, doubtless, told you of the trials attending the starting of their Refuge for the aged, of the founding of their Leper House, of the motherly eagerness with which they endeavour to snatch infants from death, these poor creatures who, according to the cruel custom of the country, are thrown, living, into the forests and condemned to be the prey of wild beasts. But the Sisters will tell you nothing of the heroic patience, of the boundless devotedness which sustain them in their too often thankless labour, of the perfect self-abnegation which guides their steps to the cabin of the poor outcast leper, and which gives them courage to touch with their hands all that is most repulsive. It is a pleasing consolation for me to be able to render them this respectful homage.

But enough of Assaba. Let us pass on to our new stations of Eboo and Illah. Eboo presents the most striking and realistic picture of the establishment of a new Mission. A cabin of bamboos, thatched with leaves and built in the centre of a forest glade, this is what at present serves as a dwelling for the good God and the Missioner; there is the most absolute poverty, privations the most extreme, a complete lack of the strict necessaries of life. The table upon which the Father takes his meals is composed of two rough planks which he himself fixed upon four stakes planted in the earth in the middle of his room. His bed is composed of bamboos bound together, scarcely concealed by a mat, and fixed, like the table, upon thick stakes not too firmly fastened in the earthen floor. It would be vain to look for two chairs; a few old cases, containing the church furniture and the Father's linen, complete the entire worldly goods of the Mission of Eboo. But what is most disheartening of all, is the obstinate resistance which the Missioner meets with from the savage, cruel, and barbarous people. Human sacrifice is the order of the day, and although the tribe is a very small one, a single month does not pass without the sacrifice of many heads, victims to the beliefs of these blinded beings.

When will Divine Grace change these men of savage hearts into lambs?

A modest cabin is already erected beside the Missioner's dwelling: this we dignify with the title of "Refuge," and two or three other similar constructions are being built near the first. Abandoned old people, who run the risk of being sacrificed, and deserted lepers come here to seek a refuge, and this is the work which wins us the pagan's heart. How does the Father manage to support them? I do not know. I dare not even ask him, for I am aware that the supplies which he receives from the Mission barely suffice for his own meagre sustenance. Yet I can guess: that handful of rice which should make a meal for him, he manages to share with his poor outcasts. Quite recently, I saw him weep with joy when I announced to him that a charitable person in Europe had destined the sum of eighty francs (about three guineas), for his station. I am certain that God will bless this work, and I have even reason to believe that the day is not far distant when the labours of this Father will begin to be crowned with success. In fact, here is what he wrote me only two weeks ago:

"Although I never despaired of my poor savages, my heart now feels greater confidence. You know that up to this there have been few visitors to my little chapel, but for the last three Sundays God has sent me a great consolation.

"A man, a poor pagan, belonging to that part of the tribe at war with those amongst whom I live, has been touched by my care for a member of his family whose body was covered with terrible sores. He could not come to the Mission during the day, for, if he were discovered on the way, his head would pay for his temerity. Now, this brave heart, who is determined to hear the instructions and to assist at the Holy Sacrifice, leaves his cabin by night and, taking advantage of the darkness, passes through the thickest part of the forest by paths only known to the wild beasts, that he may come unseen to the Mission. With the exception of my old people, he is the only outsider who assists at the Sacred Mysteries. He hides all day and returns to his village the following night. When I turn round to say the *Dominus Vobiscum*, and that I see this man, my voice dies upon my lips..."

I cannot tell you how happy that letter made me. This man, the first catechuman, who thus exposes his life for the salvation of his soul, is, in my opinion, an incomparable conquest. What a joy for the Missioner will be the day upon which he can pour the waters of regeneration upon the convert's head.

The people of Illah are sympathetic, and the number of pagans who regularly frequent the church is constantly increasing. This post has been only a short time established, and there have already been fifty baptisms. The foundation is not magnificent, as it consists of but one bamboo cabin. The people call loudly for the Sisters, for the fame of the "Refuge" which they have opened at Assaba for old people and lepers, has reached even this place.

To the Sisters who urge me to establish a Mission here, I am always obliged to reply by a sorrowful refusal.

The influence of our holy religion has just won a magnificent result.

After many difficulties and struggles, Father Voit writes to me that the chiefs of the town have, at his request, decided to abolish the sacrificing of slaves.

God be praised that He has chosen us as the instruments of His paternal goodness!

MISSIONS OF AMERICA.

VICARIATE-APOSTOLIC OF ATHABASKA-MACKENZIE.

The long and interesting correspondence which Mgr. Grouard sends us, introduces us to the principal stations of the Vicariate-Apostolic of Athabaska-Mackenzie.

Nothing can be more edifying than the examples of faith and piety given by the neophytes of these Polar Missions. They are well calculated to console and to encourage the valiant Oblate Fathers in their laborious apostolate.

LETTER FROM MONSEIGNEUR GROUARD,

OBLATE OF MARY IMMACULATE, VICAR-APOSTOLIC OF ATHABASKA-MACKENZIE.

Mission of the Nativity, Lake Athabaska, 16th December, 1894.

Itinerary of the Journey.—Preparations.—Great Slave Lake.

THE readers of the *Annals* who have already travelled with me over a great part of Athabaska-Mackenzie will, perhaps feel interested in following the visitation of our northern Missions; but before starting on the road, I am happy to inform them that our little steam-boat, at the troublesome launching of which they assisted, is now running most satisfactorily. Its route is: first, Lake Athabaska, which is two hundred miles in length; secondly, the river of the same name, as far as fort

Mac Murray, a distance of one hundred and eighty-nine miles; thirdly, the river of La Paix, as far as the falls, two hundred and seventy-three miles distant; fourthly, and finally, these two rivers united, as far as the Rapids of the river at Sel, Fort Smith, one hundred and two miles, but it cannot pass these limits. However, beyond that again there opens a far vaster region, which we intend entering. While awaiting the possibility of taking your readers a voyage on another steam-boat belonging to the Mission, I invite them to embark with me on the *Wrigley*, a screw steamer belonging to the Hudson Bay Company.

The anchor is weighed and we rapidly descend the Slave River as far as the great lake of this name, a hundred and ninety miles distant from Fort Smith. Having already spoken of the Mission of St. Isidore at fort Smith, and of St. Joseph's at Fort Resolution, on Great Slave Lake, I will only hail them in passing.

Behold us, then, embarked on this lake, which is like an inland sea. Up to the end of June, it is covered with ice, and navigation is therefore impossible, save during the three months of July, August, and September. The land has receded from our view, but the sky is clear, the air calm, there is scarcely a ripple on the surface of the water, and we easily make ten miles an hour.

Mission of Providence.—Our Parishioners.—The work of the Missioners.—Our good Dogs.

Before long we approach the Mackenzie. Having admired the prodigious width of its bed, a width partly concealed by islands, we arrive at the Providence Mission, where also is situated the Fort of the same name. The *Wrigley* only calls here for a few hours, which we may employ in inspecting the Mission building. They consist, in the first place, of the residence of the Fathers and Brothers, a large, handsome, two-storied house, built by Mgr. Faraud, who could handle the saw and plane as well as a French master cabinet-maker. Beside this stands a pretty chapel, in which we may admire a magnificent altar, carved by the Rev. Father Lecorre. Farther on is the convent of the Sisters of Charity from Montreal, who direct a workshop, an orphanage, a school, and even a hospital. Forty children of both sexes, and belonging to the various northern tribes, receive the devoted care of these good Nuns, and there are a few half-blood families established in the neighbourhood.

All around the Mission houses are large potatoe and barley fields, which it is surprising to find so far northwards. This is the result of the persevering labour of the Missioners, who, little by little, have entrenched upon the forest and have made the hitherto uncultivated soil productive. Fishing being the only resource of the country, it is easy to understand that when one is constantly reduced to a diet of the same fish boiled, roast, or dried in the sun, the European stomach craves some mixture of vegetable food, something which will, in a measure, replace bread. Now, potatoes thrive sufficiently well at the Providence Mission to fulfil this end, but we must, however, remember the climate and not lose courage at the occasional frost which, even in the middle of summer, plays sad havoc with our gardens. Barley also ripens fairly well, but, unfortunately, for several years past, voracious grasshoppers have settled upon our harvests, destroying them pitilessly. Doubtless, in permitting this plague God had good reasons which I do not wish to question, but we are permitted to hope that He will find others equally good for putting an end to this trial, and allow our Missioners to enjoy the fruit of their labours. A little wind-mill, long out of work, stands there, sadly extending its arms towards heaven, but let the grain only ripen, and you will soon see it shaking off its torpor and enjoying itself in the breeze.

To finish the description of this thriving Mission, we must add a forge, a cabinet-maker's workshop, a granary, a shed for drying fish, a refrigerator, and a stable with its horned inmates. For, you must know, we ambitioned having a little herd, the services of which are perhaps even more highly appreciated here than elsewhere. The oxen are useful for field labour and for drawing hay and fire-wood in winter, and the cows give a little milk, which is a great boon to the good Sisters and their scholars. Naturally, the keep of these animals requires great labour and constant care, for the country is covered with snow during eight months of the year, and it takes a great quantity of hay to feed even a few beasts during such a long winter. Fortunately, on the borders of the lakes, rivers, and swamps with which the Mission is surrounded, grass grows in abundance, and our Brothers well know how to handle a scythe. I will even confess that we tried to introduce pigs and fowl into the country, but they could not be acclimatized. Finally, we must not forget to make honourable mention of the canine race, which plays a highly important part in this country, for it is it that furnishes the steeds of the North.

The Providence Mission is well supplied in this particular, and its dogs are celebrated throughout the Mackenzie district. When the snow covers the earth and the lakes and rivers are imprisoned in their thick coating of ice, without the aid of these dogs no journey could be made, either to visit the native encampments and the sick, or to go fishing and bring home the fish. They are harnessed in fours, not abreast, but one after the other, and upon two thin boards, laid flat on the snow and curved upwards in front, they draw bed, provisions, and other baggage, securely tied up in skins. Each evening they receive as their food one or two fish, which are thawed for them, and they slake their thirst by eating snow whenever they like. They are gentle enough towards their masters, but, as all the world over, they are turbulent and quarrelsome amongst themselves. Although, as a rule, honest enough, they are not quite above suspicion, and sometimes during our sleep they take it into their heads to poke their noses into and try their teeth on the provision sack. To be even with them, we usually place this sack close to our pillows and cover it with harness hung with sleigh bells, the noise of which generally gives the alarm.

But where our dogs are really philanthropic, is when, seeing us in bed, wrapped in our blankets, they come gently to stretch themselves beside us or at our feet, and thus help to keep us from the cold. I know, for my part, that during many a night spent in the open air, with the temperature from 40° to 45° below zero, I have owed them more than one good sleep.

I have dwelt somewhat at length on these humble quadrupeds because they are a peculiarity of the country, and form one of its picturesque sides. Moreover, faithful companions and devoted servants of the Missioner, do they not also contribute to the extension of God's kingdom?

Fort Simpson.—Catholics and Protestants.—Fervour of the poor Savages.

Now that we have seen the Providence Mission, let us continue our journey and arrive at fort Simpson, situated 161 miles lower down, at the confluence of the river Liards with the Mackenzie. Fort Simpson is the head-quarters of the Hudson Bay Company in these regions. We have a Mission here, dedicated to the Sacred Heart, but, alas! there is likewise a Protestant Mission, and it is even the See of the Protestant Bishop of the country. The why and wherefore of the coming of these Reverends, to sow schism and heresy in a country which certainly offers no great attractions, is curious enough.

In order to explain their presence, we must go back to the time when the Great Slave Lake Mission was founded by Mgr. Faraud. The eagerness of the savages to embrace the Catholic Faith was extraordinary. There was a general rush of these poor tribes towards the light of the Gospel, and the officers of the Hudson Bay Company, who were then absolute kings of the country, took fright. Imbued with the most hostile prejudices against Catholicism, they wished to arrest its progress, and it was not possible to enter the Mackenzie save with their permission and concurrence, seeing that they held in their hands all means of transport. They therefore said to our first Missioners: "You shall go no farther, and if you advance another step, we will bring ministers here in opposition to you."

These threats could not restrain the zeal of Mgr. Faraud and the Rev. Father Grollier, so application was at once made to the Anglican Bishop of Red River, who immediately sent a minister to Fort Simpson. A house and chapel were built for him, and although the director of the Company advised his officers to observe strict neutrality towards the Missioners, he was at such a distance from the place that his orders were easily evaded. Thus it was that it was more than twenty years before we could get a footing at Fort Simpson. We only paid flying visits there, while the minister resided there permanently.

It is, therefore, not surprising that under circumstances so unfavourable to us, Protestantism should have many adherents there; we should rather admire how, in spite of all the efforts made to seduce them, more than half the natives remained faithful to us. At last, after long years of struggle, the Rev. Father Kerangue had sufficient influence to get, from the Company's officer, a building which he arranged as a chapel, reserving a little room for his own accommodation. Unfortunately, this good Father and the Rev. Father Leconte, who replaced him, have both been taken by God. I have placed the Mission in the charge of the Rev. Father Brochu, who will not only keep the Catholics steadily to their duty, but will also make every effort to bring into the True Fold several nomadic tribes dwelling in the depths of the forests. This prey is also coveted by the Protestant Bishop, and the poor people must choose either one side or the other. God's grace is needed that they may choose aright, and I earnestly beg that the Associates of the Propagation of the Faith will pray that it may be granted them.

Even at Fort Simpson I was witness of the marvellous effects produced by grace in these simple, guileless souls, and it is well not to allow such to fall away.

During a Mission I preached at this station, I prepared a number of natives for baptism. Amongst them was a man in the prime of life; though richer than his neighbours, he had no other clothing than a shirt, with what they call here *mitosses*, a sort of long gaiters which covered his legs, and a piece of stuff by way of loin cloth. I had been struck by his attention in listening to my words. Now, while I was administering the Sacrament of Baptism, he was so deeply moved that I saw and heard the beating of his heart, and scarcely was the ceremony concluded than he turned, with a heightened colour, towards the natives present and addressed them like one inspired :

"Relatives," said he, "behold, the Gates of Heaven are now open to me and I hope that the good God will allow me to enter them. As for you, against whom they are still shut, why do you delay in preparing for baptism, which would open them for you also?"

On another occasion, when an epidemic was raging in the neighbourhood, I visited the sick from house to house, and found one poor creature alone, without food, completely abandoned. I brought him to the hut of some other savages; having spoken with him of the principal mysteries of religion, I left him, promising to return next day and the following days in order to prepare him for baptism.

"Oh!" said he, "if you would only baptize me now; I beg of you not to wait for to-morrow!"

I comforted him, not thinking he was in any danger. Still, when evening came, the sick man's prayer recurred to my mind, and I went back to see him. He repeated his petition, and, without further delay, I poured the waters of baptism upon his forehead. What was my astonishment when a messenger came next morning to tell me the poor savage was dead!

Here is an instance of quite another kind, which will show you that our Catholics at fort Simpson can sometimes give a smart answer. Discussions occasionally arise between them and the Protestants, now upon the subject of the Blessed Virgin, now upon the celibacy of the clergy, etc. This latter subject appears to have been somewhat hotly debated. Now it happened one Sunday that the Protestants went to their place of meeting and returned home almost at once.

"Hello!" said a Catholic who met them, "your service was not long to-day! Has anything uncommon happened?"

He was told that the Reverend had scarcely begun his sermon than a servant came to tell him that his wife was ill at home and wanted him. He at once dismissed the congregation, and this explained their quick return home.

"Well," said our Catholic, "do you see now that I was right the other day? Has not Our Saviour said that no man can serve two masters? Here is your minister, who leaves God there, to run home to his wife! That is why the Priest does not get married, and when he says Mass, he can continue to the end without being disturbed!"

I must here remark that the Company's officer who is in charge of the Mackenzie district and of Fort Simpson, is a thorough gentleman, free from old-times' prejudices, liberal minded, and most kind towards the Catholic Priest.

Fort Wrigby.—Efforts suspended for want of supplies.— A heroic fast.

Before long we perceive the lofty crests of the Nahanes Mountains, counterparts of the Rocky Mountains, heights which bathe their feet and reflect their summits in the waters of the river. Soon we shall have them constantly in sight, now upon the right, now upon the left, an insurmountable barrier to the flood. Some 136 miles from Fort Simpson is Fort Wrigby, an unimportant station, mostly frequented by the mountaineers. Here we have the Mission of the Sacred Heart of Mary, a dependency upon that of the Sacred Heart, from which a Father comes every Spring, at the season of the general assemblage of the savages, that he may instruct and prepare them for baptism. The minister also comes, and the little Fort is a field of battle where Priest and English preacher fight for souls. The contest still goes on, and the final result seems yet a long way off. Curiously enough, each year the combatants are obliged to separate, for want of ammunition; that is, this station is so poorly provisioned that all, Priest, minister, and Savages, have soon exhausted their stock of food, and are obliged to disperse, in order to avoid the horrors of famine. Three years ago, I arrived at fort Rigby, with the Rev. Father Leconte, and we were unable to find a single mouthful of food. The agent and his clerks had long before cleared out the store, and, to avoid perishing of hunger, they found themselves obliged to eat the bear and castor skins collected during the winter trade, not an isolated case in this country. The natives are at a distance, hunting wild beasts for their own support, and the fish seem to have abandoned the river, so that if the agent does not take every precaution he finds himself reduced to *fasting*, as they say here, and to make his employees fast in a far more rigorous manner than that prescribed by the Church.

When I arrived, the clerks and their families had no other resource left than to follow the course of the river, digging up wild roots for food. At the same time, the mountaineers came in, but they brought nothing but their furs. The poor Savages took very little heed of this critical state of affairs, and remained several days to receive the instructions of the Priest, whom they see so rarely. Two or three days without eating is nothing for these men, hardened to all sorts of privations, but, when too much pressed by hunger, they go off to the woods, dig up some roots, and wait till Providence sends them better fare. Then, when they have killed some animal, they make a good meal, with which they quickly recoup the strength they have lost.

To be sure, all years are not alike, and sometimes game abounds in the forest districts. Then, plenty reigns and past privations are forgotten, but you may judge from this little sketch that the fur trade is not always either easy or pleasant. Moreover, the motto of the Company says it plainly enough: *Pro pelle cutem:* a man must give his skin to take a skin! What a lesson for us! And for how much stronger reason should the Missioner brave every peril to save these immortal souls purchased by Our Saviour at the price of His Blood!

The Mission of Saint Teresa.—The Great River Lake. —The Puffing Holes.

A hundred and eighty-four miles separate Fort Wrigby from Fort Norman, the site of the St. Teresa Mission. It is at this spot that the river of the Great Bear Lake joins the Mackenzie. The Fort and the Mission did not always occupy their present position, as, for several years, they were established on the shore of the Great Bear Lake; but the river, which must be ascended in order to reach that spot, is so rapid and so dangerous for navigation that the Company finally decided upon fixing its station on the banks of the Mackenzie. Moreover, very few skins are to be had in the district around the Lake. It is only amongst the sterile plains, where frost reigns almost from one end of the year to the other, that they are to be had. It is but for one month that the

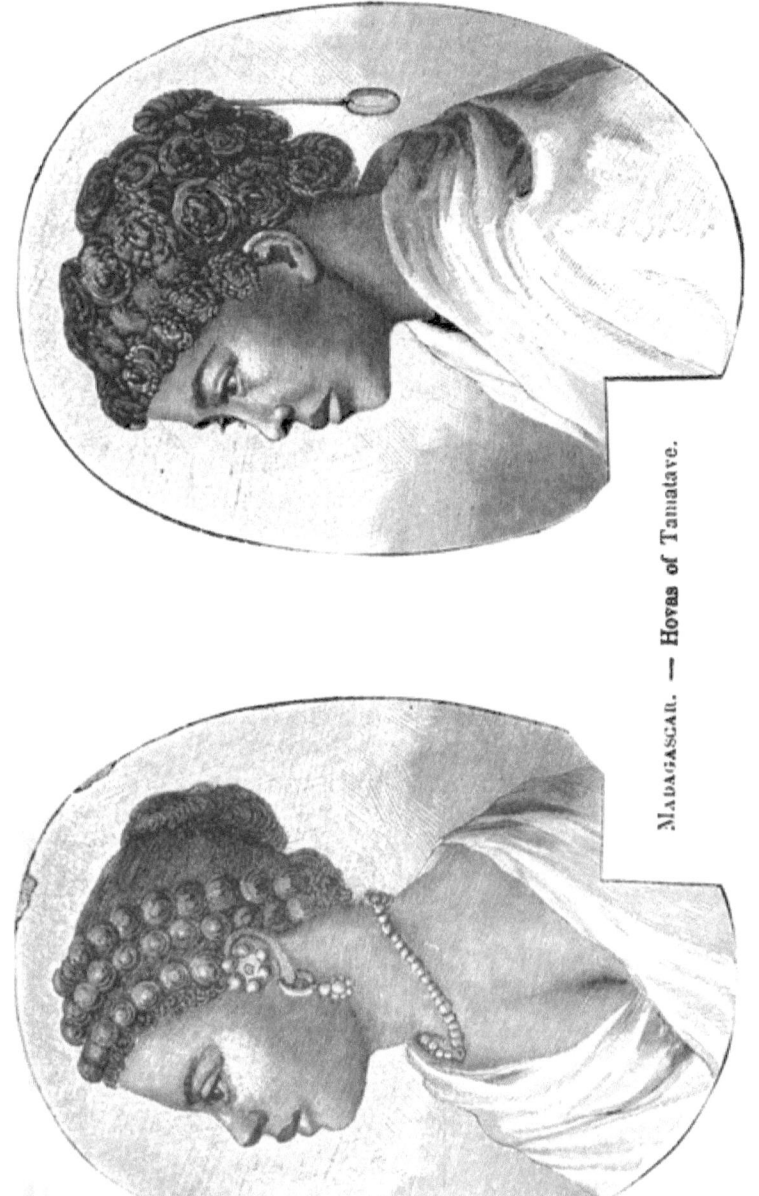

Madagascar. — Hovas of Tamatave.

Lake itself, one of the largest in the North, is almost free of ice. It abounds with fish : herrings are plentiful, and trout of an unrivalled flavour are taken in its waters. But as the beaver does not frequent it, the Company thought it best to abandon the fort they had built there, the Mission was obliged to follow their example, and it also is established on the banks of the Mackenzie and the Great Bear River.

These changes have retarded both the moral and the material progress of our establishment. Protestantism has profited by these circumstances to come also and make a settlement at Fort Norman, where it has won some followers amongst the Slaves of the river district. Besides the Slaves, the population is composed of mountaineers who live to the west, and of the Hare Skin Tribe; the latter, with the natives of the Bear Lake, occupy the northern side. The Rev. Fathers Ducot and Douy, assisted by a worthy Brother, devote themselves altogether to the evangelization of these peoples. Living poorly, often reduced to distress, exhausting their health and their strength in visiting the native camps, in spite of the excessive rigour of the cold, in their long journeys, sometimes exposed to death from hunger, like Father Ducot, who for several days had no other food than a candle, they have succeeded in converting a great number of these poor savages, whom they keep faithful to the duties of the Church, in spite of the seductive means employed by the Minister.

For, it must be confessed, it is not the Protestant religion which charms the few Slaves baptized by the Reverend, although it does not impose any very serious restraint upon them ; in fact, they do not understand it. It is the presents of tea and tobacco which are, with them, incontrovertible arguments, and which have the whole merit of their so-called conversion.

It is in the neighbourhood of Fort Norman that are seen the puffs of smoke and the wild-fires produced by gases escaping through crevices in the earth along the shores of the river, and which indicate that coal exists in the Mackenzie valley. It may be that God is reserving this provision of fuel for a more or less distant future. When civilized countries shall have exhausted their resources of this nature, they will doubtless come to seek the as yet unknown riches of the far North. I fancy, too, that the Mission garden would attract the notice of the good French people, who have no idea that it could be possible to cultivate this soil to so high a degree as to make it produce good vegetables.

On the way to Good Hope.—Our Surroundings.— A Stag Hunt.

Let us push on towards Good-Hope, distant 174 miles from Fort Norman. I will not delay to describe the incidents of the voyage, the varied scenes which charm the eye, verdant isles, picturesque shores, presenting, at each bend of the river, a fresh panorama, a hundred varied pictures of wood and forest, undulating country, and changing lights; here, the landscape half veiled in distant haze, there, bold outlines of massive rocks proudly raising their crests towards the clouds. The river also regulates its course by the nature of the soil: sometimes it hurries and rushes along, sometimes it rests a while, spreads wide its limpid wavelets and flows slowly and leisurely on its way. Here and there a little hamlet of the Indians conical huts is seen upon the shore.

At sight of the steamboat, light canoes, rowed by agile oarsmen, put out from shore and eagerly vie with each other in the race to reach us and offer us fish or venison, either fresh or dried. We at once lie-to and give them time to make their exchanges. They invariably ask for tea or tobacco, so the captain always has an abundant supply of these commodities at hand. Sometimes it happens that canoes not bringing anything for barter come out to the boat, just like the beggars who accost a traveller on the road, and we hear a confused babel of cries, in the midst of which the following refrain is always distinguishable:

"—Give us tea, give us tobacco; have pity on us, we have not had a smoke this long time!"

But the captain turns a deaf ear, and the light canoes return whence they came, no richer than before.

All at once, a deer is sighted; he is either wandering along the shore or else he essays to breast the current. Rifles and carabines are at once levelled at him, and, as soon as he is within shot, a regular volley greets him. In spite of his efforts, it is impossible for him to escape so many enemies, and he falls at last. A rope is attached to his horns, and he is consigned to the larder. Farther on, a bear attracts our notice, and in his turn falls a victim to his imprudence. Still, both bear and stag sometimes succeed in making their escape, but we never stay to give them chase. Such are the excitements and encounters which help to break the monotony of the voyage.

Good Hope Mission.—The *PEAUX DE LIEVRE* and the *LOUCHEUX* Tribes.—Trial and Consolation.

Let us suppose ourselves arrived at Good-Hope. The Mission preserves the happy name of the place and is called "Our Lady of Good-Hope." It is the pearl of the North, with its fine residence for the Missioners and its still finer church, which is the admiration of all comers. The two veterans of the Vicariate, the Rev. Father Seguin and good Brother Kearney, have been there for thirty-four years, and are the faithful guardians of the post confided to them. The good God blesses their persevering efforts, and they have the satisfaction of seeing all their savages, Peaux de Lievre and mountaineers, docile sons of the Catholic Church. We may also remark that the Company's officer and his wife, Madame Gaudet, are Canadian Catholics and, by their good example, have largely contributed to the maintenance of fervour and piety amongst our neophytes.

This place is situated within the Polar circle, and yet good Brother Kearney has had the courage to make a garden here and to plant in it potatoes and turnips. In spite of the sterility of the soil, the rigour of the climate, and the often recurring frosts, he has persevered, and still perseveres in his enterprise, his labour being sometimes rewarded with astonishing success. In fact, if three-fourths of the time he has only embryo potatoes on the stalks, he has also his prosperous years, when he has a yield of potatoes as large as an egg! What good luck, especially in a country where flour still costs a shilling a pound! As for the turnips, it is not the root he counts upon, for it is rarely bigger than a finger, but the leaves, which he jealously gathers. Imagine the delicious soups he will make with them on special feast days, and how, with their aid, the Missioner at the North Pole can persuade himself that he is almost within the tropics!

Here, as at our other Stations, the principal food is fish, but the natives hunt both the deer and caribou, and, when this game is plentiful, they carry on with the Fort a trade in fresh or dried meat, part of which the Mission purchases. Unfortunately, it not rarely happens that the chase is almost fruitless; then, if the fishing has not been favourable, famine seizes upon this unfortunate country and, adding its hardships to the already terrible severity of the cold, finds but too many victims amongst our Indians. From time to time, Providence sends them most useful aid by multiplying the hares, of which they make a double use, feeding on their flesh and making clothes of their skins, hence their surname, Peaux de Lievres, or Hare Skins. The women prepare these skins, cut them in thin strips, plait them skilfully, and shape them according to fancy. Nothing can be warmer than the clothes and bed-covering thus made; the same may be said of the rein-deer and caribou skins, and we cannot sufficiently admire the goodness of God, who, in every country of the globe, thus furnishes man with the best means for sustaining and preserving life. To the carelessness and want of forethought of the savages, must be attributed a great part of the evils to which they are exposed.

But we have not yet reached the last stage our journey. We have still to accomplish a distance of 282 miles before arriving at Peel's River fort, the most northern of all the Stations, whither the Loucheux and the Esquimaux repair in order to barter their furs.

As I have already observed, certain of the Company's agents, through hatred of Catholicity, introduced Protestant Ministers into the Mackenzie, which they would have wished to make their own exclusive property. We have seen how their project has, thank God, hitherto been a miserable failure. I must, however, acknowledge that they have, by the exercise of their tyrannical power, succeeded better in closing to us all access to a part of the Loucheux nation. Here is, in a few words, what has happened in these distant regions.

When a Minister went there for the first time, Father Seguin accompanied him. Both went as far as Fort Youkon, in Alaska, where, it seems that, with the consent of Russia, then mistress of this country, the Hudson Bay Company carried on an important commerce. The two Missioners wintered at fort Youkon, but under very different conditions. The Minister was, in fact, comfortably installed in the agent's own house, and the interpreter was appointed to give him exclusively his services; the natives, placed in communication with the minister alone and kept apart from the Priest, who had found a lodging in the house of one of the employees, were urged to declare themselves the Minister's followers. It would be impossible to describe the mental pain Father Seguin suffered during this winter, in what we may call his prison.

God, however, did not leave such a sacrifice without a recompense, and comforted His apostle in an unforeseen manner. An employee, an English half-breed who had come from Red River with his family, abjured Protestantism, along with his wife and children, on account of a dream in which the Blessed Virgin appeared to him, holding in her hands a rosary and a scapular. So the Father's journey to Fort Youkon was not quite useless, but the many obstacles opposed to his zeal for the conversion of the savages caused his Superiors to decide upon no longer sending him there, and he received an order to visit the Peel's River Loucheux only. There also, the Company's agent, an ignorant and fanatical Scotchman, did all in his power to stay the progress of the Faith. Seeing the poor Indians ardently inclined towards the Catholic religion, he plied them with promises, then with threats; he even went so far as to refuse powder and ball, which were absolutely necessary for hunting, to such as would not attend the Minister. But all in vain. There were amongst these poor Indians the elect of God, and more than half the Loucheux remained unshaken. Father Seguin built them a chapel, and continued to go each year to Good-Hope, for the purpose of visiting and instructing them. Nowhere have I seen better Christians.

The Midnight Sun.—Two months of Night.—Return.—Hopes.

I have said nothing of a natural phenomenon known to everyone, yet which never fails to interest those who see it for the first time. I mean the midnight sun. Even at Good-Hope we could already observe it, as we there entered the Polar circle. But this day without night grows longer according as we advance towards the Pole, and at Peel's River it lasts for nearly two months. I remember, the first time I visited Peel's fort and spent three weeks there, with what pleasure I used to go each evening to a sun-dial placed in the centre of the fort, in order to time the exact hour of midnight, indicated by the sun.

But if the sun is prodigal of its light and heat in summer, there is another side to the picture, and during two winter months it pitilessly refuses to show itself. For that time, a more or less luminous twilight alone marks its presence below the horizon. True, when the sky is clear, the moon and the aurora borealis give out a certain splendour, which the whiteness of the snow reflects and increases; but when the weather is dark and thick clouds fill the air, what a long, sad night hangs over these desolate regions! And what can I say of the terrible cold which then reigns supreme? Suffice to say that last winter the thermometer remained for whole months at 40° below zero, and that for several days it fell to 50°, 55°, and even 56° below zero.

But it is time to close this already too long letter. Missioners and traders fall back into their loneliness, broken by our passing visit. In fact, what are the three or four hours that *Wrigley* has been able to stop at each Station? Oh! how I long to have at my disposal a little steam-boat which could convey me along this giant river, and leave me free to pass some days with my Missioners and in the midst of our Christians.

THE ENCYCLICAL CHRISTI NOMEN

AND THE

EPISCOPACY.

The Holy Father concludes with the following words his Encyclical addressed to the entire Catholic Episcopacy, in favour of the Association of the Propagation of the Faith:

"Assuredly, Catholics will be profoundly touched when they learn that nothing can be more pleasing to Us and more useful to the Church than that they should enter into a zealous rivalry in collecting the funds necessary in order to bring about the successful accomplishment of the projects We have formed for the welfare of the Eastern Churches."

The Bishops have hastened to make this important document known to the faithful. We have already received some of their pastoral letters, and we feel pleasure in giving extracts from them, reserving for future numbers extracts from those which may come in later on. Need we add that we shall be happy to translate letters written in foreign languages. France has doubtless the honour of having been the cradle of our Association, but, to quote the words of Gregory XVI, the Propagation of the Faith knows no frontier, for, like the Church, it is Catholic.

His Eminence, Cardinal Langenieux, whom the Holy Father has particularly associated with his projects for the East, publishes the Encyclical in his Lenten letter, and has prefaced it with a highly interesting sketch of the actual condition of the Church throughout the world, of its conquests, its trials, its hopes. He concludes by the following appeal to France in favour of our Work.

"Sons of the Catholic Church, proud of the preponderant rôle assigned by Providence to her for the welfare of humanity and for the honour of our Faith 'at the dawn of a new era,' as Leo XII says, we respond to his call with all the greater generosity, inasmuch as we ourselves have greater need of mercy. Our Missioners shall be the most numerous, the most holy, the most ardent: our alms the most abundant, especially those destined for the East; and it shall be this eagerness to labour for the extension of the reign of Jesus Christ in the world and for the pacification of dissentient Churches which shall merit the Christian regeneration of our own country."

His Grace the Archbishop of Albi devotes a special pastoral letter to the Encyclical *Christi Nomen*.

"We have no hesitation, he says, in complying with the obligation imposed upon us of making you acquainted with a new Encyclical of Leo XIII., which, in an urgent manner and in moving terms, appeals to our zeal in order to obtain abundant aid in the apostolic work of bringing back to the Fold those Eastern countries which have separated from the centre of Catholicity, and to bring them back by means of Missions, Diocesan institutions, and Works like our own.

"We shall then respond to the ardent wishes of the Holy Father in multiplying our appeals, our recommendations, our ways of working out and making his wishes known. We shall realize his dearest wish by inviting the Priests and faithful to subscribe yet more generously to the Association of the Propagation of the Faith.."

His Grace the Archbishop of Aix retraces the origin and aim of our Work. The following are a few extracts from his letter:

"Leo XIII. recommends to you to-day a Work which is at the head of all other works, the *Association of the Propagation of the Faith*; it is the continuation and the application to infidel peoples of the Work of Redemption. Its aim is to invite them to a knowledge of the Gospel, to teach them to know, to love, and to serve God, and thus to merit life eternal. God has created men only that they might be saints. All else is absolutely nothing...

"Do you desire, my brethren, that I should more clearly explain to you what a magnificent act you do when you participate in the Work of the Propagation of the Faith?

"When St. Lazarus, St. Maximus, St. Trophinus, St. Martha, and St. Madeleleine came to our Provence, their compatriots, relatives, and friends in Jerusalem did not let them set out without the necessary provisions for their long and perilous journey; they furnished them with clothes, food, and all that was necessary for the celebration of Mass. Holy souls resemble each other in all times and in all countries. Our ancestors in the Camargue and in our southern provinces did not receive them badly: our Provencals have never been inhuman, but they had nothing to offer them;

the Apostles had to bring all they needed with them, as Missioners must do in those regions as yet unillumined by the light of the Gospel.

"Through the Propagation of the Faith, we pay back that which we received eighteen hundred years ago: we pay our debt of gratitude; it is an old debt, and interest has accumulated on it; we shall find it difficult to pay in full all we owe. But, once more, let us call to mind the widow in the Gospel: Our Lord Jesus Christ was a merciful creditor. Without doubt, she was deeply in debt, like all of us..."

His Lordship the Bishop of Vannes, when publishing the Encyclical, exhorts his diocesans to continue to cherish and aid the Association of the Propagation of the Faith.

"It is a great honour and a great joy for us all, adds the venerable Prelate, to know that our diocese has not fallen off in sending its relatively large contingent, both of men and money. Notwithstanding the slenderness of your resources, and all the moral and physical miseries that surround you and claim your generosity, you never refuse your alms for the great works of the Catholic Propaganda, well knowing that, from a certain point of view, you have the care of souls, according to these words of the Holy Ghost: *God has commanded that each one of us should have a care for the needs of his neighbour.*

"More than that, the most pious families will make it their glory to enroll one of their number in this heroic phalanx of evangelical labourers, ardent pioneers of true civilization, indefatigable explorers in Africa, in Oceania, in North America, in the far East, wherever, in fact, God *makes His sun to shine upon the good and upon the wicked.*

"We may well be permitted, then, to share in the congratulations addressed by the Pope to the whole Christian world..."

In a letter, the entire of which we would gladly quote, his Lordship the Bishop of Valence points out to his beloved diocesans the means by which they can respond to the appeal of Leo XIII.

"We are going courageously to work that we may recruit new members and increase our resources. Each new Associate of the Propagation of the Faith will be a new recruit for the army of civilization, and each one will have his share in the merit and the glory of the peaceful crusade preached by Leo XIII. For this, it is only necessary that each member of a Circle of Ten should take upon himself to collect, in subscriptions of a half-penny, or a penny, a sum equal to that which he himself pays annually into the treasury of the Association. There is no difficulty in this. Everyone could do it, even school children and those attending catechism. In this manner resources will be doubled and the Holy Father's end attained.

"Take advantage of the approaching Lent to undertake this work, no matter how displeasing or unpleasant it may seem. It will be a highly meritorious mortification to become the mendicants of Jesus Christ, and expose yourself to many a humiliating refusal. In giving your own alms through the medium of your usual offering, you will, moreover, participate in the merits of all those whom you shall have induced to subscribe, and who, for the most part, would not have done so but for you..."

His Lordship the Bishop of Versailles, having spoken of the dignity of the Eastern Churches, and published the Pontifical Encyclical, reminds us of the noble words which he addressed to all his diocesans, in the second year of his Episcopate.

"In order to respond, he writes, to the appeal of the Holy Father, it is not necessary to make any fresh innovation amongst us. The Association of the Propagation of the Faith and the Work of the *Schools of the East* already exist... What is then to be done? Recruit new adherents for these works, in order that the total of the receipts may mount up. To this end, we address ourselves to the zeal of the Parish Priests and of those devoted Christians who have the love of God in their hearts, and who are desirous of responding to the wishes of the Sovereign Pontiff. There are many parishes in which there does not exist a single Associate, and many others wherein the number might easily be increased. There are less populous and poorer dioceses than Versailles, yet which subscribe much larger sums. Why should not we make the effort necessary to raise us to our proper place?..."

In picturesque words, full of unction and lofty eloquence, his Lordship the Bishop of Carcassonne brings before us the beginnings and subsequent development of the Association, then, speaking of the duty incumbent upon Catholics of associating themselves with this crusade of civilization by prayer and alms, he thus expresses himself:

"To prayer should be added the alms, the slender offering asked. We read in the Gospel that during the preaching of His public life, Our Saviour met with pious women who aided Him from their private means, and the Annals of Christianity show us messengers of the Sacred Word, apostolic men, always assisted and supported by other children of the Church. It is in virtue of this tradition that an offering is invariably asked of the faithful: this is the half-penny a week. Where is the man of toil, where is the humble workwoman who cannot spare this half-penny from the fruits of their labour? Is it not this modest offering that is the sole resource of the Missioners; is it not this half-penny which, being multiplied, fills the war chest of the army of the Apostolate, the budget of the Preachers of the Gospel, the "civil-list" of the martyrs? By this simple weekly half-penny, the poor are associated with the merits of the evangelical labourers, as well as are the rich by their larger donations; constituting Himself their Banker, God, through their hands, performs actions for which He takes upon Himself the payment, both of principal and interest, in Heaven, most assuredly, but also, and oftener than we imagine, in this earthly life."

The appeal addressed by his Lordship the Bishop of Langres is truly touching:

"No matter how closely we may limit his supplies, the apostle needs the necessaries of life. He must have them for the Nuns, whom he gives as mothers to the orphans; he has need of means that he may carry on his schools, his hospitals, in a word, for the organization of his Mission. Yes, for the Propagation of the Faith we must have gold; transfigured by charity, gold itself becomes an apostle. Created by God, Dispenser of all good, gold must pay tribute to the Sovereign Lord of all things, by serving to spread the glory of His name... How can we but be moved on seeing, by the receipts of the Association of the Propagation of the Faith, how many millions are given, half-penny by half-penny, by labourers and poor servants? What a permanent commission from the people to proclaim the sovereignty of Jesus Christ over souls! "*Regi sæculorum imortale!*" Are we not edified in witnessing the generous gifts made by Christians who have inherited riches through the care and industry of their ancestors? What a noble tax in this tribute voluntarily levied upon luxury for the Propagation of the Faith!

"It is therefore to be hoped that the funds of this splendid Work will grow from year to year. That, as a river whose waves are formed of millions of drops of water, brings fruitfulness in its course, all the alms of Christian people may unite to carry the Christian Faith to all nations."

His Lordship the Bishop of St. Flour, gives a complete account of our Work, its excellence, its usefulness, its advantages. Let us quote the following fine passage:

"Which of you, dearly beloved brethren, when reading, with recollection and lively faith, the Annals of our Missions, has not exclaimed, in admiration mingled with pious regret: my God! how beautiful are the feet of these apostolic labourers who teach the Gospel of peace, who bring to men the good things of Heaven! Why am not I called to share their labours, their struggles, their triumphs? Well! to you, happy Associates of the Propagation of the Faith, to you is permitted to aspire to this dignity! From the moment that you rank amongst its members, your prayers and your alms entitle you to all the fruits, to all the merits, all the glory of the Work itself; merits of apostles, merits of confessors, merits of martyrs. You teach, you preach, you baptize by all these mouths and all these hands, the instruments of your zeal; you triumph by all this courage which your charity sustains; you have your part in all they undertake, in all they accomplish, in all they suffer, in all they sacrifice for the honour of God and the salvation of souls. If, therefore, each day and each hour, so to speak, your treasury is filled by more hidden merits, attached to the fulfilment of the duties of your condition, without quitting home or country, without losing your rest, risking dangers by land and water, so also, almost without a thought, you lay up the treasures won by the exercise of the most heroic virtues.

"Do not think you have done enough for this admirable Association in giving it your personal support, aid it by your recommendations as well as by your example. Make friends for it, make converts for it of all those who are attached to you by ties of relationship, of affection, of dependence, of neighbourhood...."

In future numbers we will continue to give extracts from the pastoral letters devoted to our interests by the Bishops throughout the universe. To-day, along with the eloquent words of Mgr. de St. Flour, we will crown our quotations with a few lines borrowed from Mgr. Freppel:

"May God's kingdom come! May it come for those infidel peoples still living in darkness and in the shadow of death! May it come for those idolatrous races who know not Jesus Christ, who are deprived of the light and the consolations of the Faith; who have not, like us, those Divine remedies against sin that the Church offers to its children! May it come also for those countries in the East which tremble at this moment in the life-giving breath of

God; may it come for these perishing branches which for centuries have been detached by schism from the trunk of Catholic Unity! And, finally, may it come for our separated brethren in Europe who have retained but a few shreds of doctrine and some semblance of Christian life! *Adveniat regnum tuum!* Then, when this glorious day shall have dawned upon the world, this day of spiritual birth for some and of resurrection for others, if we would wish to know the source of these Divine blessings, we shall find, I say it, at God's Right Hand, the Association of the Propagation of the Faith. This will be its terrestrial crown, whilst awaiting the time when it shall please God to grant its active and zealous members their eternal reward."

CHRONICLE OF THE WORK.
Association of Tens.

At a time when the Holy Father asks the concurrence of the Association of the Propagation of the Faith to aid him in his vast projects in the East, we may be permitted to urge upon our zealous correspondents the utility of forming new circles of Ten. How many of those friendly to the Missions, how many wealthy families would charge themselves yearly with an entire Ten (£1 1s. 0d.), if the idea were suggested to them. Doubtless, the simple subscription of a "half-penny" a week is the basis of the Work, but God, Who blessed the widow's mite, did not reject the offering of Zacheria. Moreover, in the designs of Providence, are not the rich obliged to participate in works of charity in exact proportion to their wealth.

The Journal of *LES MISSIONS CATHOLIQUES.*

We have been applied to for a great number of the *specimen* copies of the *Missions Catholiques* and many have sent in subscriptions for our weekly illustrated Bulletin. It is rapidly becoming known that this Review is the auxiliary of the *Annals;* that at a time when the Press occupies such an important place, and particularly now that Colonial questions interest all Europe, the Catholic Missions fix public attention upon the labours of the apostolate and frequently give the most accurate and impartial information upon Colonial affairs.

We gave this year, as a prize for all our subscribers, and we still offer to all who shall become subscribers to our journal for the year 1895, a fine map of the Sahara which enables readers to follow the work of the White Fathers and the path of explorers.

We again remind all that a specimen copy will be sent free. The Annual Subscription is 10 francs (8s. 4d.) for France, and 12 francs (10s.) for the Postal Union. Address: M. le Directeur des *Missions Catholiques,* 14, Rue de la Charite, Lyons.

NEWS OF THE MISSIONS.

THE MISSIONERS OF CHINA AND JAPAN AT THE THEATRE OF THE WAR.

The remarkable feature of the Sino-Japanese war is the courteous attitude of the belligerants towards the Missioners and the religious establishments. Besides an imperiol edict commanding the Chinese authorities to protect European Priests and institutions, we learn from an authorized source of a proclamation issued by the viceroy of Moukden in Mandchouria, where the last act of this great struggle between two great nations is being played.

"It is," writes our correspondent, " energetic and couched in the strongest terms, and has greatly contributed to the tranquility which the Christians have enjoyed ever since the war began. They have, it is true, frequently been menaced by the undisciplined hordes from the Interior; but the local authorities have always protected them. . ."

We unite our thanks to those of our esteemed correspondent and we congratulate China and its authorities on having understood that the Missioners are in their hearts attached to the country of their adoption, and that the Catholic Church is the high school of patriotism.

MADAGASCAR MISSION SINCE THE DEPARTURE OF THE JESUIT FATHERS.

Monsieur Chalain, merchant, President of the Catholic Committee, deputed to watch over the interests of religion amongst the Betsileos, writes to Mgr. Cazet:

"Nothing which concerns the Catholic religion has suffered. So far, all remains in the most perfect order, thanks to the good-will of our government, which shows itself favourably disposed towards the Catholics; the churches in the country districts remain open and the Sunday meetings take place uninterruptedly; the schools have been re-opened and the pupils are as numerous as before. As to us, here in the city, we have only to thank God for the grace which He grants us, for we meet daily for morning prayer, which is accompanied by the singing of canticles. The classes of the Brothers and Sisters are somewhat empty; the reason of this is that all the boarders belonging to these schools live in the country with their parents and, as they are at some distacne, they cannot easily come to school, but the children attend every Sunday at seven o'clock, to assist at prayers.

"As to what concerns Fort Dauphin, the governor has publicly declared that, by order of the minister, it was absolutely forbidden to meddle with the Catholic establishments, as they belong to the Queen. In fact, according to the terms of article 8, in the treaty of 1868, the churches, schools, and hospitals are royal property, but with this clause, that the sovereign cannot change their destination. In reminding the people of this article of the treaty, the government has taken excellent measures for insuring our establishments against pillage; in fact, who would dare touch the property of the Queen?"

At Tananarive, the schools and Sunday meetings continue as heretofore. Let us hope that, by the mercy of God, all will remain thus until it be possible for the Missioners to return and take up their work.

A CYCLONE IN THE FIDJI ISLANDS.

Mgr. Vidal, Bishop of Abydos, Vicar-Apostolic of the Fidji Islands, writes to the Rev. Father Hervier, Procurator for the Missions of the Marist Society.

"I write to you, suffering from the blow of the most cruel trial that has ever yet fallen upon the poor Fidji Mission since I have been in charge of it. On the 6th. and 7th. of January, a terrible cyclone, the most violent within the memory of man, fell upon our Archipelago and mercilessly ravaged most of the Islands.

"Every day I receive letters from the various Stations, and the news contained in them only confirms the extent of the disaster.

"So far, happily, I have not received notice of the death of any of our Fathers or Sisters, although the hurricane buried a number of Europeans and natives under the ruins or in the floods.

✢

NECROLOGY.

MGR. JOSEPH ZAFFINO,
ARCHBISHOP OF ATHENS, APOSTOLIC DELEGATE TO GREECE.

A despatch from Athens announces the death of Mgr. Zaffino, Archbishop of Athens.

Mgr. Zaffino was born at Corfu on the 26th May 1826, and studied at the College of the Propaganda at Rome. In 1875, Pius IX. appointed him Archbishop of Naxos. After the death of Mgr. Marango, Pius IX. called him to the See of Athens and he was proclaimed Archbishop on the 29th April 1892.

MGR. SEMPRINI,
FORMERLY VICAR-APOSTOLIC OF SOUTHERN HOU-NAN (CHINA).

Born on the 18th December 1823, Father Eusebius Maria Semprini entered the "Reformed Minors" in 1846, and went to China in the month of April 1858. His residence was burned by the rebels in 1860, and he was saved, as if miraculously by flying to the mountains and hiding in caverns infested by serpents and wild beasts. The Pope rewarded his apostolic zeal by proclaiming him, in 1876, Titular Bishop of Tiberiopolis and Coadjutor to the Vicar-Apostolic of Southern Hou-nan, Mgr. Navarro, whom he succeeded on the 18th September 1877. He founded a great number of churches, orphanages and convents for Nuns, built a seminary, and was the means of innumerable conversions. Worn out by the fatigues of a laborious apostolate, he tendered his resignation to Leo XIII. who appointed Mgr. Fantosati as his successor. Mgr. Semprini remained among his converts, working as a simple Missioner to the last. He died on the 8th. January 1895.

MGR. BAX,

OF THE FOREIGN MISSIONS, SCHEUT-LEZ-BRUXELLES, TITULAR BISHOP
OF ADRAS, AND VICAR-APOSTOLIC OF CENTRAL MONGOLIA.

The Belgian monthly Bulletin of the Missions of the Congregation of the Immaculate Heart of Mary, Scheut, announces the death of this Venerable Prelate, who, for more than twenty years governed the important Mission of Central Mongolia. Mgr. James Bax was appointed Bishop of Adras and Vicar-Apostolic of Central Mongolia on the 22nd October 1874.

DEPARTURE OF MISSIONERS.

Embarked at Marseilles, 25th December, four Missioners from Algiers for French Soudan, *via* Dakar; they were the Rev. Fathers Hacquard, of Nancy; Evaillard, of Mans; Dupuis, of Soissons, and Ficheux, of Cambrai.

The following are the names and destinations of the Missioners, Oblates of Mary Immaculate, who left for the Missions during the past months: For New Westminster, the Rev. Father Thomas, of Vannes;—for Saint Albert, Rev. Fathers Simonin, of Nancy and Lemarchand, of Mans;—for Saint Boniface, the Rev. George (Joseph), of Arras;—for Prince Albert, the Rev. Father Henry Gouan, of Vannes;—for Colombo, the Rev. Father Vigneron, of Saint-Die;—for Jaffna, the Rev. Father Olive;—for Bechualand (Free State of Orange), the Rev. Father Varnat, of Clermont;—for the Prefecture of Basutoland, the Rev. Father Dahon, of Nice;—for Natal, the Rev. Father Saby, of the diocese of Puy.

—Left Brignole College, Sale de Geneva, M. Paolo Kobielski, for New Orleans, and M. Andrew Demaurizi, for Bulgaria.

—Embarked at Marseilles, 25th November: Messrs. Couilland, of Angers,—for Northern Burmah; Excoffon, of Chambery,— for Siam; Duquet, of Besançon,—for Cambodia; Richard, of Rennes, for Siam; Pavageau, of Luçon,—for Northern Burmah; Corbel, of Vannes,—for Western Tonquin; Blancheton, of Clermont,—for Northern Cochinchina; Aubazac, of Puy,—for Kouang-Tong; Nain, of Autun,—for Malacca.—Embarked at Marseilles, the 9th December, Messrs. Morin, of Autun,—for Pondicherry; Brenguier, of Rhodes,—for Nagasaki; Combes, of Langres, for Pondicherry; Cochet, of Mans,—for Mysore; Marin, of Lyons,—for Coimbatour; Fabeyrial, of Clermont,—for Osaka; Moriniaux, of Rennes,—for Southern Thibet. All these Missioners belong to the Society of Foreign Missions, Paris.

Fifty-three Missioners of the Congregation of the Holy Ghost and the Sacred Heart of Mary embarked at the end of 1894 for the African and American Missions.

This List will be completed in the next number of the " Annals."

CONTENTS.

REPORT FOR 1894. 129

KOUANG-TONG.—*Letter from Monsieur Le Tallandier.*—Martyrdom of a Christian and four catechumens at Tan-chung. 152

UPPER NIGER.—*Letter from the Rev. Father Zappa.*—Progress of this Prefecture-Apostolic.—A model Christian.—The Nuns.—The Stations of Assaba, Eboo, and Illah. 160

ATHABASKA-MACKENZIE.—*Letter from Mgr. Grouard.*—A Pastoral Visitation.—Great Slave Lake.—The Providence Mission.—Fort Simpson.—Fort Wrigby; a heroic fast.—Great Bear Lake.—Towards Good Hope.—Good Hope Mission.—The Midnight Sun. . . 167

THE ENCYCLICAL *CHRISTI NOMEN* AND THE EPISCOPACY. 182

CHRONICLE OF THE WORK. . . . 188

NEWS OF THE MISSIONS. 189

NECROLOGY. 190

DEPARTURE OF MISSIONERS. . . . 191

1. Rev. Julius-Marius VERBIER, murdered at the tonkinese Laos.

MISSIONS OF ASIA.

DIOCESE OF LAHORE.

This diocese is one of the five Missions of Northern Hindustan confided to the zeal of the Rev. Fathers, the Belgian Capuchins. Mgr. Godefroy Pelckmans, who has been in charge of it for two years, is a native of Belgium. As assistants in his apostolic ministry he has twenty-four Franciscan Monks and a number of Nuns. A seminary has been established at Dalhousie. Of the thirty-three Christian settlements in the diocese, fourteen only possess churches or chapels. There is a relatively large European population inhabiting the Punjab, and it is these who chiefly constitute the congregations of the Bishop and the Capuchin Missioners.

LETTER FROM MGR. GODEFROY PELCKMANS,
CAPUCHIN, BISHOP OF LAHORE.

A ceremony of the highest importance for the future of the Mission took place lately at Dalhousie. On the feast of the Assumption I had the happiness of blessing the first Catholic chapel built upon the heights of this portion of the Himalayas confided to the care of our Belgian province on the 25th November, 1888. This event will mark an epoch in the annals of our Mission, for though, up to the present, this chapel serves no other purpose than that of supplying the religious wants of those European Catholics who spent the hot months of the year at this station, still it will be always a centre of action, as it were. It is a good result, after five years of struggles and various vicissitudes.

Permit me, then, to celebrate this occasion by sending you, by letter, some details of this picturesque part of the diocese, narrating for you the principal events which have marked our sojourn during the last five years.

Dalhousie.—Military Stations.—The Almoner's Chapel.

From one of the lower ranges of the Himalayas and close to the snow-clad peaks, rise three distinct summits. *Bakrota*, the principal of these, is 2,512 metres high; *Terah*, which is the centre of the group, measures 2,241 metres; and *Potreyn*, upon which are built our chapel and the residence of the Fathers, the boundary of this magnificent station, one of the healthiest in the Himalayas.

The English have converted this spot, which was quite uncultivated fifty years ago, into a perfectly enchanting resort. No words could paint the magnificent view which Dalhousie presents to the eye when, on a fine October or November morning, one gazes on these three lofty peaks standing out against a clear and cloudless azure sky, the gay and elegant villas of the Europeans appearing through the woods which clothe the mountains' sides. At an enormous cost, the English government keeps up a military station here, and hither, during the heats of summer, the sick and debilitated soldiers are sent.

Nevertheless, the rigour of the winter is sometimes a hard trial for those who are forced by duty or necessity to remain here. In 1892, we were literally blockaded in our dwelling. Impossible to procure meat, potatoes, or any such provisions; we were obliged to be content with rice and flour, exactly like the natives. In certain localities the snow-drifts were from thirty to thirty-five feet.

The buildings of the hospital, the depôt, and other offices belonging to the government and to the garrison that is encamped here in summer, or who pass the winter here, are ranged along the slopes crowning the heights of Dalhousie. It is here, within the enclosure of the military encampment, is situated the dwelling of the chaplain of the troops. In 1873, the Catholic Priest, at his own expense, built himself a modest house on a little eminence facing the hospital, hoping that some day his own means and the generous aid of the government would enable him to build a chapel in which to shelter Our Lord. Alas! up to this, his hopes have not been realized, and the Priest's small dwelling serves also as a church.

The Novitiate.—Providential Aid.—A Conversion.— The Chapel.

When, in 1889, the Belgian province sent out a caravan of young Missioners to the Punjab, Mgr. Mouard thought it best to place them in the healthiest and coolest station of the Mission. Here they could, with more freedom and facility, pursue their theological studies, gradually learn the English language, and become acclimatized to their new country. The house at Balun was assigned to them. With a little crowding and making use of every corner and angle of the little residence, our young Missioners, with light and happy hearts, considered themselves fortunate in being able thus to taste some of the sweets of poverty. Before long, God lightened these early difficulties by His Providential aid. A Catholic generously came to offer his services, and, with the most eager devotion, this Monsieur Berrill constituted himself our professor of English. His lessons in reading, orthography and grammar, his agreeable conversation and pleasant ways smoothed over the difficulties of the language for us, and soon I became in his hands the weak instrument of whom God made use in order to bring about the conversion of an apostate.

In the centre of Dalhousie, a lady, already advanced n years, had, with the assistance of her daughter, a young girl of eighteen years, opened a school for the children of Europeans residing in the station. Bring under the patronage of the Protestant minister, the course of instruction could only be acceptable to families born in this dissenting religion. The idea of visiting this school never occurred to me. One day I learned that the old lady had fallen dangerously ill, and a friend came to tell me in confidence that she had formerly been a Catholic, so, though speaking English very imperfectly, I determined upon risking a visit. The daughter received me coldly, and, on my asking if I could not see her sick mother, she answered curtly:

"—My mother cannot receive you, sir; she is asleep."

I left with the best possible grace, begging to be permitted to return the next day.

"—Willingly, sir," she replied, "but my mother is not a Catholic."

"That need make no difference; it is not in my character of a Priest that I wish to see your beloved invalid, but simply as a friend."

The following day I again presented myself. This time the young girl, though a little embarrassed, did not like to refuse my request. Admitted to the presence of the invalid, I saw, at a glance, that she was near her end. We talked on indifferent subjects, prudence dictating that I should defer to another day all conversation on religious matters.

The next day, however, I learned that the sick woman was worse, I therefore decided upon making a last attempt. Introduced into the invalid's room, I asked her plainly:

"— Madame, were you not baptized in the Catholic Church?"

"—Yes, Father, yes ... but it is twenty-seven years since I renounced the religion of my mother."

Then, with an effort drawing forth a litttle silver cross, she murmured:

"—It is the earliest token of her love. I have never ceased to wear it, and in showing it to you, Father, I make acknowledgement that in my heart I have remained a Catholic."

"—Would you not wish to die in the religion of your childhood?"

"—Oh! yes, Father, and it is . . . "

But at this moment the daughter, who from the door had not lost a single word of our conversation, rushed into the room, threw herself, sobbing, upon her mother's bed, and embraced her affectionately, crying:

"—No mamma, you are not a Catholic, you are a Protestant, and you have no need for Romish Priests."

Then, turning towards me:

"—Sir," said she, "be good enough to leave; my mother and I belong to the Church of England, and your ministrations are useless in this house."

I gently urged her to leave me at least a few moments alone with her mother, but as my entreaties were in vain, I seized the child by the arm and put her outside the door, which I at once shut against her.

To hear the dying woman's confession and reconcile her with the religion in which she had been baptized, was but the work of a few minutes. She died soon after, pressing in her hands the one object which, throughout her erring life, had reminded her of the religion of her fathers.

Acquiring possession of a House and building a Chapel.

Meanwhile, the smallness of the house in which our young students were working away assiduously, as well as its great distance from the civil station of Dalhousie, was a cause of anxiety to the Superiors, and they were on the look out for a chance of purchasing a dwelling in a more central position. Moreover, the military chaplain alone was at liberty to reside within the boundaries of the space allotted to the barracks, and from one day to another the government might raise serious difficulties. On the other hand, it was urgently necessary, for the benefit of the Catholics, that we should be able to offer them greater facilities and be more at their service. At last it happened that one of the most centrally situated houses was put up for sale, and in the month of December, 1890, thanks to the alms of our Belgian friends, we were enabled to buy it.

I at once fixed upon the spot where our future chapel was to stand, and the pick was immediately at work raising the first stones for the edifice: arduous labour, thwarted in every way by the dogged opposition of the freemasons of the municipality, by the bad faith of the contractors, and by the difficulties necessarily encountered by anyone who would endeavour to raise such a building upon the side of a mountain. With the co-operation of Mr. Cameron, a Protestant engineer in the Civil Service, Mr. Berrill undertook to direct the works which, at the end of five years, the Very Rev. Father Edward, Superior, has just brought to a happy termination. In the opinion of all, this chapel, a very tasteful Gothic construction, is truly the gem of the Mission.

While waiting, we converted one of the largest rooms of the house into a temporary chapel. There, praying and observing the rules of the regular religious life, we awaited God's own time. Amongst the first of our conversions is one which deserves special mention, on account of the tragic occurrences by which it was followed.

The Martyrs of Dalhousie.

In 1890, some Protestants from Halifax (Canada), came to settle at Dalhousie. Marsden was the name of the family. The wife, a highly intelligent person, had been educated by Nuns, and, thanks to these Catholic associations, her heart was drawn towards our holy religion. Suspecting this, her parents took her suddenly away from school and, against her will, married her to a young Protestant, the fear of offending her father and mother overcoming her resistance. God blessed this union, and, at the time of their arrival in India, six children filled their home. To remove these from her husband's pernicious influence, Mrs. Marsden managed to place them at Catholic schools. The boys were sent to the college of the Jesuit Fathers at Darjeeling and the girls were confided to the care of the Nuns in the same station. Having obtained the managership of the Dalhousie brewery, situated in a place called *Panch Pool*, Mr. Marsden settled there with his wife.

A most trifling circumstance was the occasion of our having any relations with this family. In an excursion along the wooded sides of Mount Bahkrota, the Reverend Fathers Desire and Leo lost their way one day and found themselves in a path which led directly to the brewery buildings.

A servant of the house came to ask what they sought. Meanwhile, from indoors, Mrs. Marsden had seen all, the unexpected arrival of the Fathers, their hesitation, their conversation with the servant, and, finally, their turning back to seek their mountain top. The following day I received a letter of apology, blaming the servant, who, perhaps, had not understood the Rev. gentlemen, and adding that Mrs. Marsden, although a Protestant, would have received the Fathers with pleasure.

"We must go see this lady," I said, at once, and after the solemnities of Christmas, accompanied by two of the Fathers, I descended towards the ravine in which the brewery buildings are picturesquely situated. We were received almost with cordiality, thanks to the absence of the husband, an irreligious man, full of hatred for the Catholic religion. We naturally spoke of religion, and she explained her ideas upon the Mystery of the Holy Eucharist and devotion towards the Mother of God in so orthodox a manner that I could not help saying:

"—Why, Madame, you are a Catholic."

"—No, Father, I am not a Catholic, but I have my children in schools conducted by Priests and Nuns. I should be delighted to have them become Catholics, but my husband would never consent."

She then showed us some letters which had been written to her by her eldest daughter. I remarked that under her own name,

Mabel, she signed the initials E. d. M. (Child of Mary). Seeing this, I at once assured the mother that her wish was fulfilled, and that her eldest daughter had, by special consecration, become the child of the Mother of God.

We left her, her mind divided between joy, fear, and surprise, but I promised myself to keep an eye to one on whom we already looked as a conquest to Catholicism. But why should I say a conquest? The task was, in fact, but too easy: after three months preparation, she begged to be baptized.

As it was necessary to keep the matter quiet, the ceremony was quite private. On the 1st October, 1891, having received her abjuration, I gave her Conditional Baptism and celebrated the Holy Mass, at which, for the first time, she approached the altar. If there is a true happiness, which all this world's goods could not replace, it is that which fills the heart of the Priest when he can lead to Jesus a soul won to His Truth and Love; and this joy I tasted amply on that day. But what shall I say of the pious convert? Her heart felt troubled under the silence I had imposed upon her, through prudence. Scarcely had she left the chapel than, meeting four of her friends, amongst whom was a Protestant lady (whom, later on, I also had the happiness of receiving into the Church), she threw herself into their arms, exclaiming, with tears in her eyes:

"—I am a Catholic, I am a Catholic! I have just been baptized and have made my first communion."

Alas! This spontaneous outburst cost her dear.

The whole congregation soon knew of this extraordinary conversion aud rejoiced exceedingly. Moreover, the return home of her eldest son, Robert, who was twenty years old, and of her daughter Mabel, aged eighteen, only strengthened her fervour. They all three approached the Sacraments several times a month and attended Mass during the week as often as they could do so unobserved by their father.

Still, Mr. Marsden suspected the conversion of his wife and children to the religion of the "Papists," as he always called us; on their side, they assailed him with gentleness, with kind attentions, sacrifices and concessions which had the effect of quieting him for a while. As a measure of prudence, I had dispensed them from fasting on Fridays or even hearing Mass on Sundays, but they rarely availed themselves of this indulgence.

One instance will show you the ardent piety of the young man. Rising very early in the morning, he would jump out through his window, climb the mountain at full speed, hear Mass and be home again before his father could suspect his pious escapade. One day, we found him seated on the chapel steps, saying his beads while waiting till the door should be opened.

All was therefore going on well and we had hopes that the father would end by becoming a Catholic. What gave rise to these hopes was that he found no fault with his wife when she hung up, in sight of her bed-room, a crucifix which I had given her on the day of her baptism, and, moreover, he sometimes joined in their evening prayers. Alas! Their disappointment was bitter when, suddenly and unexpectedly, they saw dissension enter their home. What had happened? It was not long before they learned the cause. Mr. Marsden belonged to the Dalhousie Masonic Lodge. Now, the brothers had got wind of the conversion of Mrs. Marsden and her children and, in their vexation, meditated revenge. One day, a zealous mason said to Mr. Marsden:

"—Listen, Marsden, if your wife was mine, I would lodge a bullet in her skull this instant."

The mischief was done. Frequently, after that day, he threatened to kill his wife and children. In the month of September, that is to say, about a month before the horrible crime, on the occasion of my first episcopal visit to Dalhousie, Mrs. Marsden, her son and daughter came to see me. On my asking how Mr. Marsden was she answered:

"—I am certain, my Lord, that one day or other he will kill us all."

"—And that is why, mamma," interrupted the daughter, "I have several times advised that we should all leave the house.'

"—No, my dear," replied the pious mother, "better suffer in silence; God will take care of us."

It was towards evening of the 10th October, 1893. The whole family were together. A quarrel, about some more trifle, arose between the father and his daughter Mabel. Mrs. Marsden thought to interfere, but he fell into a violent fury and, seizing an ink-bottle, flung it at his wife's head. Robert, seeing his mother's danger, interposed to defend her.

This intervention exasperated the father and, turning upon Robert, threw himself upon him, dragged him out of the house and flung him down a little ravine close by. The son, however, fell without receiving any other wounds than a few bruises. They re-entered the house together.

In silence, they tried to hide in their hearts the sorrow that overwhelmed them. Mr. Marsden, boiling with rage, went up to his room, and the mother retired to her own apartments. In order to dissipate the clouds of sadness, the young people tried a little music; Mabel seated herself at the piano, her brother beside her, but the joyous notes harmonized ill with the sad presentiment that troubled them. Suddenly, the father came down stairs, entered the dining-room and went straight to the apartment where the poor mother was weeping. No suspicion had entered their minds, when two loud reports threw them into an indescribeable terror. The wretched man had just lodged two bullets in his wife's head. She fell, to rise no more.

Quick as lightning, Robert rushed to his mother's assistance but two more balls stretched him dead. Poor young man! the day before he had piously celebrated the twentieth anniversary of his birth ... He was ready, Lord! and Thou didst take him from this wicked world, *ne malitia mutaret intellectum ejus*.

The young girl, stupified, stood, her mouth open, her hands clenched, before the fatal door-way through which she witnessed this horrible carnage. She uttered a cry ... the father had pierced her cheek with a ball. Vomiting blood, the poor child rushed out of the house, endeavouring, in the darkness of night, to reach the mountain-top in order to obtain aid, but, her strength failing, she fell exhausted on the path.

Enraged at not having despatched his third victim, the father pursued her furiously; a servant attempted to intercede, begging that he would not kill the young lady, but Marsden pointed his revolver a second time at his daughter, saying:

"—Now, you are sure to die."

His vengeance satisfied, the criminal re-entered his house. Would it be believed? With shocking calmness and deliberation, he sent a telegram to the proprietor of the brewery, urging that another manager should at once be sent to replace him; he wrote various letters, amongst them one to the Chief Civil Commissioner, relating what had passed and placing himself at his disposal. This done, he gave the messages to his coachman to bring to the post-office, and then, tranquil and imperturbable, he went about his business.

On the way to Dalhousie, the servant passed the spot where Mabel lay dying. Without losing a moment, he ran to tell Captain Donnelly and his family, all Irish, and good Catholics. Servants were sent to the spot, and the young girl, no longer giving any signs of life, was brought to Mrs. Donnelly. They rendered her every assistance, sent in haste for a Priest, and Doctor Keatly, son-in-law of the Donnelly's, was assiduous in his attentions. The

Doctor found that the ball, which had struck her temple and should have caused instantaneous death, had glanced along the skull and finally lodged in the back of the neck. The motherly care of Mrs. Donnelly gradually restored the wounded girl, who, two months later, was able to go down to Lahore and give her testimony before the High Court of Justice. Here I leave the narrative to one of my Missioners.

On the 6th December Mr. Marsden appeared before the Assize Court at Lahore. Naturally, this cause created a great sensation throughout the whole empire of India.

Towards mid-day, the case was opened, and Mabel, that holy child, was called before the judge to give her testimony. This is the English law. With simplicity, modesty, and candour, Mabel related the events of that awful drama, and, with a touching filial piety, she expressed the desire that her father might not be punished.

To this testimony, clear, impartial, and truthful, the father, by way of defence, opposed a series of lies, the contradictions in which were plainly apparent.

"He is innocent. He has been a freemason since 1878, and he hates the Catholic religion. Against his will, his wife and children embraced that religion. Against his will, also, his wife had placed the children in a Catholic school. Since the conversion of his family, his home had become a hell to him. True, he had killed his son, but in this sad struggle the ungrateful son had been the aggressor. He acknowledges that after that he killed his wife and that he also tried to kill his daughter, but that he was not, at the time, accountable for his acts . . . "

Enough of these lies. And now, if you please, listen to the verdict:

"Mr. Marsden has been unanimously declared not guilty of the murder of his son, seeing that the act was done in legitimate self-defence; guilty of the murder of Mrs. Marsden and of the attempt to murder Miss Marsden, but the jury consider that he committed this act in a fit of madness."

The *Indian Daily News* of Calcutta comments severely upon this verdict. The blood of these victims will not be without fruit, but will ascend towards the Throne of Boundless Mercy to implore the conversion of the unhappy man who is now working out his sentence in the prison of Lahore. This is our most ardent wish. If God sometimes permits that human justice should err in its judgments, is it not because He Himself has said : " I do not wish the death of the sinner, but that he should be converted and live."

DIOCESE OF OSAKA.

A most hopeful movement, which is spreading throughout Japan, is leading a considerable number of well-disposed souls into the true religion. The following letter gives highly interesting details as to the means employed by the Missioners in order to bring about this end. The diocese of Osaka already counts above four thousand neophytes and forty churches or chapels. Numerous catechists and twenty-four Priests are employed in apostolic labours under the direction of Mgr. Vasselon.

A MISSIONER'S LETTER,

FROM A MEMBER OF THE SOCIETY OF FOREIGN MISSIONS, PARIS, TO HIS BISHOP, MGR. VASSELON.

History of a little corner of the Father's Vineyard.

THE soldier who fights at the outposts, far from home, even though he fight under the national flag, soon finds his strength exhausted under the strain of incessant watching. Can it be otherwise with the Missioner placed in the breach in face of the enemy and obliged to be constantly on the alert that he may parry every blow and return it with interest. I calumniate no one in saying that on the Mission, each year counts as two, and sometimes more. As the bodily strength decreases, the mental faculties become weakened, and it is not surprising that one should become a little prosy in growing old. May I not then claim some indulgence if I cannot charm and interest you without also wearying you and setting you to sleep.

"This granted," as would say my early professor of mathematics, a man thoroughly conversant with the fact that two and two make four, while equally ignorant of the fact that a creature supposes a creator, I will, with your permission, tell you the history of one little corner in the Father's vineyard.

A suburb of Osaka.—The early days and dreams of a Missioner.

This little spot is nameless, although it was baptized *Tamatoukuri*, which is, in fact, but the extremity of a suburb of Osaka.

What, you say, a suburb! Yes, the extreme extremity of a suburb. I may well say I know it, for my fellow Missioners in town call me "the country Parish Priest." However, a good third of the city belongs to Tamatoukuri as its parish.

Let us, therefore, dignify this post, if you will, by the pretty name of Tamatoukuri, a name as pleasing to the Japanese ear as it sounds harsh and barbarous to the European.

Would you wish to know all about its foundation and growth, a difficult and trying undertaking, as is every fresh enterprise in Japan? Well, then, listen.

A few years ago, there was a young man who had no other thought than that of making his way, even without staff or wallet, to the pagan world, in order to plant the Cross on bare mountain tops and in fertile valleys. Well, he reached his goal, but it was the will of Divine Providence that he should first traverse four thousand five hundred leagues in a ship, without meeting any other cross than the cross-beams of the masts. Then he landed in Japan, his adopted country. Four long months were given up to refreshing his memory of the language of the country, the B-A, ba, forgotten during eighteen years. Sent to the city of Kyoto, he there conscientiously superintended the building of a church, all the time going on with his B-A, ba, and God knows all he had to look after, in his capacity of architect!

But the building of the church, all of bricks, had brought to light many talents. His gifts as a mason raised hopes that he could do something really good in the trade of Saint Joseph, so he was solemnly appointed carpenter and sent, always to "superintend" the construction of the Holy Childhood Orphanage at Osaka, Tamatoukuri, suburb of the town," as it is put.

The edifice once erected, nothing was more natural than he should be placed in it. He had, in fact, built his own dwelling. His title of "Superior of the Orphanage of the Holy Childhood" sounded very fine, no doubt; but for him who had never recognized any others than Francis Xaviers as apostles, think of it! Adieu to the crosses on bleak mountain tops and in the bosoms of fertile valleys!

At one stroke he became "father and mother" to some thirty children. History has recorded his success as a father. Nevertheless, however devoted he might be to his pupils, he could not keep from thinking of his early dreams, sometimes during his leisure hours by day, sometimes after the curfew had rung, while he slept with one eye, and looked into the future with the other.

Providence seemed determined on treating him as a spoiled child. His venerable Bishop, being of opinion that a Missioner should fill up all his spare hours, created, in the city of Osaka, the parish of Tamatoukuri, in order to lighten the burden on his own already over-charged shoulders. The announcement of the news was the signal for a *Te Deum*. At last, our Missioner was about to plant the sign of our redemption! To be sure, it was not planted on the summit of a mountain nor in a verdant valley; but what matter!

According to the episcopal ordinance, Tamatoukuri, the farthest suburb of Osaka, was henceforth to extend to the very centre of the town. Two great thoroughfares ran through it. Without delay, the spot was chosen where the Image of Our Lord Jesus, raised aloft, should attract all eyes. Alas! for a long time it was destined to be a Calvary without a cross!

Our young hero, emulater of Saint Francis, soon learned that times and men had changed since the days of the great apostle. Or could it be that times alone had changed, and not the bearers of the Glad Tidings? It would be presumption to compare oneself with the Apostle of the Indies!

Court of Justice at Lahore.

However that might be, the young Priest resolutely set himself to work, rented two houses, one in each of the thoroughfares; these, with his residence in Tamatoukuri, made three places of meeting for the pagans, or, as he called them in his own mind, three points whence the Light that the Son of God came to shed upon the world, should soon radiate and shine upon convinced and converted Japanese.

But, at this point of my story, it would need a poet to relate all the disappointments that followed, one upon the other. Let us narrate just a few facts.

Face to face with the reality.—"That will cost me my livelihood."—Hope and Disappointment.

In his fancy, it seemed to the young Missioner that it was only necessary to preach and explain the Christian Doctrine in order to see catechumens flock from every side. Up to this, he had only seen pagans in the distance, as one pictures them while one is still in the sweet land of France and looks at them through the prism of youth. Poor devils clothed with a modest cotton garment or a simple loin cloth, adoring, no matter what, simply because they know nothing at all; in a word, miserable wretches, gifted with sight, but yet in darkness.

A "bullet-headed" or "round-headed" man, as the natives indifferently termed him, a bonze, to give him his proper title, acted as spokesman at the conclusion of the first conference.

"—You are right," said he, "your religion is the only true one, but if I do as you desire, it will cost me my livelihood. Good evening to you!"

And he took himself off. You may imagine my disappointment. Perhaps he was an exception to the whole human race?

Now, another time the Missioner had talked himself hoarse for three evenings, for almost three successive nights, to the same audience of eight or ten pagans. The latter, hanging upon the lips of the orator, expressed perfect satisfaction; there was every reason to believe that the cause was won. On the third evening, towards midnight, with wearied voice and an almost suppliant air:

"—Well, my friends, it seems to me that you understand what I say. Do you wish to become Christians?"

One of them answered:

"—Father," he said, (at this word the orator started: it is rare to meet a pagan who uses this word), "Father, we thank you sincerely; your religion is glorious, it is the only true one ... (the Missioner is again moved) but it is too honest; we could no longer carry on business if we were to observe your Decalogue. Therefore ... "

The other nine signified their concurrence. The poor preacher! It was no longer one exception. They were ten.

But perhaps this might be the last of the misfortunes? Another evening, he noticed amongst his listeners a man of a different class from the others. Young, and stylish looking in his European costume, he gazed at the Father with a somewhat patronizing air. A practised eye would have noticed in his physiognomy certain signs of the seven deadly sins, but our hero, his whole heart filled with hope, said to himself: "here is a worthy soul I shall succeed in enlightening!" and he preached on, with greater fervour than ever; he must conquer, at any cost. The conference over:

"—Pastor, you have spoken very well," said the young aspirant, " and really I do not understand how it is that all of us, Japanese, do not belong to your religion, which is that of civilized countries. Still, there are a few texts from Solomon, St. Luke and St. Paul which I do not quite understand ... "

Saying which, he brought forward an enormous bible (he was a Protestant). Having become a Catholic, he exhausted all the Father's patience. One evening, it took no less than three hours to reply to all his questions on the first chapter of Ecclesiasticus alone ...

On another occasion, a Doctor presented himself, swearing that, according to science, human thought is a product of the brain, and that consequently the question of the existence of the soul is nothing but a fable invented to tranquilize humanity. Next came a disciple of Spencer, quite recently fledged in the high schools of Japan, and through whom neither science nor philosophy was in danger of becoming a bankrupt.

In the end, our Missioner had to give in. The exceptions became too numerous, and God knows if they have not multiplied since. It is a fine thing to believe, at a distance of twelve thousand miles, that the Japanese is a simple, honest being, to whom it is enough to show the Light in order to have it accepted. A nation, pagan above all things, having almost arrived at the point of treating on a footing of equality with civilized nations, yet what she has borrowed most largely from Europe is her false science. Now, Western governments having excluded God from their programme, our poor Japanese imitate them in order to lay on the outside gloss of civilization. Be it remarked that while Christian nations still retain, in spite of everything, their laws and customs born of Christianity, the Japanese, alas, have but science and paganism ... !

I remember a story I once heard. It happened at the time when Japan began to throw off its ancient prejudices against the West.

A native, wearing a tall hat and "incommoded by a pair of shoes," presented himself to the Father. "Father, you see me dressed as a European," said he. Except the hat and shoes he wore nothing but his loin-cloth; of pantaloons, coat, or even shirt not a vestige. This story is still typical of the nation. Science behold the tall hat wherewith to appear amongst civilized peoples; atheism: the shoes with which tread in the mud; of pantaloons or coat, that is to say, of religion, no vestige.

After many years experience.—We must sow with full hands.—The Missioner's Day.

But the young man has disappeared, giving place to the Missioner matured by experience. Reading the Gospels one day, he meditated on the parable of the sower. For nearly a year he had been sowing, watching every single grain to see if it would germinate. But one had fallen upon stone, that was when the listeners thought only of their doctors and philosophers. Another had not taken root, although it had fallen on good ground; it had been scattered by the winds or by the birds of the air, this was the bonze and the men of commerce. But few grains had fructified. There remained but one thing to be done, to sow with full hands, abandoning all to the winds of grace. This he did, and God blessed his efforts.

What means, then, sowing with full hands, seeing that on this depends success? Nothing less than teaching as much as possible. It meant speaking every evening and up to a late hour at night.

You will imagine, on hearing this, that our Japanese are created the contrary to all other men, as evangelization goes on during the night. I could answer by speaking of your many evening meetings, your balls and concerts, by hintings that it is only into the darkness that one carries a light, but this would be mere playing at will-o'-the-wisp. The true cause is, that our Japanese are poor, and happy is he who, in order to live, is not forced to add night work to his daily labour. Moreover, I would give you something handsome if you could succeed in finding here that family life that exists in Europe. No matter what may be said by those who do not know the reality, here woman has not her proper place, marriage is more easily broken than contracted, the number of adopted children almost equals that of children brought up by their parents; what then, is there astonishing in the fact that every Japanese considers the evenings spent at home as wearisome evenings! Besides, he has no home. Therefore, what a mercy it is when he finds some place of amusement, were it even to go listen while religion is talked! Now, however, the Protestants have so saturated them with their discourses void of doctrine, that the announcement of a Christian conference does not always suffice to draw a congregation.

Thenceforth, the path seemed cut out and secure. Behold me resolved to sow right and left, but do not imagine that we confined ourselves to conferences. If the earth is to produce fruit, it must be prepared. Listen, and you shall judge if one moment of time is wasted.

The day naturally begins, and could not begin better than by the offering of the Divine Victim, at six or half-past six o'clock. This little detail as to time has its significance when one learns the hour of going to bed. Mass and thanksgiving over, then comes the report of the previous day, a report ever old and ever new, which usually records the ending of one weary day and the beginning of another. Then it is that the Father gives his different counsels, and the list of his clients is a long one. He must encourage this, comfort that one, bring a third back to his duty, check the impetuous or ill-advised zeal of a fourth.

Then, we pass on to the pagans, and here, especially, the task becomes an arduous one; the catechists have already so exhorted and instructed, without any apparent result, that it is necessary to work up the catechist himself almost every day. Poor fellows, we must wind up their clock also!

Next comes the visitation of the sick, preparations for Confirmation, First Communion and Confession, without counting all the little miseries that require sympathy, the lukewarm who have to be stimulated, and the sinners who have to be scolded, yet scolded with sufficient tact and delicacy, so as not to extinguish the still smoking wick. Here is the daily work amongst the Christians, and when one thinks that in order to teach one page of catechism to an adult, it has often to be done orally, because he does not know how to read! It is not uncommon to see a catechist spend an hour a day for more than a month teaching the Lord's Prayer alone. What can be more wearisome than this constant labour during these months and years? Add to this, continual pre-occupation as to how to approach such a pagan, how bring him to speak of religion, how enlighten him and induce him to make up his mind to the whole decalogue and the commandments of the Church. I have not yet met two conversions similar in motive and circumstances. To attract the pagans to the conferences would seem the best means of spreading the Light.

The monotony of each day repeats itself with the night. After supper comes the meeting; four, five, or six pagans expect you at eight o'clock in the evening and you cannot leave them sooner than eleven o'clock; you would irritate them if you remained but an hour or two with them; they have taken the trouble to come, and, as your listeners are different almost every evening, they know nothing of the fatigues of the night before, so you must talk while they are willing to listen. Besides, you are not tempted to send them away; there was too much trouble in bringing them together, and who knows if we shall ever see them again? How often have I been obliged to talk for three or four consecutive hours, squatted in the midst of these good folk, smoking, in brotherly fashion, the pipe of peace with them!

Usually, the conversation does not vary, but keeps on religious topics; but sometimes excessive fatigue arrests the flow of ideas and the conference threatens to come to an end before the proper hour. Then, with what a sigh of satisfaction one hears the least timid amongst them hazard a few remarks, remarks that are oftener, indeed, more silly than profound.

This is a summary of the daily work of four years, that is, since the establishment of the station of Tamatoukuri. It has pleased God to bless our efforts, and, by dint of sowing, some grains have fallen on good ground.

Fruits gained: the Blessing of a new Church.—Future of the Labourers and their Resources.

When the station was founded, it contained twenty-five or thirty practical Christians. A hundred more names were inscribed upon the register, but they had, for the most part, left Osaka after their baptism. The following, according to the annual reports, is our rate of progress for four years.

In 1891-92, 164 babtisms; in 1892-93, 170; in 1893-94, 114. Subtracting those who died and those who, in changing their place of abode, have gone to other districts, Tamatoukuri actually contains 419 Christians, to whom we must add fifty baptized within the current year. Glory to God, who permits us to reap in joy after having sown in tears.

Four years ago, the chapel of the Holy Infancy, or, to speak more correctly, a simple room, its sole furniture a little altar and the Way of the Cross, served as parish church. There 65 to 70 persons crowded together in a space less than twenty square yards. But in proportion as the number of Christians increased, the inadequateness of the accommodation was more felt. In mid-summer (and certainly it is not cold at Osaka) 288 persons have come together in my modest oratory. But, thanks be to God, last year we had the happiness of blessing a church at Tamatoukuri.

This festival, which was one of the happiest of my life, was marked by the truest cordiality between the Fathers and their Christians.

A goodly number of pagans arrived towards the hour for the

consecration, but from the dawn the Christians had been flocking in. All had been prepared beforehand, from the innumerable garlands to the fraternal love-feast, and all at the expense of the Christians. One, a distinguished draftsman, hung from every vantage point a thousand fanciful devices in honour of Jesus, of Mary, or of St. Agnes, patroness of the church; another, less richly gifted by nature, saw to the cooking of the rice or the preparation of the fish. Each one was at his post; it was a scene of enchantment.

But the real festival, the real decoration, was the lively joy which shone on the faces of my dear Christians. These poor people, the greater number of whom had surmounted so many obstacles, had met with so many mean annoyances because they had remained faithful to a religion which had for temple only a simple and modest room, how happy they were! They seemed to understand that the blessing of a church is, as it were, officially taking possession of God. I overheard some of them say, not without a little touch of vanity which may well be forgiven them: "At last we have a church, we are like everyone else!" They meant, like the pagans, who all have their pagodas.

And now, in ending this letter I should like to speak of the present state of evangelization at Tamatoukuri. It is easy to foresee that our success cannot long continue or increase. If the conversion of a pagan is difficult, his perseverance after baptism requires still more attention. Thus, unless the number of our Missioners and our resources be increased, the more our Christians multiply, the less time have we to spare for the evangelization of the pagans.

Further, if it is easy to keep together forty or fifty Christians without establishing special works, who does not know that it is quite a different matter when they reach the number of four or five hundred? This is acknowledged at the present day in France, a Catholic country, say what one will. How much more are such works needed here, in this poor parish drowned in the ocean of paganism! Consider that we have not even the means necessary in order to found, in the town of Osaka, one single primary school that could enter the lists against the official schools! And thus, as is well known, a large number of our Christians' children escape from us; they go to the godless school, a European importation, and it is so managed that not one Missioner that I know of has been able to teach them the catechism regularly. From this you may judge of the amount of work necessary in order that our entire family, so recently converted, may have even a fair chance of perseverance!

And how follow out in the same degree the evangelization of the pagans? How create works with a view to the perseverance of the Christians, without resources, when I have nothing I can call my own but debts? That has happened to me which is the lot of every Missioner who builds; the bulk of the work is defrayed by benefactors, and unforeseen expenses are transformed into debts for the Missioner. This is my position. And to say that I still see my church without a decent altar, without a confessional, without a pulpit whence to announce the Divine Word!

It is almost a body without life!

From this to being able to develop, or even to sustain the present movement is, you will own, a long way.

And do you also think we are made " of iron," as someone has said? "The pitcher that goes often to the well breaks at last." From experience, I begin to suspect the truth of this proverb. In Japan, I repeat it, evangelization is, above all, night work. Two or three years ago I could still speak to the pagans each evening, and for several hours at a stretch. I can no longer do so. Poor human pitcher! to make it sound again would require more care than a Missioner could give it. But this is only a little matter of detail. It is permitted to believe, according to Moltke, that men are easily replaced. That which is not so easily replaced is the " war nerve."

MISSIONS OF AFRICA.

VICARIATE-APOSTOLIC OF ZANZIBAR.

An Episode in the Desert.

In the first number of last year's *Annals*, the Reverend Father Mevel described for us the founding of the Mission of Boura, whence he sends us this interesting narrative. The station established in the country of Wataita by the zealous Religious seems destined to exercise the most salutary influence in English Zanzibar. It is an intermediary post between Mombassa and the celebrated mountain of Kilima-Ndjaro, the highest mountain summit in Africa.

LETTER FROM THE REV. FATHER MEVEL,

OF THE CONGREGATION OF THE HOLY GHOST AND OF THE SACRED HEART OF MARY, SUPERIOR OF THE STATION OF BOURA.

An Apostolic Excursion.—A country ruined by Drought and by Locusts.—Numerous Invalids.

ON the first days of March I climbed the bare mountains of Boura in order to make my usual excursion in quest of souls. Already the sun, rising above the massive summit of Ndera, had chased away the morning mists which generally rest upon the mountain top. Here and there, columns of ascending smoke pointed out the poor dwellings where the Taitanes were beginning their daily routine of work, whilst the men, their hunting weapons on their shoulders, gravely descended the mountain's side.

Meeting me, they saluted me, asking where I was going. Without satisfying their curiosity, I contented myself with addressing a few affectionate words to each and we parted amicably.

Still, another time the demonstrations of joy would have been more lively. At this moment, all countenances express sadness and melancholy. Alas! these poor creatures are suffering horribly from hunger. For several months past, countless clouds of locusts have devoured the first sowings, and during this time a drought, such as has not hitherto been known, has desolated the land. A fiery sun burns up the wonderful verdure where but yesterday herds of cows, of goats, of sheep, happily grazed. To-day, the emaciated beasts, all more or less ailing, bury themselves in the valleys or the ravines, there to bronze in the shade, and through the brambles and thorns, reach some herbs that still remain green.

Near one village, a woman, lying at the foot of a sycamore, half raises herself at the sound of my footsteps, looks at me with astonishment and, without saying a word, lets herself fall back again, as if to warn me to pass on.

I hasten to uncover her face and to ask her what I could offer her to relieve her sufferings. Her large languishing eyes fix themselves on me; she smiles almost maliciously and says to me in a mocking tone:

"I willingly accept thy remedy, provided it be something to eat; it is useless to give me anything else."

She is a poor sick woman who, not being able to hunt for locusts, tries to forget her hunger in a deep sleep. I console her as best I can, give her a few of the potatoes that my two boys carry, and promise her to warn her brothers not to let her die of hunger.

A meal of Locusts.

Farther on, behind a clump of trees, a silent group of women and children was seated before a little fire. An indifferent pot was placed upon three stones, the usual fire-place of the Blacks; an old woman, shrivelled and wrinkled like parchment, from time to time stirred the contents; a child, his eyes sparkling, his teeth white as snow, profited by my conversation to plunge his hand into the dish, whence he furtively drew out a small morsel which he put in his mouth, tasting it with delight.

"—Well!" cried I, "here, at least, you are not hungry, as you are preparing a good repast."

"—Oh! Father, do not say that: our sole food to-day, consists of a dish of locusts. It is very poor fare, but when one has nothing else, we must be content, and it is better than to die of hunger. Our fields of maize, of beans, of sugar-canes, our banana trees have been completely destroyed by the locusts. The latter having devoured the bread which was intended for us, are, in their turn, eaten by us. Is it not our right? We know you are seeking for sick people. Well, we are all sick. Give us then the only remedy that can cure us, a little nourishment."

"—My good friends, you are, I know, hungry; the locusts have spread desolation through your country; but do not let yourselves be entirely cast down, rely upon the help of God. He Who feeds the beasts of the desert and the birds of the air will not let you die of hunger. But you must love Him, serve Him, pray to Him and ask Him for what you need. Just now, a great drought is paralyzing the soil: ask the good God for rain and He will send it to you. Instead of being discouraged and remaining idle, cultivate and prepare your fields, and, when the rain comes, your bananna trees will give you a great yield, your potatoes will multiply and your wants will be abundantly satisfied."

"—Yes," replied my listeners, "the Father is right; let us prepare our fields, so that when the very first rain comes we may sow them, and later on reap an abundant harvest. But while awaiting our crops, watered by the dews of Heaven, give us something to appease the cravings of hunger."

Saying which, they pointed to their attenuated stomachs, and it was easy to see the poor creatures had not satisfied their hunger every day.

I was obliged to distribute amongst them some potatoes, part of my own provision for the road, and then I continued my journey.

All the sick folk I met, as I went along, were easily cured by the same remedy; all were hungry, and all tried to quiet the cravings of nature by courting sleep, which, alas! did not always come as soon as desired.

My two companions did not regard with a favourable eye my way of curing this new kind of disease; they frowned whenever I desired them to share out the potatoes; a warning I well understood: we must not be too generous, for our turn to be hungry might come . . .

Rhinoceros hunting.—A young Black mortally wounded.

An idea struck me. Quite close to us, and extending farther than the eye could reach, spread the vast desert. Wild beasts of every size, of every colour, of every species lurked in the thick shadows of the woods. If we could bring one of them down, what a feast! How many sick people would soon recover health and spirits! We resolved to set off in search of antelopes in hope of shooting one or two. For three quarters of an hour we advanced with the utmost caution, when, to our surprise, a Taita cried out:

"Quick, quick, make for a tree!"

Quick as lightning my two companions disappeared and I also hid in the underwood. Suddenly heavy, noisy footsteps were heard and an enormous mass rushed by like an avalanche. It was a rhinosceros, just hit by a poisoned arrow, of which he vainly sought to rid himself. Two Taitas followed at a distance behind the colossal brute which, mad with pain, tore along, crushing all before it. My two youths, eager for their share of the booty, joined in the pursuit.

For my part, I continued my way slowly, when suddenly I heard a feeble moaning at the foot of a tree, to which I hurried.

It was a dying man who, in an almost stifled voice cried: "come to me, Father!" For a moment I was startled in presence of that spectre, almost reduced to a skeleton from hunger, thirst, exposure and utter neglect. I asked:

"—Who are you, and what are you doing here?"

"—Father, come here!"

He could say no more. I drew near. He seized the hem of my soutane, drew me towards him and kissed my hands. I called to my boys by firing a shot, the sounds of which was lost in the vastness of the desert. I was all alone with the dying man, and had no means of comforting or assisting him.

He must have been a youth of about eighteen, but I questioned him in vain. Too feeble to reply, he pressed close to me, kissing my hands, stroking my beard, and turning upon me glances that rent my very heart.

The sun went down behind the Pare mountains, and before long I was enveloped in darkness, alone with the dying man, who clung to me as if he would beseech me not to abandon him.

Fancying, no doubt, that I was following them, my two boys had rushed off in pursuit of the wounded rhinoceros; they had completely disappeared and gave no answer to my voice.

Already the hyena was on its nightly prowl, breaking the stillness of the night by his lugubrious cries, while, now and then, there would suddenly come from a distance the long, low roar of a lion, terrifying me in that silent hour.

The poor creature beside me tried to articulate some sounds which I could not catch, but I felt his tears flowing upon my hands, and, abandoning all to Divine Providence, I gave no further thought save to the salvation of a soul so soon to appear before its God and render account of the few short years of its existence. I attempted to explain, concisely, the principal truths of religion.

"—Father," he said, taking hold of both my hands, "yonder, yonder!"

"—Yes, above there, the good God will receive you with open arms."

Then, trying to raise himself, he repeated, while gazing towards the ravine :

"—Over there, over there !"

"—Make your mind easy, the lion will not come here, or if he should, we will die together and go together to heaven."

"—Yes, I long for God, but, there beyond . . . "

Thanks to the sudden bursting forth of the moon, I was enabled to see the pale, thin face, the swollen haggard eyes of the poor young fellow who kept on repeating : Beyond there, beyond there ! "

Seizing my rifle I tried to quiet him, telling him that if any wild beast should come near it would at once be brought down by my long range gun. But nothing could calm him, he repeated again :

" Over there, over there ! "

A shot, then a second, and a third . . . I fired in my turn : my companions were seeking me, and soon after we were re-united. They eagerly told me that the rhinoceros had fallen dead, that the Taitas awaited in order to share his flesh with me, and that they had brought a morsel for themselves and for me, but on seeing the dying man, of their own accord they offered him all their provisions. He cast on them a sad, melancholy, supplicating glance, repeating, in his weak and almost inaudible voice : " over there, over there ! "

Baptism in the Desert.—Edifying Death.

Meanwhile, we devoured some potatoes, taking care to offer some of the best to our sick lad, who was not able to swallow them.

" Yonder, over there," continued his eternal refrain.

Worn out by fatigue, I was just falling asleep when my poor foundling of the desert pulled my hand and again said : " he is over there ! " This " over there " so often repeated ended by exciting my curiosity, and I ordered the boys to go over to the spot pointed out by the sick man, whilst I prepared him to receive baptism. It was not long before they returned, terrified, and crying :

"—The rhinoceros, the rhinoceros!"

I fly to their assistance and find them perched, like apes, in the topmost branches of a tree.

"—Father, go gently; he is asleep, but he is quite near."

In fact, the monster was lying asleep. I fired twice and they did the same, but the brute did not stir, for the very good reason that it had been dead for several days, having been pierced by two arrows.

Here was the key of the enigma.

This is what had happened: the young man was hunting the rhinoceros; his poisoned arrows had pierced one which, though wounded, threw itself on him and crushed his leg by a blow of its horn, at the very moment when he was about taking refuge in a tree. The animal had continued on its way and had gone to die a little farther on. The hunter fell in his turn, and was unable to rise again. He had him there for three or four days when it pleased Divine Providence to lead me to him.

Quite proud of their discovery, my young explorers cut off the head of the rhinoceros and returned triumphantly carrying it to the dying youth, who, with a pleased smile, desired them to offer it to me. Then, a look of joy upon his countenance:

"—Now," he said to me, "I am content to die; but first baptize me, for I feel my hour is near. When I shall be no more, thou wilt relate to my father how the rhinoceros has killed me, but that it was the first to die; above all, thou wilt tell him that I breathed my last in thy arms, Father!"

And, taking my hand, he added:

"—Father, I believe all thou believest, I weep for my sins and ask pardon of God; but, quick! baptize me, for I feel that my strength is leaving me and that my life is ebbing away."

My companions, deeply moved, melted into tears, and I myself, touched to the bottom of my heart, wept with them. With difficulty stifling my sobs, I said to him:

"Take this crucifix, this image of thy Saviour, dead, in order to open to thee the Heaven where thou shalt see Him!"

3. Right Rev. Claudius Dubuis, late bishop of Galveston (United States).

He eagerly seized it, kissed it several times, and his face, although pallid, became almost smiling. One of my lads gently raised his head, whilst the other offered me his gourd, full of fresh water, which I poured upon the brow of him who on the moment became the child of God and of the Church. At this instant he opened his eyes and looked at me with a smile of joy, of peace, and of content upon his lips: his countenance already seemed to reflect his supernatural happiness.

He appeared to be sleeping tranquilly, when suddenly he tried to raise himself, murmured some words I could not catch, for a last time kissed the crucifix, gently pressed my hand, and fell asleep, only to awaken in eternity. This was at five o'clock in the morning.

When it was day, the two boys dug a grave, in which were laid the remains of the new Christian. After having recited the prayers for the dead, we planted a cross made of two pieces of wood bound together; the cross would show the passers-by that there lay a Christian, and thence we once more took our way across the forest, happy in having been instrumental in saving a soul.

A Father at once Afflicted and Consoled.

We were walking silently along, directing our steps towards the Boura mountains, whose rocky summits were already gilded by the rays of the rising sun, when one of my companions cried out:

"—What do I see over there, in the distance? One would say they were men!"

And, truly, I perceived, as it were, phantoms who appeared wandering in the desert. We went towards them, they drew near us: a few minutes, and we had met.

After exchanging salutations, the Taita who walked before the others and who appeared much troubled, asked me if I had not seen his son.

"—Five days ago he disappeared," said the father to me; "we are seeking him everywhere and cannot find him."

"—We have seen your son," I replied; "but you will never more see him in this world; he is dead!"

At these words, the Taita, usually so placid, so calm, so careless, began to weep, to utter cries, to tear his hair and his beard. I tried to console him, telling him that his son was in heaven, and that he was interred at the foot of a *baobab* tree, under the shadow of a modest cross that we had planted on his tomb. I pointed out the spot as well as I was able and made them promise to visit the grave. As for us, our provisions had long been exhausted and we hastened our march.

Some hours later, we were in the fields of maize and banana trees, and soon after at the Mission itself, where everyone was becoming uneasy at our absence. They reproached us for having passed the night out of doors without warning and without previous permission. But we gave a full account of our adventures:—two rhinoceros killed, a soul saved, a father consoled, and we were quickly forgiven. It was unanimously declared, besides, that each one, in our place, would have done the same.

PREFECTURE-APOSTOLIC OF DAHOMEY.

Now that the Mission of Dahomey, delivered from the tyranny of Behanzin, enjoys a continuous peace, the Fathers of the African Missions of Lyons are extending their work in that country and each day admit new flocks into the Divine Fold. In all important centres of population chapels and schools are rising; eight Missioners, ten Nuns, and several native catechists instruct the catechumens and the children. The number of Catholics exceeds 2,500

LETTER OF THE REV. FATHER LECRON,

OF THE AFRICAN MISSIONS, LYONS, PREFECT-APOSTOLIC OF DAHOMEY,

To the Very Rev. Father PLANQUE, Superior-General.

ONCE more I am going to speak to you of our Mission of Dahomey. I know what an interest you take in our joys and in our sorrows. From afar, you love to follow and to encourage your numerous children, while your prayers and your good wishes sustain them.

I will tell you from what we suffer greatly at this moment; but I will also show you how the good God manifests His grace to the souls He transforms and elevates.

Christian Marriages.—Hopes and Discouragements.

For several years past, we could see that the movement in favour of Christian marriage was gaining ground. Already we saw, upon the near horizon, an entire Christian society living according to the Divine precepts. This was the Church of Dahomey, which was taking form and would spread afar; these were our forces, multiplied by the influence of good example!

15 *

But our young people are overtaken by a terrible trial. On all sides, death strikes our married families. It is either the young women who die with their children in becoming mothers, or the poor little ones who have scarce seen the day. We can hardly count one amongst our Christian households where sorrow has not entered. Thus our young men and young girls, struck by these facts, hesitate before contracting a Christian marriage: " to marry in the Church brings misfortune."

Doubtless many of the accidents which happen might be quite naturally explained, and if we could shield these young women from the jealousy, the malice, the ignorance, and the false ideas of their pagan neighbours; if it were possible to surround them by experienced and reliable persons, many accidents and misfortunes would not occur.

But in the midst of these deplorable sorrows, what beautiful pages there are to write, what fine characters stand out, as if to show us, poor Missioners, that the good God wishes to make use of us as instruments of His mercy!

Story of Clare.

A little more than a year ago, we celebrated at Agoue the marriage of a young girl who had been brought up by the Sisters of the Mission. Clare was the eldest of three orphans, whose father, a merchant, being obliged to make long journeys, confided the entire care of their education to our Nuns. While quite a child, Clare was remarkable for her great goodness of heart and for her true piety. Being of an essentially active and practical nature, she drew back from no work, and she acquitted herself of all her duties with a care and an attention that merited for her the praises and the affection of her mistresses. At the age of fifteen years, Clare had already all the qualities of an accomplished mistress of a house.

At the sight of the frightful misery, the utter abandonment of the poor slaves who, because of their age or their infirmities, saw themselves abandoned by their masters and sent to die the saddest of deaths, far from all human habitation, and thrown into a corner of the brushwood, young Clare felt her heart deeply moved. We have seen her, the zealous purveyor of the Sisters' Hospital, going to visit the huts of the Blacks, seeking out slaves who were dying of want and bringing them to the Mission where these poor creatures were instructed in the principles of the Christian Faith, and, at the same time, received the care their enfeebled bodies required.

One day in particular, word was brought that an old slave was in a deplorable condition. Clare immediately set out, saying to the Sisters that she would prepare the sick woman to receive them. In a courtyard, scarcely sheltered by an old straw thatch, she found a woman whose whole body was but one wound. The sick woman was stretched upon mats that had actually rotted, while the odour that exhaled from her body banished all her Black neighbours; scarcely would they bring her a little water to quench her thirst. At the sight of such misery, Clare is deeply touched. She asks that warm water should be brought to her, and she, the daughter of a rich merchant, a young girl delicately reared, and who had a number of slaves at her service, set about dressing the invalid's wounds. A better mat is brought. Then Clare, taking this poor putrid body in her arms, gently raises it and, with truly maternal care, places it on this new couch. All this time, she has never ceased speaking to the sick woman of the good God, of her soul, and of Heaven. Her work is done: she has touched this heart. The negress wishes to be instructed, she wishes to be baptized, she longs to see *Maou* (God). And, in fact, she went to Him before three days were at an end. Her body, wrapped in a mat, was carried to the church and to the cemetery by Clare and by her companions, influenced by her example.

Clare is twenty years of age, and has just married one of our Christians from Petit Popo. In the midst of her new family and their pagan customs, she never belies her principles. How happy was the good young woman when, about Easter-time last year, I saw her approach the altar with her husband!

The month of November has come, and Clare is about to become a mother. Alas, it is the hour in which God wishes to try her, to send her agony and pain, that He may receive her soul, more beautiful and purified, into His Sacred Presence. The young mother is happy as she holds her beautiful child in her arms; she showers caresses on him, all is joy until, suddenly, she feels herself stricken down by some illness. She can no longer nurse her child. Confided to the care of a relative, the little one falls sick and dies: little angel! in heaven he will pray for his mother.

Clare is in a state of such extreme weakness that the death of her child is concealed from her. Frightful sores break out over her limbs, her impoverished blood decomposes, her flesh falls off in pieces, her sufferings are terrible. She calls for her child, she wishes to see him, but they deceive her by telling her he is well, only they have brought him to a friend's house. And this young mother, for whom the future might have so many attractions, joins her hands as she raises them to Heaven and, in an impulse of sublime faith, she offers herself to the good God: "Yes, my God, take me. I offer Thee the sacrifice of my life that my child may see Thee and possess Thee!"

And two days after, fortified by the Sacraments of the Church, she went to rejoin her child in heaven!

As for us, Missioners, who have laboured to form these young souls, and who counted upon them in these pagan centres where they seemed called to exercise a salutary influence, we might well feel sad, did we not know that Providence governs all ; it does not belong to us to scrutinize its secrets. And let us remember that the saints in Heaven pray for their families, for their country, for their benefactors.

Another touching Example.—A young man of Whydah.

The lively faith which we admired in Clare we have lately seen shining forth in a young man who died of decline, also at twenty years of age, in the town of Whydah.

This poor child, baptized shortly after his birth, left without father or mother, abandoned to the sole care of his grandmother, an old pagan who was in the utmost poverty, had received but the scantiest instruction. Allowed to make his first communion at eleven years of age, he must immediately set about gaining his livelihood. But, cast without guardianship into a world whose only care is for the material life, he soon forgot the obligations he had incurred at baptism. Still, faith remained deep down in his heart. It was but indifference that had seized upon him, or rather the kind of lukewarmness which causes so many Christians to neglect their duty.

This lukewarmness or indifference is a poison which comes to us from Brazil. It was imported by those liberated slaves who had been baptized there, but who had been left without religious instruction, without any idea of Christian morality, and who, on their return to their native country, are pagans in their lives and customs, and Christians only by baptism. Our young man had not yet entered on the fatal incline. He was naturally good, but poverty, want of nourishment and of care, imprudences of all kinds soon undermined his health and developed the germs of the malady which was to bring him to the tomb. Francis Lopez, our young man's name, was twenty years of age ; the hour of grace had come. In his long hours of sleeplessness and suffering, our invalid felt within himself some great want. Neglected by all his family, by his youthful companions (charity is not a pagan virtue), abandoned for days together even by his grandmother, who, alone, must provide for the wants of two, Francis felt this want stifling him. He wanted affection, he thirsted to hear a friendly voice.

A long time had passed thus : months of war and of a state of siege. Our Fathers had returned to Whydah; the Christians who were scattered through the farms came back to their dwellings; re-assured and feeling themselves strengthened by the presence of their Priests. If Francis had but known this, how he would have hastened to let them know that he was there, dying and abandoned! But he saw no one enter his hut, and his grandmother was a pagan. One day, an extremely violent storm of rain and wind came on. The roof and the walls of the poor dwelling are about to fall, and our invalid is in danger of being crushed to death under the ruins. He summons up all his strength, and, necessity urging him, he succeeds in reaching a neighbouring hut. They show him a kind of out-house that had been abandoned by the fowl. Francis spreads his mat and takes up his abode there as best he can, lying across, for the hut is not as long as his body, but at least he is sheltered from the wind and rain, and he is content.

Unhappily, after several weeks had passed, the incessant coughing of the sick man becomes annoying; a hint is given him to seek another retreat. The rainy season will soon be over, and he thinks that his old dwelling, which has not yet fallen, might last until the next season. He returns there, carrying his mat under his arm, bent double, stopping at each step, in order to avoid falling and to breathe more easily. People pass him on the way, but no one pays any attention to the poor dying man.

One day, a Christian passing that way and hearing prolonged moanings proceed from this hut, stopped outside. He wishes to find out who this sick man is. He enters, recognizes him, and, an hour later, the Missioners were aware of his state. Francis experienced an indescribable joy on seeing a Priest: it was, he felt, a friend, a father who came to him. What sweet tears the poor fellow shed when the Priest spoke to him of the good God, of his first communion! It was arranged that the next day his confession should be heard, and that on the following day he should receive the good God as viaticum. No, Faith was not dead in this soul!

Nothing is so uncertain as the hour of a consumptive's death. Each day he dies a little. From time to time flashes of vital strength appear, prolonging hope, until life's last flame consumes the last resource, the last atom of strength which retains the soul in the body.

For four months we admired the workings of grace in this truly pre-destined soul, which each day seemed to make a step onwards towards perfection. One morning, it was in the month of October and during the short rainy season, I found myself at Whydah, but only for a few days. The Fathers had just related to me some edifying traits of this young man's life when we saw a hammock borne by two Blacks enter the courtyard. We looked more closely and one of the Fathers cried:

"—It is Francis!"

It was indeed Francis, with his pale face, his large eyes in which all his life now seemed concentrated. It was he, covered with mud, saturated by the rain, and having more than ever the appearance of a corpse. We hastened to bring him under the verandah, give him warm clothing and some strengthening food. Poor child! How delighted he was to find himself near God's house! While this was being done the carriers explained how the torrents of rain during the night had overthrown one side of the walls of his cabin, the roof fell in, and some passers-by at day-break had heard the sound of terrible fits of coughing issuing from beneath the ruins. Searching, they found the poor consumptive crouching under what remained of the roof. The Fathers were called and two bearers were brought: Good Francis, his angel guardian had watched over him'

An hour later our invalid was sleeping in the childrens' dormitory. In the afternoon he asked to be permitted to make his confession and the whole evening was devoted to preparing him for Holy Communion, which he was to receive in the morning. He did nothing but pray.

A week later, in spite of the happiness he felt in living amongst us, knowing that his condition might be dangerous for the children coming in close contact with him, and having learned that we had repaired his hut, he desired to go to his home, and we had him carried there in a hammock. Those spots in which we have suffered much have often some especial attraction for us: he showed unconcealed pleasure in once more seeing his cabin, and looked with delight at the pious pictures with which he had hung that part of the wall near which he had laid his mat. The wall was re-built, the roof newly thatched, and the whole had assumed quite a rejuvenated air.

In the beginning of December I was obliged to go to Whydah, for on the 8th the Feast of the Immaculate Conception was to be celebrated with more than the usual solemnity, and I was to confirm a large number of children who had made their first communion. Our invalid learned this and begged as a favour that he too might receive the sacrament of the strong. It was therefore settled that I should go to his house and give him confirmation on a day to be fixed.

The following night he took no sleep. He had formed a resolution, and, at four in the morning, poor Francis set out, leaning on his stick, to walk towards the Mission. It took him three hours to walk the 1,300 yards between his hut and the Mission. Arrived at our door, he was forced to stop; a long fit of coughing discovered his presence to us. We went out to him, and scolded him a bit for his imprudence, but he answered, with a smile that showed the joy within his soul:

"Father, you do not know how I suffered yesterday because I could neither go to Holy Communion nor receive Confirmation. I could not resist coming, and here I am! I want to go to confession at once."

Half an hour later the brave lad was at the height of happiness: his longings were realized!

This was in the beginning of January, and from day to day Francis grew feebler. One evening he asked for his confessor:

"—Father," said he, "it is all over! Hear my confession; I would wish to receive my God once again to-morrow morning, for I feel that it will be my last day on earth."

He had his wish. That same afternoon he gently fell into the last sleep of eternity.

The aged negress, who watched alone in the cottage by the sick bed of her dying grandson, did not notice the moment of death not a sigh, not a murmur marked the passage from earth to heaven of that youth who, in a few short months, had tried so much to love the good God.

What an amount of good is done by such deaths; how they serve us ourselves as levers to raise up our own love of God! and how they encourage us in the midst of our struggles! Yes, each day brings us some proof that the hearts of our Blacks are capable of great faith. The greatest want of all is the presence of the Priest and sufficient instruction. Why have we not the means of founding stations everywhere, that numerous Missioners might be able to watch over the daily increasing flocks!

THE ENCYCLICAL CHRISTI NOMEN

AND THE

EPISCOPACY.

We continue gratefully to acknowledge, according as they reach us, the Pastoral letters in which their Lordships the Archbishops and Bishops promulgate the Encyclical of the Holy Father on the Eastern Churches.

As a delicate attention, His Eminence Cardinal Richard, Archbishop of Paris, dates his letter 3rd of May, the anniversary of the foundation of our Work, and gives advice as to the increase of the budget of the apostolate, to which we would wish the whole Universe to attend:

"...It is impossible not to see in these reiterated actions of the Vicar of Jesus Christ, and in the movement which is drawing the world under the influence of modern discoveries, an indication of a Providential design for the diffusion of the Gospel.

"It is for the old Catholic nations, and, we will add, for France, the eldest daughter of the Church, in particular, to respond eagerly to the call of the Sovereign Pontiff. It was in France that the Association of the Propagation of the Faith was born, it is in France that should commence the fresh development necessitated by the needs of the apostolate.

"We must not allow ourselves to be frightened by the thought that good works of every kind, frequently those most necessary, such as the giving of Christian education, appeal to us from every side. The organization and first thought of the Propagation of the Faith tends itself to further development without injury to other good works. It is not, in fact, rich offerings, large subscriptions, that are asked by this Work. It was founded on the modest subscription of *one half-penny* a week; it comes within the reach of all, of the poorest, the humblest children of the Church. This is truly a character befitting the Association of the Propagation of the Gospel, and God has visibly blessed the thought.

"We must be faithful to this Association and respond to the appeal of the Sovereign Pontiff. Let each Associate double his subscription, give *one penny* instead of a *half-penny*, and the funds of the Propagation of the Faith will be doubled...It will be easy for each member to double his subscription without letting the other good works of our parishes suffer.

"We must likewise work hard to increase the number of Associates. I would recommend you to choose a parish director from amongst your curates, and it would be useful, as is the case in some parishes, to have a Committee of zealators and zealatrices to propagate the Association and distribute the *Annals* and the *Missions Catholiques* published by the Central Councils.

"We are convinced that by labouring for the Association of the Propagation of the Faith we shall draw down fresh benedictions from God upon all our diocesan and parishional works. I have always remarked that those dioceses which subscribe most generously to the Missions are blest in their clergy, and that Priests multiply in them. Let us give our offerings generously to the Propagation of the Faith and God will multiply the means for our other works."

In a communication of which we would gladly publish the whole, his Lordship, the Bishop of Oran, speaks of the origin and the good results of the Work:

"Its history," says the Venerable Prelate, "is the history of the mustard seed in the Gospel.

"The 'tens,' originally organized by four working women, insensibly increased around them; the circle of action went on enlarging: Lyons took up the generous idea; France adopted it; the whole world imitated France, and to-day, after seventy-two years of existence, there is not a corner of the Universe that does not accord its sympathy and its praise, its prayers and its alms to this Association.

"The little coin, upon which our Lord cast that beneficent glance with which, in olden times, He regarded the widow's mite, that little half-penny has produced the astonishing figure of above *two hundred and eighty millions of francs.*

"This is the material result of this Work.

"God alone could count the blessings of salvation it has worked.

"Who can tell how many Levites of the sanctuary owe their vocation and the honour of the sacerdoce to this Association? How many Missioners has it enabled to cross the seas in search of nations still living in the shadow of death? To how many has it furnished the modest income allowed them that they might not perish of hunger on inhospitable plains, in wild forests, in the vastness of the desert.

"Who could count the churches erected by this Work to the glory of the True God in spots for centuries dedicated to the worship of false deities? The hospitals and hospices that it has built up in the very midst of barbarous peoples, to whom it has revealed what charity means, and whose souls it has won while caring, saving the body? the schools with which it has endowed poor savages of every nation, these grown children, whose intelligence it has awakened, in order to prepare them for the light of the Gospel? in fine, the ransoms it has paid in order to break the ignoble chains of slavery and give back to its victims human dignity and the freedom of the children of God?

"Faith, morals, regeneration, civilization, liberty, salvation, such are the results of this admirable Work.

"Everywhere, therefore; in our ancient Europe, amongst the islands of the ocean, on the prairies of America, and amongst the jungles of Asia, from the shores of our lakes and the sands of our deserts, there comes a cry proclaiming aloud that to the Association of the Propagation of the Faith is well due the gratitude of all humanity.

"And to this hymn of thanksgiving from earth, respond the hosannah's of Heaven, which owes to this Work such a phalanx of apostles, a multitude of confessors, legions of martyrs, thousands and thousands of the elect who, thanks to it, have learned to know Jesus Christ their Saviour.

"Glory be to God, whose goodness and infinite power can, from such insignificant things, produce such wonders of salvation!

"Could our beloved Pontiff place in better hands than those of the Association of the Propagation of the Faith the realization of his vast project for the resurrection and regeneration of the Eastern Churches? Could he recommend to our generosity a Work more worthy of our sympathies? . . .

"We are aware, dearly beloved brethren, that this Work is no stranger to you.

"But a still more generous aid should be the response to increased necessities, and you have seen that the Sovereign Pontiff confides to this Association the realization of his views for the East, at the same time that he expresses an earnest hope that the Association will not be obliged 'to restrict its beneficent influence throughout the rest of the Universe.'

"In the name of the Sovereign Pontiff, then, and with all the ardour of our heart we beg of you, we beseech that you will give the utmost assistance in your power to the Association of the Propagation of the Faith."

After making a warm appeal to his diocesans, urging all to inscribe their names as Associates of the Work, his Lordship, the Bishop of Oran commands his Priests to add to the usual prayers of the Mass, during one year, the prayer *Pro fidei Propagatione*, and exhorts them to speak frequently from the pulpit and in conversation on the subject of the Association of the Propagation of the Faith in order to have the *Annals* distributed with as little delay as possible.

Few letters other than those from which we have quoted have reached us from Europe. Now, as we have frequently repeated, we shall be happy, and it is, moreover, our duty to publish documents addressed to us by the Bishops and members of the apostolate all over the world. We will undertake to have them translated.

On the other hand, most valuable recommendations come to us from the Missioners' countries.

In his Lenten Pastoral, Mgr. Meurin, S.J., Archbishop of Port Louis, made a warm appeal in favour of the Propagation of the Faith.

"This Work," says the Venerable Prelate, "formerly so flourishing in this diocese, but now so languid, is called upon to aid in the conversion of the pagan by means of its prayers and its alms. Christians should not, either through negligence or carelessness, allow paganism to triumph over Christianity in this beautiful island. Gratitude towards the Church, which has rescued them from ignorance and religious error and guides them to the eternal happiness of Heaven, should urge them to share the great benefits of our holy religion with all who are unfortunately still dwelling in darkness and in the shadow of death.

"Try, therefore, to re-animate throughout the diocese that Christian charity which offers all its sacrifices to God in order to increase His glory by means of the holy faith which gives life to the world.

"There will never be wanting zealators or zealatrices for this eminently apostolic Work."

Mgr. Ludden, Bishop of Syracuse (New York State), addressed to the clergy of his diocese a pastoral letter entirely devoted to the Propagation of the Faith. The following is an extract:

"On the first Sunday of Lent in each year a collection will be made in all the churches, the proceeds to be divided equally between the Association of the Propagation of the Faith in general and the Missioners charged with the evangelization of the Negroes and Indians of this country. Be pleased to make the necessary arrangements and to earnestly invite the faithful to contribute generously. We must not forget that it is to such works we owe that we are no longer barbarians, like the people of the Dark continent, like innumerable pagans in the East, or like the Red-Skins of our forests. If we are blessed with Christ, if we enjoy Christian civilization, if we rejoice in the hope of a happy immortality, let us humbly thank the Lord, who, in His impenetrable Wisdom, has preferred us to so many other members of the human family, has endowed us with the gifts of faith, hope and charity. And, as we received this inestimable favour gratuitously, we shall but imperfectly express our gratitude by aiding in supplying the wants of the Missioner who abandons country, family, and friends, to bear the light of Christianity amongst the snows of polar regions or the burning sands of the equator, to peoples seated in the darkness of the shadow of death."

On the occasion of the terrible cyclone which ravaged the Fidjian Archipelago on the 6th of January, 1895, Mgr. Vidal addressed a touching pastoral to all the Missioners labouring for the glory of God and the salvation of souls under his jurisdiction. The Venerable Vicar-Apostolic, having enumerated the disasters caused by the hurricane in a few hours, adds:

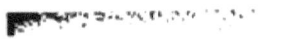

4.   Dahomean cabecere at Whydah.

"We must have assistance to rebuild our churches, our residences, our orphanages, our schools; to re-construct our embarkations, so indispensable to the Mission, and also to provide food for ourselves and our school children until the next harvest.

"And whence will come this assistance?

"Your hearts have already answered that it will come from our mother, that is from the Association of the Propagation of the Faith, which is, in truth, the Missioners' mother. What should we do without her? Oh! it is most especially in such times of trial that one feels the want of this truly divine Work, without which many of the Missions could never repair their losses nor raise aloft again the cross lying buried beneath the ruins.

"We have hastened to write to this devoted mother and we hope for speedy aid from her...."

CHRONICLE OF THE WORK.

73rd Anniversary of the Founding of the Work.

On the 3rd of May, a date blessed above all others, the entire Catholic world celebrated the glorious anniversary of the foundation of our Work. Masses of thanksgiving were everywhere said in presence of vast assemblies of the faithful, and it gives us pleasure to thank their Lordships, the Archbishops, Bishops, and the Parish Priests for the sympathy accorded us and for the zeal shown by them for our Missions.

At Lyons, the Archbishop being desirous of celebrating the festival with great solemnity, an immense audience filled the Primatial Church to hear the Abbé Fremont, one of our greatest preachers.

We shall not endeavour to give extracts from this splendid discourse, which we have much pleasure in placing at the disposal of our readers (1). But simply to read this fine oration can give no idea of the eloquence of diction, aided by dignity of gesture, charm of voice, in a word, by all those qualifications which make the great orator.

The exordium is a happy exposition of two glorious pages of the History of the Church, recalled by the same date:

"I do not know if there exist two festivals more touching to the heart and more suggestive of a grand lesson for the soul than those which we celebrate this evening; above all, I do not know if the connection of these two great events has already revealed to you the full depth of its symbolism: the discovery of the True Cross by Saint Helen and the institution of the Association of the Pro-

---

(1) To be had at our Offices, 12, Rue la Sala, Lyons; 20, Rue Cassette, Paris; at the *Missions Catholiques*, 14, Rue de la Charite, Lyons, for 5d., by post 6d.

pagation of the Faith upon the anniversary of that memorable discovery...

"As the Cross, bedewed with the Blood of Christ, had remained buried beneath the ruins with which a pagan Cæsar had covered it, so millions of souls whom this redeeming voice desires to reach are, so to say, engulfed in barbarity and infidelity. They must be brought back to the Light, as Saint Helen brought back the Cross; they must be delivered from those heavy burdens of savage fetichism under which they groan; they must be taught the truths which save, which enlighten, which console, which enable man to become, by adoption, that which Christ is by nature; that is to say, the child of God. And this is the sublime aim which the Association of the Propagation of the Faith proposes to itself."

Having shown, by the clearest reasoning, that there is no antagonism between the natural order and the supernatural, the the orator demonstrated the necessity of faith in the natural order. It is the primary condition of all our great efforts, the fundamental spring of our activity, the law of our nature. Then, passing to the supernatural order, he draws a striking picture of all the wonders that have taken place since that far off day of Pentecost, and on to the twentieth century, the first faint dawn of which is beginning to appear upon the horizon:

"Here, Gentlemen," he exclaims, "I enter the domain of your glory. It is thanks to your Association that, for more than seventy years, there has overflowed upon the world the stream of those redeeming alms which have borne the benefits of Christian civilization to the most remote confines of barbarism. How many nations and peoples, miserably plunged in the darkness of error, owe to you the consoling light of the Gospel! How many martyrs have died, bequeathing to you the preservation of their work! And you have never failed. Wherever the Catholic faith marches to new triumphs, you are to the front. And who is there that does not congratulate you on being associated more intimately than ever with the designs of the Pope for establishing unity in the Eastern Churches! Who does not feel happier for seeing your great Association seconding at Constantinople the efforts of that Holy Father whose sole aim is but the regeneration of the Christian religion in the very place of her birth ..."

The Abbé Fremont concludes by a warm appeal to the charity of the faithful :

" Pour out," said he, " in lieu of your blood, your gold, your savings, be they great or small, for the eternal salvation of souls and the extension of God's reign. And thus the Work of the Propagation of the Faith, always worthy in itself, will continue to be an honour to the Holy Church."

The Central Council of Paris did not celebrate the festival of the 3rd of May with less earnestness and solemnity. Mass was said at Saint Sulpice in presence of the Directors of the Association and the representatives of those Missioner Societies which have houses in Paris, the celebrant being Mgr. Jourdan de la Passardiere, Titular Bishop of Rosea. After the Holy Sacrifice, his Lordship pronounced an eloquent allocution.

The Weekly Illustrated Bulletin, *LES MISSIONS CATHOLIQUES.*

We have received a number of letters asking if, when subscribing in the middle of a year to the *Bulletin illustré de l'Œuvre de la Propagation de la Foi*, one could date his subscription from the 1st of January, and if so, should one receive the two prize maps presented to our readers. We are happy to reply in the affirmative.

Besides, it is an advantage to take the entire year, for each year forms a handsome volume of more than 600 pages and 200 engravings, and one has the entire of the serials which generally begin in the first January number.

We again remind our readers that a specimen number will be forwarded free. The price of the Subscription is 10 francs (8s. 4d.) for France, and 12 francs for the Postal Union. Address: M. le Directeur des *Missions Catholiques*, 14, Rue de la Charite, Lyons.

LES MISSIONS CATHOLIQUES in the 19th Century.

We have already announced the magnificent work by Monsieur Louvet and have published the first recommendations which saluted its appearance.

We thank the *Semaines Religieuses* and the journals and reviews which have echoed these authorized praises.

Distinguished personages in the literary and political worlds urge us to circulate this fine work by means of a popular edition. Meanwhile, as the season for the distributions of prizes is approaching, we commend it to educational establishments (1).

Important advice to our Benefactors.

From various sides we have been informed that Nuns or Priests from countries in which Missions are established solicit alms for particular wants, in the name of the Propagation of the Faith.

We believe it our duty to warn our Associates against such proceedings, which are very injurious to the Association which has received from the Holy See the special mission of collecting and centralizing the alms destined for Missions, in order that they may be shared amongst all the Catholic establishments.

We therefore beg our readers to reply to those who think they ought to make use of such means, that they will themselves forward to our offices the alms asked of them for such or such special work.

This is the most certain way to insure that these gifts shall arrive at their true destination.

---

(1) When obtained from our offices, it is sold entirely for the benefit of the Missions. In paper cover: 15 francs; bound: 25 francs.

NEWS OF THE MISSIONS.

ASIA.

APOSTOLIC LABOURS OF THE MISSIONERS FROM THE SEMINARY, RUE DU BAC.

The Report of the results gained during 1894 by the Missioners throughout the 27 Missions confided to the Society of the Seminary of Foreign Missions, Paris, has just been published.

Nothing can be more encouraging than the examination of these statistics, which contain a sketch of the progress made up to a recent date in the work of evangelization in Japan, in 23 Missions in India and Indo-China, and in 10 Missions in the Chinese Empire, wherein 28 Bishops, 918 European Missioners, 519 native Priests, and 2,511 catechists, instruct the faithful, who number 1,078,767; serve 8,929 churches or chapels, and teach 1,762 ecclesiastical students in the 38 seminaries. 240,000 baptisms were administered, of which 29,000 were baptisms of pagans and 171,000 baptisms of the children of pagans *in articulo mortis.*

MASSACRE OF A MISSIONER AT TONQUIN.

M. Mollard, President of the Seminary of Foreign Missions sends us the following letter from the Venerable Vicar-Apostolic of Western Tonquin, Mgr. Gendreau, who is at the head of the Mission amongst the Tonquin Laos.

" The unfortunate district of Chau-Laos has lately been the scene of a fresh disaster. Here is the despatch that I have just received.

"Father Soubeyre to Mgr. Gendreau, Hanoi.

"'Sunday, the 10th inst., at 9 o'clock at night, a band of robbers, consisting of about fifty well armed men, attacked the Mission at Yen-khuong. Father Verbier was massacred. Two catechists and two servants have disappeared. I have taken refuge at the French post of Chieng-trai. On the way I met Inspector Cavelier coming to our assistance. Details later on.'

"Since their return amongst the poor Christians of Lower Laos, our brethren had never mentioned being threatened by any impending danger. True, we were aware that Camba-thuoc, the chief of the robbers of the district, regarded the return of the Missioners with an unfriendly eye; but his hordes had been dispersed in the beginning of 1894 by the militia in the service of France.

"We also knew that a chief of the apostate tribe was strongly opposed to the return of the Missioners amongst the Muong-ding, and that he was in communication with Camba-thuoc, but nothing pointed to such an immediate catastrophe.

"Whoever may be its instigators, the blow is a terrible one for the Laos Mission, and one which throws me into great perplexity. Father Verbier knew and was beloved by the Laotians. They had confidence in him, and his influence increased from day to day. One hour has sufficed for the overthrow of all our hopes.

"But God is master of all. Let us adore His impenetrable designs and submit..."

Mr. Julius Marius Verbier, born the 10th of August, 1864, at Labruguiere, diocese of Albi (Tarn), entered the Seminary, Paris, the 12th of September, 1883, and was ordained Priest on the 24th of September, 1887. He left for Western Tonquin on the 30th of November following.

AN EPISCOPAL VISITATION IN INDIA.

M. J. Le Tohic, of the Society of Foreign Missions, and native of the diocese of Vannes, writes, on the 12th December, 1894, from Mercara to Mgr. Becel:

"Praying, in the first instance, that your Lordship will bless your Indian Missioner.

"Mgr. Kleiner, my Bishop, has been with me here for the last eight days giving confirmation, and must remain a week longer, for my parish is quite a little diocese in itself, and we must run hither and thither that we may be within reach of the people.

"Already Mgr. has administered confirmation in two villages, and God knows what trouble the Christians take to give a worthy reception to the *great souamiar* or the *metraniar*. What numbers of pandels (canopies of green branches and leaves) placed at intervals along the way, at the entrances to villages, at the church gates! What garlands of flowers hung around the Bishop's neck! Add to all this the sound of tam-tams, drums and trumpets, bag-pipes and old clarionets—charming music (in Indian ears).

"When the church is reached, the Christians recite the *Salve Regina* in their own tongue and the Bishop announces the reason of his visit. Then it is with difficulty he succeeds in reaching the presbytery; all are eager to kiss his hands, his feet, his soutane, and it is very difficult to make them kiss the ring alone. Then comes the work of immediate preparation, which consists in teaching the prayers and catechism, or at least the essential points. Those present are instructed, the absent hunted up, and at the end of two or three days confirmation is given. Then the Bishop leaves the village to the sound of drums, trumpets, bagpipes, old clarionets, not to count hymns composed for the occasion and sung to the accompaniment of violin and tambourine. The same routine in all the villages. Yesterday the reception was at Mercara, the principal quarter of my parish, and it was really magnificent; I was proud of my Christians who had taken so much pains. His Lordship is delighted..."

AFRICA.

MADAGASCAR.

Most satisfactory news come to us from the Christian settlements in Madagascar. At Tananarivo and in the provinces from which the Jesuit Missioners were obliged to withdraw, the Catholics continue to assemble together and are protected by the Malgache authorities, who express great sympathy with them.

Mgr. Cazet reached Marseilles on the 20th May, on his way to Rome and Paris on business connected with his extensive Mission.

HONOURS PAID TO MISSIONERS IN AFRICA.

Amongst those to whom gold medals have been awarded for the year 1895 by the Geographical Society of Paris, we notice the name of the Rev. Father Colin, S.J., "for his observations and triangulations in the province of Emyrnes (Madagascar)."

Other honorary distinctions accorded to Missioners are as follows: M. l'Abbe Bombard, Parish Priest of Saint-Croix, Tunis, and Monsieur Delpech, principal of the Congregational School at Sfax, have been named officers of the academy.

A CHAPEL IN THE AMPHITHEATRE AT CARTHAGE.

Cardinal Lavigerie more than once expressed a strong desire to see a chapel for pilgrims amongst the ruins where were martyred so many Christians, St. Perpetua and St. Felicity especially.

In 1881, the excavations carried on in the amphitheatre brought to light an underground vault which had served as a prison for the martyrs, or else as a cage for wild beasts.

Thanks to the assistance of Mgr. Combes, this vault has been transformed into a chapel. An altar, made of antique marbles has been erected, and henceforth the holy sacrifice of the Mass can be offered there.

It was on the 7th March, the feast of SS. Perpetua and Felicity, the anniversary of their martyrdom, that this chapel was opened. After the blessing of the sanctuary, the first Mass celebrated in the amphitheatre was said by His Grace the Archbishop, Primate of Africa.

THE EGYPTIAN ORPHANAGE AT SAMANOUD.

The Rev. Father George Vogt, of the African Missions, Lyons, writes from Samanoud:

"I and another Father have charge of directing the orphanage which we founded at Samanoud, an important market town on the left bank of the Nile. We have at present thirty little foundlings of every creed, Jews, mussulmans, etc. There are fresh arrivals almost every day, but, both our house and our means being insufficient, we are forced to refuse them admission into the orphanage. We need money to enlarge the latter and purchase the absolutely necessary furniture. Our boarders are not reared in luxury, for they live upon vegetables and drink only water. All become converts to our holy religion. The greater number are intelligent, and the elder pupils surprise us by the progress they make."

FOUNDING OF A CHRISTIAN VILLAGE IN THE CONGO.

In the month of November the Congo Independent State granted four hundred hectares of land for the foundation of a Christian village, and the Rev. Father Cambier was appointed superintendent of the works by the Very Rev. Father Van Aertselaer. Kassongo, a native black king, had requested that the new settlement might be within his territory, and it was arranged that the village should be begun about four leagues to the south of Lusambo, on the right shore, and not much more than a hundred yards from Lubi.

At first Kassongo was delighted. But while the Rev. Father

Cambier was founding Missions at Hemptinne-Saint-Benedict, and at Merode-Salvator, the princes of the neighbouring states went to king Kassongo to advise him not to receive the Whites. They decided upon a general attack upon the day of Father Cambier's arrival. Already, the cabins built by order of Kassongo for the Missioners were in flames, but fortunately the Arm of God protected His envoys. A newly made convert betrayed the designs of Kassongo and his neighbours to Father Cambier who, with a few faithful followers, went and surprised the king in his hiding-place.

They brought him to the village, and, in presence of all his subjects, reproached him for his duplicity. Having received fresh assurances of fidelity from king Kassongo, they left.

The Rev. Father Cambier was soon after able to recommence his works and, in May last, some buildings were finished and a few hectares of land tilled, in order to spare the first dwellers the unpleasantness and dangers attending a first installation. The village of St. Trudon (the name given to the new centre) will contribute powerfully to assist the evangelistic labours of the Missioners of Scheut.

AMERICA.

PROGRESS OF THE FAITH IN PATAGONIA.

From a letter addressed to the Directors of the Association of the Propagation of the Faith, by Mgr. Cagliero, of the Salesian Congregation, Turin, we take the following passages:

"Last year was a year fecund in the fruits of salvation. Our Missioners visited the shores of the Rio Negro, of the Rio Colorado, of the Rio Menzuen, and of the Limay, several times. Moreover, during a long apostolic journey which lasted no less than seven months, two of our Fathers carried the glad tidings to the Tchuelches Indians, while others travelled through more southerly regions, the valleys of Santa Cruz, of Rio Gallegos, and the plains of Rio Chico. These excursions resulted in numerous conversions of natives and thousands of infant baptisms.

"On the eastern shores of Terra del Fuego, we have at last established the new Mission of Candelaria along the shores of the Rio Grande. 500 Onas and Alcalufes Indians who were dispersed about Ushuaia have come to settle around the houses, chapels, and schools we have built. But it is not alone the blessings of the Divine Word and of education which we must give these catechumens; we must feed and clothe them, as we formerly did at the Mission of St. Raphael on Dawson Island. The work of evangelization is equally successful in the Malouine Isles...."

OCEANIA.

A CYCLONE IN CENTRAL OCEANIA.

Mgr. Lamaze, Marist, Vicar-Apostolic of Central Oceania, writes to us from Apia :

"In a former letter I announced to you that in 1895 we would make a collection in favour of the Association of the Propagation of the Faith. We were quite determined upon it, but now, for this year at least, we find that we cannot carry out our intention.

"In the beginning of January, the Island of Wallis was again ravaged by a cyclone. Two thirds of the bread trees are lying on the ground, numbers of cocoa trees are fallen, and the *igname* plantations are destroyed. Fortunately the banana plantations are saved, the natives having cut the long leaves in time. A fourth of the huts are overthrown, and the Sisters of Sofala's new chapel ruined, as well as the residence of the Sisters at Matautu. The zinc roofs were carried off our churches, the beautiful new one at Mua being the most injured. In passing westward, the wind smashed the large window of the choir, and dashed so violently into the church that it lifted, with one rush, one hundred and eight feet of the roofing.

"Our Oceanians have good reason to call these tempestuous winds 'the spinning devil, the blind devil that carries off all, even men, in its whirlwinds.'

"I spent the last four months of 1894 at Wallis. The wreck caused by the tempest of 1883 had just been repaired; fertility was renewed; in fine, the people had just begun to draw breath, and had no idea of the visitation. In these islands, so blessed in the matter of religion, we must bear some trials. The demon is not pleased with the children of the Blessed Chanel...."

✠

NECROLOGY.

MONSEIGNEUR SNICKERS,

ARCHBISHOP OF UTRECHT,

This Venerable Metropolitan of the Church of the Netherlands was at first Director of the diocese of Haarlem for several years before being transferred to the Archiepiscopal See of Utrecht, in 1883. Pious, zealous, and charitable, he was universally beloved.

MONSEIGNEUR DUBUIS,

FORMERLY BISHOP OF GALVESTON.

Going to the United States in 1846, Mgr. Dubuis was, in 1862, nominated Bishop of Galveston. For twenty years he governed this diocese, which then embraced the whole territory of Texas, and by his indefatigable zeal transformed all the centres of population in this immense savage region into homes of Christian civilization.

This Venerable Prelate, whose state of health had forced him, in 1881, to renounce the active life of the Missions after 35 years of a laborious apostolate, died at Vernaison, in the diocese of Lyons, on the 21st May 1895.

MONSEIGNEUR PAGANI

MEMBER OF THE SOCIETY OF JESUS, VICAR-APOSTOLIC OF MANGALORE.

This Prelate, who for ten years was at the head of the important Mission of Mangalore, was born at Nocera, province of Salerno, in 1815.

Mgr. Pagani was, in 1885, nominated Titular Bishop of Tricomie and Vicar-Apostolic of Mangalore.

DEPARTURE OF MISSIONERS.

—The following Missioners left the American College at Louvain (Belgium) at the close of the year 1894 for the United States: Messrs. F. Bruch and J. A. Kagerbauer, for Kansas-City (Missouri); F. Delfosse, for Omaha (Nebraska); A. Dornseifer and J. Hildebrand, for Kansas-City; Brother Fabian, for New-York; J. Girault and J. Feurlings, for New-Orleans; M. Hennessy, for Chicago; J. Kasparek, for Philadelphia; J. Kaup, B. Hilgenberg, and G. Fillmanns, for Belleville; C. Lammert, for Santa-Fé (New-Mexico); B. Philipps, for Philadelphia; G. Pike, for Louisville; J. Schemel, for Buffalo; B. Schraeder, for Wichita; Stephens, for Ogdensburg; Vandervorst, for Covington; and Versavel, for the Indian Territory.

—In the month of January, the following left the College of Brignole Sale de Genes: M. Paul Kobielski, for New-Orleans, and M. Andrew Demaurizi, for Bulgaria.

—Embarked at Marseilles, on the 25th November, nine Missioners of the Society of Foreign Missions, Paris: Messrs. Couillaud, of Angers, for Northern Burmah; Excoffon, of Chambery, for Siam; Duquet, of Besançon, for Cambodia; Richard, of Rennes, for Siam; Pavageau, of Luçon, for Southern Burmah; Corbel, of Vannes, for Western Tonquin; Blancheton, of Clermont, for Northern Cochinchina; Aubazac, of Puy, for Kouang-Tong; Nain, of Autun, for Malacca.—On the 9th December, Messrs. Morin, of Autun, for Pondicherry; Breuguier, of Rhodes, for Nagasaki; Combes, of Langres, for Pondicherry; Cochet, of Mans, for Mysore; Marin, of Lyons, for Coimbatour: Faveyrial, of Clermont, for Osaka; Moirniaux, of Rennes, for Southern Thibet.—On the 28th April: Messrs. Leo Mavaille, of Paris, for Western Tonquin; Arthur Joly, of Langres, for Pondicherry; Louis Latscher, of Strasburg, for Siam.

—During the year 1894, there embarked at Marseilles twenty Missioners of the Society of African Missions, Lyons.—On the 25th of January, Rev. Father Arribas, of Burgos (Spain), for Benin.—On the 25th of July, Rev. Father Gros, of Belley, for the Upper Niger.—On the 25th of August, the Rev. Fathers Crobas, of Clermont, for Benin; Kapfer, of Strasburg, for the Gold Coast; Teyssier, of Lyons, for Dahomey; Adolphe Rousselet, of St. Claude, for the Upper Niger.—On the 25th September: The Rev. Fathers Bricet, of Nantes, for Dahomey; Klauss, of St. Gall (Switzerland), for Benin; Martini and Steber, of Strasburg, for the Gold Coast; Poncet, of Lyons, for Dahomey; Lichtenauer, of Strasburg, for Benin.—On the 25th October, the Rev. Father Arti, of Strasburg, for the Upper Niger.—On the 25th of November, the Rev. Father Vogt, of Strasburg, for Benin.—On the 8th September, the Rev. Fathers Rauchin, of Viviers, Pichaud, of Nantes, Stephen Kyne, of Tuam (Ireland), for the Egyptian Delta.—On the 29th September, the Rev. Father Chabert, of Grenoble, and on the 10th November, the Rev. Fathers Sironi and Rinoldi, of Milan, for the same Mission.

—Left Marseilles, on the 3rd of April, for the Missions of Micronesia, three Missioners of the Sacred Heart, Issoudun: The Rev. Fathers Edward Bontemps, Superior of the Mission of Poitiers, Fillodeau, of Rochelle, and Lebeau, from Belgium.

—The Seminary of Steyl, near Kaldenkirchen (Pays-Bays) has sent eleven Missioners to various Missions in Asia, Africa, and America.—Left Genes, on the 27th August, for Southern Chantong: The Rev. Fathers Peter Noyen, of Bois-le-Duc, Augustus Hortsmann, of Münster, and George Froevis, of Brixen.—On the 11th November, from Hamburg, for Togoland: Messrs. Hermann Bucking, of Cologne, James Hoffmann, of Treves.—On the 23rd December, from Antwerp, for the Argentine Republic: Messrs. Michael Colling, of Treves, Adolphus Hegge, of Osnabruck, Hermann Lobbert, of Cologne, and on the 3rd January, 1895: Monsieur Theodore Stark, of Münster.—On the 15th February, 1895, from Hamburg, for Brazil: Messrs. Francis Dold, of Fribourg (Baden), and Francis Tollinger, of Brixen.

CONTENTS.

LAHORE.—*Letter from Mgr. Pelckmans.*—Blessing the chapel at Dalhousie.—Importance of this Mission.—Conversion of an apostate.—The martyrs of Dalhousie. . . 193

OSAKA.—*A Missioner's Letter.*—The dreams and first acts of the apostolate.—Awakenings.—The Tamatoukouri Mission, in a suburb of Osaka.—A method of evangelization peculiar to Japan. 206

ZANZIBAR.—*Letter from the Rev. Father Mevel.*—An apostolic trip.—Rhinoceros hunting.—A black mortally wounded.—A baptism in the desert.—An edifying death. 218

DAHOMEY.—*Letter from the Rev. Father Lecron.*—Christian marriages.—Touching examples.—Story of Clare and Francis. 227

THE ENCYCLICAL *CHRISTI NOMEN* AND THE EPISCOPACY. 236

CHRONICLE OF THE WORK. . . . 242

NEWS OF THE MISSIONS. 246

NECROLOGY. 253

DEPARTURE OF MISSIONERS. . . . 254

B   Right rev. DUNAND, apostolic vicar of Western Su-tchuen.

LETTER FROM
HIS HOLINESS POPE LEO XIII.,
TO THE PRESIDENTS OF THE
ASSOCIATION OF THE PROPAGATION OF THE FAITH,
LYONS AND PARIS.

We published, when it appeared, the Encyclical *Christi Nomen*, addressed to the Catholic Episcopacy and recommending to its zealous care the Association of the Propagation of the Faith. It contains these words: "the greater part of the subsidies necessary for the carrying out of Our projects for the union of the Christian Churches, We shall ask from that Association whose panegyric We have pronounced and whose aim is in exact accordance with that which We have so much at heart. Therefore, We cannot too urgently impress upon the faithful the necessity for increasing their bounty in proportion to Our wants."

At the same time that, in a most flattering letter, the Holy Father invited the Councils of the Work to become associated with his great designs, Messrs. the Directors hastened to place at the feet of the Sovereign Pontiff the assurance of their entire devotion to the cause, and they have been commissioned by the Pope to distribute amongst the Eastern Bishops designated by his Holiness Leo XIII., the sum allocated to the East, the distribution to be made in the proportions fixed by his Holiness himself.

It is as the crowning of these negotiations, in which are visible the love and delicate thoughtfulness of the father and the absolute submission of the sons, that the Sovereign Pontiff has addressed to the two Councils the following letter, which we feel happy in publishing. May it contribute to the development, amongst Catholics, of that increase of zeal and generosity which, to quote the words of the Encyclical, are rendered necessary by more urgent needs!

Dearly Beloved Sons,

We have been deeply touched by the laudable and Christian sentiments expressed in your letter, and of which, moreover, you have already so frequently given Us the most consoling proofs.

What gives Us the most heartfelt pleasure has been to see the two Central Councils of the Propagation of the Faith enter into Our views regarding the work of the Eastern Churches, and likewise cordially share the deep interest that, in Our Apostolic solicitude, we feel for these ancient and venerable Churches. It has certainly been very pleasing to you, beloved sons, to have been able, in the last distribution of your funds, to increase, in their favour, the sum you had previously allotted to them, and We, on Our side, are happy in the hope that, in the future, the piety of the faithful will enable you still more to augment your generous benefactions.

Meanwhile, and as a proof of Our especial affection, We grant to you and to all the Members of both Central Councils, the Apostolic benediction.

Given at the Vatican, 1st. July, 1895.

LEO XIII.

MISSIONS OF ASIA.

VICARIATE-APOSTOLIC OF NORTHERN CHAN-TONG.

We have received the following curious and picturesque narrative from the Venerable Vicar-Apostolic of Chan-Tong. As we are already aware, the Reverend Fathers, the Italian Franciscans, are in charge of this important Mission, which already counts above 14,000 neophytes and 360 Christian communities, 226 of which contain churches. The Bishop resides at Tsi-nan-fou, the capital of the province of Chan-Tong, one of the most populous cities of the Celestial Empire.

LETTER FROM MONSEIGNEUR DE MARCHI,

FRANCISCAN,

VICAR-APOSTOLIC OF NORTHERN CHAN-TONG

THE facts which I am about to relate are of a nature to both interest and edify the readers of the *Annals*, and, it may be, that they will obtain the precious benefit of their prayers for my Mission in general, and especially for the Christian settlement of Te-Lin.

The Missioners have frequently had occasion to speak of a curious Chinese sect, the sect of *Adorers of the Image*, the adherents of which bind themselves to a number of religious observances, such as public confession of sins, fasting, abstinence, and a special devotion towards a goddess closely resembling in many ways the Sybil of the Greek mythology, a goddess whom they venerate under the title of the Mother of Heaven. Some authors trace the origin of this sect back to the first centuries of our era, and find in its doctrine traces of Christianity disfigured by persecutions.

However this may be, Christianity has won numerous converts from the followers of this sect in various provinces of the Celestial Empire.

In the village of Te-Lin, where the facts I am about to relate occurred, one of the principal members of the sect was called Li-Tchouin-Mao. This person was specially successful in manufacturing steel weapons. For years he had been working on the fashioning of a sword, the rich ornamentation, the tempering and the strength of which were celebrated throughout the country : it was a veritable *chef-d'œuvre!* The maker loved it above all other things. His daughter had embraced Christianity and had received in baptism the name of Agnes. At first this conversion had greatly displeased Li, but, in the end, he left his daughter free to follow her convictions, and the young neophyte hoped, little by little, to draw her father into the way of salvation, by her gentleness and good example.

She was, therefore, deeply grieved on hearing him one day declare that he wished to become an anchorite, after the fashion of certain bonzes who retire into solitude in the depths of the mountains, there to spend the last years of their lives. After many prayers and tears, she at last made up her mind to reason gently with him.

"—Father," said she, "your resolve is one worthy of a noble and generous heart, but it is of no avail."

"—Why should it be useless?"

"—Because, outside of the one true religion, no penance can be pleasing to Heaven."

And she added:

"—In order to be happy after death, it is necessary to belong to this religion. Take this catechism; read it. You will see that it tells you the truth."

"—I will read your catechism; but it will be in order to refute the absurdities it contains."

In spite of his fanaticism and boasting, Li-Tchouin-Mao had an upright heart. God took pity on him and enlightened his intelligence, and, after some days of reading and reflection, Agnes had the joy of finding that her father renounced his project of leading a hermit's life. He said to her:

"—I no longer have any wish to become an anchorite like the bonzes; I will be a Catholic like you."

Li was baptized, and, in his ardour as neophyte, nothing was too much for his zeal. He preached the propaganda around him; he transformed his house into a chapel, and, in various ways, facilitated the ministry of the Rev. Father Zenon Moeltner, who has charge of that district.

Amongst the catechumens in the village of Te-Lin was one who was particularly remarked for her devotion and fervour, a young widow whose whole longing was to be baptized: "that she might go at once," she said, "to Paradise, and see the true Mother of Heaven face to face." Her only son, a youth of sixteen, was also a catechumen, but his giddiness made him a source of trouble to the whole community. He had a curious adventure one day as he was in the fields gathering dry leaves. A wicked looking stranger suddenly appeared before him:

"—Young man," he said, looking sternly at him, "you wish to become a Christian; but, believe what I say, you are deceived; the Christian sect is false and pernicious. Would you have a proof of this? You know Li-Tchouin-Mao's splendid sword; its strength is well tested. Very well! Take this in your hands. It will break into pieces. If it remains intact, you may conclude that I lie."

Terrified at this apparition and these words, the poor boy made the sign of the cross, and the stranger disappeared. But the words of the tempter kept ringing in his ears: this famous sword which was to shiver to atoms at his touch, what a marvel! To be brief, having resisted for a few days he could hold out no longer. He

mass of sores and there was no hope of saving her life. She was in despair over the absence of the Missioner, repeating that she should die without baptism, but Agnes reassured her:

"—In a case of necessity," she said to her, "the sacrament can be administered by anyone."

Agnes herself conferred it upon her. In the midst of agonizing pain, the pious neophyte was filled with joy:

"—I suffer much, but I am happy. I am now baptized and I am going to Heaven!" she exclaimed.

She was carried to Agnes's dwelling, where she died the following night.

In this death, surrounded as it was by the consolations of faith, and, doubtless, most precious in the eyes of God, the pagans found a pretext for fresh attacks upon Christianity.

"Our gods," they said, "have clearly manifested their indignation at the conduct of this woman who had deserted their altars; they have sent her many trials, one more lamentable than the other, and, in the end, have caused her to perish in a horrible manner."

They overwhelmed with reproaches a relative of the poor defunct, throwing on him the responsibility of all that had passed, accusing him of having done nothing to prevent her hateful "apostasy," a most unjust accusation, the said relative having, on the contrary, done all in his power to prevent this conversion. However, being desirous of repairing, as far as possible, the wrongs he had done the gods of his nation, he went daily to the cemetery, weeping and groaning, invoking his deities, and burning gold and silver paper on the tomb. These superstitious demonstrations won the approval of his co-religionists, but, at the end of a week, he sought out Li-Tchouin-Mao and told him that on two different occasions the deceased had appeared to him in a dream, and said:

"Cease making offerings, which are detestable to me, upon my tomb. Cease to deplore my death, for I am happy in Heaven with the true God of the Christians. Embrace the Christian religion, if you would not burn for eternity."

He had thought nothing of the first dream, but a second apparition made him reflect, and he decided upon asking to be admitted amongst the catechumens. At the present hour, he is one of our most fervent Christians.

May the true Mother of God deign to lead to the feet of her Divine Son all the *image adorers*, all the pagans of China!

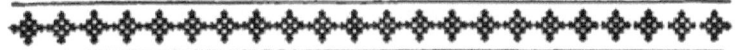

MISSIONS OF AFRICA.

VICARIATE-APOSTOLIC OF THE BELGIAN CONGO.

The various Missions known under the title of the Congo were decided on at the same time that this immense territory was appropriated and divided out amongst the European Powers. The following interesting narrative comes to us from the Mission entrusted to the Missioners of Scheut-les-Bruxelles, under the name of Belgian Congo, and especially placed under the jurisdiction of his Majesty the King of the Belgians. It is a perfect picture of the life, the resources, and the difficulties encountered by the apostles. This young vicariate already counts six hundred Catholics. It is one of the Fathers of the seminary of Scheut who has compiled this interesting work from the notes of his brethren in the Congo.

A Missioner's first Dwelling.—Commerce.—The food of the Natives.—A Market.

THE newly-arrived Missioner must not expect to find a brick house, several stories high: such dwellings are phenomenal in the Congo, and are only to be seen in some spot where a European may have lived for many years. The Missioner's habitation is a *Chimbeck*, the name usually given to the dwellings of the natives of the Lower Congo. The hut of the aboriginal is constructed of straw, is usually between six and seven feet high, with length and depth in proportion, and has a roof projecting considerably beyond the walls, in order to protect the building from the beating rain and the broiling sun. At one side, there is always a hall or verandah. Here it is that friends meet, that the fire is kindled, the cooking done, and meals eaten. The interior of the house is but very sparely furnished: a hard bed, a little common crockery, some native utensils, and, finally, a large knife hangs from the belt of the master of the house. Such is the first home of a Missioner in the Congo.

Later on, he may build a more spacious house for himself; this is usually built in the form of a horse-shoe. The Missioner occupies the centre: one side serves as an oratory for the neophytes and ransomed slave children, the other is a store for provisions or European products; all around are scattered the servants' huts, the kitchen, the goat-house, the fowl-house, and the school.

In general, the Missioner does not trouble himself much about his own dwelling, seeing that his numerous occupations constantly call him out of doors. He must oversee the workmen charged with digging up the ground and with carrying on its culture; he has to teach the ransomed children, distribute medicines, listen to the rambling tales of his negro neighbours, who pass their days in doing nothing, and who seem to think that the white man has come to Africa simply to lend his ear to their endless gossipings.

The neighbourhood of a white man's abode in the Congo soon becomes a market-place to which the neighbouring tribes resort. The women bring manioc, different kinds of bananas, lemons, pineapples, various sorts of vegetables and fruits. These are placed in a kind of large basket or ercel suspended from the head and resting upon the back, the poor women bending under their burdens, while some of them have besides a child planted astride upon their hips. The men offer tobacco, calabashes filled with *malafou*, or palm-wine, fowl, goats, smoked rats, huug on a skewer: this last named commodity is considered the *ne plus ultra* of delicacies amongst the Blacks.

European vegetables are therefore but a memory for the Missioner until he can raise them from seeds in a well prepared garden. While awaiting this harvest, he cannot even have the common luxury of bread and butter, or a potatoe; however, for want of thrushes, we eat blackbirds, says the proverb, and, therefore, in the Congo we commonly use manioc and bananas.

The manioc is the principal, if not the only, food plant of the natives. It grows in bundles of stalks which, when matured, attain a height of from six to nine feet; each stalk bears several branches, ranged alternately, and ending in a palm-like leaf. The young leaves of the manioc are used as vegetables, and, when prepared, make a dish like cabbage soup. However, the principal alimentary part is the root, which is a sort of long beet-root of a pale grey colour. This, when peeled of its bark or skin, and cooked in the ashes, has a taste not unlike that of the potatoe; of this root the natives make little loaves, which they call *chickwangues*. This is their mode of proceeding. The first operation consists in removing the husk, then they crush the root, or they grate it, afterwards passing it through several waters and drying it in the sun. In the process of washing, it is divided into two products: one is a powdery matter, which swims upon the water: this is the true tapioca; the other is a heavier substance, a very wholesome flour: this is cassava. This latter, kneaded into the form of small loaves, is covered with palm-leaves, and the entire dish, when baked in hot ashes, is called *chickwangue*. Newly-arrived Europeans generally find it detestable, for it is gluey, slimy, bitter; but when one is very hungry, one finds that, in spite of the taste and the odour, it is just as easily eaten as certain cheeses that are highly relished by our epicures. Foremost amongst the fruits is the banana, on one single bunch or branch of which are forty to fifty fruits; each fruit of the large banana measures as much as twenty-five centimetres in length, while that of the small banana, though of a finer and more agreeable flavour, is only seven or eight centimetres long.

Let us now return to the market where the Missioner must procure provisions for himself and those who depend on him. The animation of the scene at times seems something infernal: all these black folk come and go, cry out, gesticulate, laugh, dispute, beat each other, and create a fearful uproar. The duties of the Missioner who acts as purveyor are not always of the easiest, particularly as, in the absence of any money currency, traffic must be carried on by barter. The sole piece of money in use amongst the tribes dwelling on the shores of the Congo is the *mitako*. This is a simple rod, or rather wire of brass, between two or three millemetres in diameter and fifty centimetres in length. Now, it often happens either that the Missioner has no *mitakos* at his disposal or that the natives require stuffs or other products of our European cargoes. It is then the bargaining becomes difficult: the stuff is not wide enough, it is too slight in make, is not bright enough in colour; the beads are too thick or too thin; it is blue beads that are wanted, not red; instead of a bracelet, a collar is desired. Happily, the Missioner, who is well aware of the covetousness of these dark skins, remains unmoved and turns a deaf ear to all the uproar. And in the end, the market over, each one retires home content and satisfied.

A European article very much in request amongst the negresses is the mirror. Oh! what delightful moments the greater number of these black daughters of Eve pass before the polished surface which reflects their smiles and their ecstatic delight! For, believe me, coquetry is not the exclusive belonging of Europeans. The negresses who have the chance of receiving a mirror in payment of eatables, first gaze at themselves with fear, covering their eyes with one hand, but casting, through the openings-between the fingers, furtive glances on the enchanting glass. As it is always but the first step which costs, they become bolder, uncover their face, approach it to the magic mirror, press it to the glass, draw it away again, smiling and showing their sharpened teeth; then they once more become serious, then preoccupied, attentive, addressing compliments and flattering speeches to this new kind of fetich. Sometimes they become so absorbed in the contemplation of their features that they forget how time flies until, suddenly, they perceive that their companions have already quitted the market-place.

Small annoyances of the Missioners.—Insects.—White Ants.—Scorpions.—Serpents.—Rats.

But do not think that all our annoyances come only from the negros; the Missioner is greatly tormented by a crowd of noxious insects that take up their abode in his hut and sometimes cause him lively panics. Thus, he may happen to find his couch occupied by an ignoble centipede; in vain he seeks repose, being kept awake by the buzzing of some big black fly, a kind of wasp with a poisonous sting; during the night, he is unpleasantly surprised by the prick of mosquitos or by the slimy touch of the scorpion; or perhaps before daybreak he hears the well-known hiss of a serpent.

Let us pass in review some of these venomous creatures, real scourges in tropical latitudes.

First, the Missioner's habitation often becomes the resort of *salales* or white ants. These innumerable and voracious insects eat through the beams and cross wood, attack every part of the wood work, and transform the joists into a kind of sponge. A magnificent harmonium, which had been presented to the first Missioners of the Congo, was besieged by a band of these destroyers; one day, when they tried to move it, it literally fell in pieces, leaving nothing uninjured save the ivory keys and the wires. These insects also eat into the bales of stuffs and try to worm themselves into the centre of the pieces.

Very often, upon the reddish soil we see spreading out in slender spirals, innumerable processions of white ants, which go and come, enter, climb up, go out, carrying provisions, dragging bits of straw, hurrying to and fro, never stopping, always working. They construct their dwellings of a material that, when exposed to the air assumes the hardness of stone, and are thus proof against all attack. In order to escape the destruction caused by these insects, the wooden dwellings of our Nuns are raised upon iron columns, each furnished with a vessel in which the tar is every morning replenished, to prevent these unpleasant parasites from climbing up.

After the white ants, come the scorpions, millions of which haunt all buildings that serve as stores or magazines. In certain places, the ground is covered by them, and the Blacks scarcely dare to walk upon these hideous beetles, always ready to revenge themselves cruelly upon those who presume to interrupt their evolutions. The scorpion walks, crawls almost, taking care to raise the threatening claw, charged with poison, with which his long tail is armed. It is with this dart that the creature pierces the negro's foot, which is itself thick and hard as horn. This very serious sting occasions darting pains throughout the whole body. The wounded negro revenges himself, though rather late, by seizing and strongly squeezing between his fingers the claw of the scorpion, which struggles vainly and at last dies.

In offices, in kitchens, and even in wardrobes, the agile cancrelat, with its disagreeable odour, its repelling aspect, devours papers, rubbers, and household linen.

It may happen that the Missioner, going to the far end of a badly lighted apartment in order to unpack a bale of stuffs or to open a chest of European goods, suddenly, and to his great surprise, discovers a serpent, measuring a yard, or perhaps a yard and a half in length, which, lifting its menacing head, opens a large mouth foaming with whitish poison. Sometimes a well aimed blow of a cane suffices to break the spine of the dangerous intruder, at other times it has no effect.

To all these house guests, so mischievous and at times so dangerous, we must add disastrous invasions of rats, especially in the month of December. What miserable nights we sometimes pass at this season of the year! The mosquitos and the gnats are not content with obliging the European to sleep enclosed in the narrow meshes of a mosquito-net or curtain, but they vie with the rats in disturbing the sleep of the white man, exhausted by the labours of a well filled day.

It is no exaggeration to say that the rats invade the sleeping apartments in battalions. One hears them climbing on the toilet-table, noisily drinking from the water jugs, tumbling in the baths, ferreting everywhere. The noise of their claws upon the porcelain, their shrill cry, the crackling of the paper or the leather they are tearing at last oblige you to rise, furious, exasperated, to engage in the darkness in combat with the rioters, who decamp, gliding, jumping, on every side, sometimes brushing their soft, slimy bodies against the feet or the legs of their victorious enemies. Then silence reigns for a moment; but soon the rats, that have quickly recovered from their fright, again mingle with the snoring of the sleeper the devilish turmoil of their dreadful noises.

The Life of the Missioner at home.—The Palabre.— Idol Worshippers.—Burials.

It is easy to understand that with so many worries, the Missioner scarce finds very great enjoyment or much sweet repose within his dwelling, so he is glad to make frequent excursions around in order to visit his negro neighbours, in whose homes he sometimes is witness to strange scenes that make him forget the little troubles and inconveniences of his own. Let us then accompany the Missioner in one of these visits, and in his company assist at three interesting spectacles: first, a palabre, then a scene of idol worshipping, finally, an interment.

The first scene, rather a comic one, is presented to us by the palabre. Palabre is derived from the English word "palaver," which signifies a conference or *blague*. The palabre is a parliamentary reunion in the open air, and is held on some occasion of public interest: for example, the least concession asked of the chief of a tribe by a White gives rise to a palabre. Recourse is had to one in order to establish a contested right, to decide a dispute, to punish a fault or a crime, to yield up a territory or an estate, to supply porters, to sell provisions, in fine, on all social questions of any importance. It may even happen that the Blacks invite a European to preside at their palabre. The negro delights in these assemblies because he can there satisfy his two dominant tastes: boasting and drunkenness. The Black is an incorrigible boaster; besides, the palabre is almost as good as a wedding party, for a great many calabashes of palm-wine or of brandy are drunk there.

A palabre is usually fixed beforehand, and takes place with much ceremonial. It is the king or chief, the Makoko, as they style him, who convokes it and who presides. One should be a very skilful caricaturist to succeed in depicting the king to the life, and to give a faithful representation of his cap, ornamented with panther's claws or bordered with wild boar's teeth and surmounted by eagles' plumes, the strange fashion of his collar and of his bracelets, and, above all, to do justice to the startling design of his robe, a chef-d'oeuvre of needle-work, uniting in one gorgeous whole a piece of red velvet, fitted to a vest of sky blue, this again fastened to a bit of carpet and finished off by a silken scarf, pro-

Congo. — Tomb of a Bayanzi chief.

bably torn from the shaft of some European flag; from his girdle hang a tiger-cat skin and little bells which tinkle as he walks. To sum up, the perfect attire of a clown, a veritable rainbow standing out from off the back ground, a black, shining body, of which the following is a pretty fair description : head very large, abundant hair, that a good thrifty housewife would utilize as stuffing for a hair mattress; a wide face, a nose disappearing behind enlarged nostrils; fat cheeks, eyes like loto balls, and artificially darkened with soot; thick lips, showing two rows of teeth sharpened to a point; a chin endowed with the privilege of tripling itself according to the movements of its owner. Behold his Black Majesty.

The king is seated under the shade of a great tree, upon a stool covered with faded velvet taken from some ship's cabin, his feet resting on a leopard's skin. Around him are grouped, in the greatest variety of attitudes, the dignitaries of the royal suite.

When everyone is in his place, the king makes a signal for imposing silence. Then his deputy rises, coughs, and claps his hands three times. The orator begins by setting forth the question for debate; the arguments unfold with a spirit of logical deduction that is really remarkable, sometimes figurative and full of imagination. As he speaks, the orator becomes animated, interrogates with the eye and by the voice, shakes his head and ends inflammatory periods by well calculated outbursts. Briefly, he makes use, though in a somewhat rude manner, of all the means employed by our European orators. The peroration is delivered in a tone that is modulated, insinuating, always full of persuasion. Whilst the minister speaks, opinions are interchanged in a low voice amongst the public, who also permit themselves to make gestures of disapprobation.

As soon as the speech is ended, it is with difficulty an orator of the opposing party can make himself heard as he asks permission to speak. Sometimes the interruptions from both sides become sarcastic or violent: in the end, everyone rises amidst an indescribable uproar.

The decisive moment has come; the chief himself, leaning on an enormous cane, the symbol of his authority, endeavours to quell the tumult, calls for silence, apostrophises the audience, and ends by skilful manoeuvring to bring everyone to his way of thinking. If the resistance continues long, he puts the question of confidence:

"Be it so," he says, with an air of profound discouragement, "you do not wish what is for your own good, you do not listen to the advice of your father; I have nothing further to do here, and I will retire to a distant land."

This rarely fails to produce the desired effect. When the palabre is over, the decision arrived at is made known. Then everyone, delirious with joy, begins to leap, to gambol, to gesticulate, to utter ear-splitting cries.

Let us pass on to a second scene, not less strange, the actor a fetich worshipper or sorcerer physician. But first the attire of this personage deserves to be described. On his head a covering composed of feathers of the chaffinch or of the common hen, on his neck collars of thick grasses, of glass beads and of coral; around the loins a girdle of birds' beaks, joined together by a cord from which are suspended a number of fetiches, or little idols. Further, he ornaments his arms and his legs with small bells, fragments of calabashes and skins of the civet-cat; briefly, a repulsive exterior, but one that is very imposing in the eyes of the superstitious Blacks. Besides this outfit, the fetich-man's disciple carries his infernal baggage: a basket which contains medicaments for the cure of every ill: poisonous herbs, to discover a malefactor; oily plants, to preserve one from cannibal peoples; birds' claws, to make one lucky in the hunting-field; lions' manes, for giving to the warrior a courageous heart; remains of the hibou, for keeping off death; the bone of a buffalo's head, to bring success in hunting elephants; in fine, a hundred little packets, each having a different use.

The fetich priest advances imperiously into the midst of the attentive crowd. After some moments spent in laying out his diabolical stock in trade, he begins by invoking the spirits, and for this end he gives himself up to mummeries, contortions, and songs, accompanied by the most grotesque dancing. Grouped around him, the natives anxiously follow with their eyes the absurd practices of the charlatan. The presence of spirits is soon made known by repeated cries of *hou, hou, hou*, a noise that the juggler produces with the aid of calabashes through which fitting holes have been pierced.

After this introduction, the sorcerer physician proceeds to prepare a special beverage for the sick. Whilst he pounds upon a stone herbs carefully gathered beforehand, his acolyte heats upon the fire a kettle filled with water or with oil. He does not give himself the trouble of questioning the sick man; as he is a sorcerer, he must divine the illness, all the more unnecessary that he should do so, since his medicaments are warranted to cure all diseases. During the time the herbs are boiling, the fetich priest, with his wand, traces around the furnace circle after circle; sometimes he speaks in a low voice, sometimes raises his grimacing face towards the heavens, whilst he assumes the most indescribable attitudes. This farce ended, he seizes the herbs, presses out the juice with the palms of his hands, drinks three mouthfuls of this unqualifying beverage, and gives three to his patient to swallow. If the latter is not cured, then the fault is not with the sorcerer, but with the sick man. If a wound is in question, he prepares a poultice, which is applied to the suffering part. A story was told me how one day, a man having been wounded in the back, the fetich priest ran to him and began rubbing the wounded part with all his strength; none but a negro could bear such friction. Then the

18 *

charlatan, seized with sudden convulsions, rushes upon the injured man, seizes his body in his arms, presses it, and energetically sucks the wound. After some moments, the operator straigthens himself and spits out upon the ground the projectile which had caused the wound. But, O misfortune! it is a bit of copper, whilst the wound had been caused by grains of lead. But this does not cause the juggler to lose his self-possession, and, having received his fee, he retires with as much assurance and dignity as he came, discounting the credulity of the spectators.

The negros, astonished by this strange and manifest jugglery, do not the less continue to place blind confidence in the burlesque science of him whom they call the medicine man. Still, let us not laugh too much at their credulity, for in our own days, and notwithstanding our pretensions as civilized people, men who profess themselves blasés and unbelievers, put faith in the lying declarations of card-cutters and fortune-tellers. These things ought to make us indulgent towards the negros of the Congo. By coming in contact with their gross errors, more than one of us might learn useful lessons.

Since we have spoken of the fetich-man, let us add a word concerning fetiches or idols. We find, it is true, amongst the tribes of the Congo the vague idea of a Supreme Being: this is the Nzambi who, from afar off, presides over the acts of mortals, and who dwells, it appears, somewhere above the clouds. But the negros affirm that He does not concern Himself with the daily life of man. This is why they do not pay Him any special homage: there is nothing to gain by adoring Him. They address their devotions to the little guardian gods, of whom they have one for each important act of their lives.

These idols are generally fashioned from a block of wood, rudely carved in order to give it the appearance of a man or a woman: some of them perhaps reveal a certain artistic feeling, but the greater number are shapeless and often openly indecent. The natives place these fetiches in their huts, hanging them at their doors, and also carrying them about with them. After a while, the exterior forms of the idols disappear under the rags of stuff, morcels of mirrors, plates of iron, which are so many tokens of gratitude. There are even some which resemble hedgehogs on account of the numbers of nails which are driven into them. Here is the explanation:

When a poor person wishes to obtain a favour from an idol, he first makes his request, then, with his thumb he rubs its brow and its breast, in order to awaken its attention and to impress upon its memory the object for which he asks. If the idol remain deaf to his prayer, he drives a nail in the arm or in the leg, that the painful sensation it will cause may prevent it from forgetting his petition. Poor ignorant beings! When shall these silly beliefs disappear? When shall these gross frauds cease? There is but one means: it is civilization through religion.

Let us conclude by a third scene, a burial. When some notable person of the tribe dies, his corpse is placed on a kind of gridiron made of palm-branches, under which is lighted a fire that is fed by scented wood which emits a pungent and thick smoke, so that the corpse is transformed into smoked bacon! Slave women are charged with keeping up the fire; others, provided with small brooms, must keep away the flies. After having thus *smoked* the corpse, it is enveloped in stuff. In certain places, stuff of a red colour envelopes the head, the arms, and the chest of the deceased; blue calico is wrapped around the legs, some fragments of white calico represent the eyes, the nose, the ears and the mouth; thus is formed, as it were, a mannikin, which is exposed in the square in the centre of the village. In other neighbourhoods, the remains are rolled up in an enormous quantity of cotton stuffs: it is calculated that two-thirds of the European stuffs imported into the Lower Congo are employed in the embalming of the dead bodies.

On the day appointed for the funeral, all the members of the tribe make it a duty and a pleasure to attend it. For the occasion, the women have donned their finest attire, and, consequently, they are a little more hideous than usual. A smearing of tar drips from their heads, their brows, and necks, down upon their shoulders and upon the handkerchiefs which serve them as clothing; a circle of red ochre makes their eyes appear as if starting from their heads. Inside the cabin where the corpse lies, a number of women are ranged near the catafalque; crouched low, with their elbows on the ground, their faces supported by their hands, their business is to weep and moan; while some are sobbing aloud, others are tranquilly smoking their pipes and laughing heartily, then, after a while, these latter replace the others and become mourners in their turn. In passing before the corpse, they stop to chant, to dance, and to gesticulate with a simulated grief, their hoarse, strident voices and forced tears being due to libations of palm-wine and the pungent smoke of their pipes: one would fancy he saw a horde of infernal furies. Amongst these women are young mothers who, in their false delirium, shake their unfortunate infants, and it is these infants who utter the only really sad or mournful note that is heard. The men, stationed on the opposite side of the catafalque, yield in nothing to the women; two of them frantically beat the tam-tam, two others ring bells, a fifth blows a trumpet, while a sixth, whom they call the fool and who well deserves this epithet, never ceases posturing and jumping: he shakes like one possessed, throws himself on his back, utters piercing shrieks, as if trying to drown the discordant sounds of the instruments, and strikes himself upon the arms and legs. All this is kept up with such energy that before long the performers are teeming with perspiration.

When all assembled have paid their respects to the deceased, the funeral procession is formed and the body is carried to a neighbouring field, in which it is to be buried. The same deafening noise goes on at the interment, the whole assembly shouting simultaneously. As the cortege advances, a lugubrious and monotonous chant is kept up by some of the professional mourners, whose throats are indefatigable, and the dirge is repeated at random, and without any attempt at unison, by the whole assemblage, to the discordant accompaniment of drums, trumpets, fifes, and tam-tams. This uproar only ceases on arriving at the grave destined to receive the remains, the pit being dug some seven feet deep. Formerly, before burying the deceased, a certain number of women were sacrificed in the grave, but, since the arrival of Europeans, the natives no longer dare to raise these bloody hecatombs; the women now simply gather around the pit and cast in their girdles. When the ceremony is ended, all quietly seat themselves around, smoking and drinking, while the grave-digger fills up the grave. All is not over, however, for amongst the negros there is no festival without a dance. Therefore, at nightfall a musical prelude fills the air with strange harmonies, inviting the inhabitants to gather round the tomb. The leader of the orchestra stands and beats the drum; around him are grouped musicians, blowing into gourds of different forms and sizes and each pierced with two or three holes. At the first notes of the orchestra, the dancers of both sexes range themselves in two circles, each dancer holding in his hand a gourd filled with pebbles or hard grains which he shakes like castanets. The dance opens by the performers advancing, retiring, a step to the right, then to the left, slowly at first, then faster and faster until at last it becomes a perfect whirl. The air is filled with deafening notes and cries; in a cloud of malodorous dust, these creatures, their bodies shining with grease and striped with red paint, whirl, spin round, advance, retire, cross and re-cross. The final galop is a general bacchanalian melée, during which there reigns a horrible babel of cries, tinklings of bells, singing, howling, while the frantic roll of the drum grows quicker and quicker.

. Let us pray, let us pray earnestly for these poor degraded beings, that faith may dispel their sad errors and that religion may lead them to a state of morals more in accordance with the dignity of the human race!

VICARIATE-APOSTOLIC OF TANGANIKA.

Tanganika, in which there are now six hundred Catholics, is situated on the confines of the Belgian Congo. This Vicariate is in the care of the White Fathers, who, with the assistance of the brave Captain Joubert, have been enabled to found a Church that is already flourishing. The Bishop, Mgr. Lechaptois, has considered this an opportune time to call to his aid the White Sisters of Algiers, a congregation which also was founded by the illustrious Cardinal Lavigerie. From the journal of these first Missioner Sisters, we give the following pages to the readers of the *Annals*. They will admire how, sustained by the grace of God and their own zeal, these Sisters have been enabled to brave the fatigues of so long and perilous a journey. With the aid of a map, the readers may follow their route, which, for several months, lay across immense lakes and unexplored deserts.

LETTER FROM A NUN.

THE FIRST MISSIONER SISTERS TO TANGANIKA.

I.

From Zanzibar to Chinde.

IT is the 2nd. September, we embark on board the *Caul*, a first-class English vessel. The island of Zanzibar, with its numerous tall cocoa-nut trees, is soon out of sight. The sea is beautiful; on the 5th., we reach Mozambique.

Here, we are forced to remain for a week. Impossible to find room in any hotel, and Monseigneur Lechaptois was becoming very uneasy on our account when the French Consul offered us apartments at the consulate. Mozambique is a small city of about ten thousand inhabitants, some of whom are Europeans, the greater number of these being Portuguese, the rest of the population consisting of negros and Moors.

To fill up our leisure time, we take walks in the neighbourhood; one day Mgr. Lechaptois brings us to the fortress, to see a chapel where St. Francis Xavier said Mass when passing through this place. Until quite lately, the chalice and crucifix which he used were preserved here, but these sacred relics have been sent to Europe. Another time, we visit the negro and Indian quarters and, what is very rare in Africa, the cleanliness here is remarkable. Among the Indians, the worshippers of the sun are distinguished by their fanaticism. They burn their dead, they eat no animal food, neither do they use milk nor eggs, and they can eat nothing in presence of those who differ from them in faith; if surprised during a meal, they throw away all that is not yet eaten. Each day, at fixed hours, they pray to and prostrate themselves before the sun. What a field would be here for a Missioner!

At last, on the 13th., the Consul announces that the *Wissmann* will leave in the evening.

It being low tide, we are obliged, in order to reach the boats which are to bring us on board, to get into *machillas*, a kind of long chair or hammock, suspended from a thick pole carried on the shoulders of two negros, the Missioners mounting on the negros' backs. This singular embarkment takes place by moonlight. Before long, the water is so deep that our Blacks are obliged to raise the *machillas* above their heads and we are so nicely balanced that it is rather nervous work, but at last we arrive at the boats, safe and sound, and finally embark on board the *Wissmann*, a little German steamer.

Next morning, we touch at Parapat, and as there is a delay of twenty-eight hours, we land, in order to get some relief from our sea-sickness, but here there are no *machillas*, and we have to be content with the strong arms of our bearers, who cross their hands to make a seat. Parapat is situated on a hill, from which there is a splendid view, and the vegetation is luxuriant. We pass through native huts and before long a procession forms at our heels and grows larger at every instant, the natives appearing to be very gentle, but, unfortunately, we can neither speak to them nor understand them; they burst out laughing if they only see us smile, and they do not leave us until the very moment of departure.

There are ten thousand negros here, and not a single Missioner! My God, deign to send labourers for Thy harvest!

It is the evening of the 10th., and we are before Chinde, but cannot land without a pilot, and Chinde can only be entered with a high tide and at certain hours. The sea is rough and, moreover, the entrance to the port always presents certain dangers, on account of the bar. No pilot. The wind is rising, the waves wash over the deck, and we are knocked about like ninepins; thus passes the night. What a night! Great God! what a night!

Six o'clock in the morning, and still no pilot in sight; in vain we search the horizon, everyone is on thorns, for there will be a change of moon to-morrow, and if we do not get into port to-day we cannot land for another fortnight. The hour of the morning tide has already passed; we urge the captain to try and pass the the bar without a pilot.

"Impossible," he says, "we should risk our lives; many a better vessel than this has sunk at that bar; it is scarcely a week since the last was lost. To go in boats is certain death. I see only one thing to be done: it is to take you south to Beira; thence you can return to Mozambique in a large vessel belonging to the Mosambique Company, and then, in a smaller one, you will come back to Chinde, which you cannot now enter sooner than the 15th of October."

What a prospect! Go back to Mozambique, that we were so delighted to leave! and then what a delay and what expense!

Monseigneur endeavours to get the captain at least to bring us back as far as Quilimane, which is less distant than Beira.

"I cannot," he replies, "I could get no coals there, and then I could not reach Beira, where I must positively be in two days; the utmost we can hope for is that we may meet some small steam-boat which might take you on board."

We offer up fervent prayers; three shots are fired: no sign of the pilot. So we must only be resigned; the boat starts.

But what a strange trick the ship plays! Soundings are taken, the officers seem alarmed; what a surprise! we have actually faced round towards the north. Can it be true?

It is a critical moment, for we are almost on the dangerous bar! Our prayers are redoubled.

" God does nothing by halves" says Monseigneur; " We are in!"

And, in fact, we cross the bar, seeing, as we pass, the masts of the foundered vessels, and, as we anchor, the captain says to us in German:

"—Now perhaps you are satisfied; it was with the energy of despair I risked the attempt!"

Still it was impossible to land that evening, so we had to pass the night on the *Wissmann*; but what matter? we were at Chinde, and before daybreak we had transported all our baggage to the *Bruce*, a little English steamer which was to bring us to Zambeze.

II.

From Chinde to Lake Nyassa.

Here we are then, on board the *Bruce*, a little flat-bottomed steamer. Our cabins are raised about two feet above the water, and over the cabins is a little pavilion which serves as chapel and refectory; the rest of the boat being the kitchen and eating places of our black cooks.

At first we sail up the smallest arm of the Zambeze, which is called the Chinde, and before long find ourselves upon the Zambeze proper, a majestic river, tranquil as a great lake.

The country, at first rather flat, grows more picturesque as we advance. There are multitudes of pretty birds; some, as large as thrushes, have the head and neck red and the tail a brilliant green; other little green birds flutter about like large butterflies; farther on are wild ducks, herons with magnificent plumage, and fisher eagles, with blacks bodies and white necks and breasts, said to be more beautiful than the royal eagle itself.

In the English Territory.—The Machillas bearers.

On the 24th. we leave the Portuguese territory and enter the English, halting at Port Herald. It is very curious to see our negros' encampment around which numbers of the natives gather and join our people, all bounding, dancing and singing as they bring up great pieces of burning wood to add to the fire at which all are cooking.

On the 30th. we are afoot before four in the morning and by evening reach Katinga. Here we are lodged in a house built of open reed work, where we are not safe from inquisitive eyes, but in God's care! I may add that it is not without disgust that we lie down to rest, having seen numbers of big lizards crawling up and down the bars of our cage; still we fall asleep lulled by the cries of hyenas, for all day long our eyes were burned by a fiery sun and we are actually dropping from fatigue.

Next day we are to leave at nine o'clock, and are to travel from Blantyre in machillas. The greater number of the carriers go on before, but we are obliged to wait for our machillas-bearers. Here they come at last, ten in number, of all ages, of all colours, of all types, and in most primitive costumes; some carry sticks, some lances, some knives: others have a hare or rabbit-skin hung from the arm; the same variety in hair-dressing: some have their hair cut in the form of a helmet, some wear it in little locks about six inches long and rolled up in straw, others have fine plaits wound around the head, while more have it confined by a comb which serves as an ornament. Each one also carries his own food, which consists of some ears of maize, tied to a stick attached to a piece of iron, on which to roast the corn. Finally, we set out at seven in the evening. It is dark, not a ray of moonlight, and the sirocco blowing. At this season, the natives burn the tall grass in order to manure the soil, so, from place to place along the mountains, are seen huge fires enveloping the neighbourhood in thick smoke through which one fancies he sees a little town, well lighted up and covered with a white coating of snow: a winter landscape with sirocco heat.

Our carriers go gaily through their work, relieving each other frequently, and, by way of keeping up their courage, they sing or scream like veritable savages. From time to time their sweet voices join in chorus, but at other times they imitate the cries of wild beasts or birds. The poor fellows are tired, for they come from a distance, so we have pity on them, and, besides, we ourselves do not ask better than to go part of the way on foot. As we journey on, we pass the camp of the baggage-carriers, some of whom are crouched around the fire, others lie at full length on the ground, wrapped in a piece of stuff. Towards eleven o'clock we halt, our negros light fires and roast their corn, which we share with them, afterwards they fill their gourds with water, and then we once more set out on foot, making two similar halts before sunrise. The night is dark, not even sufficient light to see where to set one's foot, but our negros are most attentive and point out every stone, every inequality in the road.

At last day breaks and the 250 Blacks who surround us salute its advent with sweet songs, executed in perfect harmony.

But the road is becoming hilly, our bearers are eager to reach the station with their burdens and we are obliged once more to mount our *machillas*. Four bearers at a time take the poles and set out running, relieving each other at every moment without interrupting their pace; but the poor burden gets rather a shaking.

Going down hill it is well enough, but going up, the heels are higher than the head, and, besides, a jolt sometimes pitches you against the sides; our good negros do their best to avoid hurting us and are greatly frightened if an accident occurs, but this does not prevent occasional mishaps. At last, at about half-past five in the morning, we reach Mandala, an English station where we are able to rest awhile.

English comfort makes its way even so far as Mandala, at the Equator; fine trees, cotton trees, eucalyptus, gigantic cypresses, make a delicious oasis; a beautiful public garden ornaments the square; there are a number of European dwellings, a market-house, and a Protestant church where service is held four times a day. Alas! that Missioners should expatriate themselves and take so much trouble to disseminate error! and what a sorrow for our Catholic hearts to see ourselves preceded in the apostolate.

A Warm Welcome.—Favourable Dispositions of the Natives.

At last, after eight days' rest, we once more set out on a fine morning, still in our *machillas*.

The Blacks whom we meet on our way are gentle and polite and never fail to salute us, calling us *dona* (a name they give to the Protestant deaconesses) or *fuma* (master). One of them, dressed in a black costume bordered with gold braid, stopped the machillas to salaam before us.

In the evening, we encamp at Matope, and on the following day resume our journey in boats. Three days pass in this way without anything remarkable occurring. On the fourth we enter the great lake Pamalomba, formed by the waters of the Chire. These waters are so limpid that one may count the grains of sand at the bottom and the banks are covered with pretty aquatic plants, especially a species of green rose which would delight a naturalist. In the distance a belt of beautiful mountains forms a semi-circle around us; thousands of birds and ducks of every variety cover the islets and sandbanks, pelicans being especially numerous.

Next day being Sunday Monseigneur celebrates Mass under the tent before the negros are awake.

At six o'clock we are again under weigh for Fort Johnston, where we arrive before mid-day and spend the night, and next morning two boats bring us to Lake Nyassa, where the steamer belonging to the German government awaits us and in which we have been given free passage.

III.

From the Nyassa to Karema.

In our rere the banks of the Chire seem to meet in the form of a semi-circle, from two sides of which rise high chains of mountains in graceful and varied forms. Before us an inland sea stretches interminably and the air is so transparent that the horizon appears boundless. In the midst of this calm and majestic nature our little packet boat glides silently and swiftly over the waves.

On the 25th., we land at Karonga, to the north of Nyanza, and here we are to form a caravan to travel to T'anganika. We have plenty of porters but no *machillas*, so, as Monseigneur urges us to make them, behold us hard at work until ten o'clock at night.

Next morning we set out at six o'clock under a burning sun; from time to time the tall grasses and shrubs strike sharply against us, and sometimes our bearers knock us violently against the trunks of the trees, but these are only the pleasures of travelling.

The feast of All-Saints we celebrate in the midst of the mountains.

At last, on the 2nd. we reach Mambwe, the first Mission station which we meet on our journey. The Missioners hasten forth to receive Monseigneur, and what is our joy to see them accompanied

Congo. — A Chimbeck hut.

by some thirty young girls, very neat and clean and in holiday attire, who hold out their hands to us, saying:

"Yambo, Sister!"

We pass a few days at Mambwe, going about with the children, who long to keep us here. They are all very young and yet some, of them are affianced, and these are known by their fine pearl necklaces. We also visit their houses, where they busy themselves with their housekeeping, while some old women quietly smoke their pipes and look after them.

The environs of Mambwe are infested by lions which commit great ravages; three of them were killed during our stay, for they boldly attacked the labourers in the fields and accidents are of frequent occurrence.

First Sight of Lake Tanganika.—A Halt at Kala.

It was with difficulty that a sufficient number of bearers were got together for our departure, which took place on the 9th. Numbers of the inhabitants have deserted our village on account of the famine, and our poor starving bearers fill our hearts with pity for them.

"*Mama*," they sometimes say, "we are your children; then give us food!"

While Sister Phillipa was suffering from a terrible fever, her bearers twice let her fall on her head. The unfortunate creature who was the cause of this accident was himself utterly exhausted, having eaten nothing for three days. Alas! the famine is not nearly at an end, for clouds of locusts cross our path from time to time, literally darkening the air, and vultures follow in their wake, awaiting their prey.

In other places we pass through beautiful woods and travel across mountains by roads no better than goat paths. From the crest of a mountain we suddenly perceive Tanganika and involuntarily exclaim, as did Stanley on his first journey: "hurrah! Tanganika!"

At last we are at Kala. The bearers, several of whom belong to the place, run before to announce our arrival. Women and children rush out, screaming and rubbing their cheeks with two fingers. Suddenly, a fusilade is heard; it is the Watoto firing a salute in honour of Monseigneur's return, and instantly men, women, and children, some dressed in brilliant stuffs, others covered with skins, some without any clothes, surround us on all sides; the air resounds with the cries of the women, the songs of the men, the noise of fire-arms, and is darkened by clouds of dust raised by the frantic crowd who dance and gesticulate, fire off pistols, and brandish lances, pretending to charge violently upon us, then, with a bound, turning and retreating suddenly. Monseigneur is enveloped in a cloud of smoke from the powder and is dragged by the men across fields and manioc plantations, through which they rush, heedless of pathways, while the women fling themselves upon us with war-like gestures; hatchet in hand, they pretend to be about to smash in our heads, while the infants on their backs, frightened at the scene and violently shaken, mingle their cries with the general harmony. Our first impression is a feeling of terror, but the smiling faces and words of welcome re-assure us. We are conducted by this turbulent crowd to the hill upon which the Mission stands, and presently we are within the enclosure which renders the station a little fortress; here, to the left, is the chapel, to which we at once repair to sing the *Te Deum*.

The present chapel is but a temporary one, and another, twenty-six yards, has just been built. It is constructed of bricks, roofed with tiles, and has a choir and three altars, the interior of the building being divided into beautiful aisles, formed by square pillars. The Missioners had been awaiting Monseigneur's visit in order to have it blessed, so the ceremony took place during our visit, when all the chiefs of the surrounding districts came, at the head of their warriors, to attend the ceremony. These poor people are well disposed, but, the Mission being newly founded, they are yet only catechumens.

The Father Superior told us that it frequently happens that he would have just ended the catechism class in a neighbourhood when the inhabitants of some more distant village would arrive.

"—The instructions are over, my poor children; you have come too late."

"—Father, begin over again, for we come to be instructed."

In order to observe the Sunday strictly and come regularly to the Mission, the negros, not knowing how to count, make knots on a cord as a guide. At the feast of All-Saints, seeing that it also was a holiday, they made additional knots, which so complicated their accounts that they celebrated three Sundays that week.

We remained four days at Kala, during which time ten petty kings of the district came to pay their respects to Monseigneur, and some of them brought their wives, whose hair is so profusely oiled that the grease trickles down their faces and necks. All welcomed us cordially, begging that we would remain here and distribute ourselves amongst their States:

"Five at Karema, and none here; that is badly arranged," they say.

Navigation of the Lake.—Arrival at Karema.—Enthusiastic Reception.—Beginning the Apostleship.

Monseigneur likewise brought us to visit several villages in the neighbourhood, one of which is appropriated altogether to the sick. These are lepers, but differ from other such cases inasmuch as their sores are said to be curable; still, the horrible malady has had many victims, and the sight of the poor creatures is most appalling.

On the 19th. embarkation for Karema.

As we leave, the sea is calm, the night dark, the darkness illumined at every moment by flashes of lightning. Our oarsmen commence praying aloud, invoking the aid of the Blessed Virgin and their guardian angels. Monseigneur's boat has disappeared; we stop, hail, the call is not echoed; seeing a fire in the distance, we steer towards this beacon, but the bark is not there, so we move onward. Towards three o'clock in the morning the storm lulls and we perceive a second light at the end of a bay worn in the rocks. Approaching, we find that this strange illumination is a candle stuck in a hat, and that Monseigneur and a Missioner are here and very uneasy on our account; but God had us in His care. In order to reach the shore we have to board another little canoe hollowed out of the trunk of a tree and full of water, in which, standing, we are with difficulty shoved on by the negros.

The sun is low when we once more start on our journey, rowing the whole night through, and landing on a savage island towards morning. Great black phantoms, moving amongst the rocks, illumine the scene of our disembarkment with torches of grass and wood; one would fancy the spot an opening in hell, but, raising our eyes, we see a cross upon the summit of a rocky peak, and this sacred sign of our redemption makes our hearts bound with joy.

We spend the feast of the Presentation of the Blessed Virgin in this island, and two days later, at three o'clock in the afternoon, after many adventures, we reach Karema.

The Missioners, escorted by the orphans, male and female, and by a crowd of men and women, hasten out to welcome Monseigneur, all kneeling on the shore to receive his blessing, and then we disembark, the negros carrying us, one after the other, in machillas, their astonishment at seeing white women being something marvellous. We start at once for the Mission, followed by some forty orphan girls bearing banners and flags, which to honour us, they hold above our heads, even before our faces, so as almost to blind us.

Going straight to the cathedral, Monseigneur entones the *Te Deum*, whilst our hearts overflow with gratitude.

Having taken a slight repast at the Mission, his Lordship and the Rev. Father Dupont conducts us to our dwelling, which, for the time being, is the old chapel divided into apartments by partitions constructed of bamboos.

At last we are alone, preparing for our night's rest. Numbers of spiders crawl up and down the walls, rats and other little animals are scratching all around and bats fly over our heads; but we did not come all this way to yield to fear, and so we fall asleep, in spite of our numerous visitors.

Two days after our arrival, we open a Refuge to which the catechist brings in thirty infants, whom we clothe, first of all, thus making thirty happy little beings. Three days after, there are forty children in the Refuge, and to-day there are eighty.

We are moved with joy every time we reflect on how God has chosen us to be the instruments through which He is known and loved by all these poor Blacks. We suffer a little, it is true, but not enough to cause you unhappiness on our account; must we not, moreover, win Heaven? and our personal merits are so small!

scholars who formerly came, not to learn religion, but to learn French: at the end of two or three months, finding that they had not succeeded, they took themselves off. Now they come, not to learn French but to be instructed in religion, and already many of them know their prayers and several chapters of the catechism."

Amongst other facts in support of this, Father Suas cites a noble act of fidelity on the part of two young natives living with him.

"A few days," he says, "after the departure of our neighbours for Port Sandwich, and while the earth was still oscillating fearfully, we received a letter. In reading it, I may have shown emotion; I do not know, however that may be the two children were frightened and asked if the letter did not direct us to save ourselves and seek shelter at Port Sandwich. I took advantage of the occasion."

"—Certainly," I said, "this letter tells us to leave; we have been here now two years and hardly anyone comes to school: is it worth our while to expose ourselves to being swallowed up in the volcano?... This settles the matter, we will leave to-morrow morning; you will have Missioners no more."

At this two great tears rolled down little Benjamin's cheeks; he had barely sufficient voice to say:

"Father, I will go with you."

And when, next day, I asked him why he was willing to leave all and come with us, he answered that it was not from fear of the earthquake, but from fear of hell. To be sure, this was not the height of perfection, but it was, at least, the beginning of wisdom.

First Converts.—Nealeguette's Conversion.—Marriage of Thomas.

We ask permission to tell of three neophytes who, each after his own manner, gave edification to this Christian community, so long strangers to grace, and who give promise of becoming fervent apostles.

"At Port Olry," writes the Rev. Father Pionnier, Pro-Vicar of the Mission, "several adult baptisms are soon to take place. One of these, a youth of between thirteen and fourteen years, named Nealeguette, came last month to Mallicolo, along with Father Perthuy who was going to his annual retreat. The opportunity was a favourable one for letting the neighbouring tribes see the interesting ceremony of an adult baptism."

When Father Perthuy asked his young catechumen if he would wish to be baptized in presence of the Missioners who had assembled for their retreat, tears of joy were, at first, his only reply, and the Father had to wait some moments before Nealeguette, deeply moved, was able to reply in a few broken words of joy and hope.

Our retreat was to close on the festival of the Sacred Heart of Mary, and this day was fixed upon for the baptism of our young Santo. The question was, how to surround the administration of the sacrament with proper solemnity?

The only chapel possessed by the Mallicolo Mission at Port Sandwich is a room about five yards square. Within such narrow limits, we cannot even teach catechism on Sundays to our natives, who have to find place, as best they can, under the verandah of the house, so we could not dream of carrying out any ceremony in the chapel. The rich and luxuriant Hebridean vegetation came to our aid.

In a few days a roof was thatched; all around banana trees, crinums (the Oceanian lily), and gigantic scarlet blossomed guillenias formed improvised decorations that would be the envy of the finest Parisian churches (we envied them many another thing! . . .) For carpet, on the bare ground we had plaited palm-leaves. Such was the temple in which Nealeguetto received baptism before the solemn Mass. Moved to tears, the neophyte, who received the name of Francis in baptism, answered the questions of the ritual in Latin, and the Missioners who assisted at the ceremony were struck with the absolutely celestial light that illumined the happy child's sweet and candid countenance.

All the inhabitants of the neighbourhood, assembled to assist at the ceremonial, appeared to be seized with curiosity and, at the same time, to be full of respect and scarce concealed envy. The greatest impression was made when Francis appeared, robed in white, and when he received, as a memorial of his baptism, a pretty rosary, the gift, as was also his white robe, of some generous souls devoted to our Missions.

Kainas's Conversion.—His Baptism.—His Zeal and his Self-Sacrifice.

Nothing could be more touching than the story of Kainas; nothing has so contributed towards awakening at Ambrym the happy movement of grace for which our Fathers are never weary of thanking God.

"Kainas," writes Father Suas, "has spent eighteen years in service at Noumea and is, perhaps, the only native of the New Hebrides who has known how to profit by his contact with civilization."

Not content with learning to speak French, he learned also to read and write it. On returning to Ambrym, instead of going back to Canaque customs, like all the rest of his people, he built himself a house like those of the Europeans and set about making money. But he was of too generous a nature to think of himself alone; the idea of labouring in order to communicate the blessing of the Christian faith to his fellow-countrymen occurred to him and he formed the project of setting up a school.

Without delay, he sought out the Rev. Father Doucere at Port Sandwich, laid his plan before him, and asked for a Missioner and books. Father Doucere encouraged him, gave him reading cards and promised him a Missioner.

Returned to Ambrym, Kainas set to work to prepare the way. One year, two years, three years passed; the Protestant ministers of the neighbourhood did all in their power to win him over, but he remained steadfast, working on, and always hoping for the promised Missioner. Last month, coming from Port Sandwich, an adverse wind caused me to tack towards Porama. Thus I landed at Kainas's very door. His delight at seeing me was great, thinking that I had come to stay. On the contrary, I proposed to him to come himself and spend some months at our residence at the other extremity of the island, there to receive baptism and be thoroughly instructed in religion, in order to be able to teach his fellow-countrymen. He no doubt understood that this was the best means of hastening the arrival of the much longed-for Missioner.

"—Give me only one month," said he, "to put my affairs in order, and come back for me in July."

But an unfortunate mishap was before us.

At the end of June, our boat was smashed to pieces during the night by the Protestants of a neighbouring village. We were obliged to repair her ourselves and, as she was greatly damaged, this took us nearly two months of hard and incessant labour. It was therefore impossible to go for Kainas at the date fixed. God doutless wished to try the patience of the good catechumen. At last, on Friday, 7th of September, Father Jamond set sail in the newly painted boat for the southern coast and, on Sunday the 9th, he returned with Kainas and three children from his village.

We had not to make him wait long; filled with sincere and ardent longing for the grace of baptism, he had himself learned the catechism and the history of the Bible.

Rosary Sunday was the day fixed for the ceremony.

It was the first time that an adult baptism was witnessed in the Island of Ambrym. The natives were not without endeavouring to dissuade him from receiving the sacrament, telling him, over and over again, that baptism would cause his death. They gathered in crowds on the day fixed, in the hopes of seeing their prophecy fulfilled.

The holy water has flowed upon his brow; he lives as before. May this edifying example bear fruit!

We gave him the name of John Baptist, for is he not called upon to fulfil, in his own country, the functions of the precursor while awaiting the much longed-for Missioner?

It was not long after the departure of John Baptist for the southern coast, until we felt the effect of his sojourn in our district. It would seem, as if this were the hour marked by Providence, for the awakening of our poor New Hebridians. In a few days the number of our scholars was prodigiously increased.

It is not men only, as in former times, but women and children, all coming from the surrounding districts to be instructed in religion. The sacred fire is spreading: distant valleys on the western coast are begging of us to build schools for them. Three of these huts are already constructed; may we soon be able to establish catechists in them, for, on account of the distance, our visits can be but rare and of short duration.

On returning to his village, John Baptist Kainas became a zealous and intrepid catechist. In less than three months, he had built an immense school-house and gathered around him a hundred disciples, while on Sundays he brought together as many as five hundred. What Missioner to the New Hebrides will ever have such a congregation!

Unfortunately, John Baptist's health is far from robust, and we fear that the mission which he fills with such ardour may be far beyond his strength. If God should take him, it would be a great trial, for John Baptist is struggling all alone on that coast against the influence of the Protestants.

The following are the words in which Father Suas tells of a visit paid to John Baptist by the Fathers on Thursday, the 8th of January in this year:

"We land and inquire for our dear John Baptist, astonished at not seeing him come to meet us. Alas! he is sick. We hasten to his house, where we find him in a sad state of weakness, the cause of which we soon discover to be want. He is, in fact, in a state of extreme distress. Formerly, the *coprah* trade brought him in some income, but to-day no more *coprah*, no more flour, no more rice, no more tobacco with which to buy cocoa-nuts, in fact, he has scarcely any clothing left. Would it not be our duty to assist him, who has been so entirely devoted to the Mission? and yet we are reduced to a state of utter inability to do so, having barely what will keep ourselves from dying of hunger. The thought of this rends our hearts!

It was a sore trial for us to be obliged to leave our beloved John Baptist without being able to procure any assistance for him, in return for all the bodily strength he has expended, for his entire devotedness and self-sacrifice, in the cause of the establishment of the faith in this region."

GOLDEN JUBILEE
OF HIS EMINENCE
CARDINAL LEDOCHOWSKI,
PREFECT
OF THE SACRED CONGREGATION OF THE PROPAGANDA.

On the 13th July, his Most Reverend Eminence Cardinal Miecislas Ledochowski celebrated his sacerdotal golden jubilee.

We beg to offer, on this solemn occasion, in the name of the Central Councils of the Association of the Propagation of the Faith and of all our readers, our respectful congratulations to the illustrious Prefect of the Sacred Congregation of the Propaganda.

We have not forgotten the flattering welcome accorded to the choice of His Holiness Leo XIII., on the death of the pious and venerated Cardinal Simeoni. Confessor of the faith in Prussian prisons during the reign of the Kulturkampf, the former Archbishop of Posen appeared to the heroic army of Missioners as a model and chief of whom they might justly feel proud. For our own part, we have long been aware of the deep attachment His Eminence feels for our Work; great, therefore, was our joy when, on the very day following his election, he replied to the congratulations of the Councils by a letter from which it gives us pleasure to quote the principal passages.

"It is to you, Gentlemen, I address my first letter after having accepted the charge imposed upon me, for in you I recognize one of the most efficacious auxiliaries of the Church in its great mission, the evangelization of the Universe. From my earliest youth I have loved and admired your Association, and I have ever sought to be associated with you as far as the limits of my power permitted. I should never have dared to think that God would deign to make use of my declining years to draw yet closer, and in such a flattering manner, the bonds which unite me to you..."

Deign then, your Eminence, to accept, on the occasion of your golden jubilee, the expression of our gratitude, of our respect, and of our good wishes. From the most distant end of the earth, apostles and neophytes have addressed to Heaven their prayers for the illustrious chief who directs the apostolic army with such wisdom; we unite our congratulations to the general good wishes. May God spare you long to your devoted Missioners; may He grant you the joy of seeing constant progress in the faith and the Gospel everywhere preached and triumphant.

Ad multos annos!

CHRONICLE OF THE WORK.

The Association of Tens.

We have already several times called the attention of our correspondents to the necessity of increasing the slender resources of our Work by aiding the establishment of Associations of Tens. How many Christians, favoured by fortune and friendly to the idea of civilization by means of the Gospel, would gladly give a pound a year for the greatest of all Catholic works, if only asked to do so!

We are glad to see that our appeals are being attended to. The following letter comes from our respected and zealous correspondent at Venice, Monsieur Morada.

"In the last number of the *Annals*, the formation of Associations of Tens is advocated.

"I have the pleasure of announcing to you that a pious Priest, a member of the Chapter of our ancient Basilica, has already paid in, to the credit of your pious Work, 312 *lire*, a sum equal to twelve *decuries* (1). This generous offering comes from himself and has not been collected from others. During the course of the same year he likewise paid 286 *lire* as his generous donation to the Holy Childhood. This good Priest wishes to remain unknown; therefore, I cannot name him. But I am most anxious that the fact should be made known in the next number of the *Annals*, for the edification and encouragement of all.

"The zealators, all Priest, of the parishes of Venice are working earnestly to attain the much desired object of the Holy Father. I hope that we shall see the fruit of their efforts, as we have wit-

---

(1) About £12 10*s.* 0*d.*

Most rev. MEURIN, archbishop-bishop of Port-Louis.

nessed during the present year. These most worthy Priests have, at the very first request, sent me, as in previous years, one Association of Ten, composed of the Cassinisi Fathers of St. George's, and the Cavanis Fathers of St. Agnes's."

THE MISSIONS CATHOLIQUES and the Almanacs.

Amongst the means calculated to extend our Work, an extension more than ever necessary, by making it known and by calling attention to the labour of the Missioners, we urgently recommend the journal *Les Missions Catholiques* and our two Almanacs.

I.

Thanks to the active, conscientious, and enlightened collaboration of the Missioners, the *Missions Catholiques* holds a high place amongst journals of the present day, and the information contained therein is copied into the principal newspapers of Europe. Moreover the number of readers of the *Bulletin* increases daily; still, we also daily receive letters from new subscribers who express surprise that the journal is not sufficiently known; they urge us to work so as that it shall be more widely diffused for the benefit of the Association, for, now-a-days, they say, the press possesses a power it never had before, and the *Annals of the Work*, while continuing to be the principal organ of the Propagation of the Faith, should be seconded by the *Missions Catholiques*.

Thanks to modern invention, news from the Missions arrive frequently. If the great Work of the apostolate had not a means of publishing news weekly it would be out of date and would only give bi-monthly, in the *Annals*, information already contained in all the weekly religious papers.

We submit these remarks to the consideration of our pious readers, with the announcement that, at the close of the year 1895, the *Missions Catholiques* will publish, amongst other matters, a remarkable paper on Norway, illustrated by fine engravings. The author of this work is the Vicar-Apostolic himself, Mgr. Fallize.

We remind our readers that we forward free, on demand, a specimen number of the *Missions*. Address, M. le Directeur des *Missions Catholiques*, 14, Rue de la Charite, Lyons.

The subscription is 10 francs (8s. 4d.) for France, 12 francs (10s.) for the Postal Union.

II.

We likewise urge our readers to endeavour to increase the circulation of our two Almanacs, the Almanac of the *Missions* and the Little Almanac of the Propagation of the Faith. Through the medium of His Eminence the Cardinal-Prefect of the Propaganda, Rome has expressed a desire that these two publications should be spread throughout the Universe; in families, in schools, in Catholic meeting-places for the working class, etc. We cannot cite higher recommendation than this.

The Almanacs this year will be fully equal to those of former years. For example, in the Large Almanac will appear in the first page an article on Madagascar which M. Jules Simon has kindly contributed, prefacing it with a few generous words in honour of our Work and the end at which it aims.

In our November number we will give fuller details as to these two publications.

Journey to Rome

OF THE DELEGATES OF THE ASSOCIATION OF THE PROPAGATION OF THE FAITH IN MEXICO.

Mgr. Terrien and the Rev. Father Devoucoux, having just returned to Europe after having accomplished their great mission, repaired at once to Rome and were received in special audience by

His Holiness Pope Leo XIII. The Holy Father graciously expressed his gratitude for and entire approval of the enlightened zeal with which, during more than four years, they laboured to increase the resources of the apostolate. He has on more than one occasion manifested his love for the generous Catholics of Mexico who responded to their appeal.

What is done in Mexico should, believes Leo XIII., be repeated not only in the different American Republics, but wherever the Propagation of the Faith is unknown. To establish the Association everywhere, with its Tens and with its special organization should be the care of the Councils at Lyons and Paris. Now that the Holy Father asks considerable sums for the East, yet that his will is that nothing be retrenched from the old Missions; now that, each year, new vicariates needing our aid are founded, it is peculiarly necessary that our resources should be increased and that, in different parts of the globe, we should organize missions such as that of Mgr. Terrien and Father Devoucoux.

We unite our humble expressions of gratitude to the congratulations addressed by the Sovereign Pontiff to our Delegates, and we include the esteemed Father Boutry, who likewise contributed so largely to the success of the mission. He has shared the trouble, it is but just he should also share in the honour.

Letter from the Archbishops and Bishops of Albania

To the Members of the Central Councils of the Association of the Propagation of the Faith,

Being assembled in Council for the welfare of the Albanian Catholic people we consider it as a sacred duty to express our gratitude to the worthy Councils of the Propagation of the Faith for all that this Association has done, and for the many advantages it has procured for our Missions, not alone for the sustenance of our Works, but for their increase.

Since the second provincial council, held in 1871, we have seen, by the grace of God, the Catholic population sensibly augmented; the number of Priests is larger, the number of students in the provincial seminary for the diocese of Albania has increased, and pious and educational establishments are more numerous. Schools have been opened for the youth of both sexes, some of these being in the hands of religious orders. Several churches and presbyteries have been built and others restored; the word of God is preached with success and religion is progressing.

For all these blessings, and for many others besides, we render praise to God, to whom it is due, for from Him comes all good. But we likewise acknowledge our indebtedness to the Association of the Propagation of the Faith, which has assisted us to meet the expenses of the Missioners as well as many other urgent needs. Words fail us to express our deep gratitude.

But there still remains much to be done in order to place these Missions in a flourishing condition, for the clergy are too few to serve all the parishes of each diocese. There are more schools wanting in the villages for the education of youth; several populous centres need churches and presbyteries, while in others the churches want restoration and the clergy are in need of support.

During the Council we examined into all these things: all we can do is to recommend them to the charitable Association of the Propagation of the Faith. We hope that, as in the past, we shall see the subsidies continue to increase, thus enabling us to meet the increased wants of the Missions confided to our care, and which are in need of the principal and indispensable means for carrying on Catholic teaching. Being the nearest to the apostolic See, these Missions should be the most flourishing.

The only return we can make for all your benefits is our gratitude and our prayers, beseeching the Almighty to confer abundant blessings upon the Work of the Propagation of the Faith, upon its Directors and its Benefactors, hoping that this Work may become a gigantic force, ever progressing for the extension of our holy religion.

We remain your humble servants,

✠ Pascal GUERINI, *Archbishop of Scutari, President of the Council.*

✠ Pascal TROSKI, *Archbishop of Scopia.*
✠ Primo BIANCHI, *Archbishop of Durazzo.*
✠ Brother Julius MANFILI, *Titular Bishop of Antigone.*
✠ Brother Nicola MARINI, *Bishop of Pulati.*
✠ Brother Gabriel NEVIANI, *Bishop of Sappa.*
Primo DOCHI, *Abbot of the Mirdites.*
Nicolo STUFOI, *Administrator to the Bishop of Alessio.*

Letter from the Bishops of Japan

To the Members of the Central Councils of the Association of the Propagation of the Faith.

We have just concluded, with a *Te Deum* of thanks, the last session of the Provincial Synod of Tokio, which began on the 28th of April last.

Before separating, the Archbishop of Tokio and his three suffragans, desire to present their united respects and the expression of their gratitude to the worthy Presidents and members of the Central Councils and, through them, to all the zelators and Associates of the beneficent Association of the Propagation of the Faith.

Although we work at a distance from each other, it is none the less true that we all, no matter what course of action we may pursue, constitute but one body, that the same spirit animates us all, and that we are mutually dependent for the realizations of our common desire to advance the reign of God in this world.

We are happy to acknowledge that, as far as it concerns us, if our humble efforts have not been fruitless, we may attribute this, after God, to the co-operation of our generous Benefactors.

The daily bread of the Missioner, the education of native clergy, the support of catechists, the distribution of religious books journeys, charitable institutions, the building of churches, in a word, all that is necessary and useful to us, does not Providence send them to us, gentlemen, through the medium of the Work to which you have devoted yourselves?

Therefore, it is with hearts penetrated with the liveliest gratitude that we invoke abundant blessings from Heaven upon you and upon each of your Associates.

We also earnestly desire that the noble example given by the eldest daughter of the Church should be imitated with a like generosity throughout the entire Catholic world, for there still remains before the apostolate a long road to travel!

God grant that the urgent appeal made for this purpose by the Vicar of Jesus Christ may be responded to by every Christian worthy of the name. If all the faithful understood, as you do, the duty which is incumbent on them of participating in the salvation of their brothers, how eager they would be to end the long years and centuries of darkness and error that weigh so heavily on the peoples confided to our care! Brought face to face with the united efforts of Christianity, the eyes of infidels would be quickly opened to the light of the Gospel.

While awaiting this hour, so ardently desired, kindly continue the aid of your prayers and your alms, and, in return, accept the assurance of our respect, of our grateful remembrance and of our sincere devotion to you in Our Saviour, Jesus Christ.

✠ Peter Maria, *Archbishop of Tokio.*
✠ Julius Alphonsus, *Bishop of Nagasaki.*
✠ Alexander, *Bishop of Hakodate.*
✠ Henry, *Bishop of Osaka.*

NEWS OF THE MISSIONS.

EUROPE.

THE NEW SUPERIOR OF THE SEMINARY OF THE RUE DU BAC.

The Venerable Monsieur Delpech, having filled the office of Superior of the Seminary of Foreign Missions, Paris, during the full term fixed by the rules of the Institute, the Chapter, consisting of the Directors, has nominated to this important place Monsieur Armbruster, formerly a Missioner in Japan and for many years Director of the Seminary, afterwards Superior of the House of the Immaculate Conception, Bel-Air, where the aspirants go through their philosophy course.

The new Superior was born in the diocese of Langres in 1842.

PROGRESS OF CATHOLICISM IN MONTENEGRO.

In 1889, a concordat was concluded between the Holy See and Prince Nicholas of Montenegro. This was a most fortunate arrangement for the future of Catholicism in that country. Since then, the similarity of the views entertained by the Holy See and Prince Nicholas has only become more marked, and Leo XIII. has conceded to the Montenegran Catholics the privilege of making use of the Paleo-slavic liturgy. This is the best means of proving to the faithful of the Greek Church in that country that the difference of their liturgy is not an obstacle to their union with the Catholic Church. Therefore, the Latin tongue will no longer be the liturgic language of the Montenegran Catholics. A missal in the Paleo-slavic language has been printed at Rome, at the expense of the Propaganda, and on the 1st of January, 1895, the first Mass in the Paleo-slavic tongue was celebrated at Antivari with great solemnity by Mgr. Milinowich, Archbishop of Antivari. Monsieur Niegosch Petrovich, President of the Ministerial Council, assisted at this ceremony as the representative of Prince Nicholas.

ASIA.

PERSECUTION AT MADURA.

The Rev. Father Verdier, Superior of the Mission at Trichinopoly, gives the following details of a massacre of Christians which took place at Kalugumalai:

"Kalugumalai is a town of about eight thousand inhabitants. It has a celebrated pagan temple. Palm Sunday this year coincided with the pagan festival of Kalugumalai, when it is estimated that twenty thousand devotees assembled to witness the ceremonies.

"At nine o'clock in the morning the traditional idolatrous procession reached a shed erected by the Missioner before the church to protect the faithful from the burning heat of the sun. The pagans ordered the Christians to destroy the shed in order to give free passage for the car of the idol. The Christians refused, and took refuge in their church. The pagans barricaded the doors and threw lighted torches, saturated with petroleum, upon the roof of palm-leaves.

"In an instant, all was in flames, and it was by unheard-of efforts that the poor Christians succeeded in forcing a passage through the fire.

"The pagans, furious, then attacked the houses of the Christians, situated at some distance. They first pillaged all that came under their hands: corn, garments, cattle, all was carried off...the women were despoiled of the trinkets they wore, and the rioters carried their barbarity so far as to cut off the ears of several.

"A young man that escaped was followed by two pagans who knocked him down and so burned his feet and legs that it seems miraculous that the unfortunate youth survived.

"Almost dying, the poor young man was carried to Palamcottah. As soon as he could speak, he related the horrors of which he had been the victim and the witness. This was providential, for the pagans had so deceived the police and the magistrates as to make them believe that the victims were the culpable parties.

"The Rev. Father Caussanel sent assistance to the neophytes, who had lost everything!"

IMPOSING CEREMONY AT SONTAY.

Monseigneur Geudreau, Vicar-Apostolic of Western Tonquin, came lately from Hanoi to lay the foundation stone of a new church at Sontay, on which occasion the President spoke the following words:

"In the name of the people of Sontay, I thank your Lordship for the congratulations you have been so kind as to express with regard to the aid we have given towards the building of this church; a modest aid, it is true, but we give it with all our hearts...It is, I believe, an act of patriotism to recall, at this great distance from the mother-country, that the first ensign raised in France was the Cross upon the belfry of a Catholic Church. Long live France!"

"These words, which were applauded as they deserved to be," says the *Avenir du Tonkin*, "worthily concluded a ceremony which will certainly produce a good effect upon the native population."

PERSECUTION AT SU-TCHUEN.

A telegram recently announced the imprisonment of Mgr. Dunand, Vicar-Apostolic of Western Su-tchuen, and of Mgr. Chatagnon, Vicar-Apostolic of Southern Su-tchuen. The telegram added that both Missions had been devastated.

The Minister of Foreign Affairs decided to take active measures in favour of the Missioners and Christians who were in danger, and some days after the Superior of the Foreign Missions, Paris, communicated to us the following despatch:

"Paris, 27th June,
"*We have just received the following telegram from Shanghai:* Imperial Edict for the reparation of the Su-tchuen outrages."

This happy news calms the legitimate anxiety on our part for our beloved Missioners of Su-tchuen. Praise be to God and thanks to those in power who have used their influence to obtain this just reparation from China.

AFRICA.

ENCYCLICAL TO THE COPTS.

By a solemn act, His Holiness Pope Leo XIII. has once more expressed his sympathy with the Eastern Churches. On the 17th June, an Encyclical appeared, addressed to the Copts; the following is its general substance.

The Holy Father acknowledges the bonds which have always existed between the Church of Rome and that of Alexandria, founded by Saint Mark, the disciple of Saint Peter. This glorious Church has been sanctified by illustrious Bishops and by the hol hermits of Egypt.

At the conclusion of the Council of Florence, Pope Eugene the IV. re-united the Copts and the Ethiopians. Other Pontiffs have shown the same solicitude for them, and the Papacy has actually provided for their education through the Jesuit foundations and the African Missions of Lyons.

The Pope then addresses himself to the schismatic Copts, calls them his brothers and his sons, praises their good-will towards him and his envoys, and invites them to unity.

The Holy Father finally gives assurance of the preservation of the privileges of the ancient Church of Alexandria, invoking the holy patrons of the country, especially the Holy Family, who were forced to seek shelter in Egypt.

AMERICA.

PROGRESS OF THE FAITH IN PATAGONIA.

The Rev. Father William del Turco, Salesian Missioner, writes from Punta Arenas to the Very Rev. Father Dom Rua, Superior-General of his Congregation:

"I owe deep gratitude to our Superior, Mgr. Fagnano, for the favour which he lately granted me of spending a fortnight with him at Dawson Island.

"A seven hours' sail brought us to our destination. What changes during the year I have been absent! An entire city in embryo has grown up around the Mission; quay, slaughter-houses, bakeries, sheep-fold, dairy, cheese-factory, nothing is wanting. The chapel has been enlarged according to plans prepared by the Rev. Father Barnabe, and now accommodates three hundred persons.

"While the whole population hastened forth to kiss Mgr. Fagnano's hand, the college band, a real brass band, the bandsmen, young Indians, regaled us with a selection of music. In the vestibule of the chapel, one of the older pupils, Sylvester read a well written address of welcome to Monseigneur, and to this succeeded part singing by a musical society formed by Monsieur

Lafranconi. In fine, such a cordial reception could not but deeply touch the venerable Prelate's heart, but what gave him still greater pleasure was to witness the progress made in religion by all these good Indians, only four years ago plunged in the darkness of infidelity and barbarism. Some amongst them approach the sacraments frequently.

" Mgr. Fagnano had the happiness of baptizing several women from Terra del Fuego, who had been prepared for the reception of this great sacrament by the Sisters of our Lady of Succour.

" The fruits of the apostolate amongst the Indians exceed our utmost hopes. The two hundred neophytes of Dawson Island are the first fruits of an abundant harvest. The patience, devotedness and zeal of the Missioners to whom such magnificent results are due, are above all praise. But the field is immense and the necessity for a large number of apostolic labourers is keenly felt. May God deign to multiply the labourers in His vineyard ! "

✠

NECROLOGY.

MONSEIGNEUR MEURIN, S.J.
ARCHBISHOP OF PORT LOUIS.

During a lengthened apostolic career, first in India, then in the principal English islands of the Indian Ocean, this Prelate gave the highest proofs of an ardent and enlightened zeal.

Born in Berlin, on the 23rd of June, 1825, Mgr. Leo Meurin was nominated Titular Bishop of Ascalon and Vicar-Apostolic of Bombay on the 27th March, 1867. Having governed this immense Mission of Western India during twenty years, he was promoted, on the 28th September, 1887, to be Titular Archbishop of Nisibe and was transferred, the following November, to the See of Port Louis, left vacant by the resignation of Mgr. Scarisbrick. We must not forget that in his last Lenten pastoral the deceased addressed a warm appeal in favour of our Work to his clergy and and diocesans.

Mgr. Meurin, who had ample experience of the evil influence produced by the sectarian spirit amongst Christian peoples, was the author of several remarkable works in which he unmasks the aims of the enemies of God and of the Church.

We recommend to the prayers of Missioners and Associates of the Work, Mgr. Count Morandi, Prelate of His Holinesses household, Canon of the Cathedral of Plaisance, and diocesan treasurer of the Association of the Propagation of the Faith.

DEPARTURE OF MISSIONERS.

On the 3rd May, 1895, Mgr. H. A. Fraysse, of the Marists Society, Bishop of Abila, Vicar-Apostolic of New Caledonia and the New Hebrides, embarked at Marseilles on his return journey to his Mission. He was accompanied by the Rev. Fathers John de Fenoyl and Victor Mulsant, of the diocese of Lyons.

CONTENTS:

LETTER FROM HIS HOLINESS POPE LEO XIII. TO THE CENTRAL COUNCILS OF THE PROPAGATION OF THE FAITH. . 257

NORTHERN CHAN-TONG.—*Letter from Mgr. Marchi.*—Image Worshippers.—Li-tchouin-mao and his sword.—A strange adventure.—Tragic death of a Christian widow. 259

BELGIAN CONGO.—*A Missioner's Letter.*—Apostolic life.—Privations and sufferings.—Palabres and fetich worshippers.—A funeral in the Congo. . . . 265

TANGANIKA.—*Letter from a White Sister.*—The first Nuns in Tanganika.—From Zanzibar to Karema by Lake Nyassa.—Incidents of the voyage.—Enthusiastic welcome. 281

NEW HEBRIDES.—*Letter from the Rev. Father Monfat.*—Trials and difficulties.—The volcano at Ambrym.—First converts.—Zeal of Kainas. . . . 294

SACERDOTAL GOLDEN JUBILEE OF HIS EMINENCE CARDINAL LEDOCHOWSKI, PREFECT OF THE PROPAGANDA. . 302

CHRONICLE OF THE WORK. . . . 304

NEWS OF THE MISSIONS. 311

NECROLOGY.—Mgr. Meurin. . . . 317

DEPARTURE OF MISSIONERS. . . . 318

1. Right Rev. Paulus Pellet, vicar apostolic of Benin   R.

IMPORTANT NOTICE.

We have already frequently called the attention of our Associates to the advisableness of making the last payment of their subscriptions before the end of the year to which these subscriptions belong, that is to say, before the 31st of December. This is the practice in all good works, and rightly so, for if we put off to January or February the payment of the annual alms, we are naturally inclined to think that we are making this payment for the current year.

The delay in closing the accounts beyond the time indicated has yet another serious inconvenience, namely, it retards the long and troublesome labour of the annual distribution, the results of which are awaited with legitimate impatience by the heads of the Missions.

Therefore, we think it well to remind all that the month of January is reserved for Diocesan Correspondents, in order to gather in their receipts, and that such of their payments as shall not have reached the Treasurers of the Central Councils at Lyons and Paris by the time appointed, the 31st of January, cannot be entered until the following meeting; after the 20th February, it will not even be possible to insert any corrections in the Balance Sheet.

GENERAL REPORT OF THE RECEIPTS AND EXPENSES

RECEIPTS (1).

Diocese of Europe	6,175,825f.	71c.
— Asia	7,550	23
— Africa	30,553	63
— America	596,151	46
— Oceania	10,083	40
Total Receipts for the year 1894	6,820,164	43
Balance from excess of Receipts over disbursements in the account for the year 1893	1,500	34
TOTAL	6,821,664f.	77c.

---

(1) The editions of the *Annals* actually struck off every second month number 269,550 copies, namely: French, 171,000; Breton, 6,485; English, 11,500; German, 32,500; Spanish, 14,500; Flemish, 6,725; Italian, 19,800; Portuguese, 1,450; Dutch, 2,850; Basque, 650; Polish, 2,050.

In the expenses of publication are comprised the cost of transport, the purchase of paper, the printing and binding of the numbers, the translation into the various languages, and the expense of accessory printing, such as Prospectuses, Pictures, Maps, &c. We may remark that the extension of the Work sometimes necessitates several editions in the same language, either on account of distance or of high custom duty, or for other reasons. Thus, amongst the editions of the *Annals*, there are three in German, two in English.

The product of the sale of the *Annals* and the collections is included in the total receipts of each diocese in which the sale has been effected.

OF THE PROPAGATION OF THE FAITH FOR 1894.

EXPENSES.

Missions of Europe	740,061f.	65c.
— Asia	3,097,973	09
— Africa	1,455,174	45
— America	365,553	75
— Oceania	585,016	40
Expenses of publication of the Annals and other works, in France and foreign countries (1)	328,640	02
Expenses of management in France and abroad (2)	48,401	48
Total Expenses for the year 1894	6,620,820	84
Sum remaining at the disposal of the Holy Father for his Eastern Association	200,000	,,
Excess of Receipts, to be applied as the first disbursements to the Missions in 1895	843	93
TOTAL	6,821,664f.	77c.

(1) See note, page 322.
(2) In the expenses of administration are comprised not only the expenses incurred in France, but also in other countries. This outlay comprises office expenses and rent, the salaries of the employes, and the postage of letters of correspondence both with the dioceses which contribute to the Work by their alms, and with the Missions all over the globe.

The services of the administrators are at all times and everywhere given gratuitously.

We make it our duty to remind our readers that all Benefactors of the Work are especially remembered in the prayers of the Missioners.

REPORT.

The Allocation of alms among the different Missions, for 1894, has been made in the following order:—(The several sums for Masses and donations for special destinations are included in the allocations for the respective Missions).

MISSIONS OF EUROPE.

To the Right Rev. Dr. Fitzgerald, Bishop of Ross (Ireland)	1,000f ,,c.
To the Right Rev. Dr. Deruaz, for the Missions of Lausanne and Geneva	35,000 ,,
To the Right Rev. Dr. Jardinier, Bishop of Sion, for the parishes of Aigle (Switzerland)	1,000 ,,
To the Right Rev. Dr. Battaglia, Bishop of Coire (Switzerland)	7,000 ,,
To the Right Rev. Dr. Egger, Bishop of Saint-Gall (Switzerland)	2,000 ,,
To the Right Rev. Dr. Haas, Bishop of Bâle (Switzerland)	22,000 ,,
To His Eminence Cardinal Krementz, for the Missions of Cologne	5,000 ,,
To the Right Rev. Dr. Korum, for the Missions of the Diocese of Treves	5,000 ,,
To the Right Rev. Dr. Dingelstad, for the Missions of the diocese of Münster	2,000 ,,
To the Right Rev. Dr. Simar, for the Missions of the diocese of Paderborn	28,000 ,,
To the Right Rev. Dr. Hoting, for the Missions of Northern Germany	34,000 ,,
To the Right Rev. Dr. Klein, for the Missions of the diocese of Limbourg	2,000 ,,
To the Right Rev. Dr. Haffner, for the Missions of the diocese of Mayence	2,000 ,,
For the Missions of the diocese of Fulde	2,000 ,,
To the Right Rev. Dr. Sommerwerk, Bishop of Hildesheim	15,000 ,,
To the Right Rev. Dr. Wahl, Vicar-Apostolic of Saxony	4,000 ,,

To His Eminence Cardinal Kopp, for the Missions of Pomerania and Brandenbourg	37,000f. „c.
To the same, for the Missions of the diocese of Breslau	7,000 „
To the Most Rev. Dr. Stablewski, Archbishop of Posen and Gnesen	12,000 „
To the Right Rev. Dr. Thiel, Bishop of Warmia	7,000 „
To the Right Rev. Dr. Von Euch, Prefect-Apostolic of the Missions of Denmark	40,000 „
To the Right Rev. Dr. Bitter, Bishop, Vicar-Apostolic of Sweden	15,000 „
To the Right Rev. Dr. Fallize, Prefect-Apostolic of Norway	28,000 „
To the Right Rev. Dr. Jaquet, Bishop, Vicar-Apostolic of the Moldavia	10,000 „
To the diocese of Bucharest	23,000 „
To the Right Rev. Dr. Doulcet, Bishop of Nicopolis	7,000 „
To the Most Rev. Dr. Stadler, Archbishop of Serajevo	20,000 „
To the Right Rev. Dr. Markovic, Bishop of Banjaluka	5,000 „
To the Most Rev. Dr. Milinovich, Archbishop of Antivari	6,000 „
To the Most Rev. Dr. Guerini, Archbishop of Scutari	4,000 „
To the Right Rev. Dr. Marconi, Bishop of Pulati	2,000 „
To the Right Rev. Dr. Neviani, Bishop of Sappa	1,000 „
To the Right Rev. Dr. Dochi, Abbé of Mirdites	2,000 „
To the Most Rev. Dr. Troksi, Archbishop of Scopia	7,000 „
To the Most Rev. Dr. Bianchi, Archbishop of Durazzo	3,000 „
To the Most Rev. Dr. Mennini, Archbishop, Vicar-Apostolic of Philippopolis	4,000 „
To the Most Rev. Dr. Bonetti, Archbishop, Latin Vicar-Apostolic of Constantinople, for the Brothers' Schools, and for various Works of the Latin Vicariate and Delegation-Apostolic of Constantinople	136,500 „
To the Most Rev. Dr. Azarian, Archbishop, for the Armenian Catholics	59,000 „
For the Missions of the Lazarists at Constantinople, at Salonica, and Monastir, and the establishments of the Sisters of Charity	70,000 „

To the Most Rev. Dr. de Angelis, Archbishop of Athens, for the Apostolic-Delegation of Greece, and for the Sisters	15,000f. „c.
To the Most Rev. Dr. Evangelist Boni, Archbishop of Corfu	11,000 „
To the Most Rev. Dr. Boni, Administrator of Zante	4,000 „
To the Right Rev. Dr. Polito, Bishop of Syra, and for the Sisters	2,500 „
To the Right Rev. Dr. Castelli, Bishop of Tyne, and for the Sisters	3,000 „
To the Very Rev. Father Angelo, of the Mission of Candia	3,000 „
For the Missions of the Society of Jesus at Tyno and at Syra	8,000 „
For the Missions of the Lazarists at Santorin, and for the Sisters of Charity	9,000 „

MISSIONS OF ASIA.

To the Right Rev. Dr. Nicolosi, Bishop of Scio, and for the Sisters	2,000f. „c.
To the Most Rev. Dr. Timoni, Archbishop of Smyrna, for the Brothers and Sisters	29,000 „
For the Missions of the Lazarists at Smyrna, and the establishment of the Sisters of Charity	25,000 „
For the Missions of the Jesuits in Armenia	42,000 „
To the Most Rev. Dr. Altmayer, Archbishop, Delegate-Apostolic of Mesopotamia, Kurdistan, and Armenia Minor	21,000 „
To the same for the United Rites	35,000 „
For the Missions of the Rev. Dominican Fathers of Mesopotamia and Kurdistan	40,000 „
For the Missions of the Rev. Capuchin Fathers in Mesopotamia	24,000 „
For the Missions of the Rev. Carmelite Fathers at Bagdad	7,000 „
To the Most Rev. Dr. Piavi, Latin Patriarch of Jerusalem	44,000 „
For the Greek Seminary of St. Anne of Jerusalem (Mission of the Society of Algerian Missions)	23,000 „

To the Right Rev. Dr. Piavi, for the Island of Cyprus and for the Sisters	3,000f. „c.
To the Right Rev. Dr. Bonfigli, for the Apostolic-Delegation of Syria, and for the different United Rites	58,000 „
To the Right Rev. Dr. Gregory Youssef, Greek Melchite of Damas, by His Holiness Pope Leo. XIII.	100,000 „
For the Missions of the Rev. Capuchin Fathers in Syria	13,000 „
For the Missions of the Rev. Carmelite Fathers in Syria	4,000 „
For the Missions of the Lazarists in Syria, and the establishment of the Sisters of Charity at Beyrouth	46,000 „
For the Missions of the Society of Jesus in Syria	39,000 „
To the Right Rev. Dr. Montety, Delegate-Apostolic of Persia and Missions of the Lazarists	40,000 „
To the Right Rev. Dr. Lasserre, Vicar-Apostolic of the Mission of Aden, and for the Sisters	10,500 „
To the Very Rev. Father Reynders, for the Prefecture-Apostolic of Kashmere and Caffirstan	8,000 „
To the Right Rev. Dr. Pelckman, Bishop of Lahore	4,000 „
To the Prefect-Apostolic of Rajpoutana	9,000 „
To the Right Rev. Dr. Dalhoff, for the Missions dependent on the diocese of Bombay (Mission of the Society of Jesus)	18,000 „
To the Right Rev. Dr. Beiderlinden, Bishop of Poona (Mission of the Society of Jesus)	10,000 „
To the Most Rev. Dr. Goethals, Archbishop, for the Missions dependent on the diocese of Calcutta (Mission of the Society of Jesus)	45,000 „
To the Prefecture-Apostolic of Assam	7,000 „
To Right Rev. Dr. Hurth, Bishop of Dacca	25,000 „
To the Right Rev. Dr. Pozzi, Bishop of Kishnagur (Congregation of Milan)	15,000 „
To the Most Rev. Dr. Melizan, Archbishop of Colombo (Missions of the Oblates of Mary Immaculate)	18,000 „
To the Right Rev. Dr. Joulain, Bishop of Jaffna (Mission of the Oblates of Mary Immaculate)	38,000 „
To the Right Rev. Dr. Pagnani, Bishop of Kandy	5,000 „

For the Missions of the Society of Jesus in Ceylon	8,000f.	,,c.
To the Most Rev. Dr. Colgan, Archbishop of Madras	12,000	,,
To the Right Rev. Dr. Caprotti, Bishop of Hyderabad (Mission of the Cong. of Milan)	16,000	,,
To the Right Rev. Dr. Pelvat, Bishop of Nagpore	15,000	,,
To the Right Rev. Dr. Clerc, Bishop of Vizagapatam	15,000	,,
To the Most Rev. Dr. Gandy, Archbishop of Pondicherry (Cong. of Foreign Missions)	84,778	50
To the Right Rev. Dr. Bardou, Bishop of Coimbatour (Congregation of Foreign Missions)	42,196	50
To the Right Rev. Dr. Kleiner, Bishop of Mysore (Congregation of Foreign Missions)	47,751	50
To the Right Rev. Dr. Barthe, Bishop of Madura (Mission of the Society of Jesus)	74,000	,,
To the Diocese of Mangalore (Mission of the Society of Jesus)	54,000	,,
To the Most Rev. Dr. Mellano, Archbishop of Verapoly	4,000	,,
To the Right Rev. Dr. Ferdinand Ossi, Bishop of Quilon	7,000	,,
To the Right Rev. Dr. Medlycott, Bishop, Vicar-Apostolic of Trichoor	8,000	,,
To the Right Rev. Dr. Lavigne, Bishop, Vicar-Apostolic of Cottayam	8,000	,,
To the Right Rev. Dr. Usse, Bishop, Vicar-Apostolic of Southern Burmah (Congregation of Foreign Missions)	29,926	,,
To the Right Rev. Dr. Roch Tornatore, Vicar-Apostolic of Eastern Burmah (Congregation of Milan)	19,000	,,
To the Right Rev. Dr. Cardot, Vicar-Apostolic of Northern Burmah (Congregation of Foreign Missions)	37,243	,,
To the Right Rev. Dr. Vey, Vicar-Apostolic of Siam (Congregation of Foreign Missions)	47,110	,,
To the Right Rev. Dr. Gasnier, Bishop of Malacca (Congregation of Foreign Missions)	89,418	50
For the College of Pulo-Pinang (Congregation of Foreign Missions)	10,000	,,
For the Procurator of the Congregation of Foreign Missions at Singapore	10,500	,,
To the Vicariate-Apostolic of Cambodia (Cong. of Foreign Missions)	35,941	,,

To the Right Rev. Dr. Caspar, Bishop, Vicar-Apostolic of Northern Cochinchina (Congregation of Foreign Missions)	39,061f. ,,0
To the Right Rev. Dr. Van Camelbeke, Bishop, Vicar-Apostolic of Eastern Cochinchina (Congregation of Foreign Missions)	44,846 ,,
To the Right Rev. Dr. Depierre, Bishop, Vicar-Apostolic of Western Cochinchina (Congregation of Foreign Missions)	65,612 ,,
To the Right Rev. Dr. Colomer, Vicar-Apostolic of Northern Tonquin (Mission of the Rev. Dominican Fathers)	23,000 ,,
To the Right Rev. Dr. Terres, Vicar-Apostolic of Eastern Tonquin (Mission of the Rev. Dominican Fathers)	20,000 ,,
To the Right Rev. Dr. Oñate, Vicar-Apostolic of Central Tonquin (Mission of the Rev. Dominican Fathers)	34,000 ,,
To the Right Rev. Dr. Pineau, Bishop, Vicar-Apostolic of Southern Tonquin (Congregation of Foreign Missions)	44,241 ,,
To the Right Rev. Dr. Gendreau, Bishop, Vicar-Apostolic of Western Tonquin (Congregation of Foreign Missions)	69,021 50
To the Right Rev. Dr. Ramond, Vicariate-Apostolic of Upper Tonquin (Congregation of Foreign Missions)	16,000 ,,
To the Right Rev. Dr. Jackson, Prefect-Apostolic of the Island of Borneo	12,000 ,,
To the Most Rev. Dr. Staal, Archbishop, Vicar-Apostolic of Batavia	8,000 ,,
To the Right Rev. Dr. Sarthou, Bishop, Vicar-Apostolic of Northern Pé-tché-ly (Mission of the Lazarists)	23,000 ,,
To the Right Rev. Dr. Bruguiere, Vicar-Apostolic of Western Pé-tché-ly (Mission of the Lazarists)	22,000 ,,
To the Right Rev. Dr. Bulté Bishop, Vicar-Apostolic of South-Eastern Pé-tché-ly (Mission the Society of Jesus)	23,000 ,,
To the Right Rev. Dr. Scarella, Bishop, Vicar-Apostolic of Northern Ho-Nan (Mission of the Congregation of Milan)	12,000 ,,
To the Right Rev. Dr. Guillon, VicarApostolic of Mandchuria (Cong. of Foreign Missions)	36,302 50

To the Right Rev. Dr. Rutjes, Bishop, Vicar-Apostolic of Eastern Mongolia	30,000f. ,,c.
To the Vicariate-Apostolic of Central Mongolia	29,000 ,,
To the Right Rev. Dr. Hamer, Vicar-Apostolic of Western Mongolia	27,000 ,,
To the Very Rev. Father Van Hoot, Superior of the Mission of Ili	7,000 ,,
To the Right Rev. Dr. Hubert Otto, Vicar-Apostolic of Southern Kan-sou (Belgian Mission)	24,000 ,,
For the Agency of Shang-hai (Belgian Missions)	8,000 ,,
To the Right Rev. Dr. Pagnucci, Bishop, Vicar-Apostolic of Northern Chen-si (Mission of the Franciscan Fathers)	14,000 ,,
To the Right Rev. Dr. Passerini, Vicar-Apostolic of Southern Chen-si	17,000 ,,
To the Right Rev. Dr. Grassi, Bishop, Vicar-Apostolic of Chan-si (Mission of the Franciscan Fathers)	11,000 ,,
To the Right Rev. Dr. Hoffmann, Vicar-Apostolic of Southern Chan-si (Mission of the Franciscan Fathers)	15,000 ,,
To the Right Rev. Dr. Marchi, Bishop, Vicar-Apostolic of Northern Chan-tong (Mission of the Franciscan Fathers)	20,000 ,,
To the Right Rev. Dr. Schang, Vicar-Apostolic of Eastern Chan-tong	11,000 ,,
To the Right Rev. Dr. Anzer, Bishop, Vicar-Apostolic of Southern Chan-tong	21,000 ,,
To the Right Rev. Dr. Reynaud, Bishop, Vicar-Apostolic of Tché-kiang (Mission of the Lazarists)	20,000 ,,
To the Right Rev. Dr. Volonteri, Bishop, Vicar-Apostolic of Southern Ho-nan (Mission of the Congregation of Milan)	15,000 ,,
To the Very Rev. Father Saturnin de la Torre, Pro-Vicar-Apostolic of Northern Hou-nam (Mission of the Augustinian Fathers)	7,000 ,,
To the Right Rev. Dr. Fantosati, Bishop, Vicar-Apostolic of Southern Hou-nam (Mission of the Franciscan Fathers)	10,000 ,,
To the Right Rev. Dr. Carlassare, Bishop, Vicar-Apostolic of Eastern Hou-pé (Mission of the Franciscan Fathers)	15,000 ,,

REPORT. 331

To the same for the Procurator of Han-keou	3,000f. „c.
To the Right Rev. Dr. Banci, Bishop, Vicar-Apostolic of Northern Hou-pé (Mission of the Franciscan Fathers)	14,000 „
To the Right Rev. Dr. Christiaens, Vicar-Apostolic of Southern Hou-pe (Mission of the Franciscan Fathers)	17,000 „
To the Right Rev. Dr. Garnier, Vicar-Apostolic of Kiang-nan	10,000 „
For the Agency of the Congregation of Foreign Missions at Shang-hai	10,500 „
To the Right Rev. Dr. Bray, Bishop, Vicar-Apostolic of Northern Kiang-si (Mission of the Lazarists)	13,000 „
To the Right Rev. Dr. Coqset, Bishop, Vicar-Apostolic of Southern Kiang-si (Mission of the Lazarists)	14,000 „
To the Right Rev. Dr. Vic, Bishop, Vicar-Apostolic of Eastern Kiang-si (Mission of the Lazarists)	21,000 „
To the Right Rev. Dr. Guichard, Bishop, Vicar-Apostolic of Kouy-tcheou (Congregation of Foreign Missions)	42,822 „
To the Right Rev. Dr. Dunand, Bishop, Vicar-Apostolic of Western Su-tchuen (Congregation of Foreign Missions)	43,252 „
To the Right Rev. Dr. Chouvellon, Bishop, Vicar-Apostolic of Eastern Su-tchuen (Congregation of Foreign Missions)	46,779 „
To the Right Rev. Dr. Chatagnon, Bishop, Vicar-Apostolic of Southern Su-tchuen (Cong. of Foreign Missions)	42,052 50
To the Right Rev. Dr. Biet, Bishop, Vicar-Apostolic of Thibet (Congregation of Foreign Missions)	24,533 „
To the Right Rev. Dr. Escoffier, Bishop, Vicar-Apostolic of Yun-nan (Cong. of Foreign Missions)	36,040 „
To the Vicariate-Apostolic of Amoy (Dominican Fathers)	7,000 „
To the Vicariate-Apostolic of Fou-tcheou (Dominican Fathers)	14,000 „
To the Right Rev. Dr. Chouzy, Prefect-Apostolic of the Mission of Kouang-si (Congregation of Foreign Missions)	18,899 „

To the Right Rev. Dr. Chausse, Bishop, Prefect-Apostolic of Kouang-tong and Hai-nan (Cong. of Foreign Missions)	49,801f. „c.
To the Vicariate-Apostolic of Hong-Kong (Mission of the Congregation of Milan)	11,000 „
To the same, for the Italian Missions of China at Hong-Kong	3,000 „
For the Agency of the Congregation of Foreign Missions at Hong-Kong	17,960 „
To the Right Rev. Dr. Mutel, Bishop, Vicar-Apostolic of Corea (Cong. of Foreign Missions)	31,774 „
To the Most Rev. Dr. Osouf, Archbishop of Tokio, Northern Japan (Congregation of Foreign Missions)	38,548 „
To the Right Rev. Dr. Vasselon, Bishop of Osaka, Central Japan (Cong. of (Foreign Missions)	34,313 „
To the Right Rev. Dr. Cousin, Bishop of Nagasaki, Southern Japan (Congregation of Foreign Missions)	37,738 „
To the Right Rev. Dr. Berlioz. Bishop of Hakodate (Japan) (Cong. of Foreign Missions)	30,830 50

MISSIONS OF AFRICA.

To the Most Rev. Dr. Dusserre, Archbishop, for the Missions dependent on the diocese of Algiers	12,000f. „c.
To the same, for the Missions of Kabylia (Mission of the Society of Algerian Missioners)	23,000 „
To the Most Rev. Dr. Toulotte, Archbishop, Vicar-Apostolic of Sahara (Algerian Missioners).	17,000 „
To the Right Rev. Dr. Laferriere, for the Missions depending on the diocese of Constantine	18,000 „
To the Right Rev. Dr. Soubrier, for the Missions depending on the diocese of Oran	15,000 „
To the Most Rev. Dr. Combes, Archbishop, for the diocese of Carthage	20,000 „
Mission of the Franciscan Fathers of Tripoli	9,000 „
To the Most Rev. Dr. Corbelli, Archbishop, Vicar-Apostolic of Egypt, for the Schools of the Brothers and for the Establishment of the Nuns of the Good Shepherd	38,000 „

For the Missions of the Prefecture-Apostolic of the Egyptian Delta (African Missions of Lyons)   21,000f. ,,c.
For the Missions of the Franciscans of Upper Egypt . . . . .   7,000 ,,
For the Missions of the Society of Jesus at Minich   14,000 ,,
For the Missions of the Lazarists at Alexandria in Egypt, and the establishment of the Sisters of Charity . . . . .   20,000 ,,
To the Prefect-Apostolic of Erythree .   16,000 ,,
To the Right Rev. Dr. Taurin, Bishop, Vicar-Apostolic of the Gallas (for the Mission of the Capuchin Fathers) . . . .   16,000 ,,
To the Right Rev. Dr. Hirth, Bishop, Vicar-Apostolic of Southern Victoria Nyanza (Mission of the Society of Algerian Missioners) .   21,780 ,,
To the Right Rev. Dr. Guillermin, Bishop, Vicar-Apostolic of Northern Victoria Nyanza (Mission of the Society of Algerian Missioners)   38,220 ,,
To the Right Rev. Dr. Hanlon, Bishop, Vicar-Apostolic of Upper Nile . . .   10,000 ,,
To the Right Rev. Dr. Roelens, Bishop, Vicar-Apostolic of Upper-Congo (Algerian Missions)   25,000 ,,
To the Right Rev. Dr. Girault, Administrator, Vicar-Apostolic of Ounyanyembe (Mission of the Society of Algerian Missions . .   22,000 ,,
To the Right Rev. Dr. Lechaptois, Bishop, Vicar-Apostolic of Lake Tanganika (for the Mission of the Society of Algerian Missions)   27,000 ,,
For the Mission of Lake Nyassa (Mission of the Society of Algerian Missioners) . .   8,000 ,,
For the Procurator of the Society of Algerian Missioners at Zanzibar . . .   5,000 ,,
To the Right Rev. Dr. Courmont, Bishop, Vicar-Apostolic of Northern Zanzibar (Society of the Sacred Heart of Mary) . . .   36,000 ,,
To the Very Rev. Father Kerr, Superior of the Mission of Upper Zambeze (Mission of the Society of Jesus) . . .   50,000 ,,
To the Right Rev. Dr. Jolivet, Bishop, Vicar-Apostolic of Natal (Mission of the Oblates of Mary Immaculate) . . . .   20,000 ,,
To the Right Rev. Dr. Gaughran, Vicar-Apostolic of the Orange Free States (Mission of the Oblates of Mary Immaculate) . . .   22,000 ,,

To the Very Rev. Father Monginoux, Prefect-Apostolic of Basutoland (Mission of the Oblates of Mary Immaculate) . . .	23,000f. ,,c.
To the Very Rev. Father Schoch, Prefect-Apostolic of the Transvaal (Mission of the Oblates of Mary Immaculate) . . .	20,000 ,,
To the Right Rev. Dr. Strobino, Bishop, Vicar-Apostolic of the Cape (Eastern Province) .	12,000 ,,
To the Right Rev. Dr. Leonard, Vicar-Apostolic of the Cape (Western Province) .	10,000 ,,
To the Very Rev. Father Simon, Prefect-Apostolic of the Mission of the Orange River .	18,000 ,,
To the Very Rev. Father Lecompte, Prefect-Apostolic of the Mission of Cimbebasia (Congregation of the Holy Ghost and of the Sacred Heart of Mary)	18,000 ,,
To the Very Rev. Father Campana, Prefect-Apostolic of Lower Congo (Congregation of the Holy Ghost and the Sacred Heart of Mary)	19,000 ,,
To the Very Rev. Father Huberlant, Pro-Vicar-Apostolic of Belgian Congo . . .	19,000 ,,
To the Rev. Dr. Carrie, Bishop, Vicar-Apostolic of the French Congo (Congregation of the Holy Ghost and the Sacred Heart of Mary) .	21,000 ,,
To the Right Rev. Dr. Augouard, Vicar-Apostolic of Oubanghi (Mission of the Congregation of the Holy Ghost and the Sacred Heart of Mary)	30,000 ,,
To the Right Rev. Dr. Le Roy, Vicar-Apostolic of the Two Guineas (Mission of the Congregation of the Holy Ghost and of the Sacred Heart of Mary) .	33,000 ,,
To the Very Rev. Father Joseph Lutz, Vice-Prefect-Apostolic of Lower Niger (Mission of the Congregation of the Holy Ghost and the Sacred Heart of Mary) . . .	11,000 ,,
For the Mission of Fernando-Po . .	4,000 ,,
To the Very Rev. Father Pallotins, for the Mission of Cameroun	6,000 ,,
To the Right Rev. Dr. Pellet, Bishop, Vicar-Apostolic of the Coast of Benin (African Missions of Lyons)	43,000 ,,
For the Mission of the Upper Niger (African Missions of Lyons)	18,000 ,,
For the Mission of Dahomey (African Missions of Lyons)	18,000 ,,

Mission of the Gold Coast (African Missions of Lyons)	19,000f.	,,c.
For the Mission of Togoland	10,000	,,
To the Very Rev. Father Blanchet, Pro-Vicar-Apostolic of Sierra-Leone (Congregation of the Holy Ghost and of the Sacred Heart of Mary)	19,000	,,
To the Right Rev. Dr. Barthet, Vicar-Apostolic of Senegambia (Mission of the Cong. of the Holy Ghost and of the Sacred Heart of Mary)	49,000	,,
To the Right Rev. Dr. Cazet, Bishop, Vicar-Apostolic of Madagascar (Mission of the Society of Jesus)	108,000	,,
To the Right Rev. Dr. Hudrisier, Vicar-Apostolic of the Seychelle Islands	9,000	,,
For the Missions of the Indians and Chinese in the Isle of Bourbon	3,000	,,
For the Missions of the Indians and Chinese in the diocese of Port Louis (Isle of Mauritius)	3,000	,,

MISSIONS OF AMERICA.

To the Right Rev. Dr. Howley, Vicar-Apostolic of St. George's (Newfoundland)	2,000f.	,,c.
To the Right Rev. Dr. Lorrain, Vicar-Apostolic of Pontiac	2,000	,,
To the Right Rev. Dr. Langevin, Bishop of St. Boniface (Mission of the Oblates of Mary Immaculate)	19,000	,,
To the Right Rev. Dr. Grandin, Bishop of St. Albert (Mission of the Oblates of Mary Immaculate)	33,000	,,
To the Right Rev. Dr. Pascal, Vicar-Apostolic of Saskatchewan (Mission of the Oblates of Mary Immaculate)	28,000	,,
To the Right Rev. Dr. Grouard, Bishop, Vicar-Apostolic of Athabaska-Mackenzie (Mission of the Oblates of Mary Immaculate)	42,000	,,
To the Right Rev. Dr. Durieu, Bishop of New-Westminster (Oblates of Mary Immaculate)	40,000	,,
For the Indian Missions of the Society of Jesus in Canada	10,000	,,
For the Missions of the Society of Jesus in Alaska	15,000	,,

To the Right Rev. Dr. Shanley, Bishop of Jamestown	2,000f.	,,c.
To the Right Rev. Dr. Marty, Bishop of Sioux-Falls (United-States)	2,000	,,
To the Right Rev. Dr. Hennessy, Bishop of Wichita	3,000	,,
For the Missions of the Society of Jesus in the Rocky Mountains	26,000	,,
To the Right Rev. Dr. Bourgade, Vicar-Apostolic of Arizona (United States)	4,000	,,
To the Most Rev. Dr. Chapelle, Archbishop of Santa-Fé (United States)	8,000	,,
To the Right Rev. Dr. Dunne, Bishop of Dallas	8,000	,,
To the Right Rev. Dr. Meerchaert, Vicar-Apostolic of the Indian Territory	15,000	,,
To the Right Rev. Dr. Durier, Bishop of Natchitoches (United States)	6,000	,,
To the Right Rev. Dr. Healin, Bishop of Natchez (United States)	6,000	,,
To the Right Rev. Dr. Naughten, Bishop of Roseau (English Antilles)	10,000	,,
To the Right Rev. Dr. Gordon, Vicar-Apostolic of Jamaica (Mission of the Congregation of the Sacred Heart of Jesus	6,000	,,
To the Right Rev. Dr. Flood, for the Port of Spain	3,000	,,
To the Right Rev. Dr. Joosten, Vicar-Apostolic of Curaçao	12,000	,,
To the Right Rev. Dr. Wulfingh, Vicar-Apostolic of Surinam	20,000	,,
To the Prefecture-Apostolic of Oyapock	5,000	,,
To the Right Rev. Dr. Cagliero, Vicar-Apostolic of Northern Patagonia	6,000	,,
To the Right Rev. Dr. Fagnano, Prefect-Apostolic of Southern Patagonia	12,000	,,

MISSIONS OF OCEANIA.

To the Very Rev. Father Ambroise, Pro-Vicar-Apostolic of Kimberley	4,000f.	,,c.
To the Right Rev. Dr. O'Reilly, Bishop of Port-Augusta (Australia)	5,000	,,
To the Right Rev. Dr. Luck, Bishop of Auckland (New-Zealand)	14,000	,,

GABON. — Market of Libreville

To the Marist Fathers, for the Mission of the Maoris in the dioceses of Wellington and Christchurch (New-Zealand)	20,000f. „c.
To the Most Rev. Dr. Navarre, Archbishop, Vicar-Apostolic of New-Guinea	43,000 „
To the Right Rev. Dr. Couppe, Vicar-Apostolic of New-Pomerania	30,000 „
To the Very Rev. Father Bontemps, for the Mission of Micronesia	22,000 „
To the Procurator of the Fathers of the Sacred Heart of Issoudun in Sydney	6,000 „
To the Right Rev. Dr. Lamaze, Bishop, Vicar-Apostolic of Central Oceania (Mission of the Marist Fathers)	40,000 „
To the same, for the Navigators' Isles	40,000 „
To the Right Rev. Dr. Vidal, Vicar-Apostolic of Fidji Islands (Mission of the Marist Fathers)	68,000 „
To the Right Rev. Dr. Fraysse, Bishop, Vicar-Apostolic of New Caledonia (Mission of the Marist Fathers)	82,000 „
For the Agency of the Marist Fathers at Sydney (Australia)	12,000 „
To the Right Rev. Dr. Verdier, Bishop, Vicar-Apostolic of Mangareva and Tahiti (Mission of the Congregation of the Sacred Hearts)	45,000 „
To the Right Rev. Dr. Ropert, Bishop, Vicar-Apostolic of the Group of the Sandwich Islands (Mission of the Congregation of the Sacred Hearts)	47,000 „
To the Right Rev. Dr. Martin, Vicar-Apostolic of the Marquesas Group (Mission of the Congregation of the Sacred Hearts)	28,000 „

ADDITIONAL GRANTS TO DEFRAY THE MISSIONERS' TRAVELLING EXPENSES.

EUROPE.

To the Vicar-Apostolic of Sweden	300f. „c.
To the Diocese of Nicopolis	150 „
Mission of Lazarists in Santorin	200 „
„ „ Constantinople, Macedonia and Bulgaria	2,300 „
	22

ASIA.

Mission of the Lazarists in Smyrna			700f.	,,c
,,	,,	Capuchins of Mesopotamia	1,400	,,
,,	,,	Carmelites ,,	600	,,
,,	,,	Lazarists in Syria	1,500	,,
To the Delegation-Apostolic of Persia			2,000	,,
To the Diocese of Agra			3,900	,,
To the Prefecture-Apostolic of Bettiah			2,600	,,
To the Diocese of Allahabad			325	,,
,,	,,	Nagpore	1,700	,,
,,	,,	Vizagapatam	2,000	,,
,,	,,	Pondicherry	4,000	,,
,,	,,	Coimbatour	2,000	,,
,,	,,	Mysore	2,000	,,
To the Vicariate-Apostolic of Northern Burmah			2,500	,,
,,	,,	Eastern Burmah	1,000	,,
,,	,,	Southern Burmah	2,500	,,
,,	,,	Siam	2,000	,,
,,	,,	Malacca	500	,,
,,	,,	Cambodia	500	,,
,,	,,	Northern Cochinchina	1,500	,,
,,	,,	Eastern ,,	1,500	,,
,,	,,	Western ,,	1,500	,,
,,	,,	Southern Tonquin	2,500	,,
,,	,,	Western Tonquin	5,000	,,
,,	,,	Northern Tche-ly	2,200	,,
,,	,,	Western Tche-ly	2,000	,,
,,	,,	Northern Ho-nan	2,400	,,
,,	,,	Southern Ho-nan	2,000	,,
,,	,,	Mandchuria	1,000	,,
,,	,,	Eastern Mongolia	2,500	,,
,,	,,	Western Mongolia	2,500	,,
,,	,,	Northern Chen-si	800	,,
,,	,,	Southern Chen-si	1,000	,,
,,	,,	Eastern Chan-Tong	3,800	,,
,,	,,	Tche Kiang	1,800	,,
,,	,,	Eastern Hou-pé	2,800	,,
,,	,,	Southern Hou-pe	3,500	,,
,,	,,	Northern Kiang-si	600	,,
,,	,,	Southern Kiang-si	2,000	,,
,,	,,	Eastern Kiang-si	1,000	,,

To the Vicar.-Apostolic of Kouy-tcheou	2,500f. ,,0.
,, ,, Western Su-tchuen	2,500 ,,
,, ,, Eastern Su-tchuen	2,500 ,,
,, ,, Southern Su-tchuen	2,500 ,,
,, ,, Thibet	2,000 ,,
,, ,, Yun-nan	2,500 ,,
To the Prefecture-Apostolic of Kouang-tong	2,000 ,,
To the Vicariate-Apostolic of Hong-Kong	1,600 ,,
To the Vicar-Apostolic of Corea	1,500 ,,
To the Diocese of Tokio	2,000 ,,
To the Diocese of Osaka	1,500 ,,
To the Diocese of Nagasaki	2,000 ,,
To the Diocese of Hakodate	1,500 ,,

AFRICA.

To the Prefecture-Apostolic of the Egyptian Delta	1,150f. ,,0
Mission of Lazarists in Egypt	700 ,,
To the Vicar.-Apostolic of Soudan	10,000 ,,
,, ,, Upper Congo	6,000 ,,
,, ,, Tanganika	8,000 ,,
,, ,, Upper Nile	20,000 ,,
,, ,, Zanzibar	4,000 ,,
,, ,, Eastern Cape	1,000 ,,
,, ,, Western Cape	5,200 ,,
To the Missions of Cimbebasia and Cunene	700 ,,
To the Prefect.-Apostolic of Lower Congo	600 ,,
,, ,, Belgian Congo	5,500 ,,
,, ,, French Congo	6,700 ,,
,, ,, Oubanghi	6,000 ,,
,, ,, Gaboon	2,900 ,,
To the Prefect-Apostolic of Lower Niger	800 ,,
To the Vicar.-Apostolic of Coast of Benin	9,250 ,,
To the Mission of the Niger	4,250 ,,
,, ,, Dahomey	2,250 ,,
,, ,, Gold Coast	2,750 ,,
To the Vicar.-Apostolic of Sierra Leone	2,400 ,,
,, ,, Senegambia	2,900 ,,
To the Diocese of Port-Victoria	2,200 ,,

AMERICA.

To the Diocese of Green Bay	600f. ,,c.
To the Vicar.-Apostolic of Arizona	2,500 ,,
To the Diocese of Galveston	2,000 ,,
To the Diocese of Goyaz	10,000 ,,
To the Benedictine Fathers of Brazil	2,000 ,,

OCEANIA.

To the Diocese of Wilcannia	1,000f. ,,c.
,, ,, Kimberley	6,000 ,,
To the Dioceses of Wellington and Christchurch	5,000 ,,
To the Diocese of Auckland	1,000 ,,
To the Vicar.-Apostolic of Central Oceania	4,000 ,,
,, ,, Navigators' Islands	6,000 ,,
,, ,, Fidji ,,	9,000 ,,
,, ,, New Caledonia	7,000 ,,
To the Procurator of the Marist Fathers at Sydney	2,000 ,,
To the Vicar.-Apostolic of Tahiti	5,000 ,,

DONATIONS TRANSMITTED TO THE MISSIONS ACCORDING TO THE INTENTIONS OF BENEFACTORS.

Europe	.	.	.	14,111 65 ⎫
Asia	.	.	.	145,248 09 ⎪
Africa	.	.	.	285,924 45 ⎬ 488,754f. 34c.
America	.	.	.	10,453 75 ⎪
Oceania	.	.	.	33,016 40 ⎭

6,243,770f. 34c.

BALANCE SHEET.

GENERAL REPORT OF THE RECEIPTS AND EXPENSES

RECEIPTS (1).

		£	s.	d.
Dioceses of Europe		247,033	0	7
— Asia		302	0	2
— Africa		1,222	3	0
— America		23,846	1	2
— Oceania		403	6	10
Surplus carried from Accounts of 1893		60	0	3
Total		£272,866	12	0

---

(1) The editions of the *Annals* actually struck off every second month number 269,550 copies, namely: French, 171,000; Breton, 6,485; English, 11,500; German, 32,500; Spanish, 14,500; Flemish, 6,725; Italian, 19,800; Portuguese, 1,450; Dutch, 2,850; Basque, 650; Polish, 2,050.

In the expenses of publication are comprised the cost of transport, the purchase of paper, the printing and binding of the numbers, the translation into the various languages, and the expense of accessory printing, such as Prospectuses, Pictures, Maps, &c. We may remark that the extension of the Work sometimes necessitates several editions in the same language, either on account of distance or of high custom duty, or for other reasons. Thus, amongst the editions of the *Annals*, there are three in German, two in English.

The product of the sale of the *Annals* and the collections is included in the total receipts of each diocese in which the sale has been effected.

OF THE PROPAGATION OF THE FAITH FOR 1894.

EXPENSES:

	£	s.	d.
Missions of Europe	29,602	9	8½
— Asia	128,918	18	5
— Africa	58,206	19	11
— America	14,622	3	0
— Oceania	23,400	13	1¼
Charges for publication of the Annals and other prints, in France and abroad (1)	13,145	12	0
Charges for Administration in France and abroad (2)	1,936	1	2
Total Expenses for the year 1894	264,832	16	11
Sum remaining at the disposal of the Holy Father for his Eastern Associations	8,000	0	0
Excess of Receipts, to be applied as the first disbursements for the Missions in 1894	33	15	1
TOTAL	£272,866	12	0

(1) See note, page 342.
(2) In the expenses of administration are comprised not only the expenses incurred in France, but also in other countries. This outlay comprises office expenses and rent, the salaries of the employes, and the postage of letters of correspondence both with the dioceses which contribute to the Work by their alms, and with the Missions all over the globe.

The services of the administrators are at all times and everywhere given gratuitously.

We make it our duty to remind our readers that all Benefactors of the Work are especially remembered in the prayers of the Missioners.

A FEW WORDS
AS TO THE ALLOCATIONS.

EACH year the task of the Central Councils of the Association in the apportioning of the alms received becomes more laborious and more painful: more laborious, because, having only six millions of francs to distribute, while there are just claims for over twenty millions, the Directors are obliged to give three months to a minute examination of those claims, in order to take every precaution that their work shall be accomplished with that impartiality for the exercise of which they are so justly lauded: more painful, because, to Catholic hearts, what pain can compare with that of being obliged to reject petitions coming from those who, in presenting them, have no other end in view than the glory of God. Seeing that the resources of the Association remain stationary, whilst, on the contrary, the Missions each year increase in number, what can be sadder than to be forced to withdraw from Vicariates already in existence, sums which would assist in creating new centres of the apostolate? It is then, above all, dare we say it? that we cast an envious glance at the resources which Protestant England and America place at the disposal of their Missioners. Doubtless, these enormous resources usually end in sterility, as is acknowledged by even the most reliable Protestant travellers, and, if our apostles have not the riches of this world, they have the grace of Heaven, which renders their labours fruitful; but still, God, who raises up in the Catholic Church so much heroic devotion for the distant apostolate, has the right to demand of those who remain in their homes and country, that by their alms they shall aid the apostles. This is why we consider it our duty to urge and to pray again and again; this is why we once more appeal to all the friends of the Church and of civilization, and exhort them to be no longer content with their subscription of a half-penny a week, if they can possibly afford to increase it. This is why we incessantly repeat our request to families and to those favoured by fortune, to take each year the care of at least one Circle of Ten, that is to say, to contribute one pound to the treasury of the Association.

Need we add, in order to give to our humble petition the sanction of the highest authority in the world, that the Holy Father has this year deigned to make a solemn appeal in favour of the Propagation of the Faith. When he applied to us to assist him by large subsidies towards the accomplishment of his grand projects for the East, he asked for greater zeal and generosity on the part of our friends; "for," he said, "in order that existing Missions should in no way suffer by being deprived of any part of the income upon which their support depends, the Bishops cannot too strongly urge the faithful to increase their generosity towards this Work, and to increase it proportionately to our needs."

Our appeal will reach our Associates just as they are making their collections for the current year. Therefore, we cannot better conclude these remarks than by quoting the words of the same Encyclical: "Of a certainty, Catholics will be deeply touched when they learn that nothing could be more pleasing to Us or more useful to the Church than that they should rival each other in their zeal for obtaining the resources necessary to happily accomplish the projects We have formed. May God, whose glory alone is concerned in the diffusion of the name of Christian and in the unity of spiritual faith and government, deign, in His goodness, to bless Our desires, and, as a pledge of the most precious heavenly blessings, We affectionately grant you all the apostolic benediction."

MISSIONS OF ASIA.

VICARIATE-APOSTOLIC OF EASTERN SU-TCHUEN.

In this flourishing Mission of Eastern Su-tchuen, lately threatened with persecution, the Missioners find their first and sweetest reward in the faith and courage of their neophytes. The edifying story which we are about to read, shows us with what noble sentiments the grace of God fills the hearts of His elect. We cannot, without emotion, read of the life and of the death of the humble and heroic Christian of whom Monsieur Provost tells us.

LETTER FROM MONSIEUR PROVOST

To Monseigneur CHOUVELLON, Vicar-Apostolic.

AMONG the faithful in Kouy-fou whom God lately called from this life, I make especial mention of a young neophyte, aged twenty, whose conversion, last years of life, and pious death seem to call for this notice.

The Learned Yang.—A Christian Doctor.—The Designs of Providence Regarding two of Yang's Children.

In the course of the year 1885, an educated pagan, named Yang, quitted the town of Tchangcha, capital of the province of Koulan, his native place; he brought with him his wife and four children, two girls and two boys, and came to settle in Kouy-fou. He had lived there for some time when, through what circumstances I no longer remember, he became the neighbour and tenant of a

Christian doctor, a man well-known in Kouy-fou, where he has gained considerable reputation for understanding the maladies of children. We may add that this good man, whose name is Tchang-Isy-Sang, having for several years fulfilled the functions of *Baptist* for the Association of the Holy Infancy, has never failed, while practising his profession as doctor, his only means of living, to baptize those pagan children whom he considers to be in immediate danger of death. Now, considering the great number of children brought to him, or whom he visits in their homes when they are too sick to be carried to him, Tchang-Isy-Sang baptizes some two or three hundred in a year.

This was not what induced the learned Yang to become the tenant of the Tchang family. Originally from a province in which the preaching of the Gospel has never ceased to encounter obstacles of every kind, since the introduction of Christianity into China, Yang had brought with him to Su-tchuen all the prejudices, the contempt, and the hatred which animated his fellow-countrymen. Finding the rooms which Tchang-Isy-Sang let to him in his house suited his convenience, he came to reside there. He never dreamt of the merciful designs Providence had in store for two of his four children.

The eldest, a boy, was then about eighteen years of age, and his sister, of whom in particular we are about to speak, was sixteen. The learned Yang was most anxious that his eldest son should study all the classics, without a perfect knowledge of which no one in China can win literary degrees. The young sister, who was gifted with rare intellect and a remarkable memory, had, equally, with her brother, profited by the father's lessons, for he was himself his children's teacher.

Having become the neighbours of the Christian family Tchang, it was not long until young Yang and his sister began to listen to the prayers at morning, mid-day, and in the evening, and they soon remarked the religious pictures which ornamented the walls of the principal sitting room in Tchang-Isy-Sang's house. Upon an altar of sculptured and polished wood, an altar of peculiar form and size, they saw certain objects, a crucifix, candlesticks, and a holy water font and rosaries hung from the wall, for Tchang-Isy-Sang and his family were not ashamed to proclaim themselves Christians. All this attracted the attention of our two young pagans, nor did they fail to turn over the leaves of some books placed upon the altar, a catechism and a prayerbook. They longed to carry them to their own apartments and study them at leisure, but what would their parents say? The young people were aware of their aversion to, their hatred of the Christian religion, and so they hid their desire to embrace it.

Yang-eul-mey, as the young girl was named, learned both the prayers and the Christian Doctrine off by heart. If a book proved too large to be hidden under her dress, she studied it secretly, page by page, and thus, in less than a year, she had read by degrees all the books of piety in use amongst the Christians. She always carried home, concealed under her robe, a page, which she returned to the Tchang's when she had read and re-read it several times. She then borrowed a new page, and thus, by such pious contrivances, Yang-eul-mey evaded her mother's observation and baffled her suspicions. As for the learned Yang, he had been for some time absent from Kouy-fou, being for a few months occupied as chancellor or assessor to the mandarin at the Prefecture of Aan-hieu.

The Doctor's Son.—A Pagan Maiden.—Influence of Christian Ceremonials.

Towards the close of the year 1889, death, which was destined to carry off, within a few years, three of Yang's four children, struck its first blow in the Tchang family. Tchang-Isy-Sang had a son, Gabriel, born of a former marriage; he was aged twenty-eight, married, and the father of two children. He was a model of piety and good conduct and was his father's joy.

All the Christians of Kouy-fou, with whom he was most intimate were unanimous in their praises of this young man, whose irreproachable conduct was a striking contrast to the dissipated and only too often corrupt life of pagan society. Yet Gabriel Tchang, so amiable and so beloved, was dying of an incurable malady.

One day, it was early in November, the lad Yang, who had not heard Gabriel's voice for some weeks, saw a palanquin carried into Tchang's courtyard and a stranger, whose features and the colour of whose hair and beard denoted a foreigner alighted. This was the Missioner, Father Besombes, who was then in charge of the district of Kouy-fou, and who came to see the sick youth and hear his confession. The following morning, the Father came again, and Yang-eul-mey remarked yet greater attention for him on the part of the Tchang family than they had shown him on the previous day; they appeared more recollected, more respectful. Two candles were lighted on the altar and all knelt down. The Missioner put on the surplice and stole and then entered the sick room, followed by the family.

The young pagan, who was obliged to observe the greatest care, in order not to awaken her mother's suspicions, remained outside, but she listened to all the prayers, recited in Latin and in Chinese by the Father and by the Christians, paying special attention to the short exhortation addressed by the Priest, in a voice of emotion, to the patient. The latter was about to receive the Blessed Eucharist, the Holy Viaticum, the true Body of Jesus Christ. The young girl already believed in the mystery about to be accomplished so close to where she stood, in the chamber of the dying man, for the salvation of the soul of Gabriel, whom God was so soon to call to Himself. As we have already said, she had secretly learned the Christian doctrine, and the chapter in the catechism concerning the Blessed Eucharist had particularly touched her heart. A few days later, on the day preceding young Tchang's death, the Missioner was seen a third time. He came to administer Extreme Unction to the dying man and to give him a final absolution and plenary indulgence.

All these ceremonies of our holy religion made a profound impression upon the young pagan. Could that religion be false whose ministers were so solicitous for the soul about to leave the body?

The prayers and chaunts of the Ritual which the Christians of Kouy-fou recited for several days beside the body of the deceased, according to the custom in our Missions, are too touching to fail in deeply moving the soul of Yang-eul-mey. Thus, the pious death and the burial of Gabriel Tchang were, for this young pagan in search of the truth, so many means employed by God to strengthen her in the resolution she had already formed of becoming a Christian.

A Year Later.—The Pagan Yang's Two Children.—Recovery and Trials.

Less than a year after the death of Gabriel, the Yang family lost the eldest of their children, the youth of eighteen of whom we spoke as being so well disposed. God would not let a soul perish that, in the midst of paganism and in a family hostile to religion, had preserved a simplicity, uprightness and candour, so rare amongst pagans. Tchang-Isy-Sang, who attended him as his physician, did not fail to speak to him of God, of the soul, of heaven, and of salvation, as soon as he saw that there was danger of death. The doctor found, as he hoped, a docile heart, well prepared for the grace of regeneration. A few days before his death, the young lad received baptism at the hands of Tchang-Isy-Sang, who, we really believe, has saved more souls than bodies during his long career as a physician.

What a consolation for the sister to see her eldest brother die a Christian! How she longed for the day when she might enjoy the same happiness of being baptized. Her wishes were not to remain long unfulfilled.

✠

In 1892, Yang-eul-mey felt herself stricken with the malady which had two years previously, as we have seen, carried off her eldest brother; and a year after a young brother of nine years had succumbed to the same disease, consumption, which was hereditary in the family. Thus, in less than three years, three coffins had been carried out of Tchang's dwelling, and Yang's eldest daughter was apparently soon to rejoin her three young companions who had preceded her to the cemetery.

In the beginning of February, 1891, the patient's state was so serious that doctor Tchang, fully persuaded that she was dying, believed it his duty to baptize her, she having been prepared for a considerable time. Before her illness, she had often expressed a desire to be baptized at the Oratory, in presence of all the Christians, but the suspicions and watchfulness of her parents had made it impossible for her to go to the Missioner.

Become a child of God and of the Church, the young girl, whom we shall henceforth speak of as Marie Yang, contrary to the expectations of all, suddenly found herself restored to the life of the body, as she had just been born to the life of the soul. Before calling her to Himself, God destined her to bear trials and combats. As soon as she was sufficiently restored to make an excursion into town, the young neophyte, under the pretext of visiting a friend and relative of her mother's, succeeded, for the first time, in making one amongst the assemblage of Christians. She came to ask the Missioner to perform the ceremonies of baptism and confirmation. This was towards the end of the month consecrated to Mary.

To the questions on doctrine addressed to her by Father Besombes, she gave the most satisfactory answers, the Christians present at the ceremony being astonished to find this young girl, who had never quitted the house of her idolatrous parents, as well, if not better instructed in the truths of religion than they themselves, who had spent several years at school.

Again in her home, Marie Yang was not long in proving with what strength and courage the Holy Spirit, in the sacrament of confirmation, arms souls for combat and victory.

Yang's daughter was just eighteen years of age. Endowed with all the gifts of nature which the world admires, she could not but attract notice, and a wealthy family in Kouy-fou asked her of her parents. But it is scarcely necessary to add that the young man was a pagan: the learned Yang and his wife would never have consented to marry their daughter to one of those Christians for whom they had only aversion and contempt.

One day, Marie Yang, being in her room, heard her mother and a guest whose voice she recognized, discussing a question which interested the young girl personally. She had discovered and seen through her parents' plans; the moment for speaking had come. To keep silence any longer, would be permitting the Yangs to enter into an engagement which it would be very difficult to break off.

Marie Yang understood this, so, presenting herself suddenly before the stranger, in the presence of her mother, she declared her intentions.

"—Life is short;" said she, "only a few months ago I thought it was at an end for me. How long will it last? ... My mother, as you know, is often ailing. Who would take her place in the household? For this, and other reasons, let us at once put a stop to arrangements which can only end in nothing."

While this was passing, the parent Yang arrived from Aan-hien, not again to return there, the mandarin having been changed. This meant, before long, straitened means, if not poverty for the family, so long as Yang should be without employment. Now, we all know that in China the number of placeless educated men is almost infinite. In this difficulty, the union of their daughter with a rich family would be of the utmost benefit to the Yangs, and here was Marie refusing to marry! A less thing would irritate a father

GABON. — Pahouin woman

reduced to shifts to procure daily bread for his family, besides, they were becoming more and more suspicious of their daughter having become a Christian; her increased intimacy with the Tchang family, especially with the eldest daughter, the prayers which she said kneeling in her room often provoked anger and reprimands. They went so far as to ill-treat, even to beat her, and the blows of the learned Yang, especially when he was drunk with opium, were so violent that they were heard by the neighbours.

Marie bore all without complaint. If her mother wished to drag her before the ancestral tablets and the idols that were erected in the centre of the house, and force her to bow before these superstitious images, and to burn perfumed wood in their honour, the young girl, while avoiding all that could be construed into want of respect, still managed to avoid complying.

Often, after most painful scenes, Marie Yang, lightly crossing the court which separated her room from that of her friend, Rose Tchang, would begin a conversation on subjects totally apart from what had just occurred at her house. If questioned as to what they could not avoid seeing and hearing, she invariably answered " there is nothing the matter; it is all right. Let us talk of something else."

During these daily meetings, the two young girls talked on religious subjects as they worked, and the time passed happily. Thus the good God, witness of what she bore and suffered at home, sent the young Christian consolation in her sorrows and her trials. During the two years that His devout servant lived after her baptism, our Saviour Himself condescended to visit and strengthen her.

Pious Stratagems.—The Blessed Eucharist.—A Holy Death.

Once the Yangs were sure that their daughter had become a Christian, they watched her incessantly. If they did not forbid her intimacy and constant companionship with Rose Tchang, it was because they were under obligations to their Christian neighbours, part of whose house they occupied, though they did not pay the rent too regularly. As for excursions in the town, they were rarer than ever.

To satisfy Marie's piety, whenever, on the eve of a festival, she had been able to evade her mother's watchfulness and go to confession, a Chinese Priest brought the Blessed Sacrament to her at daybreak the following morning. The little silver pyx containing the host hidden under his robe, Father Ouang would affect a graceful air and walk while crossing the courtyard, so that the pagans should never suspect him to be a minister of the God of Heaven, while Tchang-Isy-Sang and his family, each in his way, helped to keep up a complete delusion in the minds of their neighbours as to the position of the stranger and the object of his visit. He was, they would say, a friend going to or coming from Han-Kou, some clerk in a warehouse.

Meanwhile, Marie awaited the Priest in the narrow passage to the rere of Tchang's house, and the Priest, leaving the doctor to continue in his loudest voice, the subject of the bargain in question, arrived, without stole or surplice, at the rendezvous; without holy water or the prayers of the Roman Ritual, he gave Marie the Holy Communion, and then returned to listen to Tchang-Isy-Sang's conversation.

The young Christian, her treasure in her heart, would return to the house and withdraw to her chamber, to make her thanksgiving to the Divine Guest who had visited her.

Thus did Marie Yang, like the Christians of the primitive Church, in the days of the catacombs and the persecutions, receive the Blessed Eucharist many times. One day, during the Octave of Corpus Christi, in the June of 1893, there was a great pagan festival held at Kouy-fou, as well as throughout all China. Marie could not resist so good an opportunity for asking her mother's leave to go into town and look on, from the ramparts above the blue river, at the boat-races, or regattas. The young girl, who really cared but little for these worldly amusements, having paid a short visit to her parents' friends, was carried in her chair through a number of narrow streets, as far as a girls' school, taught by a young Chinese maiden, her godmother. It was near mid-day. As she was fasting, she begged to receive Holy Communion when she had made her confession.

A few months later, we saw her for the last time. Already suffering from the malady which was to end her days, Marie could scarcely walk; her quick breathing and a constant cough showed how serious was her case. No longer doubting that her end was near, she still wore the same calm, joyous look of six months before. She knew that she was soon to die and rejoiced in the thought, thanking Our Lord for it. She dreaded recovery, for what would become of her if, regaining health, her father should go back to Han-Keou, to that immense city of Tchang-Cha, where there is not a single Catholic; she would far rather die at Kouy-fou, and God granted her prayers.

In the first weeks of January of this year, the invalid's state was hopeless. One day doctor Tchang came to beg of us to go and administer the last sacraments to Marie Yang, who might die any day. But there was one great difficulty in the way.

The young girl could no longer take even a few steps without the assistance of her mother and another person. How then was the Priest to gain access to her? Ask her parents' permission? It was not to be thought of. These people, firm in their pagan prejudices and their religious hatred, rather than acknowledge that their ill-treatment and brutality had shortened their daughter's days, attributed her sickness, the recent death of their two boys, all their misfortunes, in fact, to our holy religion.

Still, Marie wished to go to confession and to receive the Holy

Viaticum and Extreme Unction, and her faith suggested to her the following expedient. She begged of her mother to help her to rise, then to support her: "she wanted to go to the other side of the court, to go to her friend Rose Tchang; she would be better there, she said, than in her own room, on her own bed, where she was dying of loneliness." The mother refused; Marie returned to the charge and begged so hard that at last the favour she asked was granted.

Stretched upon the bed of her friend, who was only too happy to give up her couch to her, the sick girl made up her mind not to return home until she should have received the last sacraments. The Chinese Priest came in the evening, and fortunately it was not Father Ouang, whose frequent visits had in the end excited suspicions. His successor, Father Hiong, made his first appearance in the Tchang household. Welcomed as Father Ouang had been, after the pipe and tea, the Priest, seizing a moment when Yangs wife was at the far end of the court, talking with the doctor's wife in a room opening off the street, went to |the dying girl's room, heard her confession, administered the last sacraments and left her, promising to bring the Holy Viaticum in the morning.

Before the hour of rising, always a late hour in winter amongst townsfolk, Father Hiong returned with the Blessed Eucharist. The sick girl, who had spent the night in Rose Chang's room, was ready for this final communion, the last of her life. Having administered the Holy Viaticum, the Priest gave her a plenary indulgence.

Marie Yang had nothing more to wish for. Death might come. Carried to her home, she expired there gently, on the 28th January, invoking the holy names of Jesus and Mary.

MISSIONS OF AFRICA.

VICARIATE-APOSTOLIC OF GABOON.

The Mission of Gaboon, which extends throughout the whole portion of the territory comprised between Cameroun in the north and French Congo in the south, is evangelized by the Fathers of the Holy Ghost, and has Mgr. Le Roy as its Vicar-Apostolic. Above seven thousand natives have been converted; eight churches and ten chapels have been built. The Missioners, twenty-three in number, are assisted in their apostolic labours by numerous coadjutor Brothers, by catechists, and by the Sisters of the Immaculate Conception, Castres.

LETTER FROM THE REV. FATHER MONNIER,

MEMBER OF THE CONGREGATION OF THE HOLY GHOST,

To the Directors of the Propagation of the Faith, Lyons.

FOR the last nine years I have been in the sacred ministry at Gaboon, and for the last five have been stationed at Libreville, the head quarters of the Christians and centre of government for the French Congo; it seems to me, then, that I may speak with at least as much confidence as many travellers who, having passed once through the principal street of the place or assisted at a nocturnal drumming party in a village of doubtful fame, take it upon themselves to speak slightingly of our Christians and of our institutions.

I.—DEPLORABLE CONDITION OF PAGAN WOMEN IN GABOON.

The Spirits and the Idols.

In Gaboon, the woman who wishes to become a convert to Christianity has, as in all pagan countries, to get rid of the superstitions in which she has been reared, and this is the first obstacle to her conversion.

Fetich worship is a veritable idolatry, a veritable homage paid to certain spirits, or to the souls of ancestors, by means of sacrifices and symbols, or superstitious objects. It constitutes a great obstacle to Christianity, especially amongst the negresses.

The female mind is, in fact, the weaker and more timid, and everything in fetichism tends to act upon this weakness, their very ignorance as to the spirits to whom their worship is paid and who are to be feared, as well as all the mystery with which their religion is surrounded increases their superstitious dread. Above the god *Anambye*, who is the creator of all, is the great spirit, *ombwini*, the genius of the village, the house, and the river, who has established his residence, no one knows where, in a tree, in a sacred grove, upon a rock, and there are also the *abambo*, the shades, the spirits of ancestors which are always fluttering about in the midst of the people and who have the ordering of good and evil, storm and sickness. To show respect for them, or to appease their anger, it is necessary to take part in the ceremonies and mysteries performed in their honour by the fetich priest and to wear objects which show devotion to and fear of them. Moreover, no one knows exactly what these fetiches (*simonda*) are; that is the secret of the fetich priest.

There are ashes, wild herbs gathered at certain phases of the moon, parings of nails, hair, bits of bones which were once a part of certain renowned chiefs; all these are enclosed in tigers' claws, in the horns of deer, of antelopes, sometimes merely in a rag, but all, according to the Black, are terrible and endowed with great

The Priestess.

Having such ideas, the men in Gaboon, as in Ogowe, have kept women in servitude, through the fear of certain masks, or figures of *Okukwe* and *Yasi*, whom they are forbidden to name or to look upon under pain of death. Accustomed to these mysteries from infancy, the women end by devoting themselves to the worship, body and soul. They are often themselves the priestesses in the ceremonies, and, when come to a certain age, they would rather die than abandon their fetiches. For a long time to come, this will be a great obstacle to conversion in the interior of the country, amongst the Rungus and certain families in Ogowe and Fernan-Vaz.

I remember catechising a woman for six months; she had one of these fetiches called *mbwiri*. To get the little presents of manioc and dry fish with which I nourished her, she would promise me every day to get rid of it. Her end came, and she had never consented to give it up; the fetich had been her guardian during life, it would be her guardian after death.

Just before my return to France, I went to see another of these persons devoted to the *ndyembe* and the *iloyos*. I had taught her the rosary and I counted on the aid of the Blessed Virgin to convert her. I mentioned baptism. "Ah," said she, "don't you know that this is the first quarter of the moon and that the power of my fetiches increases with her; wait till she is on the wane, perhaps they would go away then and you would find me ready."

Office of the Missioner.

As a rule, no one could form an idea of the power wielded by these superstitions in pagan countries, and it is only little by little they can be overcome. Still, at Libreville we already see the fruit of grace and of the labours of the early Missioners. The cases of refusal of baptism through attachment to fetichism are becoming daily rarer. If they still occur, it is in some *mpindis* or villages of the interior, the special dwellings of some sorcerers, and these are only consulted in cases of sickness, because they possess the secrets of curing.

Social Condition of Women.

A yet more serious obstacle than fetichism, or rather the true obstacle to the regeneration of the pagan woman is her unhappy state in regard to marriage, according to the laws, manners, customs, and traditions of the native tribes.

Throughout the Congo, amongst the tribes of the Mpongive or Myesne race and amongst the Pahouin savages, woman is simply a marketable article. In the various tribes, the value differs, the dowry, or the purchase price varies, the education is more or less gentle or harsh: the result is the same.

Once the property of her husband, be he young or old, comely or deformed, pleasing or repugnant, whether she will or no, the wife is his property for life. It is her parents who make the bargain and hand her over, whether she likes it or not. One thing which proves that their wishes are little consulted is that the customs or laws of certain tribes allow rich women also to purchase, like the men, and with the same privileges, other young girls whom they dispose of as they like, and children, over whom they have the same power.

The Education of Young Women.

Moreover, it is usually at a very early age a young wife is bought. For this it is sufficient to pay the parents the dowry by instalments of salt, tobacco, plates, brandy.

She is left with her mother until she is six or seven years old; she then goes to the family of her intended. Here she is reared as one of the children of the house, and it is sought to inspire her with affection for her future husband and to lead her to share his tastes. She is not ill-treated, but is left at liberty to amuse herself with her dolls and play in the sun with her new brothers and sisters, but she is also taught to assist in the household cares.

Under the tuition of the grandmother, she learns to dry fish, to grind manioc, to dry mango nuts for chocolate, to extract palm-oil from the kernals, to cook her master's meals; she goes fishing, works in the fields, and draws water.

She it is, moreover, who carries the burdens or goes of messages requiring the greatest speed and activity. In the village, it is she who lights her master's pipe and presents it to him on her knees or with a low reverence. When travelling, she carries his umbrella or holds it over him while he takes a sleep in the canoe.

Little by little, she is also initiated into all the secrets of the family religion and is obliged to adopt it and worship their fetiches. At the age of fifteen or twenty, she is the life of all the *ndyembe* dances, or secret ceremonials in which the women consult together to consider what they shall decide upon or do for or against their husbands.

The Marriage and Dowry.—A Base Traffic.

It is about this age that usually takes place the official ceremony of marriage, which ceremony principally consists in the handing over of the marriage portion, and is celebrated by nocturnal dances, to the sound of the tam-tam, to which dances all the friends and relatives of the families are invited.

The fortune varies according to the tribe: amongst the Mpongwes it is two pounds; amongst the Bengas, Bulus, Bakelais, and Bungus it sometimes amounts to eight pounds, twenty pounds, and even thirty-two pounds. Amongst the Pahouins it varies from sixty pounds to eighty pounds.

Besides this, the husband is never done paying. He is obliged to participate in all the happy or sorrowful events of his wife's family by paying his quota, and if he has the misfortune to fail in paying up, the wife at once runs away to her people who keep her until the sum claimed has been obtained. It is further understood that the bargain may be cancelled if there are blows or wounds, or even violation of the laws and customs of the country. Now, cupidity easily induces the parents to invent all sorts of accusations in order to condemn their son-in-law and bring about fresh bargaining.

We may easily imagine the endless palaverings and difficulties, wars, and divorces that these complications bring about. Let us add, however, that in a pagan country, this marriage portion has certain advantages; it is often a guarantee to the parents who are giving up their child for ever to the bondage of a capricious and cruel master.

Sad Effect of these National Laws.

But the odious part, the iniquity of these customs is that the young girl is only an article of traffic for her parents, a plaything, an object of luxury or pleasure for her husband.

As soon as she has been purchased, she has neither soul, nor dignity, nor name, nor country; she is obliged to adopt the manners and religion, the hatreds and affections of her master; during his life, she is his sole wealth, and, at his death, she increases the fortune of his parents, brothers, or cousins, to whom she passes as an inheritance. And yet, the hardness of this condition does not equal the injustice of her lot, from a Christian point of view. For, what is to be done with a child thus sold or promised even before the age of reason? What must become of the souls of these women who find themselves the second, the third, or the tenth wife of these despots, even were she ever so desirous of baptism?

The Story of Augustine.

One day I baptized a woman in danger of death, but death did not come. After her recovery, she was instructed, and for a year succeeded in hiding from her master, whose eighth wife she was.

However, she was found. What was to be done? I tried to make the husband listen to reason: impossible. I addressed myself to the government and only got for answer: "her husband paid for her, and she belongs to him until he shall be paid back her value, if he be willing to receive the price of the fortune he gave for her..."

I had not a farthing...! and, before my eyes, the master carried off by force my unfortunate catechumen, who, the tears in her eyes, struggled and cried: "Ah! Father, pardon, pardon. It is not I, pardon...!"

And what Missioner has not, in his excursions, had to reply to such laments. "Then," say these poor women, "is Heaven not for us? must we go to hell, in spite of ourselves?" And these women learn the rosary and the catechism; they have sometimes the highest sentiments and a strong wish for baptism, but their condition separates them from the Missioner, and he is powerless to deliver them.

Mother and Children.

The consequences of this social state are no less injurious to the children. They belong, in fact, like their mother, to the father only, so that, if the mother separates from her husband she by this act renounces her children. She may rear them up to the age of four or five years, but then they pass over to the paternal family, and they are forbidden to pronounce their mother's name or to go see her. How often are children brought to us at the Mission, with the words: "keep them, but if their mother comes to see them, they must not speak to her, and, above all, they must not accept anything from her, neither food nor clothes.

When they are marriageable, it is likewise the father or grandfather, or, in default of these, the paternal uncle who settles upon the marriage, makes the bargain and receives the dowry. In certain tribes it is the maternal uncle who has this power, but even then the mother is scarcely consulted, if at all.

In general, the wife no more counts in the domestic economy than in the matter of her salvation; her husband, father, or brother settle all for her.

A Deathbed Baptism.

One day I was called on by a Christian to go and baptize a dying woman of the Pahouin tribe. After two hours' walking under an equatorial sun, and by paths which were only such in name, I arrived very tired at the village. The Christian brought me to the house, but on the treshold I was stopped by the dying woman's father and husband: "You shall not baptize her," they said.

She was there before me, lying on the ground on a wretched mat, the signs of death already in her face. "Father," she cried, "do not listen to them. Give me the water which purifies, that I may go to heaven."

I entered then into treaty with my two adversaries, and at the end of an hour I had gained over one, but the other remained obdurate. I went over my arguments again, with still greater emphasis, and at last he yielded, but the first became furious: "No," said he, "you shall not baptize her, for you would cause her death, and I alone am her master."

The dying woman turned on me a supplicating look: "Baptize me, baptize me," she repeated.

I contended no longer but, at a single bound, I was beside her bed and pouring the holy water on her forehead:

"*Marie, ego te baptiso in nomine Patris et Filii,*" but at this moment I was seized round the throat by my two tigers. "*Et Spiritus Sancti,*" I murmured in a low voice, pouring the water over the dying woman, while the whole house was in a state of rage and uproar.

By sheer force of struggling, I at last got free from the strong arms that clasped me: "it is done," said I, "she is baptized."

It is impossible to describe to you the stupefaction, the fright, the fury of my two men; I took advantage of the moment to tell them.

that even if they killed me, it would be all the same, and it would be more to their advantage to win my friendship, so, with the aid of a few presents, we became good friends. I heard that a few days later Marie went to heaven.

Martyrdom in Perspective.

There is not one of our Missioners who has not such facts to relate, who has not tasted or been threatened with the knife under similar circumstances. As soon as there is question of the wife, the whole village is on the watch. This explains why, in our apostolic visitations, we have scarcely anyone attending catechism except men and children. As soon as they see us, the women remain in their homes or hide in the banana plots, contenting themselves with examining our pale faces through the crack of a door or from behind trees.

If we would progress, we must first win the men, and it is only by making a few friends amongst them that we can succeed in gaining the ear of the feminine population also.

I must beg to be excused for having dwelt so long upon this lamentable state of things, but I wish to make it known in its full reality, that we may be more generously assisted to remedy it. In Gaboon, especially, is the real slavery which we have to combat, slavery all the sadder that it has for its victim the feeblest, yet the best element of society, and that, as our venerated Vicar-Apostolic has said, it extends its influence over all that woman can give, her strength, her life, her body, and her soul.

II.—OF THE GOOD ACCOMPLISHED BY THE MISSION.

Progress made at Libreville.

However grave it may be, the evil is not without remedy, and already the good done in our various Missioner centres is a guarantee for the future. To speak of Libreville alone, great progress has already been made; half the population is Christian, and the single fact that I have been able to bring together in a confraternity, around the statue of Saint Anne, more than a hundred women, all faithful to their duties, proves that the Christian spirit already vivifies family life. These women are not to be seen, it is true, abroad in the public streets or in the market-place, but they are scattered through all the villages of Libreville, living by the work of their hands, occupied solely by their household cares.

Would you like to hear a few of their names?

Sketches of Life and Character.

Here is the President of the confraternity of Saint Anne. Mary is old and a widow; until lately, she kept a little shop, her customers being of every class: she is one to whom an unkind word has never been addressed. She hears Mass daily and is a weekly communicant. For the last seven years, she has taken entire charge of two little orphans, whom she adopted from the cradle and whom, through charity, she has ever since fed and supported, like a tender mother. Last year, she gave nearly five hundred francs worth of goods to ransom a little pagan girl and make of her a Christian who, later on, will increase the number of our Christian mothers.

Sophie had eight children, all Christians and occupying good situations under the government and in trade. Each morning she too was to be seen at Mass, and in the evening, especially after the death of one of her sons, she spent several hours in adoration before the Blessed Sacrament, praying for her family. Going to and coming from the fields, her load upon her back, she always had the rosary in her hands, telling her beads, as she said, for her children. She died last year, offering her sufferings to God in union with those of our Lord, and speaking words of counsel to all around.

And that good Madeleine, who lived in the bush, about ten kilometres from Libreville. The year of her death, she came to receive the Holy Communion at Pentecost:

" —Well, Madeleine, when will you come again to see us?"

" —Oh, soon;" said she, "on the feast of the Sacred Heart, for *I still hunger after my God.*"

Alas, she could not come, for the good God called her suddenly to the eternal banquet, on the very morning of the feast of the Sacred Heart.

Who has not seen in the roads about Libreville, our good Thais, with her little basket on her arm, carrying a sisterly alms to the poor in the backwoods, seeking out the sick, preparing the dying to receive Baptism and Extreme Unction?

Clementine Ta chiko imitated her example: through pure devotedness, and without any hope of reward, she has shut herself up with a hospital Sister, to care the lepers, her whole happiness being to see them die a Christian death.

And that young mother, Germaine, to whom I lately administered the last sacraments, and who, dying, the tears in her eyes, but strong in faith, resigned, generous, said to me: "Oh! Father, it is with joy I give my life to God, that He may guard my child and take him into His service, like you!"

Clementine has reared seven children, the eldest of whom is married to a former pupil of the Mission, who rivals his young wife in the practice of his duty. Clementine herself, though living with a husband who has greatly tried her, has never lost patience, never murmured; she found all her strength at the foot of the altar and in the Holy Communion.

One of our young girls, accosted in the street by one of those who ought to give a good example, replied to him:

" —Sir, would you be pleased if anyone said the same thing to your sister, if you had one? Know that I, too, am a young lady."

And abashed and confused, our gentleman passed on.

Needless to continue these examples! Besides, I should fear to make my sketches too personal, although I would gladly cite Pauline, Lucy, Margaret, Adela, Marie-Louise, etc.... These few lines will at least show that, in spite of difficulties, the good work goes on, and may not alone console the Missioner for his labours and trials, but encourage benefactors to continue their alms and their prayers.

And now, if you have no objection, I will say a word as to the means employed by us to win some results.

III.—MEANS EMPLOYED BY THE MISSION TO CONVERT AND SAVE PAGAN WOMEN.

The Sisters of the Immaculate Conception, Castres.

Although every work we undertake tends toward the regeneration of family life, I would particularly point out amongst those which most conduce to that end, the work of the Nuns and our teaching of catechism in the homes. Having come to Gaboon in 1848, to the number of four or five, our Nuns of the Immaculate Conception, Castres, now number twenty, and have three establishments; at Libreville, at Donghila, and Lambarene; we even hope that next year will not end without our seeing them in our stations of Fernan-Vaz and Bata.

In the principal establishment, Libreville, they have from two hundred to two hundred and fifty little girls, whose ages vary from six to seventeen and eighteen; they are divided between a primary school and an industrial school, the one succeeding the other in order to prepare them for household duties. The work is completed by a hospice, where from fifty to sixty sick people are received, and by a dispensary, where medicines are given out and about a hundred persons daily instructed in religion.

Whence come these children?

The young girls in the primary and industrial schools are, for the most part, the free children of those families in Libreville amongst whom the Christian element already dominates, or amongst whom the influence of the Mission has somewhat penetrated, and who begin to understand that woman should be something better than a slave, something more than an article of commerce. The rest are brought from various places by the Missioners, who gather

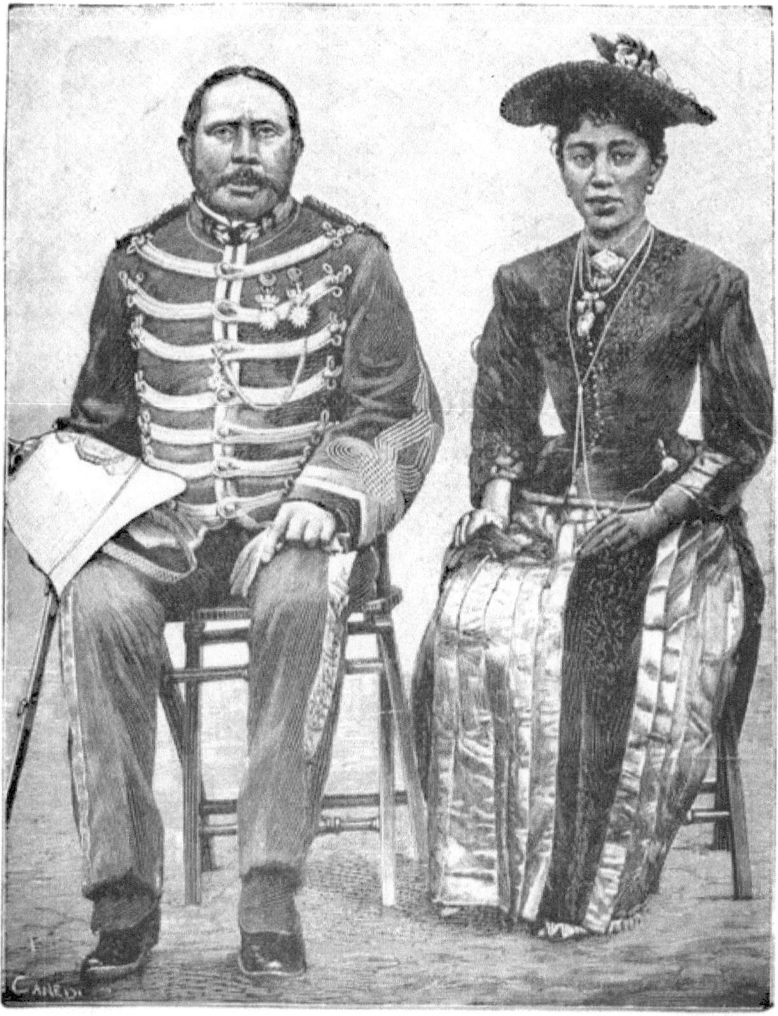

4. MADAGASCAR. — Governor of Tamatave and his Wife H.

them in while on their apostolic visitations, or got them from their parents before they were betrothed, under a formal promise that they should be left free up to the age of eighteen or twenty.

Education under the Sisters.

In the primary, as in the industrial school, the children study and work, the great object never being lost sight of: the forming of good mothers of families. They are therefore not only taught to read and write, but to wash, sew, iron, and cook, to plant and prepare manioc, pistachios, nuts, and ignames.

A proof of the strength of their Christian sentiments is that two of them have aspired to the religious life, and zealously fulfil, along with our European Sisters, their duties as infirmarians and teachers; ten other young girls are preparing to follow their example and, in their little novitiate, are already becoming accustomed to practice the virtues of the religious life.

The Work of the Missioners.

It is unnecessary to add that the Missioners do their utmost to ensure the success of these works. In one station, they have even had the courage to use the means employed by the natives in order to obtain little girls who are not yet affianced. They travel through the country from village to village and when they find one still free, they offer the parents salt, and stuffs, of which the dowry usually consists; they then have the girls reared by the Sisters and, when they have reached a marriageable age, they give them the choice of a husband, who pays the remainder of the marriage portion.

Sister Saint Charles and her Hospital.

One work which has done immense good at Libreville is the hospital with its dispensary, confided to the care of Sister Saint Charles. *Sen Shal*, as the negresses call her, has been thirty-six years at Gaboon, whither she came when scarcely twenty-two years of age, and when everything had to be done and to be begun. At first, as she herself tells, she had much to suffer, but under the firm yet mild direction of Mgr. Le Berre, she soon overcame nature and triumphed over all its repugnances, nothing, in fact, is repellant to her, neither the most purulent sores nor the most repugnant services; for her negresses, she is ready to do anything, is capable of anything. We have seen her for two hours on her knees, the crucifix in her hands, urging the sick to be converted. Her delight is to go to a distance, like the Missioners, seeking for abandoned souls, and then nothing stops her, neither the heat of the sun nor the mud of rivers or marshes: she is never happier than when, on feast days, the good God sends her a poor loathsome leper by way of bouquet.

What she has done for the conversion of poor Gabonese women is incalculable: every year she brings for baptism from forty to fifty aged and infirm adults, whom she alone knows how to find out and instruct, while the number of those whom she brings back into the paths of virtue is still greater. May God leave her long to us and may He inspire charitable souls to send her some alms in aid of her hospital and her dispensary!

The Catechists.

Our catechists also do a great deal towards hastening the conversion of the country and, through this conversion, the regeneration of woman. Amongst these catechists, I would make special mention of king Felix of Denis, and the two brothers, Benjamin and Ernest, of Evendo, in the Gaboon estuary.

Felix Denis Rapontyombo.

Felix is the son of king Denis, who, in 1841, ceded Gaboon to France. Reared, from his childhood, at the Catholic Mission, he has acquired a distinction of language, of carriage, and of manners, very rare amongst his fellow-countrymen. On the death of his father, he succeeded to his rank and power, but, unfortunately, a little unpleasantness which arose between him and a French commandant broke off his connection with Libreville.

However, in 1891, I had the pleasure of meeting him at Denis and of bringing him back into the right course, and now he could not be better disposed towards religion and the Mission. Every day he teaches French and catechism to a dozen little children and is using all his influence to induce his subjects to renounce fetichism for Christianity. Thanks to his influence, I lately baptized his eldest sister, who had hitherto been very obstinate and was the chief support of the pagan party in Denis. Her example will, I hope, induce many others to come over. Felix's great desire is to have a chapel and a Missioner near him; but it is not probable that our means will allow of this so soon.

Ernest Okioma and Benjamin Ogombe.

Ernest and Benjamin are also former pupils of the Mission, who went astray for a time but who have at last come back to the God of their childhood. They are village chieftains, and the comparative wealth which they have acquired by trade gives them influence for good around them. Benjamin's hut has been transformed into an oratory, where prayers are said morning and evening in common; in the afternoon, a little bell calls pagans and Christians to catechism and the rosary, and on Sunday Mass and Vespers are replaced by the singing of canticles, a short instruction, and the rosary.

What joy for the Missioner if he could have everywhere such good and devoted catechists! Unfortunately, all are not so disinterested as our good Ernest and Benjamin; others ask from eight to ten pounds a year, and, whether we will or no, we must count our resources.

In ending this short account of pagan womanhood in Gaboon, and the means employed for her regeneration, I beg of the generous to give a special thought to them and their Missioners. He who aids and succours the apostle, will have the recompense of the apostle.

CHRONICLE OF THE WORK.

INDULGENCES OF THE WORK.

Some of our friends have asked us if we had thought of renewing those indulgences which, according to Pontifical rescript, had lapsed. We hasten to reply, that we could never be guilty of forgetfulness in such a matter; all may therefore feel perfectly secure and continue, without anxiety, to enjoy the spiritual favours granted to the Association.

OUR ALMANACS FOR 1896.

At the same time as this number of the *Annals* reaches our Associates, the two Almanacs sold by the Association of the Propagation of the Faith will be before the public. The aim of these publications is to draw attention to our Work and to gain for it wide-spread sympathy by penetrating, under an attractive and popular form, into schools, families, sodalities, and, in fact, amongst all classes of society. In making known the civilizing work of the Missioners, these little books gain admirers and adherents for the great work of the apostolate; they therefore deserve mention, side by side with the official publications of the Propagation of the Faith: the *Annals* and the *Missions Catholiques*.

In order to give some idea of the variety and interest afforded by the contents of our Almanacs, we give the titles of the principal articles, all published for the first time, all written specially for the publications and enriched with illustrations which are, for the most part, the work of the clever and facile pencil of Monsieur Alexander Guasco, Secretary of the Council, Paris.

LARGE ALMANAC OF THE MISSIONS.

Madagascar, by Monsieur Jules Simon, Member of the French Academy.

The Place of Christianity in the World, by Monseigneur Le Roy, Vicar-Apostolic of Gaboon.

The Solitary Worm, Recitation, by X...

Moko, by M. Baulez, Missioner in Pondicherry.

Christmas amongst the Maoris, by the Rev. Father Cognet, Marist.

The Rolling Plant, by the Rev. Father Jullien, S.J.

Story of Rabah le Fezzani, by the Rev. Father Hacquart, White Fathers.

Letter from a Black Foot to the Black Robe, Poem, by the Rev Father Delaporte.

The Sacraments of Mopoko, by Monseigneur Le Roy.

Quam pulchri super montes, song for baritone, by Monsieur Eymieu.

Chronicle, etc., etc.

In a word, the almanac, which is illustrated with numerous engravings and a splendid chromo, exceeds in beauty and interest those of the preceding years.

LITTLE ALMANAC OF THE PROPAGATION OF THE FAITH.

Between the Bambinos, Poem, by Monsieur Serre.

The Antelope, by Roger Dombre.

Story of Louiset, by Monsieur Baulez.

Lost in the Frost, by Monsieur Durier.

A Lamentable Story, Poem, by the Rev. Father Delaporte.

A Parliamentary Day in Gaboon, by Monseigneur Le Roy.

Golden Locks, by Camille de Saint-Aubin.

Conversion of an old Kabyle Woman, related by a White Sister

Batignolles, Clichy, and Odeon, by Roger Dombre.

The Gloria of the Angels of Infidel Countries, chorus for children.

The Poor Wounded Man, by Monsieur Fourcade, of the Foreign Missions, Paris.

Gaboon Estuary, by Mgr. Le Roy.

Needless to repeat that we beg of our Associates and the Parish Directors of our Association to circulate these books as much as possible.

THE *MISSIONS CATHOLIQUES*.

At the same time that we beg of our Associates to spread, as far as possible, the sale of our two Almanacs, we cannot too strongly recommend to their notice the weekly illustrated journal of the Association, *Les Missions Catholiques*. We thank them sincerely for having already greatly assisted in making it known, and we have fully recognized the value of their assistance; but, in an age when the press has such power, it is important, in order to make a good work known, to circulate, as widely as possible, those journals which chronicle its triumphs and its trials.

We again remind our readers that a specimen number will be sent free. The yearly subscription is 8s. 4d. for France, 10s. for the Postal Union. Address Monsieur le Directeur of the *Missions Catholiques*, 14, Rue de la Charite, Lyons.

MONSIEUR LOUVET'S BOOK.

CATHOLIC MISSIONS IN THE 19TH CENTURY.

We have already acquainted our readers with the flattering reception accorded to this splendid book by the most competent judges and eminent personages. To this unanimous concert of well-merited praise, we are happy to add the following lines, signed with a name which gives them an especial value:

"This is the golden book of the Missions, the greatest propagandist work which the world has produced. From 1822, the date of the foundation, to 1892, that is, in seventy years, the receipts of the Propagation of the Faith have reached a sum of two hundred and seventy millions of francs; the receipts of the 'Holy Childhood,' founded only in 1842, have reached eighty-two millions. The present annual revenues are respectively six millions and a half and three millions and a half. If we add the revenues of the schools of the East and the work for the poor Churches, the total reaches eleven millions of francs. A veritable army of Fathers, Brothers and Nuns assist in the preaching and teaching: 1,000 Fathers of the Foreign Missions, 800 Jesuits, 2,000 Christian Brothers, 4,000 Sisters of Saint Joseph, 2,000 Sisters of Charity, etc. More than a hundred Priests, almost all our compatriots, victims of their Faith, have suffered martyrdom.

"Sometimes the Missioners have been reproached with a narrow and too exclusive spirit; we must not ask from men that which they cannot give. Pioneers of the Gospel, the Fathers trouble themselves little about material interests and sacrifice all to their religious convictions; their kingdom is not of this world. But this does not make them less ardent patriots, and when circumstances demand it, their aid may be relied on...

"Father Louvet's book should be consulted by all who are interested in the spread of colonization.

"LE MYRE DE VILERS."

A magnificent work of six hundred pages and two hundred engravings. Price: paper cover, 15 francs; bound, 25 francs (£1 0s. 0d.). For copies, apply to the *Missions Catholiques*, Rue de la Charite, 14, Lyons. For France, carriage extra: volume in paper cover, 1 franc, 50c. by post; bound volumes, by rail, payable on delivery.

NEWS OF THE MISSIONS.

EUROPE.

MONSEIGNEUR CAZET'S CONFERENCE ON MADAGASCAR.

Mgr. Cazet gave a lecture on Madagascar in the large hall of the Geographical Society, Lyons. Mgr. Couille, Archbishop of Lyons, and a great number of distinguished townspeople were present.

As at Paris, Toulouse, Bordeaux, and everywhere that he spoke, the venerable Bishop held his audience spell-bound by the charm of his eloquence. He spoke as an authority and with an experience of thirty-one years of apostolic work in a country towards which all sympathies turn at present.

The superiority of the Hovas over the Sakalaves, the hospitality and intelligence of these people, their peculiar aptitude for business and for the government of the nation, the prospects of commerce and agriculture after the war, all these questions were treated by the orator in a brilliant conversational style, full of charm, enlivened by a fund of anecdote illustrating the various matters touched upon.

THE CATHEDRAL OF LONDON.

On the 29th June, His Eminence Cardinal Vaughan, Archbishop of Westminster, laid the first stone of the Catholic Cathedral of London.

His Eminence was assisted by the Primate of Ireland, His Eminence Cardinal Logue, Archbishop of Armagh, and by the entire English episcopacy. Three hundred Catholic Priests, and all the Catholic Ambassador saccredited to the English court figured, besides numerous Members of Parliament and the most distinguished Catholics of the United Kingdom.

The new metropolitan Church is situated in the centre of London, in the neighbourhood of the Queen's palace, of the Parliament Houses, of the Ministerial Offices, and of the ancient Abbey in which the Kings of England are crowned, that is to say, in the south-eastern quarter, one of the most beautiful parts of London.

The Cathedral will be 320 feet long, 160 feet wide, and 100 feet high. It will be dedicated to the Precious Blood of Our Lord Jesus Christ.

ICELAND ABOUT TO BE EVANGELIZED.

This large island, which forms part of the kingdom of Denmark, in a few months will be visited by two Missioners from Copenhagen. It is the express desire of Pope Leo XIII. that a Mission should be established in this place, so long neglected by the Catholic apostolate.

The shores only of Iceland are inhabited, the natives being Lutherans. The Danish Mission abandoned this station between twenty-five and thirty years ago, but still possesses a house and wooden church there. There are in Iceland 75,000 inhabitants, divided into one hundred and fifty Lutheran parishes.

ASIA.

END OF THE PERSECUTION IN CHINA.

The journals announce the happy conclusion of affairs in Su-tchuen, even naming the sum granted by the Chinese government as indemnity to the Missions of Western Su-tchuen and Southern Su-tchuen, at the suggestion of Monsieur Gerard, French Minister at Pekin. The sum mentioned in the journals (£160,000), though apparently large, is in reality little enough, for the losses sustained by the Missioners and their numerous flocks during the late persecutions were immense.

Let us now hope that the culprits will be severely punished, for the welfare of all the Missions throughout China is concerned.

NEWS FROM TONQUIN.

Monsieur Frichot, Pro-Vicar of Southern Tonquin, writes:

"I think it well to communicate to you the latest news which I have received by mail. The movement towards conversion becomes more marked, but what obstacles stand in the way! At Kheha, Father Guignard was obliged to defend himself against pirates. The Christians killed four of them and took six living; these latter they delivered up to the Resident, and their chief swore to be revenged for the defeat inflicted on him by the Christians. At Thuong-ich, between seventy and eighty pagans, the mayor at their head, asked to become Christians. Eight days later, the mayor was seized by pirates, and three individuals sent out to seek him have also disappeared.

"At Tri-ban, two hundred households are asking to be instructed in religion. God grant we may not have to put them off indefinitely, for want of funds! I beg the prayers of your pious readers, and some assistance, which must be given to these neophytes, who are obliged, during the time they are under instruction, to abandon the occupations by which they live."

THE SANCTUARY OF SAINT VERONICA AT JERUSALEM.

This church, which is the property of the Melchite Greeks, has been solemnly blessed and opened for public worship by Mgr. Gregory Youssef, Patriarch of Antioch, whose portrait we this year published in the March number of the *Annals*. This church forms the sixth station of the dolorous way, the only one of the fourteen Stations of the Way of the Cross in Jerusalem which had not been already provided with a sanctuary.

AFRICA.

THE COPTIC CHURCH.

The Pontifical Encyclical has drawn public attention to the Coptic people, or rather the Coptic tribe, a name given by the Arabs to the descendants of the ancient Egyptians who remained Christians, and who inhabit the principal towns of Egypt. They speak Arabic, but receive religious instruction in Coptic, and their liturgy is also in that tongue. There are colonies of Copts in Jerusalem and in other localities of the Holy Land, and in these two countries it is computed that there are about two hundred thousand Christians belonging to this Rite; of these nearly twenty thousand belong to the Roman Catholic Church.

The various Coptic stations and Missions in Egypt number thirty, and several of these are exclusively reserved for native Coptic clergy; others have Priests belonging to the Latin Rite and the Coptic Rite.

The Vicariate is at present confided to Mgr. Kobes, a former pupil of the Roman College, and there are twenty-two native Coptic clergy in union with Rome. But there are in the Vicariate Jesuit Fathers, who have flourishing educational establishments at Alexandria and in Cairo, and there are also Franciscans and Priests from the African Missions, Lyons. The Seminary of the Vicariate is under the direction of the Jesuit Fathers.

It is difficult to ascertain the exact number of Copts settled in Egypt, in Palestine, and in the various countries of Asia and Africa. Some compute them at five millions, but we think this number is a great exaggeration. It is certain, however, that in Egypt proper and in the Holy Land there are about 300,000 Copts. We may hope much from these in favour of the union of Churches and of the special interests of Catholicism in the East.

THE NEW VICAR-APOSTOLIC OF BENIN.

The consecration of Mgr. Pellet, Vicar-Apostolic of Benin (of the African Missions, Lyons), took place in the Primatial Church of Lyons, on the 25th August. The consecrating Prelate was his Grace the Archbishop of Lyons, assisted by Mgr. Philippe, Bishop attached to the Society of Missioners, Annecy, and by Mgr. Belmont, Bishop of Clermont, a diocese in which the African Missions have an important apostolic school.

Monseigneur Pellet was born in 1859, at Saint-Jean-de-Bournay (Isere); he belongs, however, if not by birth, at least by his priestly education, to the diocese of Lyons.

Ordained Priest in 1883, he went to Ireland for a year, in order to become familiar with the English language. Appointed to the Missions of the Coast of Benin, he arrived at his post in 1884. It was in this immense district, which comprises a part of Dahomey, that for ten consecutive years he laboured in the severe ministry of the evangelization of the negros. An extraordinarily robust constitution saved him, for the first three years, from the fever of the country, but, little by little, he was forced to pay his tribute to the redoubtable malady. Last year he returned to France in order to recruit his health, when his Superiors placed him at the head of the Novitiate at Sassenage (Isere). The pure mountain air soon repaired the ravages of the African climate, and the intrepid Missioner was about to return to his beloved Mission when he was appointed to be head of that Vicariate in which he has already done such noble work.

OCEANIA.

NECESSITIES OF THE NEW HEBRIDEAN MISSION.

The Rev. Father Jamond, one of the Missioners of this archipelago, makes an urgent appeal to our readers in favour of the sland evangelized by him, and which seems particularly disposed to welcome the Good Tidings:

" Now, more than ever, are we in need of funds. Before long, Ambrym will abjure paganism. To respond to this consoling movement, we must have catechists. We could find families who would come and settle near our residence, if we had the means of supporting them. We divided with two families of future catechists the small sum allotted to us, and now, in the middle of the year, our provisions are already exhausted.

" A fresh expense comes upon us at the present moment: we are just finishing the translation of the catechism into the Ambrym language, and the increasing number of disciples necessitates the publication of this little work, in order to facilitate its study.

" How many things we must ask of you, for, in truth, we are in want of all! Yet, having asked our daily bread, may it still be permitted me to remind the generous hearts of our fellow-countrymen that our poor New-Hebrideans are beginning to feel shame at their nakedness. They ask for clothes, and we have none to give them. With what gratitude would we not receive orders for prints, calicos, and other cotton stuffs, to supply the most pressing needs of our poor catechumens."

✠

NECROLOGY.

MONSEIGNEUR CORDIER,

OF THE FOREIGN MISSIONS, PARIS, VICAR-APOSTOLIC OF CAMBODIA.

A telegram announces the death of this Prelate, who for thirty years governed the Cambodia Mission.

Born in the diocese of Gap, in 1821, Mgr. Marie Laurent Cordier left for Indo-China in 1848. He was nominated Titular Bishop of Gratianapolis and Vicar-Apostolic of Cambodia on the 13th December 1882.

MONSEIGNEUR MICHEL NAAMO,

FORMERLY CHALDEAN BISHOP OF SEERTH.

This Prelate, who was elected Bishop of Seerth in 1885, and gave in his resignation in 1893, died at Bagdad on the 18th of last July, after a short illness. He gave the most consoling proofs of his attachment to the Holy See.

REV. FATHER BRESSON

LAZARIST, KIANG-SI.

This Missioner was but thirty-five years of age. He died on the 19th of June, at the tribunal of Kouei-ki, where he had gone to demand justice of the mandarin.

We recommend to the prayers of our readers the soul of Monsieur Ernest Jaricot, nephew of Mademoiselle Jaricot, who, if she did not actually found the Association of the Propagation of the Faith, at least had the honour, with other ladies, of establishing the first Circles of Tens on the basis of the weekly half-penny subscription.

DEPARTURE OF MISSIONERS.

Embarked at Marseilles on the 1st of July, for the Cape Coast (Côte d'Or): the Rev. Father Joseph Gumy, of the diocese of Fribourg (Switzerland), and the Rev. Father J. Gavey, of the diocese of Tuam (Ireland), both of the Society of African Missions, Lyons.

—Forty-two young Missioners of the Society of Foreign Missions embarked at Marseilles:

On the 4th of August: Messrs. John-Baptist Joseph Geley (Angers), for Osaka; Augustus Luke Billing (Strasburg), and John-Mary Daumer (Rennes), for Tokio; John Benedict Daragon (Clermont), for Southern Tonquin; Joseph Petit (Nevers), for Western Tonquin; Andrew Joseph Chapuis (Le Puy), Emile Binder (Strasburg), and John Anthony Maillebuau (Rhodes), for Northern Cochinchina; Constantine Philomen Jeanningros (Besançon), and Paul Andrew Maheu (Paris), for Eastern Cochinchina; Stephen Maria Cellard (Lyons), for Kouang-tong; Alexis Celestine Jacquemin (St. Clande), and John Marut (Tulle), for Kouang-si Alphonsus Blondet (St. Claude), and John Joseph Chaudier (Le Puy), for Cambodia; Victor Granger (Le Puy), and Anthony Seve (Lyons), for Southern Burmah; Louis Lafon (Rhodes), and Joseph Bazin (Rennes), for Burmah; Edmund Jeantet (St. Claude), and Theophilus Thockler (Strasburg), for Siam.

On the 18th of August: Messrs. Henry Andrew Roubin (Le

Puy), and Peter Emile Villeneuve (Rhodes), for Mandchuria; Paul Augustus Monge (Paris), and Peter Marion (Grenoble), for Hakodate; Peter John Guinand (Lyons), and Peter Joseph Bouyssou (Rhodes), for the Corea; Joseph Rossillon (Annecy), and Augustus Joseph Salvat (Perpignan), for Yun-nan; George Eleusippe Aubert (Langres), for Thibet; Joseph Esquirol (Rhodes), and John Joseph Ronat (Le Puy), for Kouy-tcheou; James Victor Mary Rouchouse (Lyons), and Emile Francis Viret (Chambery), for Western Su-tchuen; Louis Leo Jouve (Montpellier), and Nicholas John Adolphus Koscher (Metz), for Southern Su-tchuen; Michael Elisee Meiller (Lyons), and John Hippolyte Mommaton (Rhodes), for Eastern Su-tchuen; Henry Peter Joseph Arthur Tignous (Toulouse), for Coimbatour; Maurice Pinatel (Bayonne), for Mysore; Joseph Mary Pinel (Nantes), and Louis John Mary Pungier (Rhennes), for Pondicherry.

INDEX TO VOL. LVIII.

GENERAL REVIEW OF THE LABOURS OF THE APOSTOLATE DURING THE YEAR 1894.	3
THE ENCYCLICAL *CHRISTI NOMEN* IN FAVOUR OF THE ASSOCIATION OF THE PROPAGATION OF THE FAITH.	65
BRIEF FROM THE HOLY FATHER TO THE PRESIDENTS AND DIRECTORS OF THE CENTRAL COUNCILS OF THE ASSOCIATION OF THE PROPAGATION OF THE FAITH.	66
THE ENCYCLICAL *CHRISTI NOMEN*, TEXT AND TRANSLATION.	68
REPORT FOR 1894.	127, 129
THE ENCYCLICAL *CHRISTI NOMEN* AND THE EPISCOPACY.	182, 236
LETTER FROM HIS HOLINESS POPE LEO XIII. TO THE CENTRAL COUNCILS OF THE PROPAGATION OF THE FAITH.	257
SACERDOTAL GOLDEN JUBILEE OF HIS EMINENCE CARDINAL LEDOCHOWSKI, PREFECT OF THE PROPAGANDA.	302
BALANCE SHEET FOR 1894.	322
CHRONICLE OF THE WORK.	57, 112, 188, 242, 304, 372
NEWS OF THE MISSIONS.	60, 115, 189, 246, 311, 376
DEPARTURE OF MISSIONERS.	63, 125, 191, 254, 318, 384

NECROLOGY.—His Eminence Cardinal Desprez, 123;—Mgrs. Raimondi, Neraz, 62;—Mgr. Colombert, 124;—Mgr. Zaffino, Sempriui, 190;—Mgr. Bax, 191;—Mgrs. Snickers, Dubuis, Pagani, 253;—Mgrs. Meurin, Morandi, 317;—Mgrs. Cordier Naamo, 382;—Monsieurs Bresson, Jaricot, 383;—Very Rev. Canon Pradel, 125.

MISSIONS OF ASIA.

CHINESE EMPIRE.

THE COREA.—*Letter from Mgr. Mutel.*—Particulars of the death of Father Jozeau, and account of the present situation of the Christians in the Corea. . . 10

—*Letter from Monsieur Villemot.*—Dangers encountered by Messrs. Villemot and Baudounet during the Sino-Japanese war.—Incidents of their flight through the districts in possession of the rebels. — Tragic and moving details. 75

SIAM.—*Letter from M. Guego.*—Evangelization of a tribe of Laos on the left shore of the Me-Kong.—The Sos.—Christian villages.—A singular vision.—The devices of charity. 18

KOUANG-TONG.—*Letter from Monsieur Le Tallandier.*—Martyrdom of a Christian and four catechumens at Tan-chung. 152

LAHORE.—*Letter from Mgr. Pelckmans.*—Blessing the chapel at Dalhousie.—Importance of this Mission.—Conversion of an apostate.—The martyrs of Dalhousie. . . 193

OSAKA.—*A Missioner's Letter.*—The dreams and first acts of the apostolate.—Awakenings.—The Tamatoukouri Mission, in a suburb of Osaka.—A method of evangelization peculiar to Japan. . . . 206

NORTHERN CHAN-TONG.—*Letter from Mgr. Marchi.*—Image Worshippers.—Li-tchouin-mao and his sword.—A strange adventure.—Tragic death of a Christian widow. 259

EASTERN SU-TCHUEN.—*Letter from Monsieur Provost.*—Interesting story of a young neophyte of Kouy-fou. . 346

MISSIONS OF AFRICA.

NORTHERN VICTORIA NYANZA.—*Letter from the Rev. Father Achte.*—Foundation of a Mission in Unyoro.—Some account of the country and its inhabitants. . . 96

UPPER NIGER.—*Letter from the Rev. Father Zappa.*—Progress of this Prefecture-Apostolic.—A model Christian. —The Nuns.—The Stations of Assaba, Eboo, and Illah. 160

ZANZIBAR.—*Letter from the Rev. Father Mevel.*—An apostolic trip.—Rhinoceros hunting.—A black mortally wounded.—A baptism in the desert.—An edifying death. 218

DAHOMEY.—*Letter from the Rev. Father Lecron.*—Christian marriages.—Touching examples.—Story of Clare and Francis. 227

BELGIAN CONGO.—*A Missioner's Letter.*—Apostolic life.— Privations and sufferings.—Palabres and fetich worshippers.—A funeral in the Congo. . . . 265

TANGANIKA.—*Letter from a White Sister.*—The first Nuns in Tanganika.—From Zanzibar to Karema by Lake Nyassa.—Incidents of the voyage.—Enthusiastic welcome. 281

GABOON.—*Letter from the Rev. Father Monnier.*—The sad condition of pagan women.—The good done by the Mission.—Touching and edifying incidents. . . 357

MISSIONS OF AMERICA.

NAPO.—*Letter from the Rev. Father Detroux.*—Missions to the savages of the Republic of Equator.—Difficulties of the journey.—Beginning and progress of evangelization. —Trials.—Present state of affairs. . . 88

OUR DELEGATES TO MEXICO.—*Letter from Monseigneur Terrien.*—Abundant fruits of the Mission of Mgr. Terrien and the Rev. Father Devoucoux. . . . 106

ATHABASKA-MACKENZIE.—*Letter from Mgr. Grouard.*—A Pastoral Visitation.—Great Slave Lake.—The Providence Mission.—Fort Simpson.—Fort Wrigby; a heroic fast.—Great Bear Lake.—Towards Good Hope.—Good Hope Mission.—The Midnight Sun. . . 167

MISSIONS OF OCEANIA.

WELLINGTON. — *Letter from the Rev. Father Coynet.* — Christmas amongst the Maoris. . . . 46

NEW-HEBRIDES.—*Letter from the Rev. Father Monfat.*—Trials and difficulties.—The volcano at Ambrym.—First converts.—Zeal of Kainas. . . . 294

TABLE OF ENGRAVINGS.

PORTRAITS.

Right Rev. TIMOLEON RAIMONDI, Bishop, Vicar-Apostolic of Hong-Kong.	1
Most Rev. GREGORY YOUSSEF, Greek Patriarch of Antioch.	65
Right Rev. HENRY HANLON, Bishop and Vicar-Apostolic of Upper Nile.	96
Right Rev. JAMES BAX, Bishop of Adrassus, Vicar-Apostolic of Central Mongolia.	129
Rev. JULIUS-MARIUS VERRIER, Missioner to Western Tonquin.	193
Right Rev. CLAUDIUS DUBUIS, late Bishop of Galveston, United States.	224
Right Rev. DUNAND, Vicar-Apostolic of Western Su-tchuen.	256
Most Rev. Mgr. MEURIN, Archbishop, Bishop of Port-Louis.	304
Right Rev. PAULUS PELLET, Vicar-Apostolic of Benin.	321

LANDSCAPES AND VARIOUS SCENES.

EUROPE.

BELGIUM.—Statue of Father Damien at Louvain.	112

ASIA.

COREA.—Mandarins and Satellites.	80
HINDUSTAN.—Court of Justice at Lahore.	208

AFRICA.

BELGIAN CONGO.—Tomb of a Bayanzi chief.	272
,, ,, A Chimbeck hut.	288
GABOON.—Market of Libreville.	336
,, Pahouin woman.	352
UPPER NIGER.—Wood of the Mission at Assaba.	144
MADAGASCAR.—Hovas of Tamatave.	176
,, Governor of Tamatave and his wife.	369

AMERICA.

CANADA.—House near the Mackenzie River.	160
EQUATOR.—Indians of Napo.	16
,, Mission-house at Archidona.	32
,, Pucaurcu, Village of Napo.	48

CONTENTS.

Balance Sheet for 1894. 322

Eastern Su-tchuen.—*Letter from Monsieur Provost.*—Interesting story of a young neophyte of Kouy-fou. . 346

Gaboon.—*Letter from the Rev. Father Monnier.*—The sad condition of pagan women.—The good done by the Mission.—Touching and edifying incidents. . . . 357

Chronicle of the Work. 372

News of the Missions. 376

Necrology. 382

Departure of Missioners. . . . 384

Table of Contents. 386

GENERAL TABLE OF THE INDULGENCES
GRANTED TO THE
ASSOCIATION FOR THE PROPAGATION OF THE FAITH,
BY
THE SOVEREIGN PONTIFFS, PIUS VII, LEO XII, PIUS VIII, GREGORY XVI, PIUS IX, AND LEO XIII.

I.—INDULGENCES WHICH MAY BE GAINED BY ALL THE BENEFACTORS.

I.—PLENARY INDULGENCES:

1. On 3rd May.—The Feast of the Invention of the Holy Cross (the day on which the Association was established);
2. On 3rd December.—The Feast of St. Francis Xavier, the Patron of the Association;
3. On the 25th March.—The Feast of the Annunciation;
4. On 15th August.—The Feast of the Assumption;

Or on any day within the Octave of these Festivals

5. On the 6th January.—The Feast of the Epiphany;
6. On 29th September.—The Feast of St. Michael;
7. On all the Feasts of the Apostles;
8. Every month.—On any two days chosen by the Associates;
9. Once a year.—On the day of the *general* commemoration of all the deceased Members of the Association;
10. Once a year.—On the day of *special* commemoration of the deceased Members of the Council, the Committee, or the Circle of ten to which he belongs;
11. The Day of admittance into the Association.
12. At the hour of death, **by in**voking, at least **in their heart, the** sacred name of Jesus;
13. The favour of the privileged Altar for every Mass said in the name of an Associate for a deceased Member.

(Children who have not made their first Communion can gain the above-mentioned Indulgences by performing some pious work appointed by their Confessor).

II.—PARTIAL INDULGENCES:

1.—Seven years and seven quarantines *every time* an Associate performs in aid of the Society any work or devotion of charity;
2. 300 days *every time* an Associate assists at the *Triduum* on the 3rd of May and the 3rd of December;
3. 100 days *every time* an Associate recites *Our Father* and *Hail Mary*, together with the invocation of St. Francis Xavier.

All these Indulgences, both plenary and partial, are applicable to the souls in Purgatory.

III.—All such persons as contribute at one time two hundred francs (£8), at the least, for the purpose of establishing a permanent fund, even though this sum should be immediately expended on the Missions, shall be regarded as Members in perpetuity of the Association, and may enjoy in perpetuity the Privileges and Indulgences

II.—SPECIAL FAVOURS GRANTED TO ECCLESIASTICAL BENEFACTORS OF THE ASSOCIATION.

I.—To every Priest who shall be charged in any parish or establishment to collect alms for the Association for the Propagation of the Faith or, who either from his own resources, or otherwise, shall contribute to the funds of the Association a sum equal to the subscription of an entire circle of ten.

1st.—*The favour of the privileged Altar three times a week.*
2nd.—*The favour to apply the following Indulgences:*
    To the faithful at the hour of death, a Plenary Indulgence; to Beads or Rosaries, Crosses, Crucifixes, Pictures, Statues and Medals the Apostolic Indulgences; to Beads, the Brigitine Indulgences
3rd. *The faculty of attaching to Crucifixes the Indulgences of the Way of the Cross.*

II.—To every Priest who is a Member of a Council or Committee appointed to watch over the interests of the Work.

To every other Priest who in the course of the year shall pay to the account of the Association a sum equal at least to the amount of one thousand subscriptions (£108 6s. 8d.) from whatever source derived

1st.—*The same favours enjoyed by Priests in the preceding category.*
2nd.—**The favour** *of the privileged Altar five times a week personally*
3rd.—*The power to bless Crosses with the Indulgences of the Way of the Cross, and, moreover, the power to invest with the Seraphic Cord and Scapular, and to impart all the Indulgences and privileges granted to such investiture by the Sovereign Pontiffs.*
4th.—*The power to bless, and invest the faithful with, the Scapulars of Mount Carmel, the Immaculate Conception, and the Passion of Our Lord.*

In case the collection of the special subscriptions should be for the moment incomplete, His Holiness prolongs the privileges of the Priest who shall have brought in the entire amount the preceding year, up to the current account.

III.—Every Priest who shall contribute once for all out of his private resources, a sum representing the amount of one thousand subscriptions, shall enjoy during his life the favours granted to the Priests who are Members of a Council.

These Indulgences are subject to the approbation of the Ordinary.

See the *Annals*, vol. xiv, p. 72; vol. xxix, p. 221; and vol. xxxv p. 65, for the conditions and explanations of these special favours.

NOTE.—It is particularly requested that all communications on the business of the Association be addressed to the Secretaries.

Right Rev. Mgr. Walsh, P.P., V.G., } Hon. Secs.
Very Rev. Canon M. M'Manus, P.P., }

Rev. James Mac Veagh, C.C., *Secretary.*

ISSUED EVERY TWO MONTHS

Vol. LVIII.—MARCH, 1895.—No. CCCXLIV.

DUBLIN:
PUBLISHED FOR THE CENTRAL COMMITTEE
OF THE ASSOCIATION FOR IRELAND,
22 PARLIAMENT STREET.

The Association for the Propagation of the Faith throughout the Old and New World has been established for the purpose of assisting, by prayers and alms, the Catholic Missioners who are engaged in preaching the Gospel. The Members say one *Pater* and one *Ave* every day; and it is sufficient, once for all, to offer for this intention the *Pater* and *Ave* of their morning and night prayers, adding each time the aspiration: *Saint Francis Xavier, pray for us.*

The Subscription is *one half-penny per week*, (or 2s. 2d. a year). One Subscriber in ten acts as Collector, and pays in the amount to another Member of the Association, who has ten such collections, in other words, one hundred subscriptions, to receive. Donations are likewise thankfully received from the Subscribers, and from others not Members of the Society.

Two separate Councils, one established at Lyons, and the other at Paris, distribute the funds among the different Missions. A report in full of the sums received, and of their distribution, is inserted every year in the *Annals of the Propagation of the Faith*. This publication, which is a continuation of the *Edifying Letters*, is lent free of charge to the Members for their perusal, and gives six times a year the news received from the Missions. One copy is supplied to every circle of Subscribers bringing in £1 1s. 8d.

The *Society for the Propagation of the Faith*, approved by the Bishops of every land, recommended by numerous Circulars and Pastoral Letters, favoured on many occasions with the benediction of the Holy See, received, finally, by the Encyclical of the 15th of August 1840, the highest approbation which a work of charity could receive. The Sovereign Pontiffs, Pius VII, Leo XII, Pius VIII, Gregory XVI, and Pius IX, by Rescripts dated the 15th of March 1823, 11th May 1824, 18th September 1829, 25th September 1831, 15th November 1835, 22nd July 1836, 17th October 1847, 10th September 1850, 31st December 1853, 17th April 1855, 7th March 1862, and 26th January 1865, have enriched it with many Indulgences. Finally, by a new Encyclical of the 3rd December 1880, Pope Leo XIII has solemnly recommended it to the entire Catholic Universe.

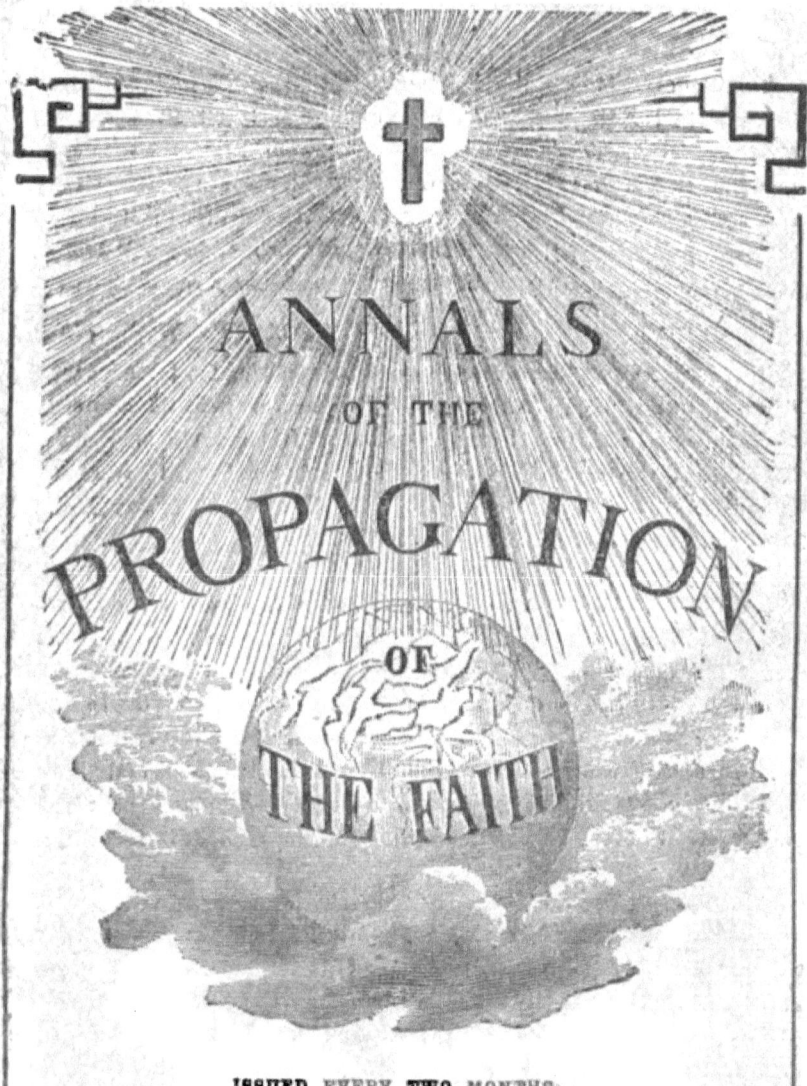

ISSUED EVERY TWO MONTHS

Vol. LVIII.—NOVEMBER, 1895.—No. CCCXLVIII.

DUBLIN:
PUBLISHED FOR THE CENTRAL COMMITTEE
OF THE ASSOCIATION FOR IRELAND,
22 PARLIAMENT STREET.

II.—SPECIAL FAVOURS GRANTED TO ECCLESIASTICAL BENEFACTORS OF THE ASSOCIATION.

I.—To every Priest who shall be charged in any parish or establishment to collect alms for the Association for the Propagation of the Faith, or, who either from his own resources, or otherwise, shall contribute to the funds of the Association a sum equal to the subscription of an entire circle of ten.

1st. *The favour of the privileged altar three times a week.*
2nd. *The favour to apply the following indulgences:—*
    To the faithful at the hour of death, a Plenary Indulgence; to Beads or Rosaries, Crosses, Crucifixes, Pictures, Statues and Medals, the Apostolic Indulgences; to Beads, the Brigitine Indulgences.
3rd. *The faculty of attaching to Crucifixes the Indulgences of the Way of the Cross.*

II.—To every Priest who is Member of a Council or Committee, appointed to watch over the interests of the Work.

To every other Priest who in the course of the year shall pay to the account of the Association a sum equal at least to the amount of one thousand subscriptions (£108 6s. 8d.) from whatever source derived:

1st.—*The same favours enjoyed by Priests in the preceding category.*
2nd.—*The favour of the privileged Altar five times a week personally.*
3rd.—*The power to bless Crosses with the Indulgences of the Way of the Cross, and, moreover, the power to invest with the Seraphic Cord and Scapular, and to impart all the Indulgences and privileges granted to such investiture by the Sovereign Pontiffs.*
4th.—*The power to bless, and invest the faithful with, the Scapulars of Mount Carmel, the Immaculate Conception, and the Passion of our Lord.*

In case the collection of the special subscriptions should be for the moment incomplete, His Holiness prolongs the privileges of the Priest who shall have brought in the entire amount the preceding year, up to the current account.

III.—Every Priest who shall contribute once for all out of his private resources, representing the amount of one thousand subscriptions, shall enjoy, during his life, the favours granted to the Priests who are members of a Council.

These Indulgences are subject to the approbation of the Ordinary.

See the *Annals*, vol. xiv p. 72; vol. xxix, p. 221; and vol. xxxv, p. 65, for the conditions and explanations of these special favours.

NOTE.—It is particularly requested that all communications on the business of the Association be addressed to the Secretaries.

    Right Rev. Mgr. Walsh, P.P., V.G., } Hon. Secs.
    Very Rev. Canon M. M'Manus, P.P., }
        Rev. James Mac Veagh, C.C., *Secretary.*

Central Committee Rooms,
  22 Parliament Street.

www.ingramcontent.com/pod-product-compliance
Lightning Source LLC
Chambersburg PA
CBHW032140010526
44111CB00035B/628